ENCYCLOPEDIA OF

HERB GARDENING

Published by Fog City Press
814 Montgomery Street
San Francisco, CA 94133 USA

Chief Executive Officer: John Owen
President: Terry Newell
Publisher: Lynn Humphries
Managing Editor: Janine Flew
Design Manager: Helen Perks
Editorial Coordinator: Jennifer Losco
Production Manager: Caroline Webber
Production Coordinator: James Blackman
Sales Manager: Emily Jahn
Vice President International Sales: Stuart Laurence

Project Editor: Rosemary McDonald
Project Designer: Lena Lowe
Consultant: Frances Hutchison
Contributors: Frances Hutchison, Erin Hynes, Susan McClure,
Patricia S. Michalak, Judy Moore, Jennie Simpson

A catalog record for this book is available from
the Library of Congress, Washington. D.C.

Library of Congress Cataloging-in-Publication Data

ISBN 1 877019 94 1

Color reproduction by Bright Arts Graphics (S) Pte Ltd
Printed by Kyodo Printing Co. (S'pore) Ltd
Printed in Singapore

A Weldon Owen Production

DISCLAIMER

This book is intended as a reference volume only, not as a medical manual or a guide to self-treatment. The information that it contains is general, not specific to individuals and their particular circumstances, and is not intended to substitute for any treatment that may have been prescribed by your physician. Any plant substance, whether ingested or used medicinally or cosmetically, externally or internally, can cause an allergic reaction in some people. The publishers cannot be held responsible for any injury, damage or otherwise resulting from the use of herbal preparations. We strongly caution you not try self-diagnosis or attempt self-treatment for serious or long-term problems without consulting a qualified medical practitioner. Always seek medical advice promptly if symptoms persist. Never commence any self-treatment while you are undergoing a prescribed course of medical treatment without first seeking professional advice.

Contents

How to Use This Book

The *Encyclopedia of Herb Gardening* is designed to encourage, help and inspire gardeners, both novice and experienced. It is packed with information about buying plants, planting, propagation, soil conditions, cultivation, harvesting, preserving and using herbs. The book is easy to read and each page has colorful photographs showing how beautiful your garden can be. Section Seven of the book is an encyclopedia of herbs to help you choose and identify them.

Each section is color-coded for easy reference.

Clear and informative text explains the subject area being covered.

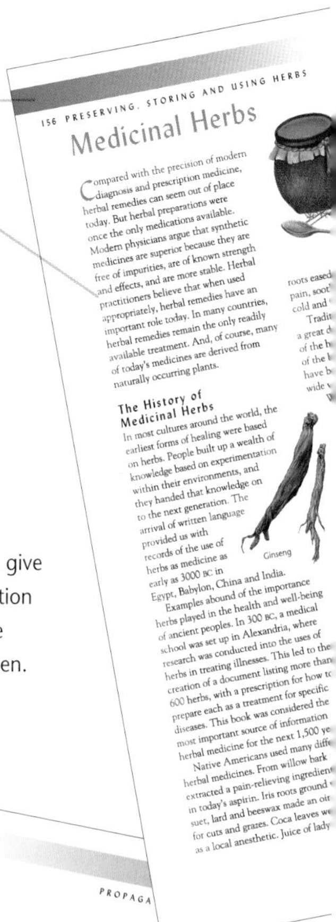
156 PRESERVING, STORING AND USING HERBS

Medicinal Herbs

Compared with the precision of modern diagnosis and prescription medicine, herbal remedies can seem out of place today. But herbal preparations were once the only medications available. Modern physicians argue that synthetic medicines are superior because they are free of impurities, are of known strength and effects, and are more stable. Herbal practitioners believe that when used appropriately, herbal remedies have an important role today. In many countries, herbal remedies remain the only readily available treatment. And, of course, many of today's medicines are derived from naturally occurring plants.

The History of Medicinal Herbs

In most cultures around the world, the earliest forms of healing were based on herbs. People built up a wealth of knowledge based on experimentation within their environments, and they handed that knowledge on to the next generation. The arrival of written language provided us with records of the use of herbs as medicine as early as 3000 BC in Egypt, Babylon, China and India.

Ginseng

Examples abound of the importance herbs played in the health and well-being of ancient peoples. In 300 BC, a medical school was set up in Alexandria, where research was conducted into the uses of herbs in treating illnesses. This led to the creation of a document listing more than 600 herbs, with a prescription for how to prepare each as a treatment for specific diseases. This book was considered the most important source of information on herbal medicine for the next 1,500 ye

Native Americans used many diffe herbal medicines. From willow bark extracted a pain-relieving ingredient in today's aspirin. Iris roots ground suet, lard and beeswax made an oi for cuts and grazes. Coca leaves we as a local anesthetic. Juice of lady

Clear headings indicate the beginning of a new chapter within one of the seven major sections in the book. The line above is the section heading.

Helpful illustrations feature throughout the book.

Colorful photographs give you practical information on how to learn more about your herb garden.

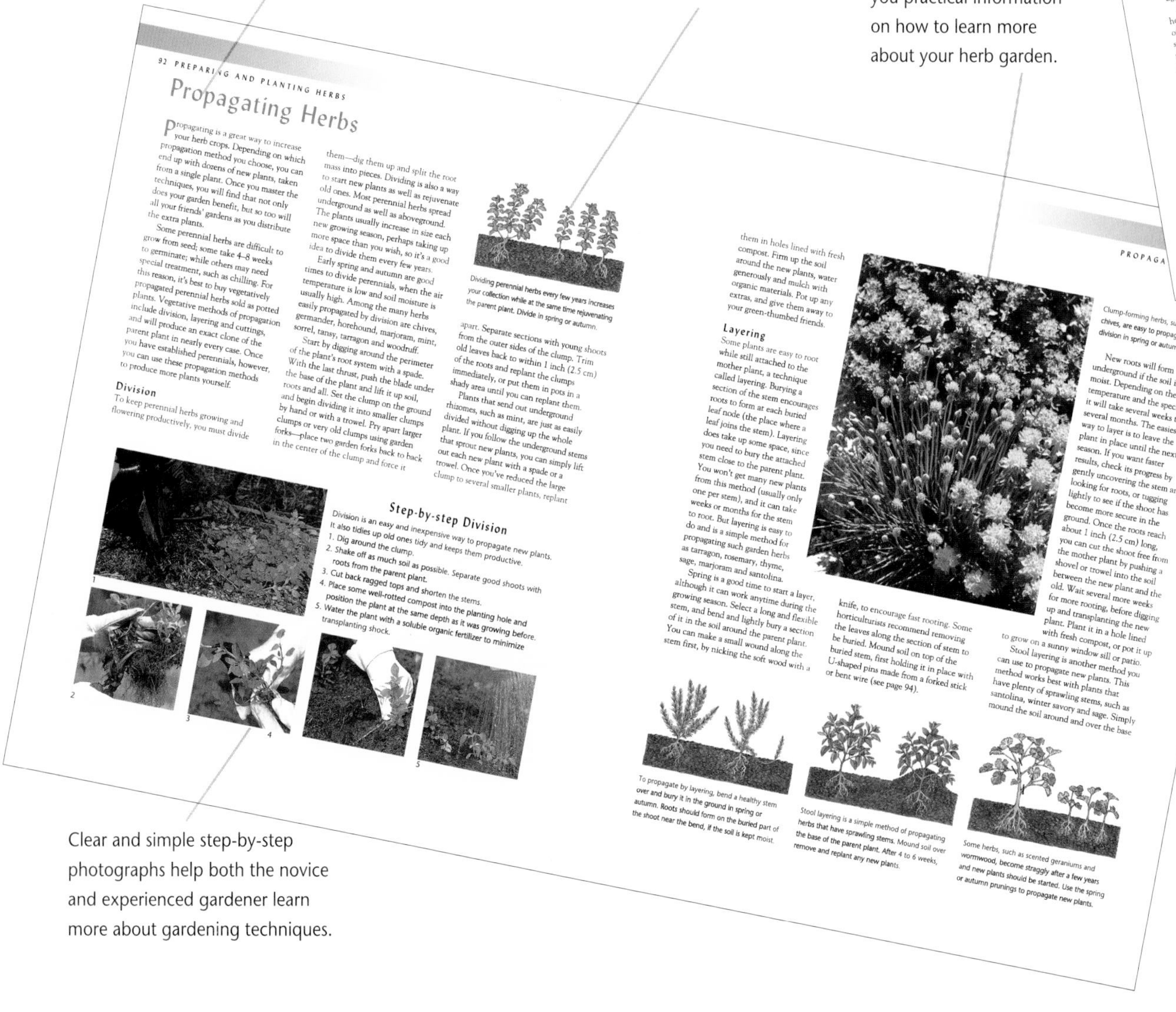
92 PREPARING AND PLANTING HERBS

Propagating Herbs

Propagating is a great way to increase your herb crops. Depending on which propagation method you choose, you can end up with dozens of new plants, taken from a single plant. Once you master the techniques, you will find that not only does your garden benefit, but so too will all your friends' gardens as you distribute the extra plants.

Some perennial herbs are difficult to grow from seed; some take 4–8 weeks to germinate; while others may need special treatment, such as chilling. For this reason, it's best to buy vegetatively propagated perennial herbs sold as potted plants. Vegetative methods of propagation include division, layering and cuttings, and will produce an exact clone of the parent plant in nearly every case. Once you have established perennials, however, you can use these propagation methods to produce more plants yourself.

Division

To keep perennial herbs growing and flowering productively, you must divide them—dig them up and split the root mass into pieces. Dividing is also a way to start new plants as well as rejuvenate old ones. Most perennial herbs spread underground as well as aboveground. The plants usually increase in size each new growing season, perhaps taking up more space than you wish, so it's a good idea to divide them every few years.

Early spring and autumn are good times to divide perennials, when the air temperature is low and soil moisture is usually high. Among the many herbs easily propagated by division are chives, germander, horehound, marjoram, mint, sorrel, tansy, tarragon and woodruff.

Start by digging around the perimeter of the plant's root system with a spade. With the last thrust, push the blade under the base of the plant and lift it up soil, roots and all. Set the clump on the ground and begin dividing it into smaller clumps by hand or with a trowel. Pry apart larger clumps or very old clumps using garden forks—place two garden forks back to back in the center of the clump and force it apart. Separate sections with young shoots from the outer sides of the clump. Trim old leaves back to within 1 inch (2.5 cm) of the roots and replant the clumps immediately, or put them in pots in a shady area until you can replant them.

Plants that send out underground rhizomes, such as mint, are just as easily divided without digging up the whole plant. If you follow the underground stems that sprout new plants, you can simply lift out each new plant with a spade or a trowel. Once you've reduced the large clump to several smaller plants, replant them in holes lined with fresh compost. Firm up the soil around the new plants, water generously and mulch with organic materials. Pot up any extras, and give them away to your green-thumbed friends.

Dividing perennial herbs every few years increases your collection while at the same time rejuvenating the parent plant. Divide in spring or autumn.

Step-by-step Division

Division is an easy and inexpensive way to propagate new plants. It also tidies up old ones tidy and keeps them productive.
1. Dig around the clump.
2. Shake off as much soil as possible. Separate good shoots with roots from the parent plant.
3. Cut back ragged tops and shorten the stems.
4. Place some well-rotted compost into the planting hole and position the plant at the same depth as it was growing before.
5. Water the plant with a soluble organic fertilizer to minimize transplanting shock.

Layering

Some plants are easy to root while still attached to the mother plant, a technique called layering. Burying a section of the stem encourages roots to form at each buried leaf node (the place where a leaf joins the stem). Layering does take up some space, since you need to bury the attached stem close to the parent plant. You won't get many new plants from this method (usually only one per stem), and it can take weeks or months for the stem to root. But layering is easy to do and is a simple method for propagating such garden herbs as tarragon, rosemary, thyme, sage, marjoram and santolina.

Spring is a good time to start a layer, although it can work anytime during the growing season. Select a long and flexible stem, and bend and lightly bury a section of it in the soil around the parent plant. You can make a small wound along the stem first, by nicking the soft wood with a knife, to encourage fast rooting. Some horticulturists recommend removing the leaves along the section of stem to be buried. Mound soil on top of the buried stem, first holding it in place with U-shaped pins made from a forked stick or bent wire (see page 94).

PROPAGA

Clump-forming herbs, such as chives, are easy to propagate by division in spring or autumn.

New roots will form underground if the soil is kept moist. Depending on the temperature and the species, it will take several weeks to several months. The easiest way to layer is to leave the plant in place until the next season. If you want faster results, check its progress by gently uncovering the stem and looking for roots, or tugging lightly to see if the shoot has become more secure in the ground. Once the roots reach about 1 inch (2.5 cm) long, you can cut the shoot free from the mother plant by pushing a shovel or trowel into the soil between the new plant and the old. Wait several more weeks for more rooting, before digging up and transplanting the new plant. Plant it in a hole lined with fresh compost, or pot it up to grow on a sunny window sill or patio.

Stool layering is another method you can use to propagate new plants. This method works best with plants that have plenty of sprawling stems, such as santolina, winter savory and sage. Simply mound the soil around and over the base

To propagate by layering, bend a healthy stem over and bury it in the ground in spring or autumn. Roots should form on the buried part of the shoot near the bend, if the soil is kept moist.

Stool layering is a simple method of propagating herbs that have sprawling stems. Mound soil over the base of the parent plant. After 4 to 6 weeks, remove and replant any new plants.

Some herbs, such as scented geraniums and wormwood, become straggly after a few years and new plants should be started. Use the spring or autumn prunings to propagate new plants.

Clear and simple step-by-step photographs help both the novice and experienced gardener learn more about gardening techniques.

...lly is used as a base in medicinal herbal ...ap. Beeswax is used in herbal ointments.

Herbal Remedies

...repare your own herbal remedies, such as infusions, decoctions, compresses, poultices and tinctures, from herbs you have harvested, to treat a number of common ailments. Refer to the "Quick Guide to Medicinal Herbs" on pages 158–159 for the appropriate herb to use.

Herbal Infusions

Infusions are made by pouring boiling water over herb leaves or flowers and steeping them for up to 15 minutes to release the aromatic oils. They are a good way of making herbal remedies at home and are best drunk fresh, while still hot, although they can be stored in the refrigerator for a day or two. If you find them too bitter, dilute them to your taste or try sweetening them with honey or apple juice. Use a glass or ceramic pot, and bottled water or rainwater if possible.

1 teaspoons dried herbs or 1–2 teaspoons of fresh herb leaves or flowers, washed and dried well
1 cup (250 ml) boiling water

Pour the boiling water over the herbs, and allow it to brew for 10–15 minutes. Strain. For infusions for external use, triple the herb quantities and steep for several hours.

Herbal Teas

An herbal tea is an infusion of aromatic herbs that is steeped for a short period of time in water. Herbal teas should be lightly colored and mild. Steep for only 5–10 minutes for the best flavor. A strong tea will be bitter and might cause unexpected side effects if the herb has medicinal properties. Herbal teas don't have to be medicinal for you to enjoy them. Drink them after a stressful day to help you relax. Use about 1 teaspoon of fresh herb leaves to 1 cup (250 ml) of boiling water. Use a china or glass pot, as metal can change the flavor of some herbs.

Herbal Decoctions

Decoctions are made from the roots, bark, and sometimes twigs, berries or seeds of herbs and need to be simmered in order to extract their active ingredients.

2 tablespoons dried herbs, or $1^1/_2$ cups fresh bark, roots or stems, washed and dried well
2 cups (500 ml) boiling water

Add the herbs to the boiling water and simmer gently for up to 30 minutes. Strain. Decoctions are used fresh.

...dicines in the world and have been used since prehistoric times to improve health. ...ave poisonous properties and should be used only under professional supervision.

Herbal Remedy Precautions

Use all herbal remedies cautiously and follow these guidelines:

- Always consult a doctor if you have painful or chronic symptoms.
- Don't mix herbal medicines with medical prescriptions.
- Take care to identify wild plants accurately and be aware of their properties and dangers.
- Avoid large doses of any herb.
- Grow your own herbal medications for the best purity and quality.
- Follow the instructions for harvesting and storing herbs properly.
- Stop using any herbal medicine if you notice any side effects, such as headaches, dizziness or nausea.
- Avoid using herbal medicines if you are pregnant or breastfeeding, unless you have the consent of an obstetrician.
- With children, always consult a doctor first before giving herbal medications. Do not give herbal medicines to children younger than two years old.

Herbal Compress

Follow the instructions for preparing an infusion or decoction, then soak a towel in the warm liquid. Wring it out and lay it upon the affected area, covering it with a dry towel. As the compress cools, replace it with a warm one. Continue treatment for 30 minutes or until the skin is flushed or tingly. A hot compress made with mustard, cayenne, garlic or ginger will improve circulation and is good for treating nasal and chest congestion. Compresses prepared with such herbs as comfrey or aloe are good for sprains and bruises.

Herbal Poultice

A poultice is similar to a compress except that plant parts are used rather than liquid extracts. They are generally more active than compresses and are used to stimulate circulation and draw impurities out through the skin.

$^1/_4$ cup dried herbs or 3 cups fresh herbs, washed, dried and minced
4 cups oatmeal

Mix the herbs and oatmeal with hot water to form a paste. Place some paste directly on the skin and cover with a towel. As it cools, replace with more warm paste. Continue treatment for 30 minutes. Don't use hot, spicy herbs, such as mustard, that may burn the skin. Poultices are used to draw out infection and relieve muscle aches.

Herbal Plaster

Place dried or fresh herbs, or a freshly mixed paste (see the poultice recipe) in the fold of a towel, then lay it on the injured area. Since the herbs don't have direct contact with the skin, plasters are useful for particularly sensitive wounds, such as minor burns. Flush with cold water, then apply a plaster of echinacea paste.

Herbal Tincture

Tinctures are made from alcohol and powdered herbs. The alcohol extracts the herbs' active ingredients.

$^1/_2$ cup powdered dried herbs
2 cups (500 ml) brandy, vodka or gin

Mix the ingredients together in a glass bottle and allow to steep in a warm place for several weeks, shaking occasionally. Strain, then store in a cool, dark place. Use approximately 10 drops either straight or mixed in 1 cup (250 ml) of hot water. Tinctures will keep for a long time due to their alcohol content.

Herbal Ointment

Mix 5 tablespoons of crushed fresh herbs with 18 oz (500 g) of lard or petroleum jelly in a bowl. Place over boiling water. Stir thoroughly. Strain while hot and pour into sterilized glass storage jars.

Herbal teas are made by infusing leaves, flowers or roots of herbs in boiling water.

Chapter heading indicates the subject being discussed within a main section.

Box information explains in more detail a particular subject or gardening topic.

Photographs of individual plants show what they look like when grown in the right conditions.

Ginkgo biloba
GINKGOACEAE

GINKGO

An ancient species of plant that is often referred to as a "living fossil," ginkgo contains a unique chemical that is important in blocking allergic responses and improving the circulation. It is important in Chinese medicine.

Best climate and site Zones 4–8. Full sun. Native of China.
Ideal soil conditions Deep, moist, humus-rich, well-drained soil; pH 5.3–6.9.
Growing guidelines Plants are either male or female. Take cuttings of male trees in summer. Female trees bear evil-smelling fruit and are therefore not desirable as a garden tree. Seed can be sown when ripe in autumn.
Growing habit Deciduous, pyramidal-shaped tree; height 80–120 feet (24–36 m). Beautiful, fan-shaped leaves up to 5 inches (12 cm) across. Leaves turn yellow in autumn. Likes a good organic mulch especially when plant is young.
Flowering time Inconspicuous, greenish flowers occur in early spring on female plants, followed by small, yellow, unpleasant-smelling seeds. Fruiting only occurs when male and female plants are grown together and if conditions are warm enough.
Pest and disease prevention Usually trouble free.
Harvesting and storing Leaves are picked in autumn as they change color and are dried. Seed kernels are cooked for use in medicinal preparations.
Precautions Excess can cause vomiting and diarrhea. The seed pulp can cause dermatitis.
Parts used Leaves, seeds.
Culinary uses Nuts or inner kernels are roasted and eaten.
Medicinal uses Internally for allergic inflammatory responses, asthma and urinary incontinence. Helps to improve circulation by dilating blood vessels.
Other common names Maidenhair tree.

Botanical name

Family name

Common name

Detailed information about each herb.

Glycyrrhiza glabra
PAPILIONACEAE

LICORICE

The bittersweet licorice root has been enjoyed as a natural confection for thousands of years. The licorice plant is a perennial legume and is native to south-western Asia and the Mediterranean.

Best climate and site Zones 8–10. Full sun.
Ideal soil conditions Deep, rich, moist soil; pH 6.5–7.8.
Growing guidelines Divide rootstocks or take stolon cuttings in autumn and spring or propagate by seed in spring or autumn. Slow to grow from seed. Remove flower heads to encourage stronger roots and stolons, unless seed is required.
Growing habit Hardy stoloniferous perennial with long, narrow, dark green leaflets; height 2–5 feet (60–150 cm). Its taproot can be up to 3 feet (90 cm) in length and has several long branches, which are wrinkled and brown with yellow flesh.
Flowering time Pale blue or purplish flowers appear in summer followed by reddish-brown pods.
Pest and disease prevention Usually trouble free.
Harvesting and storing Roots and stolons are lifted in early autumn 3–4 years after planting and dried for decoctions, liquid extracts, lozenges and powder.
Parts used Roots, stolons.
Culinary uses Used as a flavoring in confectionery, ice cream and beverages. Roots are boiled to extract the familiar black substance used in licorice candy.
Medicinal uses Internally for constipation, asthma, bronchitis and coughs but not for people with high blood pressure. Externally for eczema, herpes and shingles.
Other uses Licorice is a basis for most commercial laxatives. Licorice extracts are used to flavor tobacco, beer, soft drinks and pharmaceutical products; used as a foaming agent in beers.

Hamamelis virginiana
HAMAMELIDACEAE

WITCH HAZEL

Witch hazel is a frost-hardy, small tree with scented yellow autumn flowers and black fruits. Its forked branches are used as water divining rods and an extract from its bark has been a popular astringent for centuries.

Best climate and site Zones 5–9. Full sun to partial shade.
Ideal soil conditions Moist, humus-rich garden soil; pH 6.0–7.0.
Growing guidelines Propagate by seed planted outdoors in early autumn. Prevent seeds from drying. Germination is slow and erratic and can take 2 years. You can take cuttings or layerings from established plants. Cut back untidy growth after flowering.
Growing habit Deciduous shrub or small tree with smooth, gray to brown bark; height 8–15 feet (2.5–4.5 m).
Flowering time Autumn; yellow, threadlike petals followed by black seed capsules.
Pest and disease prevention Usually trouble free.
Harvesting and storing Leaves are collected in summer; branches, twigs and bark in spring.
Parts used Leaves, branches, twigs, bark.
Medicinal uses Internally for dysentery, diarrhea and excessive menstruation.
Externally for burns, sore throats and eye inflammations. An infusion of the young, flower-bearing twigs can be used on a compress for bruises, sprains, muscle aches and insect bites.
Other uses Witch hazel is an important ingredient of commercial eye drops, skin tonics and skin creams. Also used as an astringent.
Other common names American or Virginian witch hazel.
Gardener's trivia The twigs of witch hazel are often used for water divining.

Helianthus annuus
ASTERACEAE

SUNFLOWER

All parts of the sunflower are usable. Each flower contains over 1,000 seeds, which can be used fresh or pressed for oil. The plants have been used medicinally for over 3,000 years and were used as a treatment for malaria.

Best climate and site Zones 5 and warmer. Full sun.
Ideal soil conditions Rich, well-drained soil; pH 6.0–7.5.
Growing guidelines Propagate by seed sown in spring. Sow ½ inch (12 mm) deep and 6 inches (15 cm) apart. Thin to stand 18–24 inches (45–60 cm) apart. Cultivate or mulch. Drought-tolerant, but regular watering will produce larger seed heads.
Growing habit Giant annual with erect stems and large flower heads; height 3–10 feet (90–300 cm).
Flowering time Yellow-petaled flowers in summer with heads up to 12 inches (30 cm) across; disc flowers red or brown.
Pest and disease prevention Provide good air circulation to avoid mildew. Flowers attract beneficial insects that eat pests such as aphids.
Harvesting and storing Whole plants are cut as flowering begins. Seeds are collected in autumn. Rub the seed heads to dislodge the seeds and store them in airtight containers.
Special tips Sunflowers bloom relatively quickly but take a long time to ripen their seeds. Very heavy heads may need support.
Parts used Whole plant, seeds, oil.
Culinary uses Oil is used for cooking and salads. Seeds are used in cereals and breads, either roasted or fresh.
Medicinal uses Internally for malaria, tuberculosis and bronchial infections.
Externally as a massage oil and to treat arthritis in China.
Other uses Oil is used in the manufacture of margarine.

SECTION ONE

Discovering Herbs

Herbs were once an essential part of people's lives, and many myths and legends developed through the ages relating to their use. An understanding of herbs—what they are, a little of their history and where they grow in the wild—is not only fascinating, but also can help you in your own herb gardening.

Introduction to Herbs

People have been growing herbs for thousands of years. Herbs were once an essential part of life—used to preserve food and make it more nourishing, for medicinal purposes and for religious ceremonies. Imagine how bland food would be without all the condiments and how dull cooking would become if we didn't experiment with adding a sprinkle of this herb and a dash of that herb. Those keen cooks who are also good gardeners know the pleasure of growing these plants for their wonderful qualities such as beneficial oil-filled aromatic leaves and tasty stems, fruits or seeds.

Botanically, a herb is a plant, usually succulent and soft, that does not develop woody tissue (known as secondary growth), at any stage of its life, which can be an ephemeral season, or of several years' duration. That said, there are many plants which today we think of and use as herbs but which don't fall strictly into this botanical category. Rosemary is a perfect example. Look at the plant botanically and you will see stems that are quite woody, resulting in its classification as a shrub. However, the softer, upper sprigs of the plant have been used to flavor all manner of dishes over the years, so there's a blurring between the scientific and culinary terms of this plant we call a herb.

You don't need a degree in botany to be a successful gardener, but understanding a little about how plants are named, plant groups, the life cycles of plants and what their basic needs are can help you to be a successful herb gardener.

Mass-planted mauve lavender edges the path to the front door, skirting a sundial planted around with pink lavender. There are many lavender varieties, heights and colors to choose from.

Understanding Plant Names

At first, the scientific names of plants can seem daunting and confusing. New gardeners can sometimes feel a touch of anxiety when faced with complicated Latin names, but if you take some time to understand what is behind the name, then you will discover that it's not as daunting as you first thought. But why use a scientific name when you can use a common name? Well, you might know a particular plant by the common name of bee balm, for instance. But if you go to an out-of-town nursery and ask for bee balm, you may only get a puzzled look. Perhaps they call the plant bergamot, or maybe Oswego tea, based on the fact that American pioneers used it as an herbal tea. Or if you are looking for bee balm in a catalog, you may only find it under its botanical name, *Monarda didyma*. So, one plant can have several different common names. Likewise, one common name can apply to several different plants. For instance, you may want to grow an herb

Purple coneflowers *Echinacea purpurea* are handsome plants for the herb garden, but their roots and rhizomes are also used medicinally.

with the common name loosestrife. This can refer to a creeping perennial with golden flowers known by the botanical name *Lysimachia nummularia*; to a tall perennial with large white flowers in a swan-necked spike, *L. clethroides*; to its less invasive counterpart, *L. ephemerum*; or to a spreading, long-blooming, purple-flowered plant, *Lythrum salicaria* (which is the herb). If you order loosestrife without using a botanical name, you stand a good chance of receiving the wrong plant.

Becoming familiar with the scientific names of the plants you want to grow helps you buy exactly what you want. Most botanical names are based on Latin, so they can be a mouthful. However, the names will be the same in all countries around the world, despite differences in the native language. Botanical names rarely change, usually only when scientists update the name to better reflect what they have discovered about the plant's heritage. If you have learned an older name, you will usually find it listed beside the newer names in nursery catalogs.

As you have probably noticed by now, botanical names usually have two parts. The first name is the genus to which the plant belongs; this refers to a group of closely related plants. The second word indicates the species, a specific kind of plant in that genus. You may end up growing several different species from the same genus. For example, *Achillea millefolium* and *A. tomentosa* both belong to the genus *Achillea*, commonly known as yarrow. But the first, *Achillea millefolium*, refers to a species with finely cut leaves, while *A. tomentosa* refers to one with particularly fuzzy leaves.

Botanical names can be easier to remember if you determine what they tell you about the plant. Some refer to the person who discovered the plant or to the part of the world in which it was discovered. For instance, *Sanguinaria canadensis* is bloodroot, a native of Canada and the eastern United States. Other botanical names are descriptive. *Viola odorata* is sweet violet, which bears an especially fragrant flower.

Horticulturists and botanists recognize two other classifications of plants that you will often encounter: varieties and cultivars. Although the names are sometimes used interchangeably, plants that develop a natural variation in the wild are called varieties, and the varietal name is included as part of the botanical name after the abbreviation "var.". This is the case with American mint, *Mentha arvensis* var. *villosa*. It differs from corn mint *M. arvensis* by having hairier leaves, a pleasant aroma, and pink or white flowers rather than lilac flowers.

Cultivars, whose names are set in single quotes after the botanical names, are plants that gardeners or horticulturists have selected and propagated as part of a breeding program or that have resulted from a chance mutation. *Aster novi-belgii* 'Professor Anton Kippenburg' is a blue New York aster.

You may also come across hybrids, which are blends of two species. One example is *Anemone* x *hybrida*. The "x" indicates that this plant is a hybrid.

In the "Guide to Herbs," starting on page 172, plants are listed alphabetically by botanical name. The most widely used common name is also included. When the abbreviation "spp." is used, this indicates that several related species in the same genus are being discussed.

What's in a Name?

Learning botanical names may seem intimidating at first, but you'll be surprised at how easily you pick them up as you read. Besides being a tool for accurately communicating about plants, a botanical name can often tell you something about the plant it identifies, such as its flower color or growing habit. Listed below are some words that commonly appear in botanical names, along with their definitions.

Albus: white
Argenteus: silver
Caeruleus: blue
Chrysantha: yellow flowers
Contorta: twisted, contorted
Edulis: edible
Grandiflora: large flowers
Grandifolia: large leaves
Lutea: yellow flowers
Montana: of the mountains
Nanus: dwarf
Nigra: dark
Odorata: scented flowers
Orientalis: from the East, Asia
Pendula: hanging
Perennis: perennial
Prostratus: trailing
Pubescens: hairy
Purpurea: purple
Reptans: creeping
Roseus: rosy
Ruber: red
Sanguinea: bloody, red
Scandens: climbing
Sempervirens: evergreen
Stricta: upright
Variegatus: variegated
Vulgaris: common

Sweet cicely

Characteristics of Herbs

You can grow herbs in your garden for a variety of reasons: to use their leaves in herbal medicine, their fruits in the kitchen, their fragrant flowers for beauty treatments, their deep taproots to dye clothes or simply because they are attractive plants. No matter what your reasons are, knowing about the functions and characteristics of the various plant parts will help you identify, select and maintain your herbs most effectively.

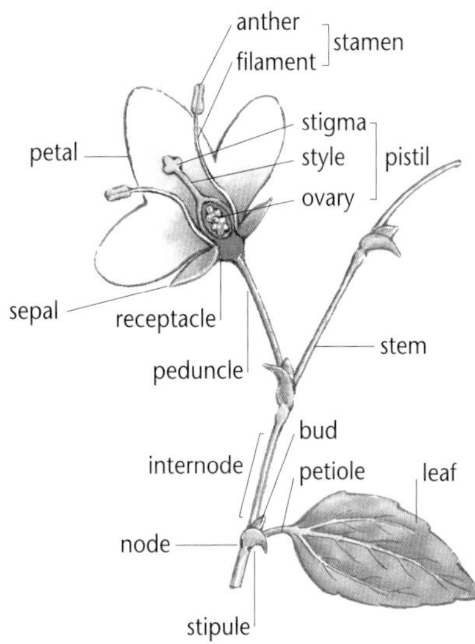

This diagram identifies some of the most common plant parts. Knowing these will help you understand the plant descriptions you read in books and catalogs.

Root Systems

As a gardener, you probably select most plants for their aboveground appearance. But when selecting and planting herbs, you should also consider their root systems. In certain plants, such as iris and ginger, the root may be the part that is used herbally.

Roots help to hold the plant firmly in the soil and provide it with a system for absorbing water and nutrients. They may also act as storage organs, as in the carrot family, holding nutrients for use during times of vigorous growth or flowering. Most herbs have a fibrous root system, made up of many fine and branching roots. Annual herbs, in particular, tend to have shallow root systems. As fibrous roots do not penetrate particularly deeply, you'll need to pay special attention to the water requirements of such plants when rain is scarce.

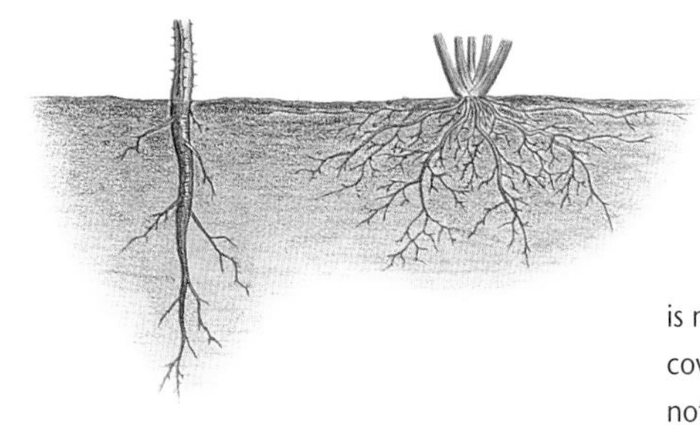

The two basic types of root system: the taproot (left) and fibrous roots (right).

Some herbs have strong central roots, called taproots, that travel straight down in search of water and nutrients. The taproot is a single, thick, tapering organ (a carrot is actually an enlarged taproot) with thin side branch roots. Taprooted plants can more easily withstand fluctuating soil moisture conditions, but many, such as parsley and lovage, are more difficult to transplant because their roots are so sensitive.

Plant Stems

The stems of your herbs not only support the leaves, but also serve as pathways for movement of nutrients and water between roots and leaves. Like roots, stems are storage organs, too. Bulbs, such as garlic and the saffron crocus, are actually specialized storage stems.

Some herbs have stems that are specially adapted for vegetative reproduction. Stolons (also called rhizomes or runners) are stems that travel horizontally along the surface of the soil. At certain intervals along the stolon, new shoots and roots will form, giving rise to new plants. Sweet woodruff and sweet violets are two examples of plants that produce stolons.

Although it grows in the ground, a bulb is not a root, but a type of stem, compressed and covered with scale-like leaves. A rhizome is also not a true root—it is an underground runner or stem that spreads just below the surface.

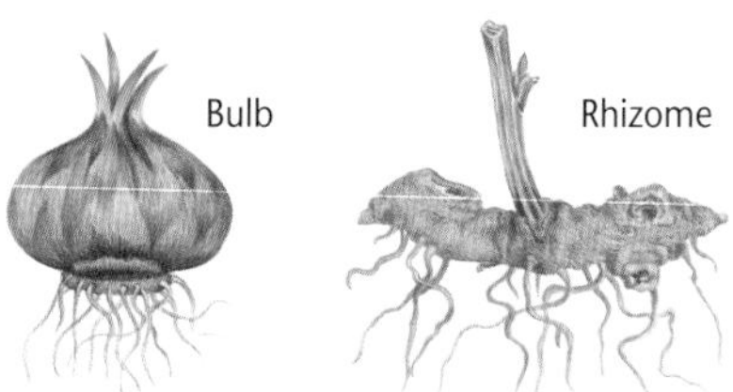

Herbs that form new plants from underground stems include mint, woodruff and violet. The creeping stems of mint spread quickly and aggressively, traveling just below the surface of the soil and rooting as they go. For this reason you may want to grow mint in containers, preferably large bottomless tubs or plastic pots or buckets. Alternatively, build a wooden barrier about 12–14 inches (30–35 cm) deep around the mint patch to keep the plants from overwhelming their neighbors.

Many herbs can be propagated by stem cuttings. Swollen buds, or nodes, located along the stems are the sites for new growth. When you take stem cuttings from your herbs to make new plants, the new root systems form underground at

The way the leaves are placed on the stem is called the leaf arrangement. Among herbs you will find an extensive range of shapes, textures and leaf colors.

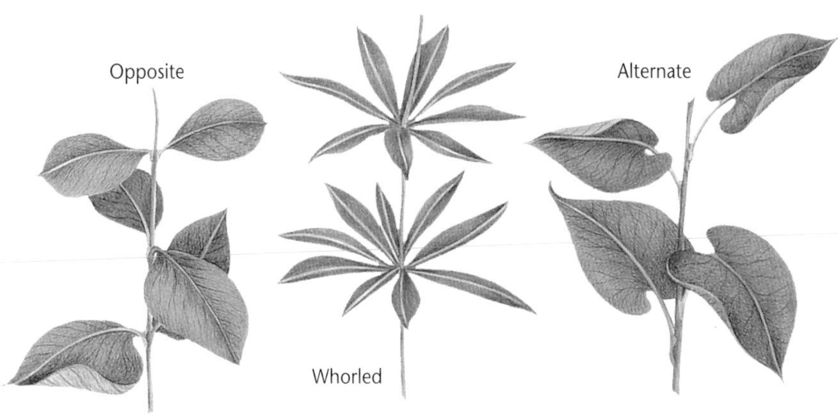

From solid simple leaves to lacy dissected ones, herb foliage comes in a variety of types and textures to enliven your garden.

When planning your herb garden, don't forget to consider colorful leaves, such as those of coleus.

Characteristics of Herbs

You can grow herbs in your garden for a variety of reasons: to use their leaves in herbal medicine, their fruits in the kitchen, their fragrant flowers for beauty treatments, their deep taproots to dye clothes or simply because they are attractive plants. No matter what your reasons are, knowing about the functions and characteristics of the various plant parts will help you identify, select and maintain your herbs most effectively.

Root Systems

As a gardener, you probably select most plants for their aboveground appearance. But when selecting and planting herbs, you should also consider their root systems. In certain plants, such as iris and ginger, the root may be the part that is used herbally.

Roots help to hold the plant firmly in the soil and provide it with a system for absorbing water and nutrients. They may also act as storage organs, as in the carrot family, holding nutrients for use during times of vigorous growth or flowering. Most herbs have a fibrous root system, made up of many fine and branching roots. Annual herbs, in particular, tend to have shallow root systems. As fibrous roots do not penetrate particularly deeply, you'll need to pay special attention to the water requirements of such plants when rain is scarce.

Some herbs have strong central roots, called taproots, that travel straight down in search of water and nutrients. The taproot is a single, thick, tapering organ (a carrot is actually an enlarged taproot) with thin side branch roots. Taprooted plants can more easily withstand fluctuating soil moisture conditions, but many, such as parsley and lovage, are more difficult to transplant because their roots are so sensitive.

Plant Stems

The stems of your herbs not only support the leaves, but also serve as pathways for movement of nutrients and water between roots and leaves. Like roots, stems are storage organs, too. Bulbs, such as garlic and the saffron crocus, are actually specialized storage stems.

Some herbs have stems that are specially adapted for vegetative reproduction. Stolons (also called rhizomes or runners) are stems that travel horizontally along the surface of the soil. At certain intervals along the stolon, new shoots and roots will

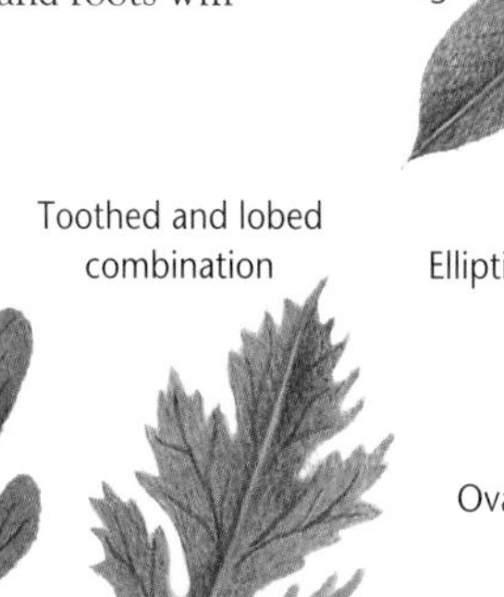

Leaf edges are a good clue to help you identify unknown herbs. By incorporating herbs with different leaf shapes into your garden, you will help to give it added visual interest.

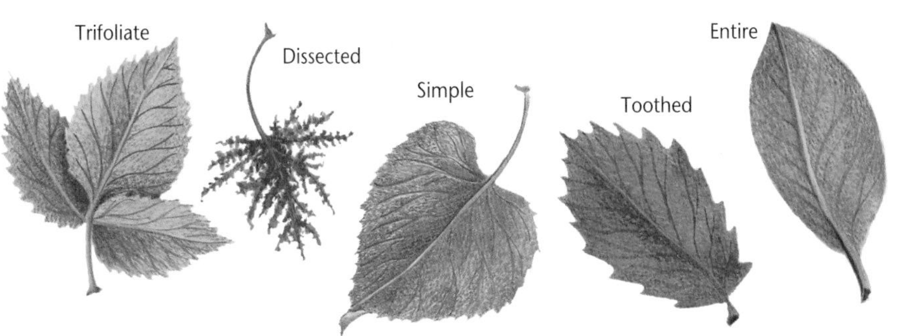

cultivars, including the yellow-and-green 'Aurea' and the cream-purple-and-green 'Tricolor'. Variegated herbs taste just as good as their green counterparts, and add color and interest to any planting.

Texture

Texture is a quality you have to feel before you fully appreciate it. Some herbs, such as borage, have large, bluish-gray leaves covered in hairy bristles that can become quite coarse as they age. By running your hand over the leaves you'll soon realize why the younger leaves are best to pick fresh for salads. Other herbs, such as the crinkled leaves of the common mint, give a delightful added sensation when floating in a cool summer drink. Think, too, of textured herb foliage in combination with other plants. This is where parsley has come into focus. Planted as a border to a vegetable or flower bed, the crisp texture of its tightly curled leaves adds an extra dimension to an otherwise regimented square or rectangular garden bed.

With a chili plant growing in your garden, you will never need to rely on chili powder again.

A bountiful herb garden is planted with golden marjoram, borage, purple sage and thyme, together with vegetables and flowers. Even the smallest garden can provide plenty of plants for cooking and crafts.

Scent

Perhaps the most distinguishing attribute of herbs is the wonderful aroma or perfume that most of them exude. Who hasn't crushed the leaves of rosemary, mint or thyme and relished in the scent? So why banish herbs to the vegetable garden out in the yard? Plant a pot of these perfumed wonders where they can be brushed against, or better still, grabbed by the handful on the way to the front door after a hard day at the office.

As well as providing harmonious color, this group of chives and euphorbia has interesting texture.

In a cottage garden, flowers and herbs intermingle freely, including mint, marjoram, salvias and strawberries. If you don't have space for a separate herb garden, grow herbs among the flowers.

Flowers and Fruits

Tasty leaves aren't the only reason to grow herbs—many produce beautiful flowers as well. Most herb flowers are either single or clustered. A common clustered floral arrangement is the umbel, which is shaped like an upside-down umbrella, with clusters of dainty blossoms at the top. Members of the carrot family, such as dill and caraway, have umbels. Flowers arranged along a tall stem, such as lavender, are called spikes.

You can also grow herbs for their seeds or fruits. Some herbs, such as dill and anise, produce an abundance of seeds that are easy to see and to collect. Nowadays, most people don't know the art of crystallizing comfrey or violet flowers to add as decorations to cakes, but it is worth taking the time to use the fruit of many plants in cooking. The reward is a taste sensation that will keep you returning to the real thing. Take vanilla, for example. You will notice a difference in taste when you substitute a vanilla pod for bottled artificial vanilla. Likewise juniper berries. These are used to distil gin, something few of us are likely to do, but a few berries from your tree will enhance a game casserole. Some roses produce a tart, berry-like hip that is high in Vitamin C content, while chilies can add an eye-watering zest to an otherwise mundane stir-fry.

What Are Herbs?

The terms "herbs" and "herbaceous" are often confused, but generally a herb is a plant valued for its flavor, scent or medicinal properties. The term covers a diverse range, from small plants or parts of a plant found growing in mountain crevices to tall trees growing in moist valleys. "Herbaceous" refers to perennial plants that have a long-lived root system which sustains recurring annual aboveground foliage and flowers.

Sage

Potted basil and parsley

Versatile Herbs

Herbs vary enormously in their characteristics and size. One of the smallest herbs is Corsican mint *Mentha requienii*, which forms a close carpet of tiny, fragrant leaves and can be used to make an herb lawn. Among the largest herbs is bay *Laurus nobilis*, with a height of 10–50 feet (3–15 m), leathery, pointed, aromatic leaves and small creamy spring flowers. The fact that both are herbs shows how difficult it is to define this group of plants. Although spices are often considered to be derived from roots, fruits or berries, and herbs from leaves, the distinctions are not clear even here, when many fruits, including rose hips and bramble fruits, are included among the herbs.

Poisonous Herbs

Anyone who has made potpourri knows how powerful the essential oils of herbs are; this intensity indicates how toxic herbs can be if used unwisely. Some have potent and poisonous ingredients, and delightful though a plant's scent may be, it can be downright dangerous to ingest parts of it or apply them to the skin. Among the most poisonous herbs are foxglove (left), monkshood, Madagascar periwinkle, lily-of-the-valley and opium poppy.

A Wealth of Choices

In this book you will find a wide-ranging list of herbs, including not only the commonly known culinary and medicinal herbs, but also some other plants that are very familiar from the kitchen or garden, but whose herbal uses may be less well known. For example, oat *Avena sativa* is listed in "A Guide to Popular Herbs" starting on page 172. Although a staple on the breakfast menu, this grain is not normally thought of as an herb. It sits, possibly, on the boundary between food and herb. Yet Nicholas Culpeper, an English astrologer-physician in the early 17th century, thought it could be used externally as a remedy for freckles, wind or "the itch." Modern herbalists see it as a heart tonic.

Blackberries have been eaten since the time of the Greek physician Hippocrates and enjoyed for their flavor, yet both the berries and fruits have herbal uses too, as an astringent and tonic. The roots make a natural orange dye. Wild celery, the species from which our cultivated varieties are derived, has beneficial effects against osteoarthritis, rheumatism and gout. Lemon has long been valued for its germ-fighting qualities and its cooling effect on the body. Lemon water is still used to counter fevers today.

"A Guide to Popular Herbs" includes some more unusual plants, such as *Astragalus gummifer*, a plant you are unlikely to grow in your own garden but one that produces gum tragacanth, an excellent fixative for potpourri. The gum is also used in food and toothpaste.

Treat Herbs with Caution

Herbs give us delicious food flavorings, powerful fragrances and remedies for various ills, but most—even familiar herbs such as thyme or rosemary—can have unpleasant, even dangerous side effects if taken in excess. They contain volatile oils that are poisonous if taken in large amounts. In small amounts they may contribute to our health, but herbs are not a cure-all for serious diseases for which medical diagnosis and treatment must be sought.

Some herbs are very poisonous and must never be ingested. These include familiar plants such as foxglove and lily-of-the-valley. These make beautiful garden flowers, but be aware that they are poisonous. Other herbs, such as rue, can cause skin allergies. Be particularly careful when growing any of these plants if there are young children or animals about. Sometimes there are warning labels on plants or seed packets to alert gardeners, but it is sensible to always use caution if you are unfamiliar with a certain plant.

Changing Uses of Herbs

Uses of herbs change over the years. No one today would be convinced that eating sage would turn their hair black or that marjoram could cure deafness, but that is what was once believed. Rhubarb was once used only for medicinal purposes in France, being popular as a laxative, so a travelling Frenchman was, not surprisingly, horrified to see the uncivilized English eating it as a fruit. "These prudish people openly advertise the defects of their most private internal economy by their shameless partiality for this amazing fare," he wrote in his journal.

Bay leaves were popular with the ancient Greeks and were woven into laurel crowns that symbolized wisdom. The Greeks also believed that bay leaves prevented lightning strikes.

Bee balm (bergamot) tea was a popular colonial herbal tea in America, and once formed part of every bride's dowry.

Sweet bay

This informal garden combines herbs such as lavender, geranium and thyme with other plants, including deadnettle, mallow, lady's mantle, stonecrop and pinks.

Always check for restrictions and warnings when you buy.

Very often, knowledge of herbs is built on old wisdom. But now, as more and more herbs are becoming part of mainstream medicine, scientific research can sometimes supply the facts on both why herbs are beneficial, and why they can be dangerous to use. In some countries, certain herbs are subject to legal restrictions on cultivation and use. The opium poppy *Papaver somniferum* and hemp (marijuana) *Cannabis sativa* are two examples. But on the whole, the herb plants on the nursery shelves are likely to be perfectly safe to grow.

Versatile Garden Plants

Even as garden plants, herbs are surprisingly versatile and can be grown in dozens of ways. They flourish in pots, can be used as groundcovers, trimmed into hedges or naturalized in a wild garden. They grow by ponds or on dry banks, or cover stone walls. They are particularly good for growing in the well-drained conditions of raised beds, which makes them useful plants for wheelchair gardeners. They are also excellent plants to use in a garden for the blind, having an astonishing variety of textures and aromas; many of the latter are released just by touching the leaves.

Among the herbs that are useful in water-conserving gardens are the Mediterranean shrubs, such as thyme, rosemary and lavender. These are of the Lamiaceae, or mint family, which includes many herbs, such as basil, catmint, mint, oregano and lemon balm. Growing and grouping herbs in families is another interesting way to garden. The Apiaceae family includes herbs such as chervil, coriander, dill and parsley that carry delicate flower heads in flattish domes, called umbels. These stand out among the other meadow wildflowers in their native habitats. Then there are the Alliaceae, or bulbs—garlic, chives and onions—and the underground stems such as ginger and galangal. Learning about the diversity of herbs can become a fascinating pursuit, but the first and most practical step to take is simply to plant your own herb garden.

Like most herbs, parsley, chives, thyme and sage are quite versatile, and will flourish in pots or in garden beds.

Herbs in the Wild

Herbs are a diverse group of plants found in all countries and used by indigenous peoples on all continents. You may have considered some well-known herbs to be native to your own country, but it's more likely that many of these herbs were originally found growing wild only in concentrated areas. As their culinary and medicinal qualities were appreciated, they became valuable trading commodities. Many herbs were taken to Britain by the conquering Romans as part of their quartermaster provisions. Similarly, the Pilgrim Fathers took traditional herbs with them across the Atlantic before they discovered that there were American herbs greatly valued by native tribes.

Plants from Europe

Many of the familiar herbs are spread across vast areas of the Northern hemisphere but it is only specific species, generally found in the wild around the Mediterranean, that are used in our cooking. For example, the sun-drenched, well-drained hillsides of that region are home to a number of species of thyme, including common thyme *Thymus vulgaris*. Other European favorites, such as rosemary and sage, also grow on the rocky terrain of the Mediterranean. Their natural habitat gives us ample clues to the type of conditions they need in which to flourish.

Across northern Europe, stretching from the Alps to Lapland and across much of Russia, where an altogether different climate prevails, meadow grasses—such as nettles, caraway, chervil, horse parsley and sweet cicely—once yielded plants that helped supplement and flavor the meager rations that were then available. Forerunners of the popular hybridized celery and carrot, vegetables that we take for granted today, still grow wild in grasslands where their fine white flowers billow above finely divided foliage in late summer. In the Middle Ages, people trying to find relief from the plague sought angelica growing beside streams in northern Europe, where it is thought to have spread from Syria. Today it can still be found growing beside streams and rivers in Britain. In the alpine regions of central Europe, lady's mantle and monkshood can be found growing wild in moist, humus-rich soil.

Monkshood

Fennel is native to the Mediterranean and grows wild on hillsides in dry, sunny positions, especially near the coast. It is one of our oldest cultivated plants.

Herbs from the Americas

While many of these plants were being used by Europeans, native peoples of other continents had their own herbal plants which over the years had proven beneficial. Native North Americans, for example, burnt sage brush or wormwood *Artemisia tridentata* along with other plants, to purify the air and repel insects. The also used teasel *Dipsacus fullonum*, a plant now much sought after by cottage garden enthusiasts, as an eyewash and for the removal of warts. And they knew all about the medicinal qualities of the purple coneflower *Echinacea purpurea* long before Europeans discovered them.

Research has proven that many of these plants belong to the same family as those long known in the Old World for their healing properties. The North American variety of wild mint, *Mentha arvensis* var. *villosa*, has similar growing needs to its relatives in Europe and shares their aromatic nature. It was used medicinally by native Americans, while a different variety of the same species in Asia was used in Chinese medicine.

South America has also contributed many of the herbs we know today. Early Spanish explorers discovered the vanilla vine *Vanilla planifolia*, a member of the orchid family, in Mexico, where the seed pods were used by the Aztecs as a flavoring. As demand for the essence distilled from the vanilla pods grew, farmers in tropical countries tried to grow the vine as a commercial crop, though without success, because it would not produce pods. Almost 300 years later, it was discovered that this was because pollinating insects were found only in the vine's native habitat. As a result, the flowers were then pollinated by hand.

Sorrel

Further south in Chile and Peru, lemon verbena *Aloysia triphylla* was found to have medicinal qualities that stimulated both the stomach and skin. Nasturtium *Tropaeolum majus*, found originally in the wild in Peru, Colombia and Bolivia, has been much hybridized, but leaves and flowers of the cultivars still provide a good substitute for pepper.

Loosestrife is native to Europe, Asia, northern Africa and Australia and has spread worldwide in damp places and wetlands. Its importation is restricted in some areas.

Herbs of the World

With Asian cuisine sweeping the world, Western countries have been introduced to many of the herbs originating in tropical areas and growing throughout southeast Asia, such as the caffre or kaffir lime. The citrus group of trees has been cultivated for so long its origins have been lost, while members of the ginger family, such as galangal and turmeric, can still be found growing wild across large areas where there is heat and humidity. The curry-leaf tree has spread from its native India and is found growing wild in many of the more tropical regions. The Malabar coast of India is also the original habitat of the pepper vine *Piper nigrum*.

Anise is one of many herbs originating in the Middle East, from where it is claimed to have spread to Egypt in 1500 BC. It was subsequently sought after in Rome for its digestive qualities.

In Australia, the value of indigenous herbs and native vegetation has only recently been recognized by Europeans, who have coined the term "bush food" to distinguish the many varieties of edible native plants. Seeds, roots and bark are still being sourced from the wild by Aboriginal populations, while plantations of some plants with proven qualities, such as some of the eucalyptus species, have been established to provide valuable oils. Recent interest in indigenous food has popularized such flavors as lemon myrtle, and such foods as wattle seed.

Herbs Through the Ages

Herbs have been used for many different purposes through the ages and their healing qualities have been known since prehistoric times. Through trial and error, the beneficial qualities were passed on to early generations and were written by the Sumerians onto stone tablets around 6,000 years ago. These tablets recorded that around 250 herbs were known, including the poppy, which was used as a narcotic and tranquilizer. There is evidence from around 2000 BC in Egypt that garlic and onions were used to feed the workers who built the pyramids. An Egyptian document known as the Ebers Papyrus, which dates from around 1500 BC and was discovered by archaeologists in 1874, lists medical prescriptions for hundreds of herbs for embalming, cosmetic, fumigation and medicinal purposes. One of these, combining field herbs, honey, dates and a grain known as *uah*, was required to be chewed for a day "to empty the belly and clear out all impurities from the body."

As well as the many plants that could relieve pain, it was also learnt that some herbs could have strange effects on the mind, while others could prove fatal. This knowledge became very valuable to early cultures, for whom there were no divisions between medicine, religion and science. In Egyptian culture, the goddesses Isis had the power to renew life and was reputed to have given this secret to mankind. One of her gods, Thoth, was responsible for prescriptions; today, the symbol of a physician is represented by Thoth's staff, around which a serpent is coiled.

Ancient Greece

The ancient Greeks began to ascribe a scientific basis to the medicinal qualities of herbs. The earliest Greek "herbals" (books detailing the culture and properties of herbs) were written around 300 BC and listed 500 plants based on the writings of Aristotle as well as his observations and the reports of travellers. In the first century AD, Dioscorides, in his *De Materia Medica*, described over 600 plants and detailed how they should be prepared for medicinal use and the effect that each had. This became the standard reference for over 1,500 years and many of the plants listed, such as dill, thyme and ginger, are still listed in herbals today.

After the fall of the Roman Empire, scientific research and writing in Europe came to a halt during the Dark Ages. During this time, however, in the Arab cultural centers of Baghdad and Damascus, scholars translated the works of the Greeks and added their own research, resulting in a number of popular herbals. This knowledge was eventually translated into Latin, the language of monastic scholars in medieval Europe.

Hippocrates, known as the father of medicine, used over 500 different drugs, mainly of herbal origins.

Early Herb Gardens

In Europe, herbs were first gathered from the wild, then cultivated around temples to ensure a ready supply for use in religious rituals. Plans exist of a herb garden created in St Gall, Switzerland, by the Benedictine monks in the 10th century.

By the 13th century, herbs were beginning to be cultivated in orchards for household use. As medicine and its ally botany were being taught in universities, gardens were being filled with plants sourced from around the world. The first such "physic" garden, with plants laid out to a simple plan, was established at Padua, Italy, in 1545. Such gardens became the botanic gardens of today. On a domestic level, these medieval gardens became more intricate, evolving into the elaborate knot gardens of Elizabethan times and the parterres of the châteaux in France.

It was believed that mandrake resembled the human form with its forked root and foliage.

In 1907, Gertrude Jekyll designed a decorative herb garden that became the basis for many gardens in Britain and America. In 1919, Maude Grieve, founder of the British Guild of Herb Growers, exhibited an herb garden at the Chelsea Flower Show. These events led to a renewed appreciation of herbs as decorative, useful garden plants.

Today, herbs can still be grown in intricate gardens as in the past, but increasingly they are planted among flowers, used as border plants or, as gardens become smaller, grown in containers.

Herbal Scents for Health

In former times, herbs were hung as fumigants to banish vermin and smells in ill-ventilated houses. Well-to-do men and women carried aromatic herbal posies or pomanders—small balls of ambergris with herbs and perfumes added—to mask unpleasant smells and ward off infection. Incense was not used just for religious ceremonies, but was commonly burnt to scent homes, keep away disease and perfume clothing. Early doctors prescribed its inhalation for medicinal purposes.

Culinary Usage

Before the days of refrigeration, when salt was used to preserve meat, herbs were added for flavor. Many of these only grew locally, but as exploration opened up the world, new plants were introduced into the Northern hemisphere from South America and added to the cooking pot. The English cook Mrs Beeton, in her renowned cookbook, referred to potatoes, onions and wild celery as "pot herbs"—a term from the days when these plants were mainly used for flavoring and had not been hybridized into the larger vegetables we know today. The definition of an herb is still evolving as plants that until recently were unknown outside a particular country are finding their way into everyday cuisine.

One of the wonderful aspects of globalization is the range of culinary herbs now readily available. One night, a Mediterranean-style meal can be prepared using herbs traditionally gathered from that region's dry hillsides, while the next evening, a Thai meal can be prepared using a number of herbs originally sourced from the lush, tropical fields of Asia.

With the development of electric drying midway through last century, herbs began to be green-dried and this led to a massive resurgence in their culinary use, as reflected on the shelves of our local supermarkets. But there is nothing to compare with using herbs straight from your garden—you can taste the difference.

This anonymous 18th century French painting illustrates the reception room of a master apothecary where drugs were made and dispensed.

Herbs in Myths and Legends

It's not surprising that the fragrant plants we call herbs were thought by ancient peoples to possess mystical properties. Today, we know these properties to be volatile oils and other chemical compounds. Scientific research into these substances is proving many of the tales of legend and folklore to be well founded.

Herbs of Honor and Courage

The list of herbs used in times gone by is long and interesting. Every culture used readily obtainable plants, and myths and legends grew up around their usage. For instance, today we use bay leaves *Laurus nobilis* mainly as a flavoring in cooking. In ancient Greece, however, they were associated with loyalty and honor and were dedicated to Apollo, the god of healing and prophecy. Branches of bay leaves were woven into wreaths and crowns for heroes and poets to wear—the term "poet laureate" stemmed from this custom. The Romans continued the association with bay or laurel berry, which they called *bacca laurus*, a name from which the academic terms "bachelor" and "baccalaureate" are derived.

Yarrow

Herbs for Healing

Yarrow, botanically named *Achillea millefolium* for the Greek hero Achilles, was said to be used to heal wounds during the Trojan War around 1260 BC. In medieval times, the finely divided leaves, which have blood-stanching qualities, were used to stop nosebleeds, and garlands of the herb were hung to protect homes from both disease and evil spirits.

Likewise, thyme was found to have numerous qualities, not least among them its use by ancient Greeks as a cure for a hangover. Indeed the herbalist John Gerard wrote in 1629 of thyme that it would weary both the reader and the writer to "sett downe" all the attributes of this wonder herb. The Greeks also held rue in high regard, using it as a remedy for indigestion, which they believed was visited upon them by witches rather than by over-eating. Later, Gerard wrote, "If a man be anointed with the juice of rue, the poison of wolf's bane, mushrooms, or todestooles, the biting of serpents, stinging of scorpions, bees and wasps will not hurt him." And Leonardo da Vinci claimed rue improved his eyesight and creative inner vision.

In more recent times, the Australian native blue gum *Eucalyptus globulus* was given the name "fever tree" when it was planted in Algeria in 1857 as a possible remedy for the tropical disease malaria. It dried up the marshy lands in which it was planted, thus eliminating the mosquitoes' habitat. Prior to this, however, it had been used in a more traditional healing sense by the Australian Aborigines as an antiseptic and to treat fevers.

Lovage

Love Potions

Besides the aptly named, heady-scented modern rose 'Love Potion', roses have been synonymous with sensuous potions for centuries. Petals of one, *Rosa* x *damascena*, were strewn over a canal during the wedding procession of a Persian princess. As it was a hot day, the oil from the floating petals mixed with the water, so that when the princess dipped her hand into the river, she smelt the exquisite perfume we know today as rosewater.

The origin of the common name lovage, given to the herb *Levisticum officinale*, has been lost in antiquity. Perhaps it, too, was used as an ingredient in potions of the heart. Similarly quinces, sent as presents in Roman times, were considered tokens of love. Up until the Middle Ages, quinces were presented at wedding feasts, according to Grieve, "to

In *The Annunciation* (attributed to Antoniazzo Romano), the Virgin Mary is presented with a madonna lily *Lilium candidum*. This flower, symbolizing purity, is closely associated with the Virgin Mary.

Herbs in Literature

Throughout history, writers and poets have used the language of herbs in various analogies.

"There's rosemary, that's for remembrance,
pray, love, remember,
and there is pansies, that's for thoughts."
SHAKESPEARE *Hamlet*

"Amongst my herbs sage holds the place of honor;
of good scent it is full; virtue for many ills."
WALAFRED STRABO, 9TH CENTURY ABBOT OF REICHENAU

"Better a dinner of herbs where love is,
than a stalled ox and hatred therewith."
The Bible, Proverbs

Sage

"I know a bank whereon the wild thyme blows,
Where oxslips and the nodding violet grows,
Quite over-canopied with luscious woodbine,
With sweet musk-roses, and with eglantine."
SHAKESPEARE *A Midsummer Night's Dream*

"How vainly men themselves amaze,
To win the palm, the oak, or bays;
And their incessant labors see,
Crowned from some single herb or tree."
ANDREW MARVELL *The Garden*

Rosemary

"For you there's rosemary, and rue,
these keep
Seeming and savor all the winter long."
SHAKESPEARE *The Winter's Tale*

RIGHT: John WIlliam Waterhouse, *Ophelia*

be a preparative of sweet and delightful dayes between the married persons."

In Norse folklore, a dart made from the mistletoe tree was used to kill the gentle god Balder, after which it was only allowed to grow high up in a tree and those meeting under it were required to kiss as a sign of love.

Ritual and Magic

Along with the development and use of herbs in religion and medicine, magicians and witches also used them in their rituals. The white flowers of hawthorn or may *Crataegus laevigata* were used in crowning the Queen of the May in pre-Christian times before she was sacrificed. No wonder the lovely white blossoms were thought of as bad omens in traditional British life and were never allowed over the threshold.

Mandrake *Mandragora officinarum* was one of the most magical and feared plants in the world. Its forked root was said to resemble the human form, and because the plant was thought to emit shrieks fatal to humans when uprooted, it was always dug up by a dog.

Legend states that winged serpents protect the frankincense and myrrh trees, which provided oil for rituals in ancient China, Egypt, Greece and Italy. In ancient Egypt, the sacred lotus flower *Nymphaea caerulea* was used as a garland in funeral rites and was also associated with Isis, the goddess of fertility.

Elder *Sambucus nigra* is thought by many cultures to be a magical plant. Gypsies considered it sacred, and in Germany one had to doff one's cap when passing by an elder bush. Because these trees are reputed to be a favorite haunt of witches, legend says that you should always ask permission before pruning one, lest you cause offence.

SECTION TWO

Planning and Design

When gardening, you need to take time to plan and design a garden that will fulfill your needs. Herbs can be planted in a garden on their own, tucked into existing flower beds or grown in decorative pots. But in this planning stage, keep in mind the two most important natural resources—your local climate and your soil.

Understanding Your Garden

You may have some idea of what you want from your herb garden, but do you know what kind of growing conditions you have to give your herbs? Learning about your garden, including its climate, topography, sunlight and soil, is critical for success in herb gardening. No matter what you plan to grow, you'll find that working with, rather than against, these factors will help you avoid many gardening problems.

The two most important natural resources to consider are your local climate and your soil. You might think that there is nothing you can do to change your climate (short of moving), and this is almost true. What you can do is grow the right plants at the right time and in the right place. All plants have basic requirements for temperature, moisture and light. Your gardening success depends on how well you understand these needs and the way plants interact with soil. If you understand how the environment works to make plants grow, you'll get the greatest rewards from gardening.

Good soil is like money in the bank. You'll have to make deposits (of organic matter and plant nutrients) before you can make withdrawals (of plentiful harvests). The "interest" that herb gardeners earn appears as healthy, pest-free plants and a soil that continues to improve with each gardening season.

Garden planning is one step that too many gardeners take lightly. Especially if you're a beginner, you should take the time to decide exactly what plants you want to grow and how you would like to grow them. Consider your future garden design plans as well. Most gardeners find that their landscape changes with each new growing season, simply because there's always something new to try. Make a rough garden plan and list the goals you'd like to accomplish each year. Gardens aren't completed overnight, but continue to grow and develop.

Keep track of new gardening methods and developments by subscribing to horticultural magazines. Some specialize in herbs, some in organic gardening, and so on. The organic method is gaining more attention and a wider following. Organic herb growers are increasing in numbers, so you'll have lots of company. Whatever your interests, compare notes with other gardeners; their knowledge and experience are other valuable resources.

Starting from Scratch

If you've just moved into a new development, built a new house or inherited a particularly uninspired all-lawn landscape, you may be staring at bare soil or an expanse of grass where you want a garden to be located. Most people want to jump straight in and begin gardening right away, but the best way to start is not to start—at least for a year or so. If you can stand it, try to live with the existing landscape for one full year. This way you can understand more about your garden before you begin. See where water puddles

TOP: Herbs in attractive containers are good for small spaces or as accents in larger gardens.
RIGHT: Keep in mind existing structures, such as garden paths, when planning your new design.

after storms or where it runs off quickly, taking valuable topsoil with it. Note where structures and trees cast shadows on your property through the seasons. See how traffic patterns develop. Where do you always walk to reach the car? Where do visitors walk on their way to the door? Where's the best place for the clothesline? And what about the children's playing area? All these are important considerations to plan for when you come to designing your garden.

Adapting an Existing Landscape

In some ways, adapting an existing landscape is more challenging than starting from scratch. Although your yard may have desirable features, such as large trees or an established lawn to work with, you also have someone else's mistakes to undo (or perhaps your own, which are even harder to face.)

One of the beauties of gardens is that they are not static, but change over the years.

If you've lived with the yard for at least a year, you are probably acutely aware of its troublesome areas or high-maintenance points. Don't try to change the whole yard at once, or you may create more headaches than you solve. Identify the elements you want to change, and choose a few (or one major one) to work on each year.

Trees and Shrubs

Whenever possible, try to keep existing trees and shrubs. If shrubs are overgrown, give them a facelift with a drastic pruning. If you do decide to remove a tree or shrub, make sure you dig out the stump—it's a lot of work, but it will save you time in the long run as you won't need to deal with suckers sprouting up from the roots. If you are tired of pruning hedges, consider replacing these high-maintenance elements with an informal herb hedge, such as a bay or lavender hedge.

Lawns

If you don't like to mow, you can replace some of the lawn with shrubs or trees, but you can also plant an herb lawn. Every time you walk over the ground, an herbal aroma will be released. If you have dry conditions, try growing chamomile or creeping thyme. For moist areas, plant mint or pennyroyal. Or you could put down some paving stones and plant thyme between the pavers.

Flowers

If your garden has existing flowers that are overgrown, dig them out and replace them with herb perennials. Or divide ones you want to keep and replant the vigorous outer parts in enriched soil. If you have favorites that aren't thriving, they may be in the wrong spot, so dig them up in spring and move them to a more favorable site.

Paths and Walkways

If your existing paths are in the wrong spot, or made from the wrong material, it's best in the long run to rip them up and start again. The paving material you choose should complement the style or color of your existing landscape or home. For example, a brick path looks good with a brick home, while a stone path complements a country cottage. Make sure you keep the path well drained so you can use it during wet weather.

Hints for Easy Herbs

When planning your garden and choosing which herbs you want to grow, check out their maintenance considerations below.

Basil For best leaf production, you will need to pick off flower heads as they form (every few days). You will need to water basil regularly.

Chives Easy to grow, but can reseed prolifically if you don't clip off spent flowers.

Dill Let a few plants self-sow the first year, and you'll probably never need to replant. Pull seedlings from where they're not wanted, or remove flowers if you don't want seedlings.

Mint Most species tend to spread rapidly unless contained. Plant in bottomless pots sunk in the soil to 1 inch (2.5 cm) below the rim. Or grow as container plants.

Oregano Needs well-drained soil and organic matter added each year. Plant in sandy soil for best results.

Parsley Seeds are slow to germinate and seedlings can get swamped by weeds. Often easiest to start from transplants.

Rosemary In cold climates, treat as an annual and buy new plants each year.

Sage Start from transplants; easy to grow.

Thyme Won't compete well with weeds, so keep weeded until plants become established.

Chives

Garden Planning

For an herb garden to be effective, it has to match your site conditions, your style, the amount of time you can set aside for gardening and the results that you want to achieve. Do you want a separate herb garden or would you prefer to incorporate herbs into other plantings? If you're planning a new herb garden, you'll need to consider your garden's location, size, shape and design. Start out simple. Seek inspiration from books and experienced gardeners. If you enjoy formal patterns, plan your garden along the lines of an Italian Renaissance garden or a knot garden, in which intertwining miniature hedges of different herbs create a knotlike shape. For something easier and more informal, think about planning a cottage garden. Or perhaps you would prefer to specialize and grow a kitchen garden full of culinary herbs, a scented garden, a medicinal herb garden, or simply a wild garden with a variety of different herbs.

Where your garden space is limited, a decorative and practical solution is to use pots and hanging containers brimming with herbs. Pots are also good for growing invasive herbs, such as mint.

The Garden Site

First decide where to locate your herb garden. You could reassign a section of your existing vegetable or flower garden, or perhaps create a whole new garden devoted to herbs. Or you may choose to place herbs in several different small sites around your garden. If you're starting from scratch, put as much thought as you can into site selection. You can avoid many problems by choosing a good location, especially if you plan to live in the same place for several years.

Your garden site has to suit the plants you plan to grow. If your site is shady, choose herbs that will tolerate shade. If your site has wet conditions part of the year, choose plants that can tolerate this. If you have a range of possible sites, choose the one that provides as closely as possible the specific requirements of the plants you want to grow.

An ideal site will also correspond with your ideas of what a garden should be and where it should be. It may be most convenient for you to have your herb garden located near the kitchen door. Or perhaps you'll get most enjoyment from one that may be viewed from indoors through a window.

To choose a site, begin with a tour of your garden, keeping in mind the following considerations:

- If possible, choose a level site with good drainage, since it is easier to garden on flat surfaces and soil erosion won't be a concern for you.
- Avoid hills that lose moisture quickly.
- Stay away from pockets of low-lying land, where poor drainage and inadequate air circulation could encourage related disease and pest problems for your plants.
- Plan to garden across slopes, rather than in rows running up and down them, to prevent erosion.
- Avoid areas where the soil is compacted and therefore hard to dig.
- Be sure that you have proper access to your garden site. You may only need room for a wheelbarrow to move between rows or beds, or you may need to provide access for a truck to deliver a load of soil.
- Clear rocks and brush from the site before you start your garden.
- Avoid planting in the root zones of trees, as digging around the roots could injure the trees, and the trees will compete with the herbs for moisture and nutrients in the soil.
- Be sure you have access to an adequate water supply.
- Choose a site where your plants will get adequate light for at least part of the day.

Garden Size

The size of your herb garden will be determined by how much you want to grow and harvest, the suitable space available to you, the amount of time you have and the availability of resources. If you're a beginner, it may be best to start with a small garden and work with this until you gain experience.

When deciding on the size of your herb garden, you must think realistically about the time you have available to tend your garden. The time any garden needs varies with climate and season, as do the tasks to be done. You'll need to prepare the soil by

When planning your garden, take into consideration the space, size and look you want to achieve. Ideally, the well-organized garden will include culinary herbs, such as chives, as close as possible to the kitchen.

digging and adding nutrients where necessary, plant your seeds or seedlings, and perform regular maintenance tasks, such as weeding, watering, pest control and harvesting. The work will be slower and heavier if you're using hand tools than if you're using powered tools, such as a rotary tiller.

How much you want to harvest will influence the size of garden you need. One or two plants of an herb you have not grown before will usually be enough, but you will soon develop favorites and learn which grow well in your garden. You may know that you want to grow enough basil to make a batch of pesto sauce each week. Or you may want to have a variety of herbs available for drying to make potpourris. Your plans must allow space for the plants you want your garden to produce for you. Parsley, for example, is a popular and nutritious herb with many culinary uses, so it is worthwhile having a dozen plants at a time to ensure a good supply. A dozen basil plants would not be too many for your weekly pesto sauces. In the garden, a dozen parsley plants would require 3 square feet (about .3 sq m) of space, and a dozen basil plants would need about 2 square feet (about .2 sq m). A larger perennial, such as angelica, would need about 4 square feet (about .4 sq m), while a wide shrub, such as barberry, would need 6 square feet (about .6 sq m). The spacing guidelines on the seed packet, or in "A Guide to Popular Herbs," starting on page 172, will give you an idea on how much space your herbs will need.

Matching Resources

If soil moisture is limited, due to climate, soil type or topography, you will have to devise a way to supply water. A large garden will require more water than a small one. Mulching is an excellent way to control weeds and conserve soil moisture, but if you plan to mulch, how much material will you need? If you are starting a herb garden, how much of an investment can you afford to make in soil amendments, plants, seeds, watering equipment, tools and structures during the first year? If you're unsure of the answers to these questions, it's probably best to keep it small and simple the first year and extend as you gain experience.

Garden Style

Regardless of the size, shape or location of your garden, its style is a reflection of your own tastes and is a chance to add a personal touch. At one extreme are the formal gardens with their angular knots and pruned hedges, and at the other are random groupings of whatever suits the season. The number of possible herb-garden styles is limited only by your imagination, creativity and the effect you want to create. You can plan one or more theme gardens to concentrate on a particular aspect.

Formal Gardens

Formal landscaping uses straight lines, sharp angles and symmetrical plantings with a limited number of plants. They are usually laid out in squares or rectangles with low hedges of clipped evergreens or brick walls to define different areas of the garden. The key to success with a formal garden is uniformity—you want the plants to be evenly spaced and evenly developed. Often the beds on either side of a straight central path are planted with the same sequence of plants, thus forming a mirror image of each other. Formal designs tend to have a restful feel. But they may not be as restful for the gardener, because you'll need to clip, stake and weed on a regular basis to keep the plants looking perfect.

Informal Gardens

Informal landscapes use curving lines to create a more natural feeling. They tend to have few permanent features, such as walls or hedges, although elements such as rustic split-rail fences and wood-chip paths add greatly to the informal feel. These kinds of gardens generally include many different types of plants—trees, shrubs, annuals, perennials, herbs and vines. Informal designs are relaxed and lively and are better suited to the ordinary small backyards of many houses today. Herbs can be planted in any part of the garden—beds, borders, raised beds or containers—to blend in with the overall garden design. Since the plants are free to spread and sprawl, they tend to need less regular maintenance to still look well tended. You won't need to keep sharp edges on the beds, and the few weeds that pop up won't be immediately obvious and ruin the look of the garden.

This cottage garden groups annuals, perennials and shrubs around a structural focal point.

Mixed Gardens

It's difficult to mix informal and formal areas effectively, but sometimes the classic formal garden can seem a little too rigid. The modern approach is to plant sections of a formal garden with a touch of informality by maintaining the basic geometric shapes but softening the angles with creeping and trailing edges.

Cottage Gardens

The ultimate in informality, cottage gardens display a glorious riot of colors, textures, heights and fragrances. Cottage gardens defy many gardening "rules": plants are packed closely together, ignoring standard spacing; colors aren't organized into large drifts; tall plants pop up in front of shorter ones; flowers are allowed to grow through each other to create a delightful, casual mixture. While cottage gardens may appear effortless and unorganized, they need to be planned, planted and maintained just like any other garden.

For a formal look, include such elements as straight paths, symmetrical plantings and tightly clipped, closely planted low hedges.

Bog Gardens

While most herbs prefer warm, well-drained positions, some have an affinity for wet ground and will thrive at the edge of a pond or in a boggy or marshy area. Such plants as irises, horsetail and marsh mallow will grow well in these moist areas. If you do not have a naturally wet area but enjoy the beauty of bog plants, keep this in mind when designing your garden, as you can create your own.

The classic cottage garden is an eclectic collection of plants, including perennials, annuals, herbs and roses, allowed to ramble and intertwine. Cottage gardens usually are at least partially enclosed within walls, hedges or fences, making them a natural choice for a small suburban house or a contemporary townhouse with an enclosed garden. You might allow the plants to spread unchecked or to self-sow, letting the seedlings grow where they want. For this to work well, though, you must be willing to do some rearranging if the plants pop up where they're not wanted. Unify the scene with a permanent focal point, such as a path that marches through the garden's center to a door, patio or bench.

Elaborate knot gardens of interwoven herbs first became popular in the 15th century in Europe.

Knot Gardens

If you like garden beds formed from simple geometric patterns, why not try an even more elaborate, eye-catching design and plant a knot garden? Knot gardens were first recorded in the 15th century and are one of the most traditional styles of herb garden planting. Hedges or border plants are used to create ribbons or knots of color, forming intricate designs.

Shrubs and Trees

When planning your herb garden, try to include some shrubs and trees for variety. Some plants we think of as herbs, such as rosemary and thyme, are in fact shrubs, as they have woody growth. If conditions are to their liking, they can live for years. Trees, such as bay or the caffre (kaffir) lime, are long lived and need careful positioning not only for you to pick the leaves but also to prevent them shading out your herb garden. They also make ideal container plants, and can be positioned in a sunny courtyard just outside the kitchen door. For extra visual interest, trim them into neat mounds or fun lollipop shapes.

If this type of garden appeals to you, try to keep the pattern relatively simple, as the more intricate designs can end up looking muddled and the more complicated the design, the more work is needed to maintain it. An important point to keep in mind is that knot gardens are best viewed from a height. Try to place them where they can be viewed from an upstairs window or a higher part of the garden, to get the best effect. A center feature also works well in knot gardens, such as a statue, sundial or large flowering plant in a pot—anything to catch the eye.

Herbal Potager

The word "potager" is French for a kitchen garden, but the meaning of the word has changed over the years. Such gardens date back to medieval times and were once walled gardens used to grow medicinal herbs, adjacent to churches. Today, "potager" refers to a kitchen or herb garden laid out in a formal pattern based on geometrical shapes, mainly circular, square, rectangular or triangular. Potagers include a number of different beds with mixed plantings of herbs. Paths or hedges divide the beds. Hedges can be grown from a variety of plants, including box and lavender, and the paths between the hedges can be covered with gravel or wood chips. Herbal potagers don't need a lot of room in the garden—a small potager for the most common culinary herbs can be planted near the house so herbs can be cut fresh and used immediately.

Whatever the garden style you choose, remember that most herbs have originated from warmer, Mediterranean climates and will require at least five or six hours of sunlight a day. Keep this in mind and consider shadows from the house, garage, fences and tall trees already in the garden. Also think about the exciting visual effects that can be created by placing together herbs of vivid, contrasting tones, or, if you would prefer, more muted complementary colors.

Garden Shapes

The simplest gardens to set out and manage are square or rectangular. If you must take advantage of every available bit of space, it makes sense to closely follow the general outline of your property. Because land is most often sold in boxlike shapes, laying out your herb garden with square or rectangular beds not only may be the most practical way, but also can

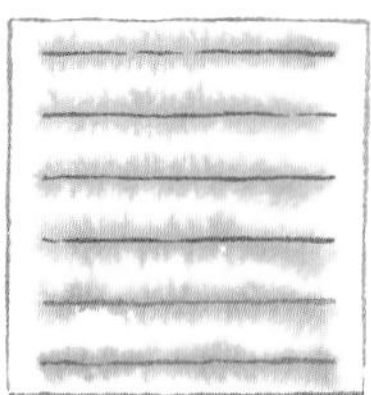

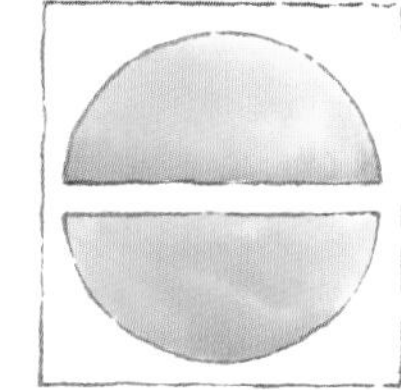

These four diagrams show practical approaches to designing an herb garden.

give the garden a formal look that appeals to many gardeners.

Of course, squares and rectangles aren't the only shapes. You may choose to lay your garden beds following the curve of a hill, stream, fence or stone wall, or design them to accent the shape of a building. If you want to be especially creative, garden within unusual boundaries, such as circles or ovals. You can make a garden in the shape of a spiral with one continuous bed beginning in the center and spiraling out in circles. (It is best to avoid circles and curves if you have limited space.) A book or magazine on garden landscaping will offer you examples to follow in shaping your garden beds.

If you choose to garden in several small patches, position plants that need daily attention or frequent picking close to the house. If space is limited, take advantage of borders along paths and fences. At the least, you can dress your windows outdoors with boxes of luscious herbs close at hand.

Paths

For convenient access, herbs need to be planted no more that 2 feet (60 cm) from a path, so unless you plan to insert stepping stones, beds should measure no more than 4–5 feet (1–1.5 m) across. Paths are important in your overall garden design for the effect they can bring, as well as the way they can define shapes. Try to avoid paths that go straight across the garden, as this suggests rushing ahead. An herb garden needs to create a feeling of a place where you want to linger. Instead, incorporate curving paths or change the direction of a straight path; break the flow by changing the pattern of the paving material, or add a birdbath or sundial.

Walls

An important aspect of a traditional herb garden is some type of enclosure, such as a wall or hedge. Enclosures can reduce wind damage to your plants and raise the overall average temperature. A solid garden wall can increase the temperature around it to the equivalent of moving 200 miles (320 km) closer to the equator. Walls also give a feeling of privacy and solitude and can help contain the perfume of your aromatic herbs. When constructing a wall, choose materials that will match the texture and color of your house and other hard surfaces, such as terraces or paths. Plant sun-loving herbs at the base of the wall. If you are planning a rock wall, include herbs such as chamomile, which enjoy rocky, dry locations and will grow in all the nooks and crannies.

Hedges

Once established, hedging is a great long-term enclosure. You can use a variety of herbs as hedges. Hedging can be neat and formal or soft and wild, depending on the type of plants you choose and how you trim them. For low hedges, try growing lavender, santolina and rosemary, but make sure you check whether the particular species can survive the winter conditions of your area. For higher hedges, box *Buxus sempervirens*, yew *Taxus* spp. and sweetbriar rose, with its apple-scented leaves, are good choices.

An eye-catching central feature, such as a sundial, works well to unify a garden.

Fences

If you don't want a hedge for a boundary, select fencing, such as timber or bamboo, that will harmonize with the color and softness of your herbs. Solid paneling gives the greatest amount of privacy and allows climbing plants to climb up it, but solid fences do block out light and cast shadows over your garden. Open fencing, such as post-and-rail or pickets, allows light to reach your garden and also allows better ventilation for your plants and so reduces the risk of plant disease. Whatever type of fence you choose, it will require ongoing maintenance, so choose the best quality materials you can afford.

Formal gardens tend to use straight lines; informal gardens have curved lines and less rigid plantings.

Garden Design

With all the ideas you now have for your herb garden swirling around in your head, go outside to your chosen site and outline the shape of the planting area with a flexible hose or rope. Step back and walk around the garden to see how the dimensions look from several different viewpoints (including the view through your windows).

Check your garden layout with a hose, buckets and other items to represent the various plants.

Put Your Ideas on Paper

If you are happy with what you see, you can start putting your plans down on paper. Sketching garden designs will allow you to try out different ideas on paper, without physically digging up your backyard. Measure the length and width of the area you have targeted for the herb garden. Determine an appropriate outline and draw it to scale on graph paper. Choose the largest scale that allows your design to fit on one sheet: 1 inch (2.5 cm) on paper to 1 foot (30 cm) of planting area works well for gardens smaller than 10 feet (3 m). Draw in the major existing features, such as buildings, trees, shrubs, fences and paths. This is also a good place to jot down notes about the soil conditions in the various planting areas: is it frequently wet, often dry or evenly moist? Note also the amount and type of sunshine available: does the garden get full sun, just a few hours of morning or afternoon sun, or no direct sun at all? Do neighbors' houses cast shadows over the garden? Are there any hills or slopes you need to consider?

Make several photocopies of your base plan, or lay sheets of tracing paper over the original sketch. This way you'll always have a fresh base plan to work with.

Start sketching your designs. Mark in your garden beds and paths. Paths are a necessity in your garden. For both work and leisure, make garden paths 4–5 feet (1.2–1.5 m) wide. If you're planting in beds, keep them under 5 feet (1.5 m) wide, not more than twice the distance you are able to reach from the side. You'll want to avoid walking on beds as you work.

Once you've located your paths, garden beds or rows, begin selecting and arranging your plants. Prepare a list of the plants you want to grow, along with their growth habits, size at maturity, and special soil, space, or environmental requirements. Refer to "A Guide to Popular Herbs," starting on page 172, for specific information about each herb's requirements. Remember that single plants tend to become lost in the crowd; it's more effective to plant in groups. It's generally best to plant the tallest herbs at the back and the shortest in the front.

It's important to keep the following points in mind when you plan the design of your garden:

- Use your site's limitations to your advantage. If you're confined to gardening in the shade, use the opportunity to grow as many shade-loving herbs as possible. Include angelica, chervil, lemon balm and sweet cicely. In wet areas, select from the wide assortment of plants in the mint family. Among the herbs, you'll find plants to fill just about every niche of your garden.
- Divide a large garden, or create several small gardens, by grouping herbs that serve particular purposes. Medicinal, dye, fragrance and culinary gardens are some examples.

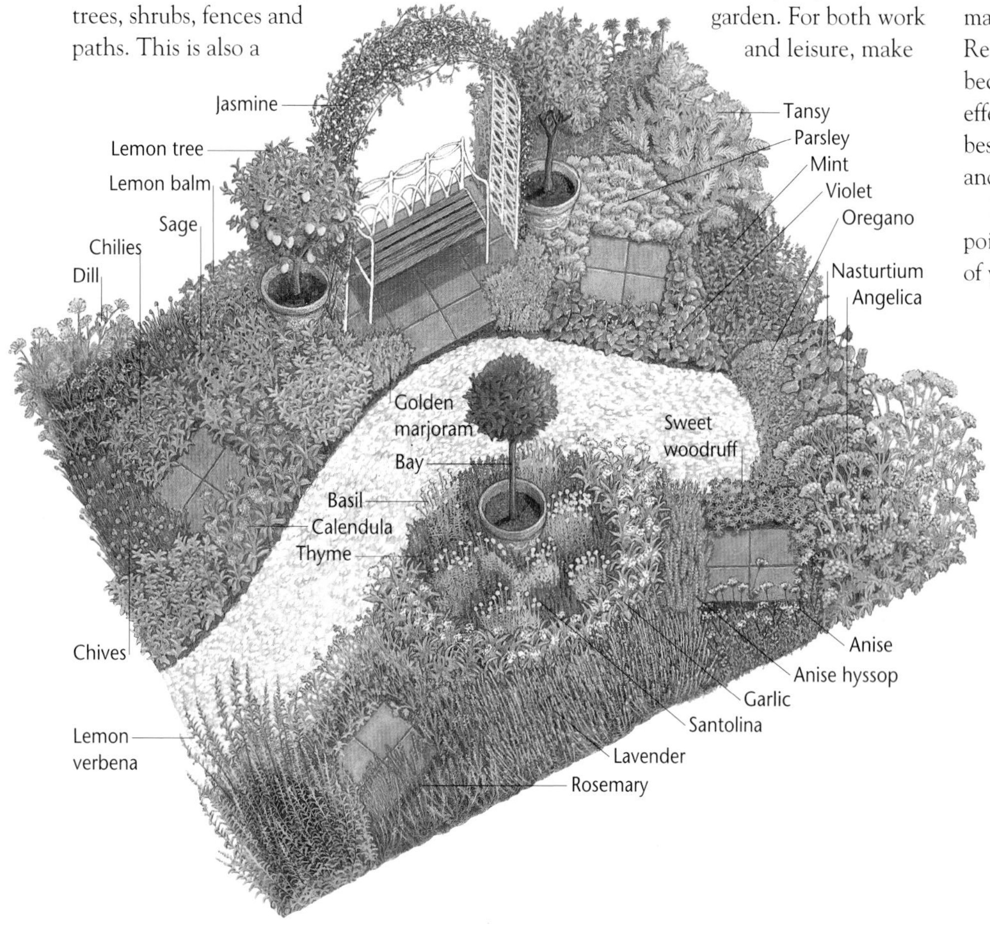

Jasmine
Lemon tree
Lemon balm
Sage
Chilies
Dill
Golden marjoram
Bay
Basil
Calendula
Thyme
Chives
Lemon verbena
Rosemary
Lavender
Santolina
Garlic
Anise hyssop
Anise
Sweet woodruff
Angelica
Nasturtium
Oregano
Violet
Mint
Parsley
Tansy

Water features give a sense of coolness to your garden. Plant moisture-loving herbs nearby.

- Select herbs that flower at the same time or are the same color. Lavender and blue themes especially are easy to create with herbs. Or focus on foliage, and plant blue-green or silvery herbs mixed with darker greens for contrast.
- Try to group perennials together, because they tend to have similar requirements and this will help you with maintenance. If you're planning to grow invasive perennials, such as mint, among other herbs, plant them in buried containers, such as clay pipes or bottomless large pots, that are at least 1 foot (30 cm) deep.

Tansy, parsley and bee balm (bergamot) are plants that have similar growing requirements. Grouping plants together with similar needs helps you conserve resources in your garden.

This aromatic herb border is brimming with fragrant herbs such as lavender, parsley and plants from the onion family. Themed gardens are a delight for both the gardener and visitor.

Planning Your Plants

As you finalize your plant list, start thinking about how to organize the different plants in the garden. To visualize possible color combinations, cut circles representing each group of flowers out of colored paper, matching the paper color to the flower color. Juggle these around until you find combinations that you like. If you have decided that you want different areas of the garden dedicated to different herb groupings, such as culinary, medicinal or fragrant herbs, cut out pieces of cardboard to represent each group. Move them around your base plan until you are happy with how they look.

Experiment with different arrangements and designs until you are happy with the results on paper. Then go out into the yard and visualize how the design will look. Place objects in the garden to represent plants to see the overall effect.

Container Herbs

If you live in a high-rise apartment building where you have no ground for a garden, you can still design your own lush herb garden using the space you have. More herbs are grown in containers than anywhere else, especially the best-known culinary herbs. So if you have a balcony, stairway or window sill with plenty of light, you can enjoy the fun of growing your own herbs as well as reaping the rewards with their aroma and taste. Container herbs fare better and look more attractive when grouped together, and they are also easier to water. Plan herbs to enhance different rooms of your house—a clipped bay or sweet myrtle in a sunny entrance hall; a mint in the moist air of the bathroom; scented geranium and lemon verbena to scent a living room; aromatic lavender in the bedroom; soothing aloe vera near the medicine chest; hanging baskets with trailing catnip and prostrate sage in the stairwell; and culinary herbs, such as parsley, chives and basil, on the kitchen window sill.

RIGHT: Climbing roses tumbling from a pergola add height and informality to this herb garden.

Design Rules for Your Garden

While designing a garden is a very personal and creative activity, following some basic design rules will give your finished garden a cohesive look, whether you are aiming for a polished feel or a more natural one. The key rules are to create balance and rhythm and to add a dominant feature to tie the garden together.

First, keep the garden in balance. Include plants with a mix of heights and sizes throughout your plantings. Don't plant all of the tall or massive flowers on one side, with a group of low, delicate plants on the other. In formal gardens, you may balance one side of the garden by planting the same design on the other, making a mirror image. For an informal garden, you can vary the plantings, perhaps matching perennial herbs with red flowers on one side with shrubs with yellow flowers on the other. In this case you are matching brighter color with larger size.

Second, create a rhythm, or a sense of continuity, throughout the entire garden. You can repeat groupings of the same plant or use other plants with identical colors or similar flower shapes. Let a middle-of-the-border plant drift from the foreground to the background, giving a sense of movement and uniting the different layers of the garden.

Third, establish a dominant feature. This focal point can be a path, sculpture, birdbath, sundial, pergola or tree with the garden built around it.

It is worth the effort to work out an initial plan for your garden. Factors to take into consideration include light, moisture, soil and topography.

Herbs for Different Plantings

Include in your design different garden themes for different herbs. You can include the following herbs:

A Cook's Garden
Angelica, basil, bay, borage, burnet, caraway, chervil, chives, cilantro (coriander), dill, garlic, ginger, lemongrass, lemon tree, lovage, marjoram, mint, nasturtium, oregano, parsley, rosemary, sage, tarragon, thyme

A Medicinal Garden
Agrimony, aloe, angelica, anise hyssop, bee balm (bergamot), blackcurrant, burdock, calendula, caraway, chamomile, chicory, comfrey, fennel, garlic, horehound, horseradish, horsetail, lovage, marjoram, nettle, rosemary, sage, St John's wort, tansy, thyme, yarrow

A Fragrant Garden
Angelica, basil, bee balm (bergamot), catnip, chives, clove pink, geranium, jasmine, lavender, lemon balm, lemon verbena, mint, nasturtium, parsley, rose, scented geranium, thyme, violet

A Tea Garden
Angelica, basil, bee balm (bergamot), borage, catnip, chamomile, dandelion, goldenrod, horehound, jasmine, lemongrass, lemon verbena, lovage, marjoram, mint, parsley, rosemary, sage, sweet cicely, tansy, thyme, woodruff

Container Herbs

Containers are excellent receptacles for growing herbs, especially if space is tight. Containers brimming with herbs look very attractive when grown near your kitchen door or in a window box. This way you can simply reach out and cut some basil leaves or a sprig of rosemary when you need it. A tub of chervil, with its feathery foliage, grown on a sunny balcony looks just as attractive as a potted fern, but chervil has practical uses, too.

Marjoram, oregano, rosemary, sage, mint and thyme will all thrive in containers. Once you have successfully cultivated herbs that you use regularly in cooking, you can go on to grow some of the more exotic varieties.

You can plant sun-lovers such as basil, sage, rosemary and thyme in the same container. If you have a partly shady area, plant lemon balm, lovage, tansy, oregano and parsley. They will tolerate as little as 4 hours of sun per day.

Mint is an ideal herb for container growing because its runners can spread too rapidly in a garden bed. Mint likes moist soil, so add water-saving granules to the container mix and keep it well watered. Place bay in a large pot and clip it to create a standard. Plant cilantro (coriander) in a large trough, but not during the heat of summer, as it will bolt to seed. You can clip the leaves as required or harvest the whole plant if you want the root. Annual dill may be sown as soon as the danger of frost is over and you can clip fresh leaves as you need them.

The natural beauty of terracotta lends itself to containers and window boxes. But make sure you keep up the water to your plants, as terracotta is porous and draws water away from plants.

Strawberries are well suited to containers. Plant them in strawberry barrels—containers with a number of holes on the side—to create an attractive and useful display.

Type of Container

The first step to successful container gardening is choosing the right pot. Large pots tend to provide the best conditions for growth, since they hold more soil, nutrients and water, but they are also quite heavy if you ever need to move them around or hang them up. For herbs, pots that hold about 2 to 4 gallons (9 to 18 l) of growing medium work best. Small trees or shrubs can start out in 2- to 4-gallon (9- to 18-l) pots, but you'll probably need to move them to larger containers after their first season. Large plants, such as gardenia or citrus trees, will be more productive if given plenty of room. Five- to 10-gallon (23- to 45-l) containers are best for such plants.

The material that a container is made from can be just as important as its size. Each kind of material has advantages and disadvantages, depending on what you are growing and where you are growing it.

Clay and terracotta pots look very attractive and are generally heavier than other materials, so that taller plants won't blow over in the wind. However, these pots are porous and lose moisture that may be needed by your plants. Another problem with clay and terracotta pots is that if you live in an area where the temperatures dip below freezing, they can crack and break when moisture in the soil expands as it freezes. To avoid this you either need to move the pots inside

Fruit Herbs for Containers

Raising fruit crops in containers is easier than putting a lot of work into growing fruit in a full-scale garden. You can have a steady supply of fresh produce right outside your door. Strawberries are a popular choice. Buy certified plants from your local garden center and plant them straight into pots.

Citrus trees are another good choice for containers. Dwarf varieties such as 'Eureka' or 'Meyer' lemon, or the typical small green Mexican lime, grow well in pots. They need plenty of sun and fertilizer in summer, along with regular watering to keep them in peak production. Move the pots inside in the cold winter months, except in areas with a mild climate.

Kumquats

Herbs will thrive in containers if placed in a sunny position and given a little attention.

during winter or empty them, and clean and store until the next growing season.

Plastic and fiberglass pots are much lighter than clay and terracotta pots, so can be moved more easily. They don't dry out as fast and are usually less expensive. However the main disadvantages are that as they are much lighter, they tend to blow over more often in the wind and they also require good drainage and soil aeration.

Wood is a good alternative for container pots, as it insulates the plant roots from overheating in summer and freezing in winter, but it tends to rot over time. If you like the look of wood, you could use plastic liners to reduce the risk of decay.

Whatever kind of container material you choose, look for pots and planters that are light in color, especially if you live in a hot climate. They help to reflect the heat and keep the roots cool. Black pots are the worst choice in hot climates, because they can absorb enough heat to damage tender roots.

Drainage

Another important factor to consider when choosing a container is to make sure it has adequate drainage holes. This is critical for healthy root growth and top growth. Medium-sized containers need at least six holes ½ inch (12 mm) in diameter. More are needed in larger pots. If you are using a pot without drainage holes, place a few blocks of wood in the base and place your potted plant on top. The wood will keep the plant from sitting in the water that collects in the base of the outer pot.

Don't overwater your herb plants, since they prefer to be slightly on the dry side rather than being continually moist. If the container mix is good quality and has adequate drainage, water will not collect in the container and the roots will not become waterlogged. How often to water depends on the size of the pot and the requirements of the plant. Unglazed clay pots are very porous, so the soil in them tends to dry out rapidly. Plants grown in these will require more frequent watering.

Container Mixes

Once you have picked the perfect container, fill it with the best possible growing medium. While soil is fine in the garden, it is a bad choice for plants in pots when used alone. The frequent watering will cause most real soil to compact into a tight, bricklike mass, or if your garden soil is very sandy, it will dry out much too quickly in a container. The answer is to use a soil mix that is specially blended for plants in containers. To make your own container mix, see "Caring for Container Herbs" on pages 112–113.

Balconies, Courtyards and Window Boxes

If you live in an apartment or house where you have no garden, you can still create a lush green oasis with container-grown plants on a balcony, in a courtyard or even on an outdoor stairway. City dwellers can grow gardens entirely in containers on building rooftops. Even if you have nothing but a wall and windows to call your own, you can fill hanging baskets with trailing plants and pack window boxes full of herbs.

Balcony Backyard

If you live in an apartment with a balcony, a clever use of containers can help create a colorful, productive area perfect for relaxing and entertaining. But before you start your balcony garden, you must first consider what amount of weight your balcony can bear. Most newer apartment balconies have concrete floors, but some have wooden floors that are not designed to support heavy weights. In these cases, use plastic containers and spread the weight over a larger area. Check that drainage is adequate and that no damage will be caused by water.

Note the direction the balcony faces, how much sun it receives and how exposed it is to wind. Keep your design simple, taking in the size of the balcony and the furniture you want to include. The last thing you want is a cluttered, busy look without room for anything else. Use hanging baskets, trellises and climbing plants to bring the walls to life.

Just because you live in an apartment doesn't mean you have to be deprived of a garden. You can still enjoy growing your own herbs. A decorative hanging basket filled with your favorite herbs can be hung just outside your kitchen window ready for you to reach out and snip off foliage as you need it.

Courtyards

A courtyard is a natural extension of the house and provides a small, enclosed area in which to create a unique atmosphere. When designing this area, think carefully if you want it to have a formal or an informal style and the type of plants you want to feature. Several large containers or planter boxes can be more eye-catching than a collection of small pots. Courtyard walls cry out for climbing plants or plants of different heights. Plant larger perennial trees and shrubs at the back and a range of herbs in a large trough at the front. Even if your courtyard does not receive a lot of sun, there are many herbs that will tolerate shade, including tarragon, thyme, chervil and mint.

Window Boxes

Nothing adds country charm to a home like lush window boxes dripping with cascades of colorful flowers and foliage. Window boxes can be made of metal, wood, terracotta, cement or plastic and can be simple and unadorned, or painted, carved and molded.

Before you begin your window box garden, there are a few points you need to consider. Make sure you will be able to reach the boxes for watering and maintenance. Also check that ledges or brackets are strong enough for the purpose. Stick with short plants. Window boxes are usually planted to be seen from the outside, but remember you still have to see out the window. Use plants about 8 inches (20 cm) in height; those much taller than this will block your view.

Hanging Baskets

Hanging baskets look great anywhere. They come in different sizes and colors and are made from a variety of materials. The true hanging-garden enthusiast usually prefers a moss basket—a wire frame lined with sphagnum moss or a layer of similar fibrous material to hold the container mix and plants. One main advantage of this type of basket is that you can poke in extra fiber from the outside if you find that water is running out of thinner sections.

Hanging baskets are great for annual herbs that grow quickly. The dry, warm conditions that are characteristic of hanging baskets suit many herbs, such as oregano, thyme, cilantro (coriander), basil and lemon balm. As these herbs will be picked often, hang your herb basket within easy reach of the kitchen. However, hanging baskets dry out fast, so remember to keep up the water.

Herbs for Balconies and Courtyard

A wide variety of herbs can be grown successfully on a balcony or in a courtyard. Try planting: Aloe, anise hyssop, basil, bay, bee balm (bergamot), chamomile, chervil, chives, citrus, cilantro (coriander), dill, echinacea, gardenia, geranium, jasmine, lavender, lemon balm, lemongrass, marjoram, mint, oregano, parsley, rosemary, roses, sage, sweet cicely, thyme.

Lemongrass

Creating a Window Box Display

You can improve the view from your window by simply planting a window box of beautiful herbs on the window sill outside. Herbs will thrive in this location if it is sunny and you provide adequate food and water. Choose a container that is in keeping with the style of your home. A simple material, such as terracotta, always looks good.

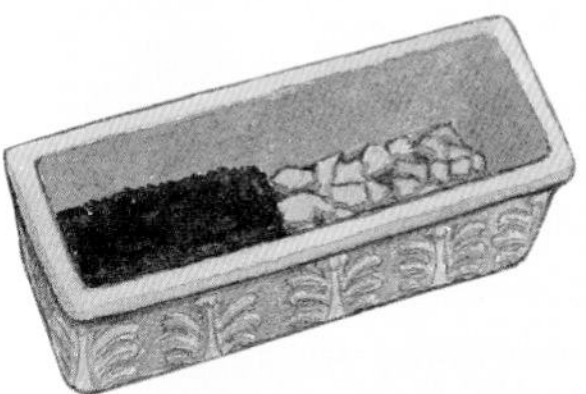

Line the window box with a layer of bark chips for good drainage. Add a 2-inch (5-cm) layer of a good container mix.

Arrange the herbs in the window box, experimenting with the design until you are happy with the arrangement.

First plant the herbs that will grow tallest, and then the lower-growing herbs. Firm up the container mix around the plants. Water well.

You can grow a productive garden of shrubs and herbs in the confined space of a balcony. Make sure you check the conditions of your balcony so you know if your plants will be exposed to high winds.

Climate

Climate—the seasonal cycles of rainfall, temperatures, humidity, frost and a combination of other factors—has a major influence on which plants will thrive in your landscape. The way temperature, moisture and wind interact in a particular region produces what is known as local climate. It is most important for gardeners to understand their local climate, as this will influence their choice of plants.

Before making your garden plans and selecting which herbs to grow, you should consider the normal weather patterns of your area. Since "normal" weather includes the unexpected, enthusiastic gardeners need to become avid weather watchers. You will have to monitor the weather in order to provide your plants with three basic requirements: a suitable temperature range, a favorable frost-free period, and an adequate supply of moisture.

Temperature Range

The leafy green exterior of any plant gives no indication of the complex chemical processes occurring within. These processes are temperature-dependent, and different plants vary in their temperature requirements.

When it comes to air-temperature preference, most plants have upper and lower limits, and are classified as cool-season, warm-season, or adaptable to both. Cool-season herbs, such as mustard and chives, continue growing even when the temperature drops as low as 40°F (4°C), but they stop growing or die during the heat of summer. Warm-season herbs, such as basil, are heat-lovers, and won't grow unless the temperature is 50°F (10°C) or above. Basil is very sensitive to the cold and usually dies with the first cold snap in autumn.

Hardy perennial herbs (those that live for more than two years) are cold tolerant and will survive the extremes of winter by becoming dormant. Dormancy means that the chemical processes normally occurring inside a plant slow down and the plant is in a resting stage. Likewise, any plant that is sensitive to heat will often become dormant in response to any high-temperature conditions.

Find out what hardiness zone you live in so you can choose the right plants for your area. Refer to the zone maps on pages 270–272 to find your zone, and try to limit your selections to plants that are recommended for your area. By doing this, you can be fairly confident that these plants will grow well. You will find that plant descriptions in this book and in many other books and catalogs give a range of zones such as "Zones 5 to 8"

ABOVE: The key to having a beautiful and productive herb garden is using herbs that are adapted to both your local climate and your garden's microclimates.
RIGHT: Nasturtiums planted around a small bay tree are grouped with ornamental cabbages, golden oregano and lavender.

Moderate-climate Herbs

These herbs prefer climates where winter temperatures do not fall below 10°F (-5°C) and that have warm, dry summers with cool nights.

Agrimony, basil (sweet), bay, calendula, cilantro (coriander), eucalyptus, fennel, fenugreek, feverfew, geranium (scented), germander, horehound, lavender (English), lemon verbena, madder, marjoram, mint, oregano, orris, parsley (curled), passionflower, pennyroyal, rosemary, rue, safflower, sage, santolina, southernwood, thyme, violet, witch hazel.

Fennell

Sage

Warm-climate Herbs

These herbs require tropical or subtropical climates, but some can be grown in cold climates in summer or as houseplants.

Aloe, cayenne pepper, coffee, ginger, lemongrass, Madagascar periwinkle.

(lower and upper hardiness). That's because cold temperatures aren't the only factor that determines if a plant will grow well in an area; heat can have a great effect, too. The upper limit of a plant's hardiness range will give you an idea of what kind of summer temperatures that plant can tolerate. However, even if a plant can tolerate the heat, it may demand frequent watering in return, and probably won't thrive. Plants that can't take the heat are a bad choice if you want a good-looking, easy-care garden. Unfortunately it is often difficult to put a number on a plant's heat tolerance. Use these recommendations as guidelines only, but also check around your local neighborhood and nurseries to see how herbs grow there before making your choice.

It's important to remember that herbs are basically wild plants that have been adapted to grow in backyard gardens, so it makes sense to grow them in conditions that compare with their original habitat. This, however, can be difficult because herbs grow in many varied habitats throughout the world. Some of the most useful are the culinary herbs from the Mediterranean, which thrive in dry, hot summers. So if you don't live in an area with hot, dry summers, try positioning your herbs in a sunny location in your garden, or grow them on a sunny windowsill.

Coffee *Coffea* is widely grown in the tropics. It can make an interesting glasshouse plant.

Cool-climate Herbs

These herbs are adapted to cool climates, where winter temperatures commonly drop below 10°F (–5°C). Most can be grown in moderate climates, too, but in subtropical and tropical climates many of them will not thrive.

Angelica, anise, anise hyssop, arnica, barberry, bearberry, bee balm, betony, birch, borage, burdock, caraway, catmint, chamomile (Roman), chervil, chicory, chives, clary, comfrey, costmary, dandelion, dill, dock, elecampane, garlic, goldenrod, hop, horse-radish, horsetail, hyssop, lady's bedstraw, lemon balm, lovage, marsh mallow, mugwort, mustard, nasturtium, nettle, New Jersey tea, plantain, red clover, roses, saffron, sassafras, savory (winter), soapwort, sorrel, sweet cicely, sweet woodruff, tansy, tarragon (French), valerian, vervain, wormwood, yarrow.

LEFT: Frost on seeding alliums and grasses.

Coastal Climates

Land by the sea has its own beauty, but it is often exposed to drying, salt-laden winds or gales, and has soil that is either sandy and poor, or rain-leached loam. Plants find this climate difficult to thrive in and will be slower to establish and grow. They may burn off at the tip, but frequently go on to adapt to their surroundings given reasonable care. A useful start to a coastal herb garden is to establish some salt-resistant plants to form a sheltering windbreak for other less-tolerant plants.

Catmint

Fortunately quite a few herbs are able to cope with exposed coastal conditions, including juniper, rosemary, artemisia, catmint, lavender, tea tree, acacias, eucalypts and roses such as *Rosa rugosa*. Buy plants when they are small—they have a better chance of adapting and forming good roots against the wind.

Some coastal areas are also very humid in summer, and the Mediterranean herbs, such as lavender, used to dry, sunny, coastal conditions, may develop fungal diseases. Don't crowd the plants and plant them in an open, airy, sunny position.

Coastal gardens have the advantage of open aspects, lack of frost and even seasonal temperatures, so with some care, most herbs can be grown.

Soil temperature also has an effect on plant growth. Roots tend to grow more slowly in cool soil, so your herbs may have trouble getting the nutrients they need for their flush of spring growth. An early spring application of compost will supply your herbs with nutrients until their roots start spreading again. You'll also want to keep soil temperature in mind when planting your seeds. Some herb seeds, such as caraway and chervil, germinate best at cooler temperatures, while others, such as fenugreek and nasturtium, prefer warmer soil. Mulches help control soil temperature. In summer, a good layer of mulch around your plants helps reduce the amount of sunlight and wind that reaches the soil, so water evaporates from the soil more slowly, keeping it cooler. In autumn, mulch can help hold in soil warmth, encouraging good root growth.

Frost-free Period

In most climates, the growing season begins after the last frost of the cold season and ends when frosts begin again in autumn. If you live in a cool climate and want to use the flowers and seeds of your herbs, the plants you decide to grow will have to sprout, flower, and set seed within this period. Plants vary in the amount of time they require to reach maturity; seed and plant suppliers usually provide information as to the number of days needed by each variety. If you're growing herbs for their foliage, they won't need to flower and set seed, so the frost-free period is less important.

Frost occurs when the air temperature around plants falls to 32°F (0°C) or below during the night, after dew has formed. The result is a lacy coating of water crystals on your plants' leaves. Plants vary in their susceptibility to frost, but in those that are frost-sensitive, such as basil, it injures internal structures and turns the foliage black. With sufficient damage, plants will die as a result of frost in spring or autumn. Hardier annuals, such as borage and dill, are able to tolerate light autumn frosts. Most perennials are frost-tolerant.

If you're a new gardener, check frost dates with your neighbors or nursery to find out the length of the growing season in your area. You can extend the growing season of your herb garden by selecting plants suited to the conditions, planting them at the right time and shielding them from the cold spring or autumn temperatures. Look for cultivars that are suited to cold conditions.

Chives do best in areas where winters are mild, but they can be successfully grown even in areas where winter temperatures drop well below freezing. Their adaptability makes chives a useful herb for all conditions.

Topography

Topography means the lay of the land. As hills and valleys dip and rise, small changes in altitude, slope and wind shelter create "microclimates" in particular areas. If your garden is on a hill or in a valley, you'll probably be faced with slightly different conditions from the average climate of your region.

Slopes and rolling terrain can add interest to your garden. If you can, save flat spots for your entertaining and play areas, and build terraces for your garden beds above.

Gardening in a Valley

Valleys tend to be cooler than the higher land around them. This happens because cool air is heavier than warm air. Cool air tends to drain toward lower ground. For this reason, gardens located at the bottoms of valleys suffer the latest frosts in the spring, the earliest frosts in autumn, and the severest frosts in winter. The absence of wind in valleys increases susceptibility to frost.

Soil tends to be wetter in a valley, since water follows the path of least resistance and flows downward. Where drainage is poor, water will puddle, creating spongy wet areas. Poor air circulation and high moisture levels in valleys create ideal conditions for fungal development, so fungal diseases of plants are more likely to occur.

You may find the best topsoil at the bottom of a valley. As water flows downhill, it washes away the slopes above and carries topsoil and organic matter away, depositing it lower down.

Gardening on a Hilltop

Air temperatures on hills tend to be lower than on flat land. You will have greater protection from frost and plant disease on a hill, compared with a valley, since air movement is greater. Excessive winds, however, can damage plants, increase soil erosion and speed the loss of moisture from the soil.

Since water drains from high ground, soil at the top of a hill will usually be drier than the land below. On hilltops, soil is generally thinner and nutrients will be lost more easily through excessive drainage and runoff.

A retaining wall, or herb and succulent rock garden such as this, helps to prevent water cascading downhill and taking with it valuable topsoil. Close planting to cover all bare soil holds it in place.

Clary prefers sun and well-drained soil, so it is an ideal herb for planting in hilltop gardens.

ABOVE: It is best to gently terrace slopes to maintain the natural drainage patterns.
RIGHT: Planting your garden so the rows run across the slope will slow water and soil runoff.

Gardening on a Slope

Gardening on a gentle slope can have advantages. Slopes are often cooled by breezes in the afternoon, while warm air rising over them in the morning keeps away frost. In cool northern climates in the Northern hemisphere, a slope with a southern exposure warms more quickly in the spring, and remains warm for a longer period. This means a longer growing season and potentially greater harvests. In a southern climate, the extra warmth may not be so vital. In the Southern hemisphere, the slope facing north is the warm, protected aspect.

Slopes, however, are subject to erosion from water drainage and from wind unless they are sheltered by natural or planted

windbreaks and terraced where they are steep. If drainage is excessive, your plants may suffer from lack of soil moisture, and you may find that topsoil is thin on a slope due to soil erosion.

The Effect of Water

Large bodies of water, such as oceans and lakes, influence the climate of the land nearby. The larger the body of water, the greater its effect. Since water temperatures rise and fall more slowly than land temperatures, they modify the air temperatures of the surrounding land. Coastal gardens, for example, do not experience the same extreme temperatures as inland gardens. Similarly, a garden near a large lake will experience less-extreme air temperatures than one further away. The effect of the water on land temperatures may be enough to hold frosts at bay, giving a longer growing season, making it possible to grow a wider range of herbs.

Exposure

Exposure refers to the amount of sun and shade that your garden receives in the course of the day. Exposure to sunlight is one of the factors that you will need to consider when adding herbs to your garden landscape. While most herbs prefer full sun, there are some that will grow in partial to full shade. The quantity and duration of light are critical factors in your garden and affect the growth of your herbs, especially their flowering and reproduction. The intensity of the light influences photosynthesis, the plant's internal process that employs light energy to produce carbohydrates or sugar for food, using carbon dioxide and water. Photosynthetic activity generally increases with greater light intensity and decreases with less.

Sunlight

The intensity of sunlight varies with the season, the geographic location and the atmosphere. In the tropics, the normal duration of sunlight is around 12 hours a day. In the areas north and south of the equator, the length of the day varies with the season and the latitude. During winter, the sun is lower in the sky than it is during summer. Sunlight travels a longer distance through the Earth's atmosphere and strikes the Earth's surface at a lower angle. As a result, it is less intense. In summer, sunlight reaches the surface more directly and is more intense.

To make sure your plants get the right amount of light, identify the direction your property faces. Consider shade from trees, buildings, fences, hedges and hills when planning your garden. How do you tell if a particular spot has full sun? Watch the spot regularly over the course of a day, checking it every hour or so. Make a note each time you check to see if the spot is sunny or shady. Plants that need full sun are able to stand uninterrupted, unfiltered sunlight from sunrise to sunset. Plants that prefer partial sun will usually be able to stand about five to six hours of direct sunlight, with shade or filtered sun the rest of the day. Place herbs that do best in partial shade in filtered, indirect light where trees provide dappled shade. Few herbs need to be in full shade, but if that is the recommendation, the plants will need just that: solid and dense shade away from all direct sun.

Shady side Northern hemisphere,
Sunny side Southern hemisphere

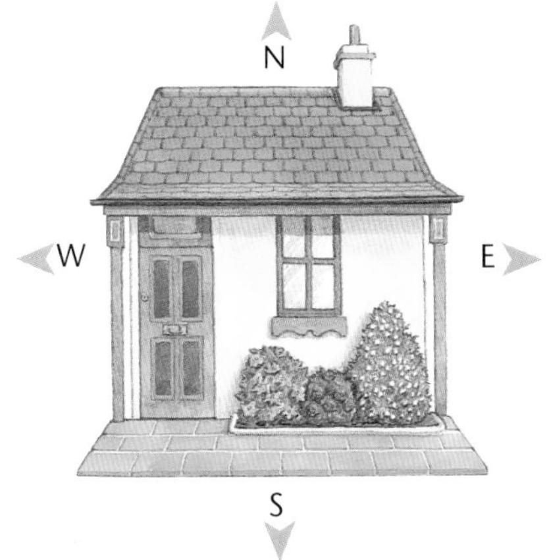

Shady side Southern hemisphere,
Sunny side Northern hemisphere

By identifying the direction your house faces, you can make sure your plants get the right amount of light, sun and shade, depending on the aspect.

Garden Location

Locating a garden on the south side of your house ensures the maximum amount of light in the Northern hemisphere, while planting on the north side provides the most light in the Southern hemisphere. Many plants thrive in eastern exposures where they receive up to half a day of direct light and are sheltered from the hot afternoon sun. Western exposures can be a challenge to many plants. Such sites are generally cool and shady in the morning, but the temperature can change dramatically when strong afternoon sun hits. When a plant receives too much sun, leaves may wilt and it may develop a scalded appearance and grow poorly. With too little sunlight, on the other hand, plants become lanky, flower poorly

Plants need sun or shade according to how they grow in the wild, although some can adapt. They will always do best given the right conditions.

Wind Exposure

Another element to consider in exposure is wind. Is your garden exposed to strong winds, or is it fairly sheltered? Strong winds can quickly dry out plants and erode bare soil. Where winds are strong, protect your gardens by locating them on the sheltered side of walls, buildings, fences or hedges. In exposed areas with cold winter winds and no consistent snow cover, choose plants that are rated for at least one zone colder than yours to be on the safe side.

LEFT: Geraniums, lobelia, heather and borage.

or not at all, and lack vigor. Space your plants correctly and weed regularly to reduce competition for sunlight.

The daily cycle of light and dark influences several plant functions, including seed germination, root initiation and the growth of blossoms, fruits and bulbs. Some plants, such as chrysanthemums, require short days and longer nights to bloom and are called short-day plants. Plants that flower when the days are long and the nights are short are known as long-day plants. Long-day herbs include most of the annual herbs. Other plants, such as roses, are unaffected by day length and are called day-neutral.

RIGHT: There's no need to despair of growing herbs if you have shade. Many, such as foxgloves, thrive in full or at least partial shade.

BELOW: Coastal gardens have sea winds and salt, but a more even and often frost-free climate.

Moisture

A garden that is actively growing and flowering will need a source of moisture at all times. Plants are dependent on water. They cannot absorb nutrients and maintain essential processes unless they receive adequate moisture. If water is in short supply, flowers and flower buds are the first to suffer damage. If water is over abundant, plant roots rot. You will have to fine-tune your watering depending on several factors, including the type of soil you have, the amount of natural rainfall, the plants you grow, and the stage of growth the plants are in.

If you don't mind lugging a hose around the garden and watering frequently, or if you plan to have an automatic irrigation system, you may choose to grow plants that need extra water. However, if your goal is to save time, money and natural resources, you'll definitely want to include naturally adapted plants in your landscape. Do a little research to find out what herbs will thrive best in your garden. Many herbs have small, fuzzy or silvery leaves, which are fairly reliable clues that a particular plant is adapted to low water conditions. One of the best ways to get ideas on what plants will grow well in your garden without extra water is to investigate what's growing in local natural areas or parks.

Unsure about your soil's moisture content? Check below the soil surface by digging a small hole to see if the root zone is dry.

Plants with small or silvery leaves, such as eucalypts, are often well adapted to drier conditions.

As a general rule, herb plants will require the equivalent of 1 inch (25 mm) of rainfall each week. Rain is the best source of moisture during the growing season, but you will need to supplement this by irrigation or hand watering if rains fail or are inadequate. In some climates, snow contributes to a great part of the annual water supply. Even though snow usually falls when most plants are dormant, it still contributes to the water reserves held in the soil below the surface.

Consistently inadequate moisture levels may cause irreparable damage to plants. The first sign is wilting foliage. Drought-sensitive plants grow slowly, become dormant, or die under dry conditions. At the other extreme, too much water may flood the root system and prevent the plant from absorbing the oxygen and nutrients it requires. Plants susceptible to flooding may also wilt, drop their leaves, and die if the excess water is not quickly drained away.

Moisture-loving Herbs

Although most herbs need well-drained conditions, there are some herbs that grow best in moist or very moist soils. Some are tough and tolerant, such as horseradish, which will grow in most conditions except badly drained clay; others are more particular. Watercress, which grows wild at the edge of flowing streams, must be flooded with clean water every day or so.

If you have moist, well-drained conditions, try growing the following herbs: angelica, basil, bee balm, catnip, chamomile, chervil, chives, comfrey, elder, feverfew, horseradish, lemon balm, lovage, marjoram, mint, parsley, rose, sweet cicely and woodruff.

Watercress

Keeping Track of Rainfall

Monitor the rainfall in your garden. You can tell how much rain has fallen if you leave out a rain gauge, which is like a narrow measuring cup with inches (millimeters) of rainfall marked on the side. If you don't want to buy a rain gauge, you can place a small, clean can out in an open part of the garden and use a ruler to measure how much rain water collects in it. Check your rain gauge once a week to keep track.

Rain gauge

Soil Moisture

If you do not already know how moisture-retentive your garden is, it is time to find out. For instance, will it provide reserves of water for one week after a good drenching or will most of the moisture drain away within a day? To answer this question, water a portion of your garden thoroughly. After 48 hours, dig a small hole 6 inches (15 cm) deep. If the soil is reasonably water-retentive, the earth at the bottom of the hole will still be moist. If it is not, you can improve its water-holding capacity by working in lots of organic material, such as compost. This organic matter acts like a sponge, holding extra

Sweet basil will thrive in moist, warm conditions.

moisture reserves that plant roots can draw on. If you do add a great deal of organic matter, you won't need to water as frequently.

Different Herbs Have Different Needs

Some herbs, such as basil and chives, thrive in moist soils. Others grow weakly or rot where water is abundant. It's important to group plants with similar water needs together. For drought-tolerant plants, such as lavender and purple coneflowers, you can let the soil dry out more between rainfalls. These plants will probably need no more than about ½ inch (12 mm) of water per week. However, for such herbs as comfrey, elder and horseradish, which thrive in moist conditions, you will need to keep watering them regularly between periods of rain.

You have to expect to coddle new plants until their roots establish and spread far enough to support the plants. If the weather is warm and dry, you may have to water daily until drenching rain comes. If the season is cool and rainy, you can let nature handle the irrigation.

Wind

Wind is another factor you will need to consider when watering your garden. Herbs will require more water under windy conditions, as wind draws away moisture released through pores faster than normal. When the weather is both cold and windy, water is often drawn out of exposed plant tops and roots faster than it can be replaced. This can lead to severe damage or to death of your plants. If you live in a windy area, wind shelter is important for your more sensitive herbs. You can protect your herb garden by locating it on the sheltered side of the house, or planting it along a fence. See "Exposure" on pages 50–51.

All plants depend on water so they can maintain essential processes. If rainfall is erratic in your area, or if you are growing moisture-loving herbs, you may need to supplement with hand-watering.

All About Soil

Good soil is the herb gardener's key to success. Besides providing physical support for plant roots, soil contains the water and nutrients plants need to survive. A good soil is loose and well drained, but it also holds enough water and air for healthy root growth. Before you start digging, it is helpful to take some time to learn about the physical characteristics of soil so your herbs can get off to a flying start.

Healthy soil builds healthy plants. You need to understand your soil so your garden will thrive.

Soil Composition

Soil is actually a mixture of mineral and organic matter, water and air. In general, soil contains approximately 45 percent mineral matter, 5 percent organic matter, 25 percent water and 25 percent air. Organic matter is an essential part of the soil makeup because it supplies nutrients to the plants and can help to improve drainage. Soils that contain a lot of organic matter are usually dark in color.

Sand

Silt

Dark gray clay

Soil Texture

Soil texture is determined by the proportions of different-sized mineral particles in the soil. At one extreme are microscopic clay particles, and at the other are coarse sand particles easily seen with the naked eye. Silt (the very fine soil often found in riverbanks) falls between these two extremes.

Soil texture can have a great effect on the growth of your plants. Roots will spread easily in open sandy soil, but water will drain away quickly, so your plants may need more frequent watering. In a tight clay soil, roots cannot penetrate so readily or widely and the soil will tend to become waterlogged. Also, in a clayey soil, water is so tightly held by the soil particles that it may not be able to enter the roots freely.

You can easily check your soil's texture. Take a handful of your damp garden soil and squeeze it. If it crumbles slightly when you release your grip, its texture is probably satisfactory; if it runs through your fingers, it is too sandy; if it forms a sticky lump, it is too clayey. In general, loamy soils, which contain moderate amounts of clay, silt and sand, often suit most plants best.

Soil Structure

The structure of soil depends on the way the various particles—sand, silt and clay—come together to form clumps or aggregates. Most plants prefer a soil with a loose, granular structure. This type of structure has lots of open space (called pore space) that can hold air or water. The water forms a thin film around the granules and holds dissolved nutrients, such as calcium and

To check the texture of your soil, take a handful of damp garden soil and squeeze it. A soil that crumbles slightly in your grip is the most ideal. Clay soil forms a sticky lump when compressed.

Taking Soil Tests

To get the most accurate information about your soil's chemical properties, it is worth taking a little time to collect good samples and have them tested by a professional soil laboratory. You can collect a soil sample anytime, although before planting in the spring is often best. The soil should be just moist enough to form a loose ball when you press it in your fist, then crumble when you open your hand and poke the soil ball. You'll need a clean trowel for digging the samples and sealable plastic bags to send your samples off to the laboratory.

Scrape away leaves and other plant debris from the surface where you plan to dig. Use a spade or trowel and dig a hole about 6 inches (15 cm) deep.

Shave a small slice from the edge of the hole. Collect another five samples from different sites around your garden. Mix samples together.

Spread on newspaper to dry. Place a sample of the soil into a sealable plastic bag, picking out stones and other debris. Send off to the laboratory.

potassium. Plants can take up these nutrients when tiny hairs on the tips of their roots enter the water film between the soil particles.

Unlike soil texture, structure can change depending on how you manage the soil. Working the soil when it is wet can break down the aggregates and destroy soil structure. Adding plenty of organic matter is an easy and effective way to promote a good soil structure.

Organic Matter

Organic matter in the soil consists of the remains of plants and animals at various stages of decomposition. Decaying organic matter adds minerals essential for plant growth, such as nitrogen and potassium, to the soil. It also improves soil structure by increasing pore space so that roots can spread easily and water and air can move freely in the root zone.

Most plants thrive in soils that are rich in organic matter. Soils with a lot of organic matter are usually dark in color (often a rich brown) and open and light in texture. They crumble easily between your fingers. Add organic matter to your soil in the form of compost, manure or green manure crops. See "Adding Organic Matter" on pages 84–85.

Air and Water

Your plants will require a good deal of water but they must also be able to take in air (for oxygen) through their roots. Oxygen is plentiful in loose, well-drained soil with good soil structure. Most garden plants grow best in well-drained garden soil. They don't like to have wet feet, since flooding cuts off the supply of oxygen to the roots. Plants obtain their oxygen from air-filled pores in the soil and, during the daytime, take in carbon dioxide from the air. Oxygen they can't use is given off from their leaves during the daytime.

Soil Nutrients

The availability of soil nutrients depends on the interaction of various factors, including the texture and structure of the soil, the amount of moisture and organic matter, and the pH. A fine texture, a loose structure, ample moisture, high organic matter content and near neutral pH are all conditions that make the most nutrients available to your plants. One of the most important plant nutrients is nitrogen, which is found in soil in various chemical combinations that plants can absorb. Keeping an adequate supply of nitrogen in the soil can be a challenge, since nitrogen is used up very quickly by plants. It also dissolves in water and leaches out of the soil. For plants to

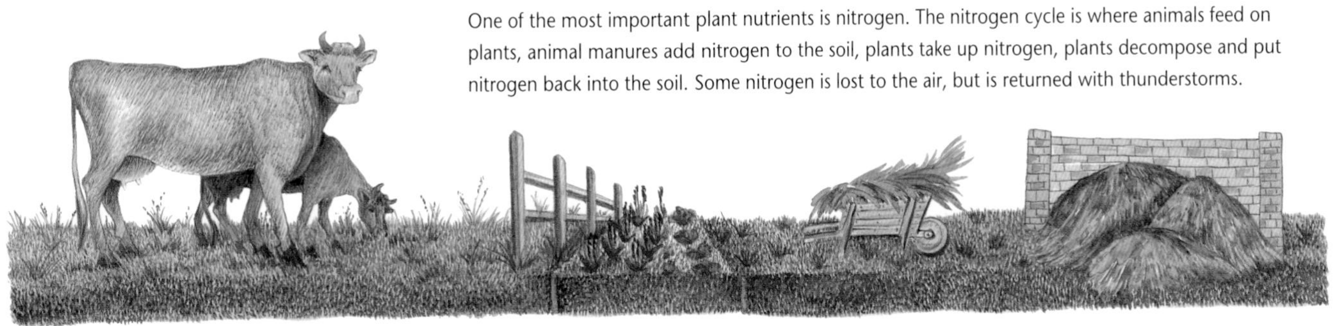

One of the most important plant nutrients is nitrogen. The nitrogen cycle is where animals feed on plants, animal manures add nitrogen to the soil, plants take up nitrogen, plants decompose and put nitrogen back into the soil. Some nitrogen is lost to the air, but is returned with thunderstorms.

thrive, nitrogen must be continually replenished. This is often why heavy applications of nitrogen fertilizers are used in commercial agriculture. When they are washed out of the soil, their destination is often the groundwater, which may be the source of your drinking water. The best and most natural way to build up soil nitrogen is to grow green manure crops. See "Manure" on pages 86–87 to learn how to grow and use them.

To check the nutrient content of your soil, it may be worthwhile to have a laboratory test your soil before you begin serious gardening. Even soils known to be highly fertile often lack specific nutrients or essential minerals that your herbs will need. Private soil-testing agencies will conduct tests on samples of your soil and provide you with a statement of your soil pH and the relative amounts of essential plant nutrients, including nitrogen, phosphorus and potassium, in the soil. They will also point out any specific deficiencies. This will show whether your soil is of high, medium or low fertility. You can test it again in a few years' time to monitor the results of your gardening practices, then make adjustments if necessary. The laboratory will also recommend rates of application of fertilizing substances and lime based on the plants you have decided to grow, since different crops will vary in their requirements. Make sure you ask for recommendations for organic fertilizers.

The dried red flowers and leaves of bee balm (bergamot, Oswego tea) are infused to make a soothing tea. In America, it became popular as a tea substitute after the Boston Tea Party in 1773.

Hydrangea arborescens is a traditional American herb used medicinally to treat kidney stones.

Soil pH

It is helpful to know how acid or alkaline your soil is. If you have the soil tested, the results will include pH, which is the measure of acidity or alkalinity. Soil pH is important because it influences soil chemistry. Plants can absorb most nutrients from the soil when the soil pH is in the neutral range, around 7. Plants cannot absorb nitrogen and sulfur, for example, if the soil pH drops far below 8, while iron and magnesium are less available as the pH moves above 8.

Many herbs prefer a soil on the slightly acid side, with a pH around 6. Plant nursery operators know the approximate pH level that suits the plants they sell. Heavy, dense, clay soils are often more acid than is desirable. Lime or dolomite will make them less acid and improve their structure. If your soil is too acid for the plants you plan to grow, the laboratory will be able to tell you how much lime to add. If your soil pH is high, you can lower it by adding a sphagnum peat substitute or sulfur. It's important not to add lime or sulfur unless it has been advised.

Puzzling out pH

Herbs can absorb most nutrients from the soil when the soil pH is in the neutral range (around 6.5 to 7.0). When the soil is either very acid (with a lower pH) or alkaline (with a higher pH), some nutrients form chemical compounds that make them unavailable to your herbs. A home test kit, which you can buy at your garden center, or a laboratory test will provide specific information on your soil's acidity or alkalinity. The pH scale is as follows:

1–5 = strongly acidic
5–6 = moderately acidic
6–7 = slightly acidic
7 = neutral
7–8 = slightly alkaline
8–9 = moderately alkaline
9–14 = strongly alkaline

ABOVE: Checking up on the type and depth of your soil is a useful first step in establishing any garden. If you have deep soil, you will be able to grow a wide range of different herbs, including trees and shrubs. If your soil is shallow, you will be more limited in your range.

Soil Depth

The actual depth of your soil has an impact on root growth and this in turn affects what plants—either deep- or shallow-rooting—will thrive in your garden. In some regions, the soil is merely a thin dust over bedrock. In others, thousands of years' worth of plant decay have formed soils 6 feet (1.8 m) deep. It's easy to tell which conditions you have—just dig down into the soil in your garden with a shovel. If you can go 2 feet (60 cm) without hitting a sheet of rock or a band of dense, tightly compacted soil, you'll be able to grow a wide range of herbs without any trouble. Larger plants, such as shrubs and trees, generally require soil that's at least 3 feet (90 cm) deep to have vigorous growth. Soils less than 2 feet (60 cm) deep are not as hospitable to root growth; they may also be prone to waterlogging, and often have fewer nutrients than deeper soil. If your soil is shallow, you may decide to build raised beds and fill them with a good soil to provide more area for root growth. A 6-inch (15-cm) high bed should accommodate most annual herbs. But note that raised beds can dry out quickly, so you may have to water more often.

SECTION THREE

Creating Your Herb Garden

You can choose to grow herbs for a variety of reasons—for their culinary uses, attractive foliage or fragrant flowers, or perhaps for their medicinal properties. Whatever your reason, it's worth knowing a little about their life cycles and their origins, and how to buy healthy plants to ensure your herb garden gets off to the best possible start.

Choosing Your Plants

Before you race out and start buying plants for your herb garden, it's worth taking some time to work out the type of garden that you want and the types of plants to grow in it. Being well informed will help you choose plants that will make your garden a success and fulfill your needs. You can choose herbs for their useful fruits, attractive leaves, fragrant flowers, or perhaps for deep taproots that cope better with a poor water supply. If you want your herb garden to be attractive all year round with minimal work, you may want to concentrate on perennials rather than annuals and biennials. If it's your first herb garden, you may want to choose a cross-section of herbs with a bias toward culinary use, because the more you use your herbs, the more you will understand their growing conditions.

An enormous number and variety of plants are grown worldwide, in a huge range of different habitats. By knowing the origins of your herbs, you will better understand how to care for them. Herbs that originated in a hot, tropical climate may require special treatment if you live in a cold climate. Take the following information into consideration when you visit your local garden center and you will be well rewarded.

Life Cycles

Knowing about the life cycles of your herbs can give you many clues to their needs and characteristics. The term "life cycle" refers to the amount of time it takes for a plant to grow from seed, flower, set seed and die. Annual herbs, such as borage and calendula, complete their life cycle in one growing season. Biennials, such as parsley and caraway, produce only leafy growth the first year, and complete their life cycle in the second growing season. Perennial herbs live for more than two years, producing leaves, flowers and seeds each year. Herbaceous perennials, such as bergamot and tarragon, have stems that usually die to the ground in winter and grow again in spring from a persistent rootstock. Woody perennials, including barberry and rosemary, have stems that expand each year as they build up woody growth.

As you plant and maintain your herb garden, though, it's not enough to know just what a plant's natural life cycle is. It also helps to know how the plant grows in your climate, and how you plan to use the herb. Some herbs that are normally

If you consider what you want from your plants and what growing conditions you have available, your herbs will fulfill your needs and provide years of enjoyment. Here, a walled gardens shelters roses on a pergola and in beds, sweet Williams, lavender, campanula and lamb's ears.

The flowers and berries of elder *Sambucus nigra* are used medicinally and in wine, jam and jellies.

perennial in warm climates, such as marjoram and chiles, cannot survive the winter temperatures of colder climates. Gardeners in cold-climate areas must treat these warm-climate herbs as annuals, and grow them from seed each year. And how you grow a biennial herb depends on what you want to harvest from it. Parsley, for example, is commonly grown for its first-year foliage, not for its second-year flowers and seeds. So even though parsley is technically a biennial, you'll need to start new plants each year if you want a good supply of foliage. If you are not sure what categories your herbs fit into, look them up in "A Guide to Popular Herbs", starting on page 172.

Annuals

Annuals germinate, flower, set seed and die all within one year. They are generally easy to grow and offer the herb gardener a wide range of plant sizes, colors and shapes. In a new garden they are especially useful for filling spaces between perennials that are just newly planted. Many annuals bloom all season and then propagate themselves by producing lots of seeds. Some, such as borage, will reseed before the end of the season and their offspring will germinate in the following season.

This cottage-garden style border features an exuberant yet harmonious mix of white carnations, catmint, white and pink roses, irises, alliums, poppies, foxgloves, artemisia and peonies.

Popular Perennial Herbs

Perennial herbs are those that live for more than two years. There are two types, woody and herbaceous.

Woody perennials: Barberry, bay (sweet), bearberry, birch, cascara sagrada, coffee, eucalyptus, geranium (scented), lemon verbena, New Jersey tea, passion-flower, rosemary, rose, sassafras, witch hazel.

Herbaceous perennials: Agrimony, aloe, angelica, anise hyssop, arnica, bergamot, betony, burdock, catmint, chamomile (Roman), chicory, chives, comfrey, costmary, dandelion, dock, elecampane, feverfew, garlic, germander, ginger, goldenrod, hop, horehound, horseradish, horsetail, hyssop, lady's bedstraw, lavender (English), lemon balm, lemongrass, lovage, madder, marjoram, marsh mallow, mint, mugwort, nettle, oregano, orris, pennyroyal, red clover, saffron, sage, santolina, savory (winter), soapwort, sorrel, southernwood, sweet cicely, sweet woodruff, tansy, tarragon (French), thyme (garden), valerian, violet, wormwood, yarrow.

Angelica

Lemon verbena

Easy Annuals and Biennials

Annual and biennial herbs are among the easiest herbs to grow. Annuals, such as basil (above), germinate, flower, set seed and die within one year. Biennials take two years to complete their life cycle. Both annuals and biennials grow quickly from seed. A few short-lived perennial herbs—including fennel, plantain and vervain—also grow quickly from seed, so you can treat them as annuals.

Annuals: Anise, basil (sweet), borage, calendula, cayenne pepper, chervil, cilantro (coriander), dill, fennel, fenugreek, mustard, nasturtium, plantain, safflower, vervain.

Biennials: Burdock, caraway, clary, parsley.

Nasturtium

The leaves and seeds of anise *Pimpinella anisum* have an interesting licorice flavor.

Most annuals require full sun and are shallow-rooted. This means that they will require plenty of water, since their roots remain near the surface. Many annual seedlings can be planted directly outdoors in garden soil, but others will require a warm start indoors. Whichever type you choose, remember you will have to water them regularly.

Some annuals, such as basil, need plenty of space, while others, such as dill and chives, form clumps. If you are going to be planting herbs in pots, it's important to keep this in mind. Plant seedlings that need space separately in pots. Seedlings of clumping herbs can be sown thickly in pots.

Annuals grow quickly from seed, but remember that easy-to-grow doesn't always mean easy-to-get-going. If there's no information with the seedlings you buy, ask the garden center for guidance on whether your annual seedlings need to be carefully nurtured indoors before being planted outside, or whether you can plant them directly outside.

Biennials

Biennial herbs have a life span of two years. During their first year they produce plenty of foliage and strong root systems. Many biennials depend upon nutrients stored in their large roots to survive the period of dormancy in the cold season. Biennials flower and make seed in their second season, just before they die. If you start biennials, such as caraway and parsley, from seed indoors, sow them in peat pots that can be placed directly in the ground to avoid disturbing the sensitive taproot during transplanting. If your climate allows, sow biennials directly into the garden so you won't have to transplant them out later. This will help you avoid taproot damage.

How you grow a biennial herb depends on what you want to harvest from it. As mentioned above, most people grow parsley for its first-year foliage and not for its second-year flowers and seeds, so you may have to grow it as an annual.

Biennials are shallow-rooted, so they don't compete for moisture with a deep-rooted plant. It's a good idea to mix them with annuals as well as perennials. Start both the annuals and biennials from seed and use them to fill in any spaces between the perennials. Mix leafy biennials, such as parsley and caraway, among the more permanent perennial plantings, harvesting the foliage the first season and enjoying the flowers and seeds the second year, when the foliage will be tougher.

Perennials

Perennial herbs live for more than two years and make up the vast bulk of edible herbs. Some, such as clary and lavender, will reach their prime growth within three to five years. Growth then declines and the plants die unless they are rejuvenated by thinning and division. Other perennials, such as tansy and mint, thrive and continue growing, unless their growth is checked with judicious thinning.

Perennial herbs form the backbone of most herb plantings. They are hardy plants that return year after year, giving structure and continuity to your herb garden. You can propagate a perennial vegetatively or from seed. Vegetative propagation involves plant division, layering or taking cuttings, and is the easiest and the quickest way to increase your stock of perennials. The seeds of some perennials may be difficult to germinate and others, such as tarragon, don't seed at all. While most perennials started from seed will flower during their second year, new plants that are started vegetatively often flower in the first year.

In cold climates, some herbs that are normally perennial, such as lemongrass, cannot survive the winter temperatures and are best grown as annuals.

There are two types of perennials, herbaceous and woody. Herbaceous perennials have stems that usually die back to the ground in the winter and grow again in the spring from a persistent rootstock. Woody perennials have stems that expand each year as the plants build up layers of woody growth. By learning whether a perennial herb is woody or herbaceous, you can make the most effective use of it in your herb garden.

It's a good idea to mix herbs with different life spans. If you are going to plant annuals between your biennials and perennials, find out the particular requirements and growing characteristics of each herb. By mixing your herbs, your garden will always be productive.

Lavenders are delightfully fragrant shrubs or sub-shrubs that become leggy with age and need to be replaced every few years with young plants. These can be grown quite easily from stem cuttings.

Before You Shop

For many people, choosing and buying plants is one of the most pleasurable aspects of creating a new garden. In the frenzy of shopping, it's easy to get carried away and go home with plants you don't really want and which don't really suit your growing conditions. But with a little preparation, you can take your time and get the right plant, for the right position, at the right price. The following sections will help you to learn about choosing herbs before you rush to the garden store.

Begin your search in the depths of winter by browsing through the colorful and informative mail-order catalogs, or catalogs from your local garden center. Make a list of plants that appeal to you and that will suit your growing conditions. When the planting season begins, spend some time at nurseries, garden centers and plant sales, making note of what plants are available and their price, and reading the labels to find out about growing requirements.

Plant Origins

Many herbs that originated in warm or hot climates are widely grown in colder regions today. Pepper plants, for example, including hot and sweet peppers, are perennials in their native tropical America. They're usually grown as annuals in cooler climates because they cannot withstand frost. Basil is another cold-sensitive herb, which originated in the warm, humid tropics. A favorite with herb growers everywhere for its profusion of fragrant leaves, basil is widely cultivated as an annual during the frost-free months.

Chilies

The medicinal aloes and the scented geraniums both originated in Africa: the aloes in arid areas, the geraniums in the cooler and somewhat moister south. If you want to grow them in cold climates, you will have to bring them indoors during winter, or alternatively, use both of them as houseplants throughout the year. The origins and history of herbs are fascinating topics that you can explore further in the many herb books found in well-stocked libraries.

Hardiness

Hardiness is the quality that enables plants to survive climatic extremes, especially cold, heat and dryness. Hardy annuals and biennials, such as dill and caraway, can be sown outdoors while spring or autumn frosts still threaten. Hardy perennials, such as tarragon and chives, can be left outdoors all year round, even in the extreme winter cold. Tansy is another hardy perennial that thrives in its native cold winter.

Caraway

Half-hardy annuals require a warm environment for successful germination, but may withstand slight frosts once they're established. Calendula is a half-hardy annual that benefits from an early start indoors and can be transferred outdoors fairly early in the season.

Tender annuals and perennials are plants that are quickly damaged by frost or cold. Tender perennials include sweet marjoram, which must be brought indoors during cold winters. Basil is a tender annual that should be started and kept indoors in the spring until all likelihood of frost has passed.

It's important when planning your herb garden to consider your plants' origins and match their needs to your conditions. Herbs such as rosemary and sage prefer warm climates and well-drained soil.

Easy-to-grow Herbs

The herbs listed below all fall into the "hard to kill" category and so are good subjects for the beginning gardener.

Agrimony, angelica, barberry, basil (sweet), bee balm (bergamot), borage, calendula, catmint, chamomile (Roman), chicory, chives, comfrey, cilantro (coriander), dandelion, dill, dock, elecampane, fennel, feverfew, geranium (scented), goldenrod, horseradish, horsetail, lady's bedstraw, lavender (English), lemon balm, lovage, marjoram, mint, mustard, nasturtium, oregano, parsley (curled), pennyroyal (English), plantain, red clover, rosemary, rue, sage, santolina, savory (winter), soapwort, sorrel, southernwood, sweet woodruff, tansy, vervain.

Getting Started

Problem prevention begins long before you plant your herbs. When you're making up your list of possible plants from seed catalogs and garden books, look for plants with resistance to the pests and diseases that occur locally. Talk to your neighbors and find out from them what herbs they grow successfully. By doing this you will be rewarded with healthy, disease-resistant plants.

Now that you have done your research, make a list of the herbs you want. Check the space requirements in "A Guide to Popular Herbs," starting on page 172, and measure your growing space, to work out how many plants to buy.

Buying by Mail

If you don't have access to a local nursery, or want the best possible prices or unusual varieties, look at mail-order sources. Write for catalogs several months before you want to plant so you have time to compare selections and prices. Some catalogs are great sources of information on the virtues of specific plants and cultivars, and some have color photographs and useful information on planting and growing.

Catalog shopping is a fun way to learn about exciting new plants, it's convenient and often the prices are cheaper than at your local nursery. But on the downside, you don't really know what you are paying for until it arrives. Shipping stress can weaken even the strongest plants. If you order bareroot perennials (with roots that are wrapped in packing material), then they will need to be planted or potted up immediately.

When you order from a source for the first time, buy just a few plants or seeds and see how they look. If you are happy with the quality for the price, you can order more. If not, shop elsewhere. Remember that if an offer sounds too good to be true, it probably is!

Inspect mail-order plants as soon as they arrive. If they are damaged, you should return them immediately. Contact the company and find out how to do so. Perennials are normally shipped when they are dormant (not actively growing) and may look dead. Plant them anyway and water them well. If they don't produce any buds or new growth in a few weeks, contact the company.

Your local nursery is a good place to start when planning what herbs to buy. They usually stock a good variety of plants.

Species Chart

Herb	Growth Form and Size	Preferred Climate	Preferred Soil Conditions
Acacia farnesiana Wattle	Straggly, evergreen tree, to 23 feet (7 m)	Zones 7–9	Well-drained soil
Achillea millefolium Yarrow	Perennial, height to 3 feet (90 cm)	Zones 2–9	Fertile, well-drained soil
Aconitum carmichaelii Monkshood	Attractive perennial, to 3 feet (90 cm)	Zones 3–8	Humus-rich, well-drained soil
Aesculus hippocastanum Horse chestnut	Large, deciduous tree, to 83 feet (25 m)	Zones 3–8	Rich, deep, well-drained soil
Agastache foeniculum Anise hyssop	Perennial, height to 3 feet (90 cm)	Zones 6–10	Rich, well-drained soil
Agave americana Agave	Perennial, spread of 6 feet (2 m)	Zones 9–10	Well-drained soil
Agrimonia eupatoria Agrimony	Perennial, height 2–3 feet (60–90 cm)	Zones 5–9	Light, well-drained soil
Allium ampeloprasum Leek	Perennial, height to 3 feet (90 cm)	Zones 6 and warmer	Loose, rich, well-drained soil
Allium cepa Onion	Biennial, height to 4 feet (1.2 m)	Zones 4 and warmer	Rich, well-drained soil
Allium cepa Shallot	Firm bulbs in sets, height 8 inches (20 cm)	Zones 4 and warmer	Deep, humus-rich soil
Allium sativum Garlic	Perennial bulb, height to 2 feet (60 cm)	Zones 7–10	Rich, well-drained soil
Allium schoenoprasum Chives	Perennial, height 6–12 inches (15–30 cm)	Zones 5–10	Rich, well-drained soil
Aloe vera syn. *A. barbadensis* Aloe	Clump-forming perennial, to 1 foot (30 cm)	Zones 9–10	Gritty, well-drained soil
Aloysia triphylla Lemon verbena	Perennial woody shrub, to 10 feet (3 m)	Zones 9–10	Fertile, light, well-drained soil
Alpina galanga Galangal	Perennial, height to 6 feet (1.8 m)	Zone 10	Rich, moist, well-drained soil
Althaea officinalis Marsh mallow	Perennial, height to 4 feet (1.2 m)	Zones 6–9	Light, moist soil, neutral pH
Anethum graveolens Dill	Annual, height 2–3 feet (60–90 cm)	Zones 6–10	Rich, well-drained soil
Angelica archangelica Angelica	Perennial, height 5–8 feet (1.5–2.4 m)	Zones 6–9	Cool, rich, moist soil
Anthriscus cerefolium Chervil	Annual, height 1–2 feet (30–60 cm)	Zones 6–10	Moist, rich, well-drained soil
Apium graveolens Wild celery	Perennial with bulbous roots, 3 feet (90 cm)	Zones 5 and warmer	Rich, moist soil
Arctium lappa Burdock	Biennial, height to 5 feet (1.5 m)	Zones 3–10	Deep, loose, moist, fertile soil
Arctostaphylos uva-ursi Bearberry	Mat-forming perennial, to 3 inches (7.5 cm)	Zones 4–9	Acid, well-drained soil
Armoracia rusticana Horseradish	Perennial, height 1–4 feet (30–120 cm)	Zones 5–10	Fertile, moist, well-drained soil
Arnica montana Arnica	Perennial, height to 2 feet (60 cm)	Zones 5–9	Dry, sandy, acid soil rich in humus
Artemisia abrotanum Southernwood	Sub-shrub, height 3–6 feet (90–180 cm)	Zones 5–9	Average, well-drained, slightly acid soil
Artemisia absinthium Wormwood	Woody-based perennial, to 4 feet (1.2 m)	Zones 4–9	Ordinary, well-drained, slightly acid soil
Artemisia dracunculus Tarragon	Perennial, height 2–4 feet (60–120 cm)	Zones 4–9	Well-drained soil
Artemisia vulgaris Mugwort	Perennial, height 3–6 feet (90–180 cm)	Zones 5–9	Light, well-drained soil
Asparagus officinalis Asparagus	Perennial, height 3–5 feet (90–150 cm)	Zones 3 and warmer	Deep, fertile, well-drained soil
Astragalus gummifer Gum tragacanth	Perennial shrub, height to 1 foot (30 cm)	Zones 9–10	Well-drained, sandy, alkaline soil
Avena sativa Oats	Tall annual grass, 1–3 feet (30–90 cm)	Zones 3–9	Well-drained, fertile soil
Azadirachta indica Neem	Large, evergreen tree, 40–50 feet (12–15 m)	Zones 4–9	Poor, well-drained soil
Berberis vulgaris Barberry	Deciduous shrub, height to 8 feet (2.4 m)	Zones 3–9	Moist, fertile, well-drained soil
Betula spp. Birch	Deciduous tree, height 40–90 feet (12–27 m)	Zones 3–8	Fertile, well-drained, acid soil
Borago officinalis Borage	Annual, height to 2 feet (60 cm)	Zones 6–10	Rich, moist, well-drained soil
Boswellia sacra Frankincense	Evergreen tree, height to 15 feet (5 m)	Zones 8–10	Well-drained to dry soil
Brassica spp. Mustard	Annual or biennial, 4–6 feet (1.2–1.8 m)	Zones 6–10	Rich, well-drained soil
Calendula officinalis Calendula	Annual, height 1–2 feet (30–60 cm)	Zones 6–10	Average, well-drained soil
Camellia sinensis Tea	Evergreen shrub, height 3–20 feet (1–6 m)	Zones 6–8	Light, humus-rich soil
Cannabis sativa Hemp	Fast-growing annual, 3–15 feet (90–450 cm)	Zones 9–10	Moist soil
Capparis spinosa Caper	Prostrate shrub, height 3–6 feet (90–180 cm)	Zones 8–10	Well-drained, sandy soil
Capsicum annuum Pepper	Tender perennial, height 1–2 feet (30–60 cm)	Zone 10	Light, evenly moist, well-drained soil
Carthamus tinctorius Safflower	Annual, height 2–3 feet (60–90 cm)	Zones 6–10	Well-drained soil
Carum carvi Caraway	Biennial, height 1–2 feet (30–60 cm)	Zones 6–10	Light, fertile garden soil
Catharanthus roseus Madagascar periwinkle	Short-lived perennial, to 2 feet (60 cm)	Zones 9–10	Moist, well-drained soil
Ceanothus americanus New Jersey tea	Deciduous shrub, height 2–3 feet (60–90 cm)	Zones 4–9	Light, well-drained soil

Propagation	Pests and Diseases	Primary Uses; Parts Used
Sow scarified seed or take cuttings in summer	Leaf miner, borer, acacia scale, galls	Culinary, medicinal (flowers, pods, seeds, bark)
Sow seed in spring, divide clumps in autumn or spring	Powdery mildew, aphids	Medicinal, other (whole plant, dried flowers)
Sow seed in spring or divide in autumn or winter	Few or none	Medicinal (roots)
Sow seed in summer or take cuttings in winter	Japanese beetles, fungal leaf blotch, canker	Medicinal (seeds, bark)
Sow seed in spring	Few or none	Culinary, medicinal (leaves, flowers)
Off-shoots taken from parent plant in spring	Mealybugs, rot	Culinary, medicinal (whole plant)
Sow seed or divide in early spring	Powdery mildew	Medicinal (whole plant)
Sow seed in spring or autumn, or by division	Root maggots	Culinary, medicinal (stems, bulbs)
Sow seed in autumn or spring	Onion fly, maggots, down mildew	Culinary, medicinal (bulbs)
Grow from sets in spring	Root maggots	Culinary, medicinal (bulbs, young leaves)
Plant cloves in autumn	Bulb diseases	Culinary, medicinal (bulbs)
Sow seed in spring, or divide clumps in spring	Bulb and stem diseases	Culinary (fresh or dried leaves)
Replant offshoots from established plants	Mealybugs	Medicinal (leaves, sap)
Take cuttings in late spring or early summer	Mites	Culinary, medicinal, other (fresh or dried leaves)
Propagate by rhizome division	Red spider mites	Culinary, medicinal (rhizomes, oil)
Sow seed in spring, take cuttings or divide in autumn	Few or none	Culinary, medicinal (leaves, roots)
Sow seed in early spring	Few or none	Culinary, medicinal (leaves, seeds, oil)
Sow seed in spring	Aphids, crown rot	Culinary, medicinal (leaves, stems, seeds, roots)
Sow seed in autumn or early spring	Few or none	Culinary, medicinal (leaves)
Sow seed in early spring	Blights, celery-fly maggots	Culinary, medicinal (whole plant, roots, seeds)
Sow seed in early spring or autumn	Few or none	Culinary, medicinal (stems, roots, seeds)
Sow seed in spring or autumn, take cuttings in autumn	Few or none	Medicinal (leaves)
Plant root pieces in autumn	Few or none	Culinary, medicinal (leaves, roots)
Sow seed in early spring or divide plants in spring	Aphids	Medicinal (flowers)
Take cuttings or divide plants in spring or autumn	Few or none	Medicinal, other (leaves)
Sow seed outdoors in autumn, divide plants in spring	Few or none	Medicinal, other (whole plant, leaves)
Take cuttings in spring, autumn, divide plants in spring	Few or none	Culinary, medicinal (leaves, oil)
Sow seed in spring, divide plants in spring or autumn	Few or none	Culinary, medicinal, other (leaves)
Sow seed in spring or plant 1-year-old crowns	Asparagus rust	Culinary, medicinal (young shoots, rhizomes)
Sow scarified seed in spring or summer	Few or none	Medicinal (gum)
Sow seed in spring	Grasshoppers, flying insects	Culinary, medicinal (seeds)
Sow ripe seed in spring or summer	Few or none	Medicinal (leaves, bark, seeds, oil, resin)
Sow seed in spring or take cuttings in summer	Few or none	Medicinal (leaves, bark, root, fruits)
Sow seed late summer or autumn	Cankers, leaf pests, borers	Medicinal, other (leaves, bark, oil, sap)
Sow seed in spring	Foliage rot	Culinary, medicinal (leaves, flowers, seeds, oil)
Take semi-hardwood cuttings in summer	Few or none	Medicinal, other (gum resin)
Sow seed in early spring to autumn	Caterpillars, slugs, snails, whiteflies	Culinary, medicinal (leaves, seeds, flowers, oil)
Sow seed in spring	Powdery mildew, aphids, rust	Culinary, medicinal (flower petals)
Propagate by semiripe cuttings or layering in summer	Few or none	Culinary, medicinal (shoot tips of leaves, oil)
Sow seed or take cuttings in summer	Few or none	Medicinal, other (whole plant, flowering tops, seeds)
Take ripewood cuttings in summer	Few or none	Culinary, medicinal (root bark, flower buds)
Sow seed in late spring	Powdery mildew, leaf spot	Culinary, medicinal (fruits)
Sow seed in early spring	Snails, slugs	Culinary, medicinal (flowers, seeds, oil)
Sow seed in spring or early autumn	Few or none	Culinary, medicinal (leaves, roots, seeds, oil)
Sow seed indoors before last frost, plant outdoors in spring or early summer	Fungal diseases	Medicinal (leaves)
Take cuttings in spring or autumn	Scale	Culinary, medicinal (leaves, roots)

Herb	Growth Form and Size	Preferred Climate	Preferred Soil Conditions
Centaurea cyanus Cornflower	Bushy annual, height to 3 feet (90 cm)	Zones 3–8	Well-drained soil
Centella asiatica Gotu kola	Low-growing perennial, to 8 inches (20 cm)	Zones 9–10 or more	Moist, well-composted soil
Chaenomeles speciosa Flowering quince	Deciduous shrub or tree, height 6–20 feet (2–6 m)	Zones 5–10	Well-drained, acid to neutral soil
Chamaemelum nobile Chamomile, Roman	Low-growing perennial, height 6–9 inches (15–23 cm)	Zones 4–10	Moist, well-drained soil
Chimaphila umbellata Pipsissewa	Shrubby perennial, to 10 inches (25 cm)	Zones 5–8	Humus-rich, moist, well-drained soil
Chrysanthemum (Tanacetum) parthenium Feverfew	Aromatic perennial, 8–24 inches (20–60 cm)	Zones 6–10	Well-drained garden soil
Cichorium intybus Chicory	Perennial, height 1–5 feet (30–150 cm)	Zones 3–9	Neutral to alkaline, well-drained soil
Citrus aurantiifolia Lime	Small, evergreen tree, 10–15 feet (3–5 m)	Zones 9 and warmer	Light, well-drained, fertile soil
Citrus bergamia Bergamot orange	Rounded tree, height to 30 feet (10 m)	Zones 9–10	Light, well-drained, fertile soil
Citrus limon Lemon	Evergreen, subtropical tree, to 20 feet (6 m)	Zones 9–10	Light, well-drained, fertile soil
Coffea arabica Coffee	Evergreen large shrub, 15–20 feet (4.5–7 m)	Zone 10	Well-drained, humus-rich soil
Convallaria majalis Lily-of-the-valley	Hardy perennial, height to 1 foot (30 cm)	Zones 3–9	Fertile, moist soil
Coriandrum sativum Cilantro	Annual, height 1–3 feet (30–90 cm)	Zones 6–10	Fertile, well-drained soil
Crataegus laevigata Hawthorn	Deciduous tree, height 15–20 feet (5–6 m)	Zones 5–9	Clay or loamy soil
Crocus sativus Saffron	Perennial, height to 6 inches (15 cm)	Zones 6–9	Light, fertile, well-drained soil
Cryptotaenia canadensis Mitsuba	Hardy succulent perennial, to 3 feet (90 cm)	Zones 3–7	Rich, moist soil
Cuminum cyminum Cumin	Tender annual, height 10 inches (25 cm)	Zones 8–10	Light, well-drained soil
Curcuma longa Turmeric	Tall perennial, height 3 feet (90 cm)	Zones 8–9	Rich, well-drained soil
Cymbopogon citratus Lemongrass	Tender perennial, height 6 feet (1.8 m)	Zones 9–10	Rich, well-drained soil
Dendranthema x *grandiflorum* Chrysanthemum	Large perennial, 1–7 feet (30–210 cm)	Zones 4 and warmer	Rich, well-drained soil
Dianthus caryophyllus Clove pink	Small, hardy perennial, to 20 inches (50 cm)	Zone 8	Well-drained, slightly alkaline soil
Digitalis purpurea Foxglove	Biennial, height to 5 feet (1.5 m)	Zones 5–9	Well-drained, acid soil
Echinacea purpurea Echinacea	Tall perennial, height 4 feet (1.2 m)	Zones 3–8	Humus-rich, well-drained soil
Elettaria cardamomum Cardamom	Tender perennial, 6–10 feet (1.8–3 m)	Zones 10 or warmer	Moist, humus-rich soil
Equisetum spp. Horsetail	Perennial, 4–18 inches (10–45 cm)	Zones 5–9	Humus-rich, moist soil
Eucalyptus spp. Eucalyptus	Evergreen tree, 5–300 feet (1.5–100 m)	Zones 8–10	Light, loamy soil
Eupatorium perfoliatum Boneset	Rhizomatous perennial, 5 feet (1.5 m)	Zones 3–9	Rich, marshy soil
Ferula assa-foetida Asafetida	Large perennial, height 6 feet (1.8 m)	Zones 8–9	Rich, well-drained soil
Filipendula ulmaria Meadowsweet	Hardy, woody perennial, height 4 feet (1.2 m)	Zones 2–7	Rich, wet soil
Foeniculum vulgare Fennel	Semi-hardy perennial, height 4 feet (1.2 m)	Zones 6–9	Humus-rich, well-drained soil
Fragaria vesca Wild strawberry	Perennial with runners, 10 inches (25 cm)	Zones 5–10	Rich, well-drained soil
Galium odoratum Sweet woodruff	Rhizomatous perennial, height 1 foot (30 cm)	Zones 5–9	Moist, humus-rich, well-drained soil
Galium verum Lady's bedstraw	Hardy perennial, height to 3 feet (90 cm)	Zones 3–9	Deep, light, fertile, well-drained soil
Gardenia augusta Gardenia	Evergreen shrub, height 5 feet (1.5 m)	Zones 8–10	Well-drained, acid soil with humus
Gentiana lutea Great yellow gentian	Herbaceous perennial, to 6 feet (1.8 m)	Zones 5–7	Moist, well-drained, alkaline soil
Geranium robertianum Herb Robert	Annual or biennial, to 20 inches (50 cm)	Zones 5–9	Well-drained, sandy soil
Ginkgo biloba Ginkgo	Deciduous tree, 80–120 feet (24–36 m)	Zones 4–8	Deep, moist, humus-rich soil
Glycyrrhiza glabra Licorice	Hardy perennial, height to 5 feet (1.5 m)	Zones 8–10	Deep, moist, humus-rich soil
Hamamelis virginiana Witch hazel	Deciduous shrub, 8–15 feet (2.4–4.5 m)	Zones 5–9	Moist, humus-rich soil
Helianthus annuus Sunflower	Giant annual, 3–10 feet (90–300 cm)	Zones 5 and warmer	Rich, well-drained soil
Humulus lupulus Hop	Climbing vine, 20–30 feet (6–9 m)	Zones 5–9	Moist, rich soil
Hydrangea arborescens Hydrangea	Deciduous shrub, 3–10 feet (90–300 cm)	Zones 5–9	Rich, moist soil
Hypericum perforatum St John's wort	Weedy perennial, 10–36 inches (25–90 cm)	Zones 5–8	Well-drained to dry soil
Hyssopus officinalis Hyssop	Semi-evergreen perennial, to 2 feet (60 cm)	Zones 3–9	Light, well-drained soil
Inula helenium Elecampane	Perennial, height 4–6 feet (1.2–1.8 m)	Zones 5–9	Moderately fertile, moist soil

Propagation	Pests and Diseases	Primary Uses; Parts Used
Sow seed in spring or autumn	Rust, petal blight	Culinary, medicinal, other (flowers)
Sow seed or take cuttings in spring	Few or none	Culinary, medicinal, other (whole plant, leaves)
Sow seed in autumn, take cuttings in summer, layer shoots in early autumn	Fireblight, chlorosis	Culinary, medicinal (fruits)
Sow seed late spring and early summer, divide plants in early spring	Few or none	Culinary, medicinal, other (flowers, oil)
Root cuttings or divide plants in spring or autumn	Few or none	Culinary, medicinal (whole plant, leaves)
Sow seed in early spring, divide or take cuttings in spring or autumn	Few or none	Medicinal, other (whole plant, flowers, leaves)
Sow seed in spring	Few or none	Culinary, medicinal (leaves, roots)
Grafted rootstock or seed	Scale, mealybugs, caterpillars	Culinary, medicinal (leaves, fruits, peel, oil)
Grafted rootstock or seed	Scale, mealybugs, caterpillars	Culinary, medicinal (leaves, fruits, peel, oil)
Grafted rootstock or cuttings	Scale, mealybugs, caterpillars	Culinary, medicinal (leaves, fruit, peel, oil)
Sow seed in spring	Few if kept well watered	Culinary (seeds)
Sow seed in spring or divide in autumn	Botrytis, caterpillars	Medicinal, other (whole plant, oil, leaves, flowers)
Sow seed in spring	Few or none	Culinary, other (leaves, seeds, roots, oil)
Sow from seed, or graft	Leafspot, powdery mildew, rust	Medicinal (fruits)
Plant corms in early autumn	Few or none	Culinary, medicinal, other (flower stigmas)
Sow seed in spring or divide in spring	Few or none	Culinary (leaves)
Sow seed in spring	Few or none	Culinary, medicinal, other (seeds)
Propagate by root division or by seed sown in autumn	Few or none	Culinary, medicinal, other (rhizomes)
Propagate by division of older plants	Few or none	Culinary, medicinal, other (leaves, stems, oil)
Grow from root division or cuttings in early spring or by seed in late winter or early spring	Aphids, slugs, snails, mildew, virus diseases	Culinary, medicinal (flowers)
Seed, softwood cuttings in spring, layering in summer	Botrytis, mildew, leaf and stem rot	Culinary, medicinal, other (flowers, oil)
Sow seed in spring or autumn	Crown and root rot in wet conditions	Medicinal (leaves)
Seed in spring, division in autumn, cuttings in winter	Few or none	Medicinal (roots, rhizomes)
Division of rhizomes in spring, seed in autumn	Thrips	Culinary, medicinal, other (seeds, oil)
Divide mature plants in autumn	Few or none	Medicinal (stems)
Purchase nursery-grown trees or seed in spring	Few or none	Medicinal, other (leaves, oil, resin, bark, seedpods)
Sow seed or divide in spring, take cuttings in summer	Few or none	Medicinal (whole plant, roots, leaves)
Sow seed in late summer	Few or none	Culinary, medicinal (gum resin)
Sow seed in spring, divide roots in autumn	Few or none	Medicinal, other (whole plant, flowers)
Sow seed in spring or autumn	Few or none	Culinary, medicinal (leaves, stems, roots, seeds, oil)
Divide plant anytime or sow seed in spring	Very attractive to birds	Culinary, medicinal (leaves, roots, fruits)
Sow seed in summer to autumn, divide in spring	Few or none	Culinary, medicinal, other (whole plant)
Sow seed in spring, divide roots in spring or autumn	Few or none	Medicinal, other (whole plant)
Semiripe or greenwood cuttings in spring or summer	Mealybugs, aphids, whiteflies	Culinary, medicinal, other (fruits, flowers)
Seed and division in autumn, offshoots in spring	Root rot in wet conditions	Medicinal, other (roots, rhizomes)
Sow seed in spring or summer	Slugs, snails, caterpillars	Medicinal (whole plant)
Sow seed in autumn	Few or none	Culinary, medicinal (leaves, seeds)
Seed in spring, root division, stolon cuttings in autumn	Few or none	Culinary, medicinal, other (roots, stolons)
Sow seed in autumn, also by cuttings or layerings	Few or none	Medicinal, other (leaves, branches, twigs, bark)
Sow seed in spring	Mildew, rot	Culinary, medicinal, other (whole plant, seeds, oil)
Take basal cuttings in spring	Aphids, mites	Culinary, medicinal (leaves, shoots, flowers, oil)
Softwood cuttings in summer and autumn	Aphids, red spider mites, scales	Medicinal (roots)
Sow seed in spring, divide in autumn	Rust	Medicinal, other (whole plant)
Sow seed in spring, take cuttings or divide in spring	Few or none	Culinary, medicinal, other (whole plant, leaves)
Sow seed in spring, take root cuttings in autumn	Sap-sucking pests	Culinary, medicinal, other (roots, flowers, oil)

Herb	Growth Form and Size	Preferred Climate	Preferred Soil Conditions
Iris 'Florentina' Orris	Perennial, height to 2½ feet (75 cm)	Zones 4–9	Deep, rich, well-drained soil
Jasminum officinale Jasmine	Vigorous, deciduous climber, to 30 feet (9 m)	Zones 7–10	Moist, well-drained soil
Juglans regia Walnut	Large, deciduous tree, to 100 feet (30 m)	Zones 4–8	Well-drained, humus-rich soil
Juniperus communis Juniper	Upright or prostrate shrub, to 20 feet (6 m)	Zones 3–9	Adaptable to most soil conditions
Laurus nobilis Bay, sweet	Evergreen tree, 10–49 feet (3–15 m)	Zones 8–10	Rich, well-drained soil
Lavandula angustifolia Lavender, English	Shrubby perennial, 2–3 feet (60–90 cm)	Zones 5–9	Light, well-drained, limey soil
Leptospermum scoparium New Zealand tea tree	Compact, evergreen shrub, height 6–10 feet (1.8–3 m)	Zones 8–10	Adaptable to most soil conditions
Levisticum officinale Lovage	Perennial, height to 6 feet (1.8 m)	Zones 5–9	Fertile, moist, well-drained soil
Magnolia officinalis Magnolia	Deciduous tree, height to 75 feet (22 m)	Zones 8–10	Humus-rich, moist, well-drained soil
Marrubium vulgare Horehound	Perennial, height 2–3 feet (60–90 cm)	Zones 4–9	Average, well-drained soil
Melissa officinalis Lemon balm	Perennial, height 1–2 feet (30–60 cm)	Zones 4–10	Any well-drained soil
Mentha pulegium Pennyroyal	Perennial, height 6–12 inches (15–30 cm)	Zones 7–9	Moist, loamy garden soil
Mentha spp. Mint	Perennial, height to 2½ feet (75 cm)	Zones 3–10	Rich, moist, well-drained soil
Monarda didyma Bee balm	Perennial, height 3–4 feet (90–120 cm)	Zones 4–9	Rich, moist, light garden soil
Murraya koenigii Curry leaf	Evergreen, tropical tree, to 20 feet (6 m)	Zone 10	Well-drained, moist, rich soil
Myristica fragrans Nutmeg	Large, evergreen tree, 30–50 feet (10–15 m)	Zone 10	Rich, well-drained, sandy soil
Myrrhis odorata Sweet cicely	Perennial, height to 3 feet (90 cm)	Zones 5–9	Moist, humus-rich, well-drained soil
Nasturtium officinale Watercress	Aquatic perennial	Zones 6–10	Alkaline, flowing water
Nepeta cataria Catnip	Perennial, height 1–3 feet (30–90 cm)	Zones 3–10	Dry, sandy garden soil
Ocimum basilicum Basil, sweet	Annual, height to 2 feet (60 cm)	Zone 10	Rich, moist soil
Oenothera biennis Evening primrose	Tall biennial, height 5 feet (1.5 m)	Zones 4–10	Dry, sandy soil
Origanum majorana Marjoram	Tender perennial, height to 2 feet (60 cm)	Zones 7–10	Light, well-drained soil
Origanum vulgare Oregano	Bushy perennial, 1–2½ feet (30–75 cm)	Zones 5–10	Average, well-drained, garden soil
Paeonia lactiflora Peony	Herbaceous perennial, height 2 feet (60 cm)	Zones 6–8	Rich, well-drained soil
Panax ginseng Ginseng	Perennial, height to 3 feet (90 cm)	Zones 6–10	Moist, well-drained soil
Passiflora incarnata Passionflower	Climbing vine, 25–30 feet (7.5–9 m)	Zones 6–10	Fertile, well-drained soil
Pelargonium spp. Geranium, scented	Evergreen shrub, height to 3 feet (90 cm)	Zones 9–10	Rich, well-drained, loamy soil
Persicaria bistorta Knotweed	Hardy perennial, height 2 feet (60 cm)	Zones 3–8	Rich, moist, well-drained soil
Petroselinum crispum Parsley	Biennial, height 8–12 inches (20–30 cm)	Zones 5–10	Moderately rich, well-drained soil
Pimpinella anisum Anise	Annual, height to 2 feet (60 cm)	Zones 6–10	Poor, light, well-drained soil
Piper longum Long pepper	Climbing subshrub, height 10 feet (3 m)	Zone 10	Rich, moist, well-drained soil
Piper nigrum Black pepper	Climbing perennial, height 12 feet (4 m)	Zone 10	Rich, moist soil
Plantago major Plantain	Perennial, 6–18 inches (15–45 cm)	Zones 5–10	Moist, well-drained soil
Portulaca oleracea Purslane	Annual, height 8–18 inches (20–45 cm)	Zones 4 and warmer	Sandy, light soil
Primula vulgaris Primrose	Clump-forming perennial, 6 inches (15 cm)	Zones 6–9	Moist, humus-rich soil
Pulsatilla vulgaris Pasque flower	Small perennial, 6–12 inches (15–30 cm)	Zones 3–8	Average, well-drained soil
Rhamnus purshiana Cascara sagrada	Deciduous shrub, 10–20 feet (3–6 m)	Zones 7–9	Moist, fertile, well-drained soil
Rheum palmatum Chinese rhubarb	Hardy perennial, up to 6 feet (2 m)	Zones 6–9	Moist, deep, humus-rich soil
Ribes nigrum Blackcurrant	Aromatic shrub, height 6 feet (2 m)	Zones 5–8	Moist, well-drained, average soil
Rosa spp. Rose	Perennial, height varies with species	Zones 3–10	Well-drained, moist soil, rich in organic matter
Rosmarinus officinalis Rosemary	Evergreen shrub, 2–6 feet (60–180 cm)	Zones 7–10	Light, well-drained soil
Rubia tinctorum Madder	Perennial, height to 4 feet (1.2 m)	Zones 6–9	Deep, fertile, well-drained soil

Propagation	Pests and Diseases	Primary Uses; Parts Used
Divide roots in autumn every 2 years	Few or none	Medicinal, other (rhizomes)
Take cuttings in spring or autumn, layer in autumn	Red spider mites, aphids, whiteflies	Culinary, medicinal, other (flowers, oil)
Sow seed in autumn or by grafting	Leaf blot, blight	Culinary, medicinal, other (leaves, fruits, bark)
Sow seed in autumn, take cuttings in late summer	Juniper scale, mites, blight	Culinary, medicinal, other (berries, oil)
Sow seed in spring, take cuttings in autumn	Few or none	Culinary, medicinal (leaves)
Take cuttings in spring or autumn	Fungal diseases in high humidity	Culinary, medicinal, other (flowers, oil)
Sow seed or take semi-hardwood cuttings in summer	Scale, black smut, webbing caterpillars	Medicinal (leaves)
Sow seed in late summer or early autumn	Few or none	Culinary, medicinal (leaves, stems, roots, seeds, oil)
Sow seed in autumn, take cuttings in summer	Scale, root rot	Medicinal, other (bark, flowers)
Sow seed or divide plants in early spring	Few or none	Medicinal (whole plant)
Sow seed, take cuttings and divide in spring	Powdery mildew	Culinary, medicinal (whole plants, leaves, oil)
Sow seed or take cuttings in spring, divide in autumn	Few or none	Culinary, medicinal, other (whole plant, leaves, oil)
Take cuttings or divide in spring or autumn	Aphids, root and foliage disease	Culinary, medicinal, other (whole plant, leaves, oil)
Sow seed, take cuttings or divide in spring	Foliage diseases	Culinary, medicinal, other (leaves, flowers)
Propagate by seed or semiripe cuttings in summer	Few or none	Culinary, medicinal (leaves, bark, roots, seeds, oil)
Sow seed in summer, take cuttings in autumn	Few or none	Culinary, medicinal, other (seeds, oil)
Sow seed in spring, divide plants in spring or autumn	Few or none	Culinary, medicinal (leaves, roots, seeds)
Propagate by root cuttings in spring	Aphids	Culinary, medicinal (leaves)
Sow seed or take cuttings in early spring	Few or none	Culinary, medicinal, other (whole plant, leaves)
Sow seed in late spring	Common pests	Culinary, medicinal, other (leaves, stems, seeds, oil)
Sow seed in spring and autumn	Root rot, powdery mildew	Culinary, medicinal, other (oil from seeds, roots)
Sow seed in spring, divide in autumn	Few or none	Culinary, medicinal, other (leaves, seeds, oil)
Sow seed in spring, divide in spring or autumn	Few or none	Culinary, medicinal, other (whole plant, leaves, oil)
Sow seed in autumn, root cuttings in winter	Leafspot, botrytis, peony wilt	Medicinal (roots)
Sow seed in spring	Few or none	Medicinal (roots, flowers)
Propagate by seed or cuttings in summer	Thrips	Culinary, medicinal (whole plant, fruits)
Propagate by softwood cuttings in spring to autumn	Whiteflies	Culinary, medicinal, other (whole plant, leaves, oil)
Sow seed or divide in spring, take cuttings in summer	Aphids	Culinary, medicinal (rhizomes, leaves)
Sow seed in early spring	Fungal diseases, carrot pests	Culinary, medicinal, other (leaves, roots, seeds, oil)
Sow seed in spring	Few or none	Culinary, medicinal (leaves, seeds, oil)
Propagate by semiripe cuttings in summer	Few or none	Culinary, medicinal (fruits)
Propagate by semiripe cuttings in summer	Few or none	Culinary, medicinal (fruits)
Sow seed in early spring or autumn	Few or none	Culinary, medicinal (leaves, roots)
Sow seed in spring	Aphids, slugs	Culinary, medicinal (whole plant, leaves)
Sow seed in autumn or divide in spring or autumn	Rust, botrytis, aphids, caterpillars	Culinary, medicinal (whole plant, leaves, roots)
Sow seed in autumn or spring; self-seeds readily	Few or none	Medicinal (flowering plants)
Sow seed in autumn, layer in spring or winter, take cuttings in summer	Few or none	Medicinal herb (bark)
Divide roots and root cuttings in colder months or sow seed in spring	Few or none	Medicinal, other (rhizomes)
Take hardwood cuttings in winter	Few or none	Culinary, medicinal (leaves, fruits)
Propagate by seed in autumn, cuttings in autumn, or by budding in summer	Fungal diseases, aphids, mites, caterpillars, beetles, birds	Culinary, medicinal, other (petals, fruits)
Sow seed in spring, take cuttings in autumn or layer in summer	Scale pests, mildew	Culinary, medicinal, other (leaves, oil, flowering tops)
Sow seed in spring, plants will grow from roots	Few or none	Medicinal, other (roots, leaves)

Herb	Growth Form and Size	Preferred Climate	Preferred Soil Conditions
Rubus fruticosus Blackberry	Semi-evergreen shrub with biennial canes	Zones 6–10	Rich, well-drained soil
Rubus idaeus Raspberry	Deciduous shrub with suckering canes	Zones 3–9	Rich, well-drained soil
Rumex acetosa Sorrel	Hardy perennial, height 2 feet (60 cm)	Zones 5–9	Fertile, moist soil
Rumex crispus Dock, curled	Perennial, height 1–4 feet (30–120 cm)	Zones 5–9	Any slightly acidic soil
Ruta graveolens Rue	Perennial, height 2–3 feet (60–90 cm)	Zones 5–9	Poor, well-drained soil
Salvia officinalis Sage	Perennial shrub, height 1–2 feet (30–60 cm)	Zones 5–10	Well-drained garden soil
Salvia sclarea Clary	Biennial or perennial, 2–5 feet (60–150 cm)	Zones 5–10	Average, well-drained soil
Sambucus nigra Elder	Deciduous shrub or tree, to 30 feet (9 m)	Zones 5–9	Moist, rich, well-drained soil
Sanguinaria canadensis Bloodroot	Perennial, height 6–8 inches (15–20 cm)	Zones 3–9	Rich, well-drained soil
Santolina chamaecyparissus Santolina	Evergreen shrub, height to 2 feet (60 cm)	Zones 7–10	Poor, well-drained soil
Saponaria officinalis Soapwort	Rhizomatous perennial, height 1–3 feet (30–90 cm)	Zones 5–9	Average, well-drained soil
Sassafras albidum Sassafras	Deciduous tree, 20–60 feet (6–18 m)	Zones 5–9	Well-drained garden soil
Satureja montana Savory, winter	Evergreen perennial, 6–12 inches (15–30 cm)	Zones 6–9	Poor, well-drained soil
Simaba cedron Cedron (quassia)	Deciduous tree, 15–50 feet (5–15 m)	Zones 10 or more	Well-drained soil
Solidago spp. Goldenrod	Perennial, height 3–7 feet (90-–210 cm)	Zones 5–9	Average to poor, well-drained soil
Stachys officinalis Betony	Perennial, 3 feet (90 cm)	Zones 5–9	Average, well-drained soil
Stellaria media Chickweed	Annual, 4–16 inches (10–40 cm)	Zones 5–10	Any soil, preferably moist
Symphytum officinale Comfrey	Perennial, 2–4 feet (60–120 cm)	Zones 5–10	Rich, moist garden soil
Tagetes patula French marigold	Bushy annual, height 1 foot (30 cm)	Zones 9–10	Average, well-drained soil
Tamarindus indica Tamarind	Evergreen tree, height 80 feet (24 m)	Zones 10 or warmer	Light, well-drained soil
Tanacetum balsamita Costmary	Perennial, 1–3 feet (60–90 cm)	Zones 6–10	Fertile, loamy, well-drained soil
Tanacetum cinerariifolium Pyrethrum	Daisy-like perennial, to 2½ feet (75 cm)	Zones 6–10	Average, well-drained soil
Tanacetum vulgare Tansy	Perennial, height 3–4 feet (90–120 cm)	Zones 4–10	Well-drained garden soil
Taraxacum officinale Dandelion	Perennial, height 6–12 inches (15–30 cm)	Zones 3–10	Any moderately fertile, moist soil
Teucrium chamaedrys Germander	Perennial, height to 2 feet (60 cm)	Zones 5–9	Well-drained, garden soil
Thymus vulgaris Thyme, common or garden	Variable shrub, height 1–1½ feet (30–45 cm)	Zones 6–10	Average, well-drained soil
Trifolium pratense Red clover	Perennial, height 1–2 feet (30–60 cm)	Zones 6–9	Light, moist, well-drained soil
Trigonella foenum-graecum Fenugreek	Annual, height 1–2 feet (30–60 cm)	Zones 6–10	Moist, rich garden soil
Tropaeolum majus Nasturtium	Annual, height 1–2 feet (30–60 cm)	Zones 8–10	Average, moist, well-drained soil
Urtica dioica Stinging nettle	Herbaceous perennial, 2–6 feet (60–180 cm)	Zones 5–9	Most soils
Valeriana officinalis Valerian	Herbaceous perennial, 3–5 feet (90–150 cm)	Zones 4–9	Fertile, moist, garden soil
Vanilla planifolia Vanilla	Evergreen, climbing perennial	Zone 10	Loose, friable compost
Verbascum thapsus Mullein	Tall biennial, height 6 feet (2 m)	Zones 4–8	Well-drained to dry soil
Verbena officinalis Vervain	Perennial, height 1–2 feet (30–60 cm)	Zones 4–10	Ordinary, moist, well-drained soil
Viola odorata Violet, sweet	Perennial, height 4–6 inches (10–15 cm)	Zones 6–10	Well-drained, moist, rich soil
Wasabia japonica Wasabi	Hardy perennial, 8–16 inches (20–40 cm)	Zones 3–6	Rich, moist to wet soil
Zea mays Sweet corn (maize)	Large annual, height 10 feet (3 m)	Zones 7 and warmer	Deep, rich, well-drained soil
Zingiber officinale Ginger	Tropical perennial, height 2–5 feet (60–150 cm)	Zone 10 or warmer	Moist, fertile, well-drained soil

Propagation	Pests and Diseases	Primary Uses; Parts Used
Take cuttings in summer or sow seed in spring	Aphids, botrytis, viral diseases	Culinary, medicinal (leaves, roots, fruits)
Propagate by division or layering	Botrytis, cane blight, viruses	Culinary, medicinal (leaves, fruits)
Sow seed in late spring, divide plants in spring or autumn, take cuttings in spring	Slugs, snails	Culinary, medicinal, other (leaves)
Sow seed in spring	Few or none	Medicinal (roots)
Sow seed, take cuttings, divide in spring	Few or none	Medicinal, other (leaves)
Sow seed late spring, take cuttings or divide plants in spring or autumn	Caterpillars, slugs, snails	Culinary, medicinal, other (leaves, oil, flowers)
Sow seed in spring, divide in early spring	Few or none	Culinary, medicinal, other (leaves, flowers, seeds, oil)
Sow seed in autumn, take cuttings in summer	Aphids	Culinary, medicinal, other (leaves, bark, flowers, fruits)
Sow seed or divide in autumn	Few or none	Medicinal, other (rhizomes)
Sow seed late spring, take cuttings in summer to autumn, layer and divide plants in spring	Few or none	Medicinal, other (leaves, flowering stems)
Sow seed indoors before last frosts, plant out in spring, divide plants in autumn or spring	Few or none	Medicinal, other (leaves, leafy stems, rhizomes)
Propagate by seed, suckers or root cuttings	Japanese beetles, gypsy moths	Culinary, medicinal, other (leaves, roots, oil)
Sow seed, take cuttings or divide in spring	Few or none	Culinary, medicinal, other (leaves, shoots)
Division of suckers or hardwood cuttings, also by seed	Few or none	Medicinal (seeds)
Sow seed in spring, divide plants in spring or autumn	Powdery mildew	Medicinal (leaves, flowering tops)
Sow seed in early spring, divide in autumn, take cuttings in late spring or summer	Few or none	Medicinal (whole plant)
Sow seed any time	Few or none	Culinary, medicinal, other (whole plant)
Propagate by seed, division or cuttings	Few or none	Medicinal (leaves, roots)
Sow seed in spring	Few or none	Culinary, medicinal, other (leaves, flowers, oil)
Air layer, graft or sow seed in spring	Few or none	Culinary, medicinal, other (fruits)
Divide plants in spring	Few or none	Culinary, medicinal, other (leaves)
Sow seed in spring to summer, divide in spring	Few or none	Other (flowers)
Sow seed indoors in late winter, transplant in spring, divide in spring or autumn	Aphids	Culinary, other (leaves, flowers)
Sow seed in early spring	Few or none	Culinary, medicinal (whole plant, leaves, roots, flowers)
Propagate by cuttings, layering or division	Few or none	Culinary, medicinal (whole plant, leaves)
Sow seed indoors in winter, plant outdoors in late spring, take cuttings or divide plants in spring	Few or none	Culinary, medicinal, other (whole plant, leaves, flowering tops, oil)
Sow seed in early spring; may need an inoculant	"Clover sickness"	Medicinal (flowering tops)
Sow seed in late spring	Slugs, snails	Culinary, medicinal (leaves, seeds)
Sow seed in spring after last frost	Aphids	Culinary, medicinal (whole plant, leaves, flowers)
Sow seed in early spring	Few or none	Culinary, medicinal, other (whole plants, leaves)
Sow seed in spring, divide in spring or autumn	Few or none	Medicinal, other (rhizomes, roots, oil)
Take cuttings anytime; leave to dry before planting	Scale, mildew, vanilla root rot, snails	Culinary, medicinal, other (fruits)
Sow seed in spring, root cuttings in winter	Caterpillars	Culinary, medicinal (whole plant, leaves, flowers)
Sow seed or take cuttings in spring, divide in winter	Few or none	Medicinal (whole plant)
Sow seed in autumn; divide in autumn, winter, spring	Slugs, snails, mites, fungal diseases	Culinary, medicinal, other (leaves, flowers, oil)
Divide root stock or sow seed in spring	Few or none	Culinary, medicinal (roots, leaves, leaf stalks)
Sow seed in spring	Wireworms, caterpillars	Culinary, medicinal (cobs, silks, oil)
Plant rhizome indoors any season, move pots outdoors in summer	Few or none	Culinary, medicinal (rhizomes, oil)

Selecting and Buying Herbs

For many people, choosing and buying plants is one of the most pleasurable aspects of creating a new garden. If you are a new herb grower, the easiest way to start will be to purchase your first plants in pots. But consider the pot when buying. Some herbs, such as dill and parsley, don't transplant well, so look for seedlings growing in peat pots, or grow your own. This way you can plant the seedling and pot straight into the ground and avoid disturbing the root system. Otherwise, the shock of transplanting can weaken the plant and make it more susceptible to disease and pest attack.

It's a good idea to buy from reputable nurseries that take good care of their stock. If you buy healthy plants to begin with, your garden is more likely to thrive.

Buying Healthy Plants

Look for healthy, vigorous plants with bright, new growth. They should be free of insects and diseases. Without damaging the plant, check the undersides of leaves for insect pests and see that the stems are strong, with no signs of injury or rot. This way you will be giving your plants the best possible start and you will avoid importing pests and plant pathogens that could spread to other plants in your garden. Common signs of insect and other pest damage include:

- Leaves with chewed holes or edges
- Shiny slime trails
- Webs on leaves or stems
- Tiny eggs on leaves or stems
- Brown or greenish droppings
- Wilted, curled or discolored leaves

Gently remove a plant from its pot to check the roots before buying. Avoid plants with massed or circling roots.

Good–quality plants will have healthy white roots that are still growing through the soil ball.

Inspect the Roots

Strong, healthy roots are a vital part of determining plant health. In plants ready for transplanting, the root system should almost fill the pot. If a plant is growing in a plastic or clay container, gently remove the plant and look at its roots. Roots should penetrate the soil without circling the outside of the root ball. They should

Plants that look strong and healthy at the nursery are likely to grow when you get them home.

Sickly plants may be cheaper to buy, but they can bring pests and diseases into your garden.

Sunflowers are easily grown from seed, but are sometimes available as potted annuals for quick color.

be uniformly white, moist and without breaks or brown spots. Avoid plants with lots of matted roots or those that are tightly rooted to their neighbors. Check the soil, too. It should be moist just below the surface. Plants that are allowed to dry out frequently become stressed and weakened, and their growth may be stunted.

Check Plant Color

Healthy seedlings are usually deep green, although you can expect color to vary among plants and cultivars. An overall pale, washed-out appearance often indicates that a nutrient is lacking. If you're not sure what a particular plant is supposed to look like, compare it with a photograph from a book or catalog. This will help you determine if those stripes, spots, or colors are normal or if they indicate a deficiency of some kind.

Common symptoms of nutrient deficiency include:

- Fuzzy patches of fungal spores
- Dead areas in leaves or stems
- Yellowing of leaves or leaf tips
- Spotty, discolored, or wilted leaves
- Leaves, roots or stems with a soggy appearance.

Where to Buy

Most nurseries and garden centers offer a wide variety of herbs and are a good place to shop, as most have very knowledgeable staff who can help you with your inquiries. Most offer container-grown plants, which are the easiest to handle. Buying this way means that you can inspect the plants before buying them. Also, your plants won't have to suffer through shipping. On the downside, some nurseries have a more limited selection and the plants can be more expensive.

Specialist nurseries produce catalogs from which you can buy via mail order, or you can visit them to pick up your plants. Some local herb growers' associations sponsor annual plant sales that offer a wide assortment of herbs suitable for both novice and experienced growers. Most herbs are prolific, so established herb growers often have plants that they are willing to share or sell. If you buy a particular cultivar or other unfamiliar plant, make sure you ask the grower for an identification tag so you can find out about its requirements.

At the end of the growing season, some outlets may offer perennial plants at a reduced price because they have outgrown their pots. Take advantage of these if they are pest-free. If they are thickly bunched, you can slice the root ball into several sections with a knife. Plant these divisions as individual plants and water them well.

If you would prefer to start your own seedlings, see "Planting Seeds" on pages 88–91 for some useful tips. Starting plants from seeds or cuttings is an easy and inexpensive way to fill a large herb garden with a wide selection of your favorite herbs.

Buying Tips

- Select small, vigorous-looking plants. They will grow faster and be more likely to be free of pests and diseases.
- With annuals such as dill, and biennials such as parsley, look for seedlings in peat pots so you can plant the whole seedling and pot without disturbing the root system.
- Buy perennials before they bloom. That way, they can settle into the garden and establish new roots before they flower.
- With bulbs, purchase large, plump and firm bulbs with no soft spots or moldy areas.
- Try to buy plants that are not root-bound. Plants that have a lot of matted roots may go into shock when transplanted, setting them back by several weeks.
- Container-grown plants should have healthy top growth that is in proportion to the container.

Herbs grown in peat pots can be planted straight into the garden. This is useful for those, such as parsley and dill, that resent root disturbance and may transplant poorly.

SECTION FOUR

Preparing and Planting Herbs

Careful planning and plant selection are essential when starting your herb garden, but you need to follow through with good soil preparation and the right planting techniques. Regardless of whether you plan to grow herbs from seed or propagate them using other techniques, preparing the planting beds is critical to the success of your herb garden.

Choosing the Right Tools

When it comes to caring for your garden, the task will be made much simpler if you've got good tools to hand. Using the right tool makes any job easier, but a shopping trip for garden tools can be quite baffling. When faced with a wall-long display of shovels, spades, forks, rakes, trowels and cultivators, it can be hard to decide what tools, and what version of them, you need.

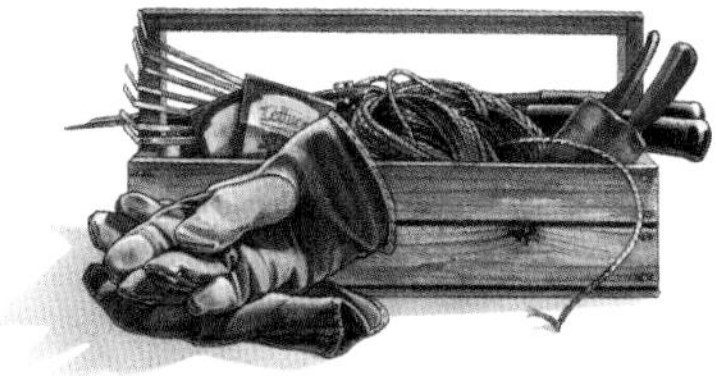

A Basic Tool Collection

Fortunately, most gardeners can get away with just a few basic tools. You'll need a spade to turn the soil, and a shovel for digging holes and for moving soil, sand, and amendments such as compost around. A spading fork is useful for turning the soil, working in amendments and green manures, turning compost, and dividing perennials. You'll also need a metal rake for smoothing the soil, a hoe for weeding and a trowel for planting and transplanting. If you garden in containers, a trowel and hand cultivator will suffice.

Shovels

Shovels with pointed blades are handy for digging holes, whereas shovels with straight blades are the best type to use for scooping up loose materials such as sand, soil, gravel or soil amendments. When digging with a shovel, use your foot to push the blade into the soil. Use your legs and arms, not your back, to lift the load. Before tossing the load, turn your whole body, not just your upper torso, in the direction of the toss.

Whether you have a whole collection of garden tools or just a few basic ones, you need to know when and how to use them properly as well as how to care for them.

Spades

A spade is used to turn soil and remove sod. The square edge and flat blade also make spades handy for digging trenches. To use, push the blade into the soil, resting your foot on the top rim of the blade and leaning your body weight onto it. Pull the handle back and down. When lifting, bend your knees before sliding one hand down the handle; if possible, brace the handle of the spade with your thigh.

Forks

Spading forks are useful in many areas of the garden. Use them for turning heavy or rocky earth, working cover crops and organic matter into the soil, fluffing compost, aerating soil, lifting root crops and dividing clumps of crowded perennials. A border fork is a smaller version of the spading fork. To turn soil or work in organic matter, use your foot to push the tines into the soil, lift the fork and then dump the load with a twist of your arms and wrists. Avoid using a fork to pry rocks or stumps out of the soil, or you will bend the tines.

Rakes

A metal garden rake is an indispensable part of any garden tool collection. Use rakes for clearing stones, leaves and sticks from garden beds and making a smooth surface for planting. Rakes are also handy for forming and shaping raised beds, working fertilizer into the soil and spreading manure, compost, mulches and other organic matter. If you are smoothing the soil before planting, try to work when the soil is slightly moist.

Buying Good Tools

There's nothing quite like the feel of working your soil with a good-quality, well-constructed tool. Here are some things to consider as you shop for garden equipment, so you'll get the best tools for your money.

Cost How much you spend on your tools depends on how long you want them to last. If you want to keep the tools for decades, get the best you can afford. If you're on a tight budget, or if you leave your tools outside all the time, buy the bargain basement kind. Be warned, though, that cost-cutting materials and designs make cheap tools more difficult to use than their more expensive counterparts.

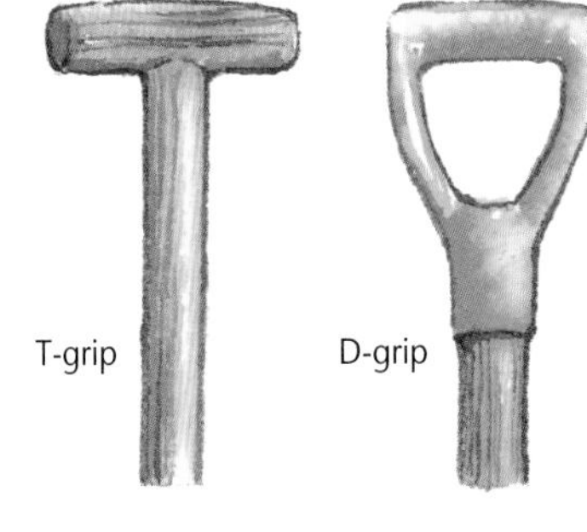

Tool handles come in several different styles of grip; choose the one that feels most comfortable to you.

Construction Read the label to see whether the metal part of the tool is stamped steel or forged steel. Forged steel is much stronger, but makes the tool cost 20 to 30 percent more. Also look at how the handle attaches to the metal part. Don't buy the tool if the metal wraps only partway around the handle; this construction leaves the wood exposed to water and mud, which can lead to rot. Instead, choose tools with metal that wraps all the way around the handle or that have strips of metal bolted to the handle.

Handles For a wooden handle, the grain should run the length of the handle, without knots. Painted handles often hide low-quality wood. Fiberglass or solid-core fiberglass handles are both stronger than wood. They also cost more, but are worth it if you want a tool to last for many years. Pick the handle length that feels most comfortable. Shovels should be at least shoulder height; rakes even longer. Short-handled tools, such as spades and spading forks, usually have 28-inch (70-cm) handles, but tall gardeners should look for larger handles. For hand tools such as trowels, choose the length that feels most comfortable in your hand. When buying a mattock or pick, choose a weight that you can lift and swing without straining your back.

LEFT: Good-quality tools can be expensive, but they are a pleasure to work with and can last for many years, provided you look after them.

Caring for Tools

Once you've gone to the trouble of buying good tools, it's worth a little extra effort to look after them. Without proper care, even the best tool can become corroded and dull after a season or two, making it unpleasant and difficult to use. It's easy at the end of a hot day in the garden to justify putting the tools away dirty. And you can even get away with it a few times. But eventually the moist soil clinging to your tools will make them rust. And once you finally do get around to cleaning them, the dry soil is harder to get off than the moist soil would have been.

For that reason it's good to get into the habit of cleaning your tools when you're finished. Use a stick, wooden spoon, or paint stirrer to scrape off the clinging soil. Or keep a heavy-duty brush in your shed to do the job. Another trick is to keep a tub of sand nearby to dip the tool in until the soil comes off. It's especially worthwhile to clean tools before you store them for the winter. Clean off the soil, then use steel wool or a wire brush to remove any rust. Coat the metal with a light oil and hang the tools somewhere for the winter.

Preparing for Planting

Along with proper plant selection, preparing a planting bed so that it contains well-drained, light, fertile soil is critical to the success of your herb garden. If you are growing only perennial herbs, or a mixture of annuals and perennials, you'll only have to consider the task of soil preparation once for each growing area. If you prepare the soil well before planting, your plants should thrive with a minimum of care. If you would prefer to grow your annual herbs separately, you'll have an opportunity to prepare the soil before planting each year.

Rotary tillers are useful in large gardens where there is a big area to dig.

Light, well-prepared soil provides ideal conditions for great root growth, leading to higher yields.

When to Start

If you can, prepare the beds at least a month before you intend to plant, to give the soil time to settle. Ideally, start in autumn for spring planting, or in spring for autumn planting.

Start digging when the soil is moist, but not wet. Digging moist soil is relatively easy, but dry soil requires extra effort, and working soil that is soggy can turn it into rocklike lumps. After two or three days without rain, dig up a shovelful in a couple of different spots and test for moisture by squeezing a handful of soil. If the soil oozes through your fingers or forms a sticky lump, it's too wet; wait a few days and repeat the test before digging. If the soil is dry and powdery or hard, water the area thoroughly and wait a day or two to dig.

Time your preparation so your new herbs will be planted in a period of good rainfall and moderate temperatures, usually the spring or autumn. Check planting instructions for what you plan to grow and refer to the Zone maps on pages 270–272 to check what climate zone you are living in.

Clearing the Land

If you are making a new garden bed, lay out the area you want to dig, as determined by your garden plan. Use stakes and string for marking the straight sides; lay out curves with a rope or garden hose. Step back and double-check your layout from all angles, including indoors. Next, clear the area, or if it is grassed, strip off the sod with a flat spade by cutting long, spade-wide strips across the width of the bed. Toss the sod into the compost pile or use it to repair bare spots in your lawn. As an alternative, you can kill the grass by covering it with black plastic. It's unattractive but effective. However, it can take several weeks or more to kill off the grass, depending on the weather. The hotter it is the faster the plastic works. Till in the turf once it has decayed. Pull out as many weeds as you can.

Making a Garden Bed

To make a new garden bed, start by outlining the shape with string. Remove any existing grass with a flat spade by cutting the grass into squares and then sliding the spade under the roots. Once the soil is exposed, add lime if a soil test indicates the site is too acid. Finally, spread a layer of compost over the surface and work it into the new bed.

Breaking up the Soil

Once you have cleared the beds, it is time to break up the soil. Consider your choice of tools carefully. If, like most people, you are growing herbs in small beds or borders, hand tools are all you need to work the soil. For hand digging, you need only a spade or shovel for digging and a spading fork to loosen the soil. If, however, you have a larger area to dig, you may want to buy or hire a rotary tiller. These machines can churn the top 6 inches (15 cm) of soil with much less effort on your part. But tillers aren't always the best choice. Excessive tilling, or tilling when the soil is too wet or too dry, will break up the good, granular soil structure into tiny particles and can lead to soil compaction. If you choose to use a rotary tiller, make sure you work the soil when it's evenly moist.

If you are using a spade or shovel, dig down as far as your spade will reach and

No-dig Garden

No-dig gardening is perfect for anyone who wants to minimize work, the elderly, or people with a physical disability. It involves building a garden on top of the existing ground so no digging is necessary. Select a sunny spot and mark out an area with pieces of wood or bricks. Lay down a layer of plain newspaper (not colored) ¼ inch (½ cm) deep. This will kill the grass below. Cover with a thick layer of compost 4 inches (10 cm) deep and then cover with an 8-inch (20-cm) layer of lucerne hay. Make slits in the paper to plant your herbs. The hay will act as a mulch and keep weeds at bay.

A no-dig garden is ideal for herbs and can be built over existing lawn, in raised beds or even on hard rocky ground.

turn over this top layer of the soil. For even better results, double dig the bed. Double-digging loosens the soil to twice the depth of single-digging, providing ideal conditions for great root growth and helping to correct heavy or poorly drained soil. See "Gardening in Problem Soils and Sites" on pages 82–83.

Once your soil is loose, mix in fertilizer to feed the plants and organic matter to condition the soil. Any balanced organic fertilizer will do. Scatter the fertilizer over the planting area at the application rate recommended on the label.

Now spread a very thick layer of organic matter over the entire area. It should be at least 4 inches (10 cm) deep to be effective. If your soil feels as loose as sand (indicating drainage that's too fast) or if puddles always remain after rain (indicating poor drainage), add even more organic matter. Use less if you want to grow herbs, such as yarrow, that grow best in dry, sunny sites.

Compost is the best source of organic matter, but leaves, straw and manure are also good. See "Adding Organic Matter" on pages 84–85. Whichever material you choose, mix it well into the top 8 inches (20 cm) of soil.

After digging in the fertilizer and organic matter, water the area thoroughly. Remember to let the soil sit for a month before planting to give the organic matter time to break down (unless you used well-decomposed compost, in which case you could plant right away). Rake just before planting to level the bed.

Double-digging helps break up compacted soil and improve drainage.

Gardening in Problem Soils and Sites

Don't let poor soil or a difficult site deter you from gardening in that area. Whether the problem is poor drainage, clay soil or rocky conditions, there are solutions. Selecting plants that are naturally well adapted to the soil type is the best way to handle most problem soils and sites. Building raised beds and tilling them with organically improved soil is another way of overcoming drawbacks. If your soil is extremely sandy or clayey, adding organic matter will help, but you will still do better to choose herbs that are compatible with the soil conditions.

Few soils are all sand, clay or silt—most are a combination. Loam is a balanced mix and is usually dark, fertile and high in organic matter. With careful management, you can develop similar conditions.

Dealing with Poorly Drained Soil

Plants need water, but poorly drained soils leave them with too much of a good thing. When the pores between soil particles are filled with water much of the time, plant roots and soil organisms don't get the oxygen they need, so plant and soil health suffer. Soil may be poorly drained because the water table is high. Raised beds (see page 83) are a good solution for small plantings, but for larger plantings you may have to look into digging a drainage ditch or burying pipes to drain excess water.

Other areas can be soggy because a layer of tightly compacted soil below the surface may be blocking water from draining. If you are willing to expend some energy, you can break it up.

Double-digging will provide ideal conditions for good root growth on deep-rooted perennials.

Double-digging

If your soil is on the clayey side and slow to drain, you may want to try a technique called double-digging. Double-digging penetrates the soil below the surface layer or topsoil, improves soil drainage, extends the depth of the root zone, and can result in greater productivity. This kind of digging is usually performed only once, and is particularly helpful if your soil has been heavily compacted.

Double-digging involves removing a layer of topsoil from the garden, loosening the layer below with a garden fork, and then replacing the topsoil. The result is a loose, deep soil that plant roots find easy to penetrate. The main disadvantages are the time and labor required.

To use this method, mark a trench about 12 inches (30 cm) wide and as long as the finished bed is to be. A flat-bladed spade is best for removing the soil to a depth of about 12 inches (30 cm); place the soil in a wheelbarrow or on a tarp laid on the ground. Once you've reached the depth, use a spading fork to loosen and aerate the soil along the bottom of the trench, but do not turn the soil. Then spread a thin layer of compost on the broken surface.

Next, move back 12 inches (30 cm) and once again remove the soil to the same depth, but this time toss the soil into the first trench. When you've reached the bottom of the second trench, aerate with the fork and apply compost, then fill the second trench with soil from a third trench. You can add more compost or organic fertilizer to the topsoil as you work. Repeat the process until you have moved across the width of the new bed, filling the last trench with the soil saved from the first trench. As you work, avoid standing on the newly turned soil. From then on, avoid walking on the soil. Rake the tilled surface smooth to prepare for planting seeds or young plants.

Managing a Clay Soil

If you listen to a group of gardeners talk about their soil, chances are that you'll hear at least a few complaining about clay.

Try not to work clay soil when it's wet or you will produce lumps that dry to hard clods.

Sandy soils tend to be light, dry and infertile, promoting short, sturdy stems on plants. Adding compost regularly will help.

To thrive, borage needs rich, moist soil with good drainage.

They may grumble about it being too wet, too sticky or too hard to dig; they may talk about it being difficult to water when dry. It is true that clay soils can be difficult to cope with, but if you can improve their structure, they are well supplied with nutrients.

Clay soil is difficult for plants. The clay particles pack tightly together so water has trouble draining. There's little space for oxygen, unless the clay has dried into a clod, leaving a big air pocket where roots dry out quickly. It's also physically difficult for roots to push through the tight soil. Fortunately it's easy to improve clay soil. To loosen it up, add organic matter and double dig. Water slowly, allowing the water to soak in, and take care not to water too often or you'll end up with waterlogged soil.

Managing Sandy Soil

Sandy soils have a lot going for them, especially when you compare them to clay soil. They are light to dig in and don't get sticky when wet. They are well aerated and warm up quickly in the spring. And it is easier to change their pH because they are not hindered by reserves of acidity or alkalinity. However, they also have their problems. They have little clay or humus to hold water and minerals, which wash quickly away between the widely spaced sand particles. With little water in the pores to moderate soil temperature, sandy soil gets hot during the day, cools rapidly at night and has little or no structure.

Compared to other soil problems, excessive sandiness is easier to remedy. If you add lots of organic matter, sandy soils can hold water and nutrients while still being well drained and easy to work.

Working with Rocky Soil

For gardens with only a thin layer of soil over rock, adding organic matter will help, but not fast enough. Plants will have problems because the roots have few places to go, and water and nutrients have little to cling to. The best approach to gardening in rocky soil is to use native plants where possible and to import soil and build raised beds. Planting from seed is also the best choice. Seeds and young plants can grow roots around obstacles in the soil rather than having to adapt an existing root system to new conditions. Or, make raised beds, if you have room; otherwise, grow herbs in containers.

Raised Beds

A good solution for poor drainage or poor soil is to raise the plant bed above the existing ground level. If you're planting perennials, trees and shrubs, build low, wide mounds of organically enriched soil and plant in these. For annual and biennial herbs, you can construct raised beds that are about 6 inches (15 cm) high in cool climates or no more than 4 inches (10 cm) high in warm climates, where raised beds can dry out quickly. If you make the beds 3–4 feet (90–120 cm) wide and leave a walkway between them, you can work the bed from either side without having to step on the soil, which can lead to compaction. For more permanent beds, frame with timber, stones or bricks. Fill with soil enriched with compost and other organic material.

Adding Organic Matter

Organic matter is the decayed remains of once-living plants, animals and soil organisms. It might not sound a very glamorous substance, but the way organic matter improves soil is so phenomenal that it's easy to overlook its humble beginnings. A layer of partially decomposed organic matter on the soil surface has enough bulk to smoother weeds and keep moisture from evaporating from the soil. Organic matter is also food for soil microorganisms. Once it decays thoroughly and mixes with the soil, organic matter works like a sponge, absorbing nearly its own weight in water without becoming soggy. This is particularly helpful for sandy soils or soils in dry regions. Decayed organic matter also loosens up clays, making them less sticky and improving soil structure. Another quality of organic material is that it holds nutrients on its surfaces, releasing them slowly into the soil water for plants to absorb. In fact, decayed organic matter accounts for half of the soil's ability to hold and release nutrients. So, it's worth learning about how to use organic matter so your garden and plants will thrive.

If you poke around in the very top soil layer in the woods or a meadow, you can see organic matter in a recognizable state. Most plentiful are decaying plant parts such as roots, stems, leaves, flowers and fruit. The deeper you dig, the less identifiable the litter becomes. That's because organisms, both visible and microscopic, have been digesting the organic residues and producing a more stable end product called humus.

Humus is sometimes used as another name for well-decayed organic matter which is dark brown and crumbly with an earthy smell. In this advanced state of decay, it is very valuable in the soil.

Organic gardeners believe that it is almost impossible to overfertilize with organic matter. They make a common practice of simply applying a fresh batch of compost or well-rotted manure to the garden at the start of each season. In garden soil with an active microbial population and with nutrients in the proper ratios for plant use, a 1–2 inch (2.5–5 cm) application of compost or other organic matter will feed the soil adequately for most garden herbs throughout the season. The great advantage in using compost or well-rotted manure is that you are adding organic matter at the same time as fertilizing.

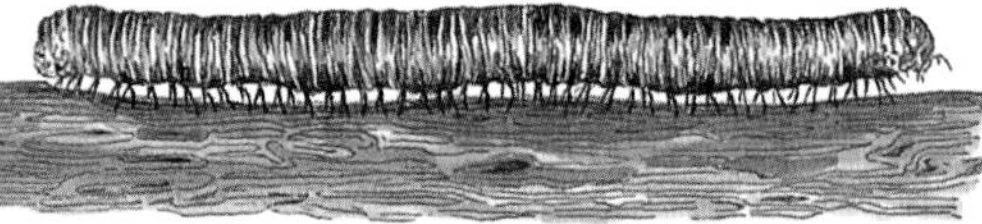

Millipedes, bacteria and other soil organisms play an important role in breaking down dead plant material in soil.

Indentifying Nutrient Deficiencies

Plants need essential elements—the so-called trace elements—in very minute quantities. Organic materials, such as compost, usually supply sufficient amounts of trace minerals to the soil. However your plants will let you know if they are suffering from nutrient imbalances or deficiencies. Look for leaves that show signs of yellowing (chlorosis). An overall yellow color may indicate severe nitrogen deficiency; yellow at the tips or edges points to a lack of potassium; yellow between the veins may result from too little iron, manganese, magnesium or zinc. A phosphorus deficiency may cause red or purple leaf coloration or premature autumn color.

If your plants exhibit signs of nutrient imbalances or deficiencies, try a foliar spray of seaweed extract (see "Fertilizers" on page 106) for fast relief. For the long-term health of your plants, have your soil tested for nutrient imbalances and apply appropriate organic material, such as compost or kelp meal, to the soil.

Natural Organic Nutrient Sources

There are a number of different substances which will add organic nutrients to your soil. Some you can make or grow yourself; others are commercial preparations.

Compost

Compost is decaying and decayed plant waste such as kitchen scraps, fallen leaves, grass clippings and shredded newspaper. The time you spend making compost and

Compost is an invaluable source of organic matter. Work it into the soil at any time of the year or leave it on the surface as a mulch.

Adding organic matter to your soil each season will encourage beneficial soil organisms and promote healthy plant growth.

applying it to your garden will be returned by improved soil and plant health. The nutrient balance in the compost depends on what you add. Well-made compost contains a small but balanced source of plant nutrients, as well as lots of organic matter. Once compost becomes well decayed, apply it to your garden. See "Compost" on pages 106–109.

Manures

The solid waste from herbivorous animals, such as cows, contains the undigested organic matter from the plants they have been eating. The amount of nutrients will vary depending on the type of animal, its diet and the amount of straw mixed with the manure. All manures add value, but you must know what you are applying and what effect it is likely to have on your plants. See "Manure" on pages 86–87.

Green Manures

Green manures are crops such as grasses and legumes that you grow and then work into the soil to add organic matter and nutrients. Like mulches and compost, green manures can do great things for your soil. The roots loosen the soil and provide organic matter while the crop is growing. Legumes add nitrogen to the soil. See "Manure" on pages 86–87.

Mulching not only helps to control weeds, but it is also important for regulating soil temperature and adding nutrients to the soil as it breaks down.

Don't throw away your prunings and grass clippings—use them as a mulch, add them to the compost pile, or work them into the soil. Chop up large pieces so that they will decompose more quickly.

Mulches

Mulching is the practice of covering the soil surface with a material that smothers weeds and prevents moisture from evaporating quickly from the soil. If you use the appropriate mulch, it can also add organic matter to the soil, improving its structure and fertility and encouraging a healthy population of microorganisms. See "Mulching" on pages 110–111.

Dried Animal Parts

The dried blood and ground bones of animals slaughtered for human food are used as fertilizers. These products are called meals, as in bloodmeal, bonemeal and fishmeal. Their nutrient content can vary widely, depending on what has been included and how it has been handled. See "Fertilizers" on pages 104–105.

Rock Powders

Rock powders are rocks pulverized to a fine powder. Reducing the rocks to such small pieces makes it easier for soil microorganisms to access the minerals that make up the rock. These minerals are released very slowly to plants. Granite meal and rock phosphate are examples of rock powders.

Applying Organic Matter

Nutrients can be worked into the soil just before planting. Spread compost or manure with a shovel, then either till it in or leave it on the surface as a mulch. You can also cover compost with another layer of mulch, such as hay, straw or grass clippings. If you're applying a powdered nitrogen fertilizer, such as bloodmeal, add it to the soil as you plant to avoid the loss of nitrogen. If plants aren't there to take it up, nitrogen tends to leach out of soil; that's why otherwise fertile soils in high-rainfall areas often lack nitrogen. You can broadcast dry organic fertilizers by hand (wear gloves and a dust mask) or with a spreader. To get the nutrients to the roots faster, scratch it into the soil, taking care not to nick roots or stems.

To feed perennial herbs, simply apply organic materials, such as compost and mulch, to the soil surface. If you use a dry fertilizer, scratch it in to a shallow depth.

Manure

There are many different types of manure, including animal manure and green manure. Both are valuable sources of organic material for your garden and if applied regularly, will ensure your herb garden thrives.

Horse manure, when collected from stables, is often mixed with straw—an added benefit for the garden. Make sure horse manure is well aged before using, as fresh manure is highly acidic and can burn foliage.

Animal Manure

The solid waste of herbivorous animals contains the undigested organic matter and minerals from the plants they eat. Some fresh animal manure, such as horse manure, is so high in nitrogen that it will burn plants if added directly to them; you either have to compost this type of manure before adding it or work it into the herb garden in the autumn after you have harvested most of your annuals. Composted manure, because it contains less nitrogen than fresh manure, is a more balanced source of nutrients.

Manure is also a good source of organic matter. The amount of nutrients in manure varies, depending on the type of animal and what it has been eating. Manure from farm animals such as horses and cows is most common, but you can also buy poultry manure and the manure of worms, bats and zoo animals. All can be valuable, as long as you know what you are applying and what effect it's likely to have on your plants.

Green Manures

Green manures are grass and legume crops that are grown for the purpose of improving the soil. You turn the crop under before it matures, and it adds valuable organic matter and nutrients to the soil as it breaks down. Common green manures are buckwheat, mustard, rye grass and vetch. Cover crops are not the same as green manures; their primary purpose is to cover the soil and protect it from damaging erosion.

Like mulches and compost, green manures can also do great things for your soil and your plants. The roots loosen the soil and provide additional organic matter while the crop is growing. If you grow a legume such as clover or vetch as a green manure, it adds nitrogen to the soil.

Different Types of Animal Manure

Fresh horse manure is high in nitrogen, but don't apply it directly around growing plants. Compost it before adding it to the soil. Once applied, it will break down quickly, adding nitrogen, phosphorus and potassium to the soil.

Cow manure contains more moisture than horse manure and less nitrogen. It decays more slowly and adds nutrients and organic matter to the soil. Add fresh cow manure to the compost pile, or work a 2–4 inch (5–10 cm) layer of fresh manure into the soil in autumn to prepare for spring planting.

Poultry manure is high in nitrogen, especially when it is fresh. It is best to compost it or to use it dehydrated to add nitrogen, phosphorus, potassium and organic matter to the soil.

Worm castings are the manure of earthworms. This is a rich source of organic nutrients and a good all-round soil improver. Work it into the soil before planting or scatter it on the surface after planting.

If you are growing annual herbs separate from perennial herbs, the soil in your annual beds may be bare between crops and during winter. Take advantage of these times to protect and improve your soil with a green manure crop.

Alfalfa

Legumes work together with certain soilborne bacteria to transform nitrogen into a form that plants can use. Different bacteria work with different legume crops. You can buy appropriate bacteria in the form of a granulated mix called an inoculant. Mixing the inoculant with the seeds before planting will ensure that the right bacteria will be there for your crop.

Green manures can choke out weeds and protect the soil from the eroding effects of wind and rain. They take up nutrients that might otherwise wash from bare soil, then slowly return the nutrients to the soil as they decay. Lastly, they provide lots of organic matter when you dig or till them into the soil.

Picking the Right Green Manure Crop

You need to consider the growing conditions of various green manures to decide which one to plant. Some manure crops, such as winter rye and hairy vetch, are planted in the autumn and turned under in the spring. Others, such as buckwheat and oats, will go from seed to usable growth in just a few weeks during the growing season. Most green manure crops grow best in well-drained soil, but some, such as clover, can take wetter conditions.

You can plant a grass or legume as a green manure, or a mix of both. Grasses are better at adding organic matter and stimulating earthworms, while legumes add more nitrogen. Dig or till to loosen the soil, break up the surface clods and rake the surface smooth. Broadcast the seed by hand or with a spreader, then dig or rake in lightly. About four to six weeks before you are ready to plant your next crop of herbs, work the green manure crop into the ground. If the growth is heavy, you may have to mow it first or cut it down by hand.

The herb comfrey also makes a wonderful green manure. Either chop up the leaves and turn lightly into the soil or make a liquid fertilizer by packing a container half full of comfrey leaves and topping up with water. Leave to soak for three weeks and apply at half strength to enrich the soil with nitrogen and calcium.

Different Types of Green Manures

Mustard This annual grows quickly, so use it to fill vacant garden space in the summer between your spring and autumn crops. It's frost hardy, so can be sown from spring to autumn.

Rye Grass Sown in late summer or autumn, rye will survive cold-climate winters and resume growing the following spring. It's a good choice where annual herbs leave the soil bare in winter.

Annual Lupins Sow in early summer or spring. Annual lupins are an annual legume, so they add nitrogen to the soil. They tolerate most soils.

Common Vetch This plant is a legume that can be left to grow for one year. Common vetch tolerates acid soils. Sow in spring or late summer.

Rye grass

Common vetch

Planting Seeds

For most of us, the garden year begins in spring. A sudden spell of warm weather makes most gardeners keen to begin planting, but don't be too hasty—the soil temperature needs to be at least 55°F (13°C) before you can begin planting. However, if you are planting tender annual herbs, such as basil, you can get an early start by sowing seed indoors first. "A Guide to Popular Herbs," starting on page 172, lists the best ways and times to sow specific herbs.

Seedlings need plenty of light for compact, sturdy growth. Near a window is a perfect spot.

Choosing Seeds

Seeds are a good choice when planning your spring crops as they are quite cheap and a single packet of seeds can produce dozens of sturdy young plants for a fraction of the cost of buying established seedlings. Starting from seed also gives you a much greater variety of plants to choose from, since most local nurseries only offer a few cultivars of the most popular types of herbs. But make sure you only use high-quality seed, packed for the current year. Buy from a reputable seed company that offers high germination rates. You can find this out if the percentage of viable (live) seeds is listed on the packet. If you have any seed left over from last year, or you have collected your own seed from previous plantings, try sprouting a few first before you sow a large number. Roll the seeds in moist paper towel and enclose the rolled towel in a plastic bag. Keep the bag warm and watch for germination over the next days or weeks. If only half of the seeds sprout, you will know that you need to sow twice as much seed to get the number of plants you ultimately want.

Sowing Seed in Trays

To help you to identify your seedlings at their various stages of development, prepare labels with the name of the seed and the date of sowing for each type of herb and use them to mark the rows as you sow. Either cluster seeds in the center of each small pot, or mark shallow furrows 2 inches (5 cm) apart in seed trays and lightly sprinkle in the seeds. For seeds that require light for germination, press them into the surface and leave them uncovered by the mix. For those that germinate in the dark, lightly cover the seeds with ⅛–¼ inch (3–6 mm) of fine soil or sand.

1. Fill the container with a moist seed-raising mix.

2. Press the mix down into the corners of the tray.

3. Level off the mix to ½ inch (12 mm) below the rim.

4. Scatter the seeds across the surface and gently press in.

5. If the seeds do not need light, cover them with a fine layer of mix.

6. Water them gently with a fine spray of water, taking care not to dislodge them.

7. Label the container with the name of the herb and the date of sowing.

8. Cover with plastic, glass or damp newspaper to maintain moisture.

Starting Seed Indoors

If you have the space, starting seed indoors will enable you to begin the new season earlier than if you wait and plant outdoors. You will also have more control over the environment, so seeds will germinate faster and the seedlings should grow more vigorously.

When to Sow

Check seed catalog descriptions or seed packets for sowing times. Sow your annual herb seeds indoors about 6 to 8 weeks before you plan to transplant them to the garden. Raising new perennials may require an additional 4 to 8 weeks if germination is slow.

Containers

You can start seedlings in just about any container that has holes for drainage. For a cheap option, you can use small plastic pots or yogurt containers with holes punctured in their bottoms. If you are planting in large numbers, it may be more efficient to purchase the conventional ready-to-use modular seed trays for sowing single seeds. If you're reusing the previous year's trays and pots, either dip them in boiling water for several minutes or rinse them in a 10-percent bleach solution (one part bleach to nine parts water) to kill any disease organisms.

Herbs that transplant poorly, such as parsley, can be sown indoors in peat pots filled with growing medium, or in peat pellets, which are advertised in seed catalogs and may be bought in garden centers. This way you can plant the whole pot or pellet containing the seedling in the ground at transplanting time.

Growing Medium

New seedlings need a light, moist growing medium for a quick start. Fill containers with a commercial seed-raising mix, or an equal mix of vermiculite or perlite and milled sphagnum moss or sifted compost. Perlite and vermiculite don't provide any nutrients to your seedlings, so once true leaves have developed, the young plants will require extra nutrients. Water them with a liquid organic fertilizer, such as fish emulsion, at half strength. Gradually increase the dose to full strength. Alternatively, you can transfer seedlings to a potting mixture with extra compost, or prepare a nourishing substitute by adding ½ cup or less of dry organic fertilizer to each 5-gallon (23-l) batch of homemade potting medium. Remember, the longer the seedlings remain in pots, the more nutrients they'll need.

Getting Started

When you're ready to sow, place your mix in a large bucket and add some warm water to moisten it. Work the mix with your hands to help it absorb the moisture. Keep adding water until it is evenly moist but not soggy. (If you squeeze a handful of mix and water runs out, it's too wet; add some more dry mix to get the balance right.)

Once the mix is moist, you can fill your chosen containers. Scoop the mix into each container and level it out to about ¼ inch (6 mm) below the top of the container. Don't pack down the mix; just tap the filled container once or twice on your work surface to settle the mix and eliminate air pockets. Prepare markers for the various seeds that you plan to sow, for easy identification when transplanting.

Sowing the Seed

The rate at which you sow will vary with the plant and the expected seed germination rate. Sow more thickly if you expect poor germination. Large seeds are fairly easy to sow and space evenly. Fine seeds, however, are more difficult to sow directly from the packet. When sowing tiny seeds, mix them with some fine dry river sand and scatter the mix over the surface with a saltshaker to get a more

There are advantages to sowing seed in individual pots. They have good drainage, are easy to clean, and can be used over again. Also, you can work standing up, which is easier than stooping in the garden.

even distribution of seed. Label the rows of seed as you sow.

If the seeds need to be covered (as indicated on the seed packet), sprinkle the needed amount of seed-raising mix over the seed. Fine seeds usually need light; just press them lightly into the surface of the mix with your fingers. Mist the surface lightly to moisten it. Seeds will rot if they are too wet. Keep seeds out of direct sunlight.

Set the containers in a well-lit spot where you can check them daily for signs of the first sprouts. Some gardeners cover the trays with plastic or glass to keep them evenly moist until the seeds germinate. Damp newspaper is another good covering material, but only if your seeds don't need light to germinate. Check every day, as you will need to remove the covers as soon as the tiny seedlings begin popping through the surface.

Once the seeds have germinated, make sure the air can circulate freely—poor ventilation may encourage fungal diseases, such as damping off. Water regularly with a fine mist to keep the seedlings moist but not soggy.

Most annual seeds will sprout and grow well at an average indoor temperature of between 60° and 75°F (16° and 24°C). In a small propagator, near a hot-water tank or on top of the refrigerator are excellent positions. Once your seeds have germinated, they will need between 10 and 16 hours of light each day, so keep them on or near a window sill.

Get a head start on spring sowing by germinating your seeds indoors under light. Or, during the heat of summer, start seeds of cool-season plants indoors, perhaps under lights in a cool basement or other cool place.

Thinning and Potting Up

Seedlings need adequate space in which to grow and so will eventually need thinning out. Once they have developed their first set of leaves, you can thin out with least disturbance by clipping some off at soil level with sharp scissors. Only healthy specimens should remain in each pot or cell. If you've started them in a nutrient-free medium, you'll now have to supplement their diet with a liquid organic plant food, such as fish emulsion, seaweed extract, or a compost or manure tea, until they are ready to be transferred out into the garden.

Thin seedlings by clipping them off at soil level with a pair of sharp scissors.

If you plan to hold seedlings for a while before transplanting them outdoors, or if your seedlings are crowded together in the tray, you'll need to transfer them to their own small pots or individual cells in a tray. About 6–12 hours before potting them up, give the seedlings a thorough soaking to ensure the stems are turgid (filled with fluid) and the roots will retain plenty of soil when the plants are lifted. Also moisten the growing medium in the new containers. Using a pencil, plant label, or other pointed stick, make a hole in the medium in the new pot. The hole should be large enough to accept the root system of the transplanted seedling without crushing the roots together. Then use the stick to carefully dig one seedling at a time from the original container. Lift each seedling by one of its leaves (not the fragile stem), and move it to its new container. Gently firm the soil around the roots of the seedling and water it in gently. Place the new containers away from direct sun and wind in a sheltered position, until the shock of transplanting is over. Feed the

Step-by-step Potting Up

If you plan to wait awhile before transplanting your seedlings outdoors, or if they are crowded together, it's a good idea to transfer them to their own individual pot or cell.

1.

2.

3.

1. Place moist growing medium into new containers. Make a hole large enough so the root system of the transplanted seedling will not be crushed.
2. Remove one seedling at a time using a pencil or pointed stick.
3. Holding the seedling by its leaves and not its stem, place it into its new container and gently firm the soil around it.

If you live in a warm climate, you can sow seed directly outdoors. Rake the soil smooth first.

young plants lightly with compost tea or liquid seaweed.

Hardening Off

Hardening off allows young plants to adjust slowly to the extremes of wind, temperature and light in outdoor conditions. At least two weeks before transplanting, gradually reduce watering and withhold fertilizer. This encourages plants to develop more roots in proportion to the rest of the plant, thus making transplanting easier. One week before you transplant, move the plants outdoors for short periods of time to a spot protected from strong light and wind. Begin with a couple of hours of exposure each day, gradually increasing the time spent outdoors. Watch the weather forecasts and bring seedlings indoors if there's a chance of a late frost. Within a week, they should be outdoors permanently. They'll need more water at this time, since sun and wind quickly dry the soil.

Transplanting

Once your seedlings have adjusted to the outdoors, you can plant them out. If they're frost-sensitive, wait until the danger of frost has passed. If they're hardy annuals or perennials, the hardening-off period should have prepared them for the garden. Follow the spacing guidelines on the seed packet or in "A Guide to Popular Herbs," starting on page 172.

Make a hole with your trowel, remove the small plant from its container, and insert it in the hole. You can plant slightly deeper than in the pot, especially if the young plant has grown tall. Firm the soil around the roots and water gently. Some herb growers water with a diluted solution of fish emulsion or compost tea. Give your seedlings a good start by transplanting on a cloudy day or in the evening to avoid the sun's drying effect.

Sowing Seed Outdoors

Some herbs, such as angelica, anise, basil and caraway, grow better from direct-sown seed because they don't respond well to transplanting. These types of herbs, along with hardy annuals, can be sown directly outdoors in early spring. Planting seeds directly outdoors is not a good idea for seeds that are hard to germinate, or, in cool areas, for plants that need a long, warm growing season.

Before the season begins, check your seed packets for the best time to plant outdoors. If you are planting seeds of frost-sensitive plants, wait until the frost season has ended.

Get ready for planting by clearing all weeds from your planting site. Prepare the soil, digging if necessary to remove clods, stones, weeds and roots. Dig in some compost or well-rotted manure and rake it smooth to create a fine-textured surface.

Sow the seeds in shallow trenches. If the seed packet doesn't indicate a sowing depth, a good rule of thumb is to plant the seed to a depth of three times its thickness. Completely cover the seeds by gently raking the soil over them and firming it down well. Keep the soil moist to encourage the best germination. Avoid watering with a strong spray that may wash the seeds out. Plant each herb species at the time and soil temperature recommended for best success.

Step-by-step Transplanting

If possible, transplant seedlings on a cloudy, moist day to help prevent them from drying out.

1. Make a hole for the transplanted seedling, wide enough so the roots won't be crushed.

2. Plant the seedling in the soil and gently firm the soil around the roots and stem.

3. Gently water the seedling.

Transplanting requires a minimum of tools—just a simple trowel or hand fork will do the job. You'll also need a watering can with a fine spray for watering your seedlings.

Propagating Herbs

Propagating is a great way to increase your herb crops. Depending on which propagation method you choose, you can end up with dozens of new plants, taken from a single plant. Once you master the techniques, you will find that not only does your garden benefit, but so too will all your friends' gardens as you distribute the extra plants.

Some perennial herbs are difficult to grow from seed; some take 4–8 weeks to germinate; while others may need special treatment, such as chilling. For this reason, it's best to buy vegetatively propagated perennial herbs sold as potted plants. Vegetative methods of propagation include division, layering and cuttings, and will produce an exact clone of the parent plant in nearly every case. Once you have established perennials, however, you can use these propagation methods to produce more plants yourself.

Division

To keep perennial herbs growing and flowering productively, you must divide them—dig them up and split the root mass into pieces. Dividing is also a way to start new plants as well as rejuvenate old ones. Most perennial herbs spread underground as well as aboveground. The plants usually increase in size each new growing season, perhaps taking up more space than you wish, so it's a good idea to divide them every few years.

Early spring and autumn are good times to divide perennials, when the air temperature is low and soil moisture is usually high. Among the many herbs easily propagated by division are chives, germander, horehound, marjoram, mint, sorrel, tansy, tarragon and woodruff.

Start by digging around the perimeter of the plant's root system with a spade. With the last thrust, push the blade under the base of the plant and lift it up soil, roots and all. Set the clump on the ground and begin dividing it into smaller clumps by hand or with a trowel. Pry apart larger clumps or very old clumps using garden forks—place two garden forks back to back in the center of the clump and force it apart. Separate sections with young shoots from the outer sides of the clump. Trim old leaves back to within 1 inch (2.5 cm) of the roots and replant the clumps immediately, or put them in pots in a shady area until you can replant them.

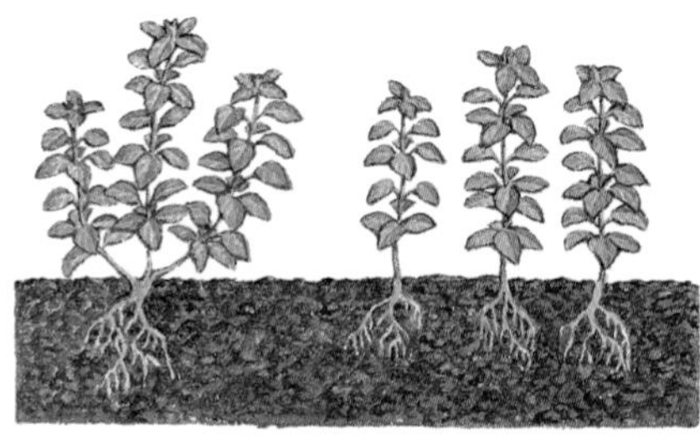

Dividing perennial herbs every few years increases your collection while at the same time rejuvenating the parent plant. Divide in spring or autumn.

Plants that send out underground rhizomes, such as mint, are just as easily divided without digging up the whole plant. If you follow the underground stems that sprout new plants, you can simply lift out each new plant with a spade or a trowel. Once you've reduced the large clump to several smaller plants, replant

1.

Step-by-step Division

Division is an easy and inexpensive way to propagate new plants. It also tidies up old ones and keeps them productive.

1. Dig around the clump.
2. Shake off as much soil as possible. Separate good shoots with roots from the parent plant.
3. Cut back ragged tops and shorten the stems.
4. Place some well-rotted compost into the planting hole and position the plant at the same depth as it was growing before.
5. Water the plant with a soluble organic fertilizer to minimize transplanting shock.

2.

3.

4.

5.

them in holes lined with fresh compost. Firm up the soil around the new plants, water generously and mulch with organic materials. Pot up any extras, and give them away to your green-thumbed friends.

Layering

Some plants are easy to root while still attached to the mother plant, a technique called layering. Burying a section of the stem encourages roots to form at each buried leaf node (the place where a leaf joins the stem). Layering does take up some space, since you need to bury the attached stem close to the parent plant. You won't get many new plants from this method (usually only one per stem), and it can take weeks or months for the stem to root. But layering is easy to do and is a simple method for propagating such garden herbs as tarragon, rosemary, thyme, sage, marjoram and santolina.

Spring is a good time to start a layer, although it can work anytime during the growing season. Select a long and flexible stem, and bend and lightly bury a section of it in the soil around the parent plant. You can make a small wound along the stem first, by nicking the soft wood with a knife, to encourage fast rooting. Some horticulturists recommend removing the leaves along the section of stem to be buried. Mound soil on top of the buried stem, first holding it in place with U-shaped pins made from a forked stick or bent wire (see page 94).

Clump-forming herbs, such as chives, are easy to propagate by division in spring or autumn.

New roots will form underground if the soil is kept moist. Depending on the temperature and the species, it will take several weeks to several months. The easiest way to layer is to leave the plant in place until the next season. If you want faster results, check its progress by gently uncovering the stem and looking for roots, or tugging lightly to see if the shoot has become more secure in the ground. Once the roots reach about 1 inch (2.5 cm) long, you can cut the shoot free from the mother plant by pushing a shovel or trowel into the soil between the new plant and the old. Wait several more weeks for more rooting, before digging up and transplanting the new plant. Plant it in a hole lined with fresh compost, or pot it up to grow on a sunny window sill or patio.

Stool layering is another method you can use to propagate new plants. This method works best with plants that have plenty of sprawling stems, such as santolina, winter savory and sage. Simply mound the soil around and over the base

To propagate by layering, bend a healthy stem over and bury it in the ground in spring or autumn. Roots should form on the buried part of the shoot near the bend, if the soil is kept moist.

Stool layering is a simple method of propagating herbs that have sprawling stems. Mound soil over the base of the parent plant. After 4 to 6 weeks, remove and replant any new plants.

Some herbs, such as scented geraniums and wormwood, become straggly after a few years and new plants should be started. Use the spring or autumn prunings to propagate new plants.

Step-by-step Layering

Layering is a slow but reliable method for propagating many kinds of herbs, trees, shrubs and vines.

1. Select a long, flexible, healthy stem about as thick as a pencil.
2. Cut off any leaves and side shoots from the section to be buried.
3. Make a nick in the soft wood with a knife to encourage fast rooting.
4. Bend the stem into the hole and anchor it with bent wire.
5. Cover with enriched soil mixture and water thoroughly.
6. After a few months, sever the stem connecting the new plant with the mother plant and transplant. Water well until the plant is established.

of already established plants. Wait at least 3 months, then slice away the young shoots that have developed their own root systems, then transplant them into pots or garden beds.

Cuttings

Cuttings of small pieces of plant stem or root are another way to propagate plants. Cuttings require more care than other methods of propagating, but if you like a challenge, you can use cuttings to create many new plants from your existing perennial herbs, such as lavender, scented geranium, bay, oregano, sage, thyme, clove pink and wormwood, to name just a few. Most herbs are easily propagated from fresh stem cuttings. The best time to take cuttings is in early spring, or late summer to early autumn, when the plants have new growth at the right stage of development.

The best cuttings are from fresh, green growth, such as tip cuttings. Softwood and semi-ripe cuttings can also be used. Cut 3–5 inches (7.5–12.5 cm) of stem cutting just below a leaf joint (node). Cut off the lower leaves. To promote root formation on slow-to-root plants, such as rosemary and bay, dip the base of the cutting into a rooting hormone preparation. Insert the cut end of the cutting in a moist, light, soil-less mix, such as vermiculite or perlite, making certain that several nodes have contact with the moist medium. Don't be tempted to use garden soil—it's too heavy for cuttings. Use small pots or any containers with good drainage. Some herb growers enclose the pots in plastic bags or upside-down glass jars to maintain humidity while the stems form new roots underground. Keep the pots sheltered, and away from direct sun. After 4–8 weeks, check for rooting by inverting the pot on your open hand, with the cutting between your fingers. Tap the edge of the pot on a hard surface then lift the pot off the plant. The young roots should be visible. Alternatively, tug gently on the cutting and if you feel resistance, new roots have formed and the cutting should be ready to transplant. Place your new plants outdoors in the shade for several days before planting them out.

Dill

Saving Seed

Although most perennial herbs are easy to propagate vegetatively, you can grow many herbs from the seed you collect if you have the patience.

Annuals and biennials, such as cilantro (coriander), dill, fennel, parsley, mustard, borage, caraway and even some types of basil, will seed themselves before the season ends. All that's required next season is patience while you leave the soil undisturbed to see which herb seedlings volunteer. Resist the temptation to dig or hoe in areas that were heavily seeded naturally the previous season.

When the new plants are established, dig them up while the weather is cool and move them as needed. Leave them in clumps or divide them up into individual plants. Water well in their new positions.

To save seeds for planting next spring, wait until they've matured on the plant before collecting. Hold the seed heads over a container and tap to release the seeds. Or you can harvest the seed heads and then hang them upside-down in paper bags to dry. It is important that the seeds are thoroughly dried before storing. See "Planting Seeds" on pages 88–91.

Growing from Bulbs

Some herbs, such as chives, saffron and garlic, grow from bulbs or similar structures. To propagate chives and saffron, lift the clumps out of the soil and divide them as you would any other plant.

To propagate garlic, harvest the bulbs as usual, allowing them to dry. Save the largest bulbs with the largest cloves for replanting and use the rest in the kitchen. There's no need to clean the bulbs you plan to replant. The more they are handled and peeled, the more likely they'll rot in storage. Store them in a dark, cool location until planting time.

To plant, divide the bulbs into individual cloves. Plant only the outer, large cloves; small, inner cloves will yield smaller bulbs or none at all. Plant the individual cloves root-side down, 1 inch (2.5 cm) deep and 6 inches (15 cm) apart in a deep bed with loosened soil. Work in plenty of organic materials, such as compost, but go easy on the nitrogen. Dig up when the tops die down.

Propagating new plants from rhizomes is a rewarding practice with a high success rate. Try propagating ginger and use it fresh in cooking—it has a zing that the powdered spice lacks.

Rhizome Propagation

It's also possible to propagate new plants from rhizomes. Plants such as ginger and turmeric have rhizomes, which are thickened stemlike organs that occur underground. Rhizomes have buds or knobs that produce new shoots and you can propagate from these.

In spring, select rhizomes that look fresh and firm (discard ones that are wrinkled and shrunken with age). Plant into pots of good-quality potting mix and keep moist and warm. Growth will be rapid and shoots will appear in a matter of days. Add a good-quality, diluted fertilizer, such as fish emulsion, once shoots have appeared. Leave in pots or plant out into garden beds in well-drained, humus-rich soil for optimum growth.

Propagating Garlic

Growing your own garlic is easy and rewarding. Autumn to winter is the best time to plant. The bulbs will produce roots and small shoots before the ground freezes. When the weather warms in spring, the shoots will start growing actively.

1. Save large, healthy garlic bulbs for replanting. Store them in a dark, cool place until planting.

2. Divide the bulbs into individual cloves. Keep the large, outer cloves.

3. Plant the cloves root-side down 6 inches (15 cm) apart, and cover with soil rich in organic matter.

Step-by-step Cuttings

Most perennial herbs are easily propagated from fresh stem cuttings. Choose a stem with at least five leaves and use a soil-less medium or a cuttings mix.

1. Select a healthy stem with good growth.

2. Cut the stem just below the leaf node.

3. Remove the lower leaves, taking care not to damage the stem.

4. Insert the cutting into a container of moist cuttings mix.

5. Cover with a glass jar to maintain humidity. Keep out of direct sun.

SECTION FIVE

Maintaining Your Herb Garden

Once your seedlings or transplants have taken hold, you need to maintain your herb garden to ensure that it flourishes. Generally, pests and diseases are not a big problem for most herbs. The best practice is to take good care of the soil, provide plenty of compost and mulch, and keep the garden well watered and weeded to ensure you grow healthy plants that do not make easy targets for pests or diseases.

Watering

Water makes up 85 to 95 percent of the weight of living plants. It's not surprising that when water is lacking, a plant stops growing and wilts. After wilting comes collapse of the cell structure in the wilted leaves and stems. After that, if much of the plant is affected, comes the death of young or delicate plants. Your goal is to water before wilting occurs.

But you also have to be careful not to overwater, as this too can stress your plants. Garden plants require about the equivalent of 1 inch (25 mm) of rainfall each week under average soil and climate conditions. Gardens in hot, dry climates will lose moisture faster and may need the equivalent of up to 2 inches (50 mm) of water each week. In cool and wet climates, plants lose less moisture and less water evaporates from the soil, so you may not have to water at all.

To monitor rainfall, purchase a rain gauge (available at most hardware stores) and place it in or near your garden. Check it immediately after rain, before water in the gauge is lost to evaporation. If natural rainfall is inadequate, you should plan to water regularly to maintain plant health and growth. Checking your soil for moisture is also a good idea. See "Moisture" on pages 52–53.

Hand watering with a hose is fine for small gardens, but for larger areas, you will probably need to use sprinklers or install soaker hoses or a drip system.

Most plant roots are in the top 12 inches (30 cm) of soil. If the soil is cool and moist and there are no signs of stress, such as wilting, you can probably hold off on the hose. A daily check is a good idea in dry weather, particularly if it is also hot. Or take a soil sample from the root zone and examine it. Dry, sandy soils will flow freely through your fingers but will stick together slightly with adequate moisture. Heavier clay soils will appear hard and crumbly when dry, and feel slick when adequately moist.

If you have plenty of time, hand watering with a watering can is often a more realistic option for irrigating small gardens, potted plants and for spot watering thirsty plants. But make sure you don't stress your plants by overwatering.

How Much to Water

You should water sufficiently to keep your plants growing, but not so much that the roots become oxygen-starved. Excess water in the soil fills the pore spaces that would normally contain air. In most soils, one good soaking is better than several shallow waterings because it encourages roots to spread over a larger area and go deeper in search of water that is farther away.

Hand Watering

Watering cans and hand-held hoses work well if you have a small garden and plenty of time. You'll know just how much water you are actually applying and where it is going. If you're tending a large garden, though, you'll probably choose sprinklers or trickle irrigation.

Sprinklers are cheap but can soak foliage. This provides ideal conditions for fungal diseases.

Soaker hoses are an effective way to water plants without waste due to runoff or evaporation.

Sprinklers

Although popular and inexpensive, sprinklers have two main disadvantages. First, they assume a plentiful water supply. In the time it takes water to reach the soil, 30 to 50 percent of the water used may be lost to evaporation on a hot, windy day. Secondly, sprinklers take longer to wet the soil, especially if the water must first penetrate a layer of mulch. Fungal diseases that thrive in moist conditions spread easily and quickly when the foliage is wet. The advantage, however, is that this type of watering system only requires an inexpensive sprinkler unit and enough hose to reach the garden.

While watering, monitor the rate of application by placing a rain gauge in your garden under the overhead sprinkler. Water for 20 to 40 minutes and check the soil again. You'll want to water until the roots receive some relief. The time required to water sufficiently will depend on your water pressure, the size of the nozzles, the diameter of your hose, your soil type, and the drying effect of wind and sun. You may need to water two or three times each week or even daily in hot, dry periods. Check the soil at root depth to be sure you're watering enough.

Drip Irrigation

Drip irrigation eliminates some of the problems encountered with overhead systems. It is the most economical system in terms of water volume used. Drip lines use less water since they apply water directly to the soil where plants need it. Less water runs off and more water sinks in. Cool water helps to keep the soil temperature low, especially if you mulch. And since foliage remains dry, fungal diseases are not encouraged. The disadvantage is that drip systems require more time and expense to install them. Once installed, however, you need only turn on the water and your herbs are irrigated most efficiently.

Soaker Hoses

You can design your own much simpler drip system by using soaker hoses. Also known as dew hoses, these are much less expensive than drip systems but provide many of the same benefits. Some soaker hoses release water over their entire length, while others spurt water through tiny holes. Make sure the holes face down into the soil when using this type of hose. A soaker hose system needs no assembly—simply lay the hoses between plants and conceal them with mulch.

Drought-tolerant Herbs

While herbs generally grow best with an even supply of moisture, the ones listed below can tolerate slightly drier soil.

Arnica, burdock, catnip, chicory, costmary, elecampane, germander, goldenrod, hyssop, marjoram, New Jersey tea, oregano, pennyroyal (American), pipsissewa, rosemary, rue, safflower, sage, santolina, savory (winter), southernwood, thyme, wormwood.

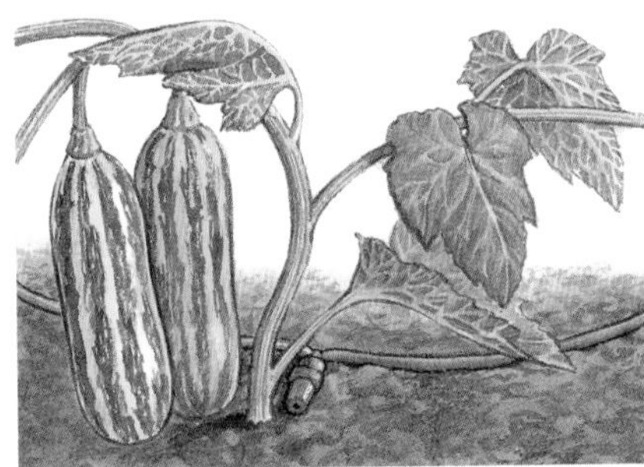

Drip irrigation systems with individual emitters deliver a supply of water directly to the plant.

How to Conserve Water

The following list gives ideas on how you can conserve water in your herb garden.

- Designate separate parts of the garden for herbs with low, medium or high water requirements and water them individually. Annual herbs will need more water than the deep-rooted, established perennials.
- Insulate the soil surface with a thick layer of organic mulch. To learn how to use mulch, see "Mulching" on pages 110–111.
- Maintain your soil's organic matter by working in plenty of compost. Organic matter holds water in the soil like a sponge.
- Eliminate weeds as they appear.
- In dry climates, select herbs that are drought-tolerant, such as burdock and germander.
- If paths are included in your garden design, use gravel or pulverized bark to pave them. A living cover, such as grass, will compete for moisture.

Drip irrigation

Weeding

Like pests and diseases, weeds can pop up in even the most carefully tended gardens. The trick is to take care of the problem early, before the weeds spread to the extent that they compete with your plants for space, light, water and nutrients. Non-gardeners may sometimes mistake your herbs for weeds, but you must know the difference. Weeds are often the most visible and persistent problem in the home herb garden.

Weeds are simply plants growing in the wrong place at the wrong time. Most are aggressive, wild plants that know a good opportunity when they find it. They usually grow rapidly and reproduce freely.

The Role of Weeds

Weeds, however, have their own importance in the plant world. Maybe you've noticed the resemblance of certain weeds to some of your herbs. Perhaps you're growing as herbs some plants that other gardeners would pull out as weeds, such as burdock or dandelion. Many of the plants we call weeds have culinary or medicinal uses that were discovered long ago. The tender leaves of dandelion and lamb's lettuce (mâche), for example, are often found in salad bowls along with lettuce. Wild comfrey was used medicinally long before modern herb growers added it to their gardens.

Weeds hold the soil in place, break up compacted soil with their vigorous root systems, and help to conserve nutrients that leach away when the soil is left bare.

It's worth trying to identify weeds in your garden so you know the best way to control them.

If you keep your plants healthy, they will be better able to compete with weeds.

Some plants that are considered to be weeds, such as clover and vetch, are also legumes and can be grown to fix nitrogen in the soil. Many beneficial insects that pollinate flowers or help to control garden pests spend part of their lives on wild plants. Queen-Anne's lace and goldenrod are dependable bloomers that provide nectar for the beneficial wasps that prey on aphids.

The presence of certain weeds indicates soil imbalances. Dandelions and couch grass, for example, thrive in soil that is compacted and low in oxygen—think of them as red flags for areas that need extra organic matter. Yellow sorrel flourishes in acidic soil, indicating that it's time to have the soil pH tested.

On the negative side, weeds are major garden pests when they compete with your garden herbs for nutrients, moisture and light. They often harbor diseases or insect pests that can easily find their way to your herb plants. Some weeds, such as poison ivy, horsenettles and nightshade, are poisonous. Other, nonpoisonous weeds can cause allergic reactions in people with sensitive skin.

Controlling Weeds

Your first step in the battle against weeds is to identify the ones you need to control. Learn to recognize the annuals and perennials so you'll know whether you can dig them in (the annuals) or must pull them out (the perennials). You also need to learn to recognize juvenile weeds; otherwise, you may end up weeding out your herb seedlings by mistake.

Annual Weeds

Annual weeds live only one season, but this is long enough for them to produce lots of seeds that can sprout next spring. The seeds can also remain dormant in your garden soil for as long as 100 years, coming to life when you dig a new garden patch. They don't have the invasive roots of their perennial counterparts, but they will reproduce themselves hundreds of times over from seed, often growing fast and spreading far. The summer annuals begin life in the spring and die in autumn. Winter annuals, such as chickweed and yellow rocket, sprout in late summer and survive severe winters in a dormant state, flowering and seeding the following spring and summer before they die.

Pulling, hoeing and cultivating are often sufficient to control annual weeds. If you do this early enough, you will stop the weeds from setting seed. If the original plants die without making seed, they won't come back the following year.

Biennial Weeds

For biennial weeds, such as Queen-Anne's lace *Daucus carota* var. *carota*, the seed-to-seed cycle spreads over two years. These weeds sprout from seed in the spring or summer, then usually grow into a ground-hugging circle of leaves called a rosette. The leaves produce sugars that move down to the roots and are stored as starch. The next spring, the plant uses the stored food energy to send up a flowering stalk, which may or may not have leaves. The plant flowers, sets seed, then dies.

You have two main options for controlling biennial weeds. You could dig out the rosette, roots and all, the first year. Or you can wait until the second year and cut the plant down to the ground. If you wait until the weed is just about to flower, the plant will have used up nearly all of its stored energy and will be unlikely to return.

Hoeing once or twice early in the season can control weeds until your plants fill in to cover the soil.

Perennial Weeds

Perennial weeds, such as wild garlic *Allium vineale*, can live for more than 2 years, and are especially troublesome because they can reproduce sexually by seed, or spread vegetatively with their specialized root and stem structures. Perennials, like biennials, store carbohydrates to fuel early growth the next spring. The food energy may be stored in taproots, in rhizomes, or in spreading aboveground runners or stolons. Or it may be in a tuber (such as a potato) or a bulb (such as an onion). Perennials are generally the most difficult weeds to control. They shouldn't be dug in, as this distributes their hardy root pieces, each of which will sprout into new plants. You need to either dig up all of the underground structures or force them to use up their food reserves by repeatedly removing their aboveground growth.

When not maintained, fence lines and pathways can become ideal sites for weeds to take over.

How to Weed

The particular weeding technique you use will depend on how many weeds you have to control, what type of weeds they are, how large an area they cover and how much time you want to spend on them.

Control Problems Early

Weed control should start while you are preparing the bed for your new herbs. Digging and composting can remove many of the existing weeds. As you dig, keep an eye out for long white roots of spreading weeds. Thoroughly remove any of these roots; if you leave even little pieces, roots can quickly sprout into new plants.

Once your herbs are established, you can control most weeds if you mulch and weed conscientiously for the first year or so and compost regularly. If you keep your plants healthy, they will be better able to compete with weeds. Mulching covers up weed seeds, stops sunlight reaching the weed roots and gets in the way of emerging weed seedlings. Either the seeds don't sprout at all, or the seedlings use up all their energy and die before they reach the sunlight.

Pulling and Digging

These techniques are simple and effective for getting rid of a few weeds but are pretty tiring when you are weeding large areas of the garden. Pulling gets rid of

A well-chosen mulch will not only look good around your plants, but will also help you to control your weed problems.

Thoroughly hand-weeding the garden bed before you plant will help you get your new herbs off to a weed-free start.

Solarizing the soil by laying a sheet of clear plastic over it during hot weather is an effective method of eradicating weeds. The weed seeds die as the soil heats up.

annual weeds well, especially if the soil is damp enough that the roots come up. If you pull annual grasses, get as much of the roots as possible; the growing point of grasses is below the ground, and the plant might resprout if you just remove the aboveground portion.

Always try to pull annual weeds before they begin to flower and set seed. If they have already started flowering, collect the pulled weeds in a bucket; don't leave them on the ground, since their seeds could still ripen and drop onto the soil.

Digging is a better choice for perennial weeds, assuming you get all the buried portions. Use hand tools to dig out small or shallow-rooted perennials. You may need a spading fork, spade or shovel for tough deep roots.

Hoeing and Tilling

When the weeds are too numerous to pull, or the area is too large, hoeing is a good solution. In most cases, hoes are best for young or annual weeds. But you can also deal a damaging blow to some established perennials, especially those with thin or soft stems, by forcing them to use food reserves to replace the decapitated top growth.

To eliminate weed seedlings, scrape the soil surface with a hoe each week. Choose any blade, but to avoid straining your back, make sure the handle is long enough. Your motion should be more like sweeping the floor, rather than chopping wood. Use a hand fork to dig out older weeds that escape the hoe, before they have a chance to flower and set seed.

Mowing

If you have a large area to weed, then mowing is a good option. Mowing doesn't remove the roots but it can keep all but the lowest-growing weeds from setting seed. And if you mow often enough, it weakens perennials by making them use up their food reserves to replace the top growth that you keep removing.

Organic Weed-control Techniques

Mulching with organic or synthetic materials is one of the easiest ways to keep weeds under control. Organic mulches, such as straw, compost and shredded leaves, help to keep weeds down while adding organic matter to your soil. Apply a layer 3–7 inches (7.5–17.5 cm) deep, because it will settle to a thin layer over time. Black plastic can also be used, but it requires annual replacement and it can be difficult to apply in a mixed planting of annuals and perennials. See "Mulching" on pages 110–111.

Other weed-control techniques include digging or cultivating and using cover crops. When digging or cultivating, try to work as shallowly as possible. This will avoid bringing dormant weed seeds to the surface, where they will germinate when exposed to light. If you are starting a new garden area, or if you have one that you use only for annual herbs, you can try controlling weeds with a cover crop of green manure. These crops grow quickly and out-compete native weed populations. See "Manure" on pages 86–87.

If a garden bed has a serious weed problem, you may just want to start over in that area. Dig out any herbs you want to save, and then use a process called soil solarization to destroy weed seeds that are close to the surface. You do this by laying a sheet of clear plastic over moist soil. Tuck the edges of the plastic into a shallow trench, and cover them with soil. As solarizing only works when the weather is consistently clear and fairly hot, it's best to solarize close to midsummer. The soil under the plastic will heat, and this will kill most of the weed seeds (as well as insects and disease organisms) in the top layer of soil. Avoid turning over the soil after you solarize it, or you'll just bring up a new crop of weed seeds.

Fertilizers

Supplying your plants with the nutrients they need is a critical part of keeping them healthy and vigorous. How much fertilizer you should add to your garden will depend on how fertile the soil is and which plants you're growing.

The texture and natural fertility of your soil will have a great impact on how much supplemental nutrients you need to add, and how often. A sandy soil will hold fewer nutrients than a clayey soil or a soil that is high in organic matter, so you will need to fertilize and add more nutrients to a sandy soil.

Different Plant Needs

The amount of fertilizer you use and how you apply it will vary whether you are growing annuals or biennials, perennials, bulbs, or shrubs and trees.

Annuals

Annuals grow quickly, so they need a readily available supply of nutrients for growth and flowering. In spring, scatter a layer of compost over the bed and dig it in as you prepare for planting. Or, if you are planting annuals around perennials and other permanent plants, mix a handful of compost into each planting hole. If you don't have compost, use a general organic fertilizer. Once or twice during the growing season, lift back the mulch and scatter some more compost or fertilizer around the base of each plant.

Fertilizing your herb garden will ensure it thrives, but don't harvest plants for sometime afterward.

For most annuals and biennials, this will provide all the nutrients they need.

Some annuals, however, appreciate extra fertility or may be looking a bit tired by midsummer. You can provide a quick nutrient boost by spraying the leaves with diluted fish emulsion or compost tea. To make compost tea, see "Compost" on pages 106–109.

Perennials

Perennials stay in the same place for years. Since you only have one chance before planting to get the soil into good condition, take the time to prepare their beds well. Once they are established, most perennials will grow happily with a light layer of compost applied once or twice a year.

Some perennials, such as yarrows *Achillea spp.* and sages *Salvia spp.*, should receive no more than an annual layer of compost otherwise they become leggy and topple over from too much fertilizer. But you can give other perennials a little fertility boost to encourage new growth or rejuvenation. Fertilize in spring as the plants begin growing, as well as after planting or dividing, and after deadheading or cutting back.

To meet the requirements of heavy feeders or to encourage exceptional blooms from perennials such as pinks or lily-of-the-valley, use extra fertilizers. Lift back the mulch or compost first and add phosphorus and potassium as well as any other nutrient recommended in your soil test; see "All About Soil" on pages 54–55. Apply them just as the plants begin

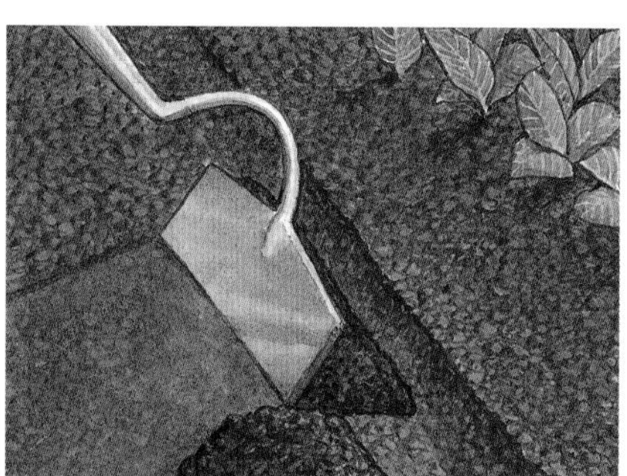

Most fertilizers can be worked into the soil just before planting. Side dressing is an easy way to fertilize herbs growing in rows. Spread it along the row and scratch it into the soil with a hoe.

A simple way to fertilize herb gardens that are already established is to evenly scatter a dry fertilizer over the soil surface. Nutrients will be slowly released as they dissolve in soil moisture.

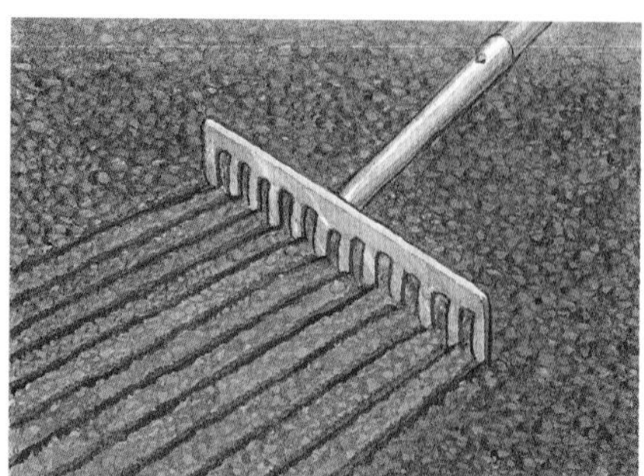

To get the fertilizer closer to the roots, scratch it into the soil with a metal rake. Work it in just lightly enough to avoid damaging established plant roots with the rake.

Organic Fertilizers

There is a wide variety of organic materials available for correcting nutrient deficiencies. Before you buy any fertilizer, check the label for information about nitrogen, phosphorus and potassium content. This is indicated by a series of three numbers, such as 5-10-5. This means that 100 pounds (45 kg) of a fertilizer with this formula contains 5 pounds (2.25 kg) of nitrogen, 10 pounds (4.5 kg) of phosphorus and 5 pounds (2.25 kg) of potassium. Compost is one source of many plant nutrients. Other possible preparations are:

Bloodmeal: 12-0-0, contains nitrogen plus iron.

Bonemeal: 1-10-0, contains about 20 percent calcium. If processed with meat or marrow, it will contain more nitrogen.

Fish emulsion: 3-1-1, releases most of its nitrogen quickly. It is sprayed often onto leaves for a fast-acting nutrient boost.

Fish meal: 5-3-3, contains both immediately available nitrogen and a slow-release form of nitrogen that supplements the soil for up to two months.

Seaweed extract: 1-0.5-2.5, usually made from kelp, provides trace elements and natural growth hormones. Use liquid kelp as a foliar spray.

Seaweed

Applying the Fertilizer

Whichever fertilizing method you use, make sure you always follow the instructions and application rates given on the package. Adding too much fertilizer can actually harm your plants.

Scatter dry organic fertilizer over the soil to slowly release nutrients.

Or apply the dry fertilizer in a ring around the base of the plant.

Spray liquid fertilizer on the leaves for an immediate nutrient boost.

setting flower buds. Scratch the fertilizers into the soil lightly with a gardening hoe or fork, then replace the mulch.

Trees and Shrubs

Once trees and shrubs are established, your fertilizing chores will be minimal. Most trees and shrubs don't need more than a layer of compost or well-rotted manure applied once or twice a year. However in the first year or two after planting, their young root system may not yet be able to reach all the necessary nutrients in the soil and they will need supplemental feeding.

Bulbs

Bulbs, such as garlic, usually grow well without you having to add a lot of extra fertilizers. Working compost or organic matter into the soil when planting, and using it as mulch, will provide much of the nutrient supply your bulbs need. For extra growth, you can sprinkle an organic fertilizer over the soil around the bulbs, following the package directions.

Applying Fertilizers

When you fertilize, you can eliminate deficiencies by applying either liquid or dry fertilizer, or both. If you decide to use a combination of fertilizers, make sure you don't apply more than your plants need. Too much fertilizer can be as bad as not enough, leading to weak stems, rampant sprawling growth and disease problems.

Liquid Fertilizers

Commonly used liquid fertilizers include fish emulsion, liquid seaweed and compost tea. Use a single dose for a quick but temporary fix of a nutrient shortage, or apply it every 2 weeks for a general plant boost. You can spray these fertilizers directly onto the plants, which will absorb the nutrients through their foliage.

Dry Fertilizers

These are released more slowly than liquid fertilizers. Scratch them into the surface of the soil in a circle around the perimeter of the plant's foliage, so that the nutrients are released gradually as they dissolve in soil moisture. This encourages roots to extend outward.

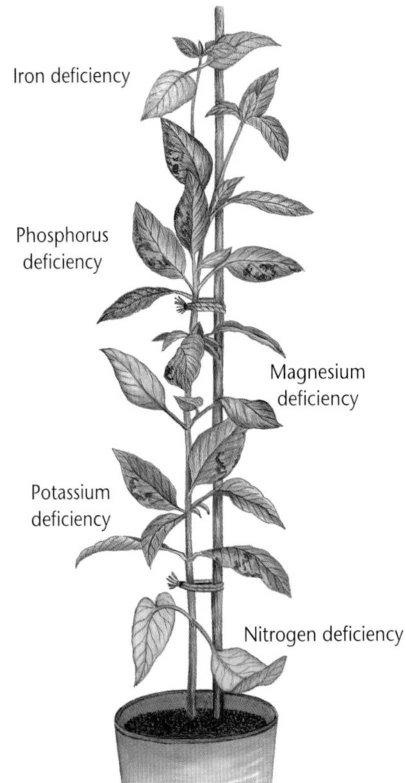

Compost

Compost is the key to success in any kind of gardening. It is a balanced blend of recycled garden, yard and household wastes that break down to dark, crumbly organic matter. Whether your garden is large or small, it's worth devoting some space to a compost pile to convert otherwise wasted products into the ultimate soil amendment. Worked into the soil or used as a mulch, compost can add nutrients, loosen up clay soils, and increase the water-holding capacity of dry, sandy soils.

Compost is a key part of a healthy garden. You can work it into the soil, use it as a mulch, and even make compost tea to give your plants a liquid nutrient boost.

How to Start

Making compost is like cooking—you mix together ingredients, stir them around and let them "cook". But with a compost pile, the source of heat isn't electricity or gas—it's the activity of decomposer organisms, such as bacteria and fungi, that live in the soil and break down dead plant and animal tissues. These organisms work best when given a warm and moist environment, with plenty of oxygen and a balance of carbon and nitrogen.

Save any organic wastes that you would normally discard, such as vegetable scraps from the kitchen, grass clippings, fallen leaves and soft plant clippings. Don't use waste products containing fats, bones or meat scraps, as they decompose very slowly and may attract scavenging animals and slow down the process of decomposition. If you have access to manure from animals such as chickens, rabbits, cows or horses, you can add this as well, but avoid human, dog and cat feces. Also avoid pesticides, and pesticide-treated plant material, such as grass clippings from treated lawns. Don't add weeds or insect-infested or diseased plants unless you have a hot compost pile (you can learn more about hot and cold composts on pages 107–109). It is also not a good idea to add roots of perennial weeds in case they survive the composting process and are then distributed throughout your garden as you spread around the finished compost.

Compost can be in an open pile, but bins look neater and help keep animals out of the compost. You can choose from a variety of commercially sold containers made from either timber or plastic, or you can make your own from timber, cement blocks, bricks or even chicken wire nailed to garden stakes. If you have the space, a multi-bin system is ideal, so when one bin is full, you can make use of completed compost while other heaps are at different stages of decomposition.

If you have the space, an ideal way to make compost is a multi-bin system. When one bin is full but still needs time to break down properly, you can start on the next. Eventually you will have compost ready for instant application whenever you need it.

Whatever design you choose, find a sunny, level, well-drained spot for your compost pile. For your convenience, put it as close to your garden as possible. A coarse material, such as straw or sunflower stalks, is best as the bottom layer of the heap so that air can circulate freely.

A wood-and-wire bin is a good way to keep your compost contained and easily accessible.

Compost Ingredients

Material	Nitrogen	Carbon	Comments
Bread, cakes, etc. (stale or mildewed)	High	Low	May attract vermin; break into pieces and mix well into the compost.
Coffee grounds	High	Low	Acidic; use in compost for acid-loving plants or mix in a little lime to raise pH.
Eggshells	Low	None	Slow to break down; crush before adding to compost; rich source of minerals.
Fallen leaves	Low	High	Also an excellent mulch for acid-loving plants.
Floor sweepings	Low	Low	Mainly inert material but may be high in minerals.
Garden prunings and clippings	Low	High	Woody materials are slow to break down; feed through a chipper or cut into short lengths.
Kitchen scraps (peelings, roots, stems)	Medium to low	Medium to low	Easy to compost.
Overripe or damaged fruit or vegetables	High	Low	Can attract fruit flies; best in a closed bin or tumbler at high temperatures.
Paper and cardboard	None	High	Wet thoroughly and mix with high-nitrogen ingredients; should not be more than 25 percent of the pile.
Potting mixes, used	Low	Low	Risk of transmitting plant diseases and pests; these are best composted at high temperatures.
Weeds	Medium	Medium	Compost at high temperatures to kill seeds and roots.

If all the green material added to your compost is relatively moist, it will not be necessary to add extra water. If materials have been allowed to dry out, you may need to moisten them for effective breakdown. By adding a few shovelfuls of good garden soil or finished compost to the pile, you will add to the micro-organisms that help carry out the composting process. If the weather has been dry and hot, each time you add new materials, such as soil and composting ingredients, sprinkle the compost pile with water. This will make sure the pile contains the moisture that is necessary for even decomposition.

Don't make your compost pile too large. Ideally, it should be around 3 feet (90 cm) on each side, and no higher than 6 feet (1.8 m) to break down properly.

There are two types of compost heaps: hot compost and cold compost. Hot compost is a more complex and faster process and involves composting at high temperatures, while cold compost is a simpler and slower process.

Keep a container in your kitchen to collect compostable food scraps and paper.

Hot Compost

Hot composting takes some work, but it will provide you with high-quality compost in a matter of weeks. There are many different systems of hot composting, but they tend to have some elements in common. Most require building a large pile of different layers of high-nitrogen and high-carbon elements, along with some soil or finished compost to make sure the right decomposers are present. Turning the pile every few days or weeks, to provide the decomposer organisms in the pile with oxygen, is another critical part of encouraging fast breakdown.

To create a hot-compost pile, blend both soft and green (high-nitrogen) plant scraps, such as lawn clippings, lettuce scraps and dandelion leaves, with tough and brown (high-carbon) scraps, such as fallen leaves, straw and woody flower stalks. The moist, green items provide the

Circular woven bins are easy to make and use. The large stick helps direct water to the center of the pile.

decomposers with the nitrogen they consume as they break down the high-carbon materials.

The key to hot composting is getting a balance between the two types of materials. Chop up the debris you plan to compost and combine in equal amounts in a pile about 3 feet (90 cm) high and wide. Smaller piles won't heat as efficiently, while anything larger can become a little unmanageable when turning the material over to redistribute and aerate.

Making Hot, Fast Compost

1. Build your compost heap with equal amounts of high-carbon and high-nitrogen materials; add in layers or mix them up.

2. As you add new materials, sprinkle them with water to keep the compost pile moist and to encourage decomposition.

3. Aerate the compost pile by turning it once every couple of days using a garden fork. This hastens the microbial activity.

Pile up these elements in layers or just jumble them together. Add a shovelful of soil or finished compost in between each layer and enough water to keep the pile evenly moist. Turn the pile with a pitchfork every few days to add oxygen. If all goes well, your compost should be ready in a few weeks. The material may break down more quickly in hot weather or more slowly in cold weather. You can use a compost thermometer to monitor your pile's temperature. The ideal temperature is below 160°F (71°C), since higher temperatures will kill important decomposer organisms. The turning process helps maintain a constant temperature. If you are in a hurry for finished compost, turn the pile every few days until it stops heating up; it will break down more quickly. If odor is a problem with your hot compost, the pile needs to

Homemade wire mesh bins are cheap. Line them with plastic to help decomposition in cool weather.

Tumbler bins enable you to turn your compost regularly and aerate it for faster decomposition.

To have nutrient-rich compost you need to put nutrient-rich materials into the compost pile.

Compost is an ideal soil-building mulch for both herb and flower gardens.

be turned and aerated more; if it is too wet, mix in more dry materials and cover the pile with a tarp. If the breakdown is too slow, add more green or nitrogenous material or water the pile to keep it evenly damp.

Cold Compost

Making cold compost is easier than making hot compost, but it is a much slower process of decomposition and requires no turning over with a garden fork. A cold-compost pile won't really feel cold; it just doesn't get warm like a hot-compost pile. Since the period of decomposition is extended by up to a year or so, more nutrients can wash away in rainwater. You'll have to leave more space for the slower decomposing piles, and you'll have to wait much longer until it is ready. Cold compost will not heat up enough to kill seeds or disease organisms, so don't add mature weeds or diseased plant material to the pile.

To create a cold-compost pile, choose a shady, well-drained spot in your garden. Over time, add your waste material, building up a pile about 3 feet (90 cm) wide by 3 feet (90 cm) high and simply wait 6 to 12 months. After this time, the original materials should be broken down, although the compost will probably still be fairly lumpy. When your compost is fully decomposed, you can use it as it is or screen out the lumps.

Sunflowers can grow in poor soil but look their dramatic best when given composted soil and regular watering.

Using Compost

There are many different ways to add compost to your garden. If you are preparing a new bed, work it in as you dig. In an established garden, spread compost over the surface of your beds each year. As a general rule, cover the bed with 2 inches (5 cm) a year to maintain fertile soil. Or you can use compost as a mulch. Use more if you are growing moisture-loving perennial herbs, such as elder, or less around such perennials as yarrow, which prefer drier, less-fertile soil. Compost breaks down gradually over the growing season, so add more as needed. Use compost indoors as potting medium or for starting seeds.

Compost Tea

Compost tea is a liquid fertilizer made by soaking compost in water. Put a shovelful of compost into a bag made of cheesecloth or burlap. Tie the bag firmly at the top and suspend it in a bucket or watering can filled with water. Keep it covered for a few days. Nutrients from the compost diffuse into the water from the bag. Dilute the liquid until it is the color of weak tea before using it on young plants, as strong water can burn seedlings.

Compost Troubleshooting

If your compost pile isn't behaving like it should, check the list below to see what the problem is.

- **Pile doesn't heat up.** Add more high-nitrogen material. If the pile is dry, add water. Or try turning the pile.
- **Pile smells bad.** Add more high-carbon material. If the pile is too wet, turning may help to add more air.
- **Finished compost is covered with seedlings.** If your compost doesn't heat up enough, seeds of weeds and other plants may survive. Either avoid adding materials with seeds or make sure they're in the center of a hot compost pile.
- **Material doesn't break down.** Woody stems, prunings and dry leaves may be slow to break down; shred or chop them into smaller pieces before adding them to a pile. Adding more high-nitrogen ingredients can help balance these high-carbon materials.

Dig compost into a new garden bed or spread it over the surface to instantly enrich the soil.

Mulching

Mulching simply means covering the surface of your garden soil with a layer of organic or inorganic material. Mulching keeps the soil warmer in winter and cooler in summer, helps retain soil moisture thereby reducing the need for you to water, keeps dirt off you and your plants, and protects soil from erosion. A layer of mulch applied after the soil freezes in late autumn will prevent the soil from thawing and refreezing, which can damage tender roots. In hot-summer climates, mulching will slow the rapid decay of organic matter added to the soil, so each application will last longer. Mulching will also inhibit the growth and germination of weeds. By putting mulch on top of the soil, you cover up weed seeds so the seeds either don't sprout at all, or the seedlings use up all their energy pushing through the mulch and die before they reach the sunlight. So mulching saves you time and labor.

Mulching Tips

If you are planting in early spring, wait until the soil warms up before mulching. If you are planting in autumn, apply the mulch right after planting. You should mulch earlier in dry climates to trap the moisture from spring rains. In wet climates, mulch a bit later in the season to give the soil a chance to dry out. If you've kept your perennials mulched throughout the winter, pull the mulch away from them in the spring to allow the soil to warm and to promote growth. A light-colored mulch, such as straw, will keep the soil cool and promote the growth of plants, such as mint, that prefer cooler temperatures. A dark-colored mulch, such as black plastic, will keep the soil warmer for heat-loving plants, such as basil. Always weed the soil before mulching, and provide a 3–7 inch (7.5–17.5 cm) layer of mulch to keep weeds down. Shady areas are less conducive to weeds and will require less mulch. Don't mulch around plants until they are tall enough so that the mulch won't smother them. Organic mulches can harbor snails and slugs and promote rot when wet, so keep mulch away from the stems of your plants.

All plants appreciate a generous layer of mulch.

Choosing a Mulch

The time you take to choose the right mulch for your needs is time well spent. You want a mulch that not only looks good, but is free of weeds. Cost and availability may also be important factors in your choice. There are two general types of mulch—organic and inorganic. Both will help to control weeds and hold moisture in the soil, but organic mulches will also add all-important organic matter to the soil. Inorganic mulches don't improve the soil, but they will last longer than organic types.

Use grass clippings as a mulch or work them into the soil to add valuable organic matter.

Organic Mulches

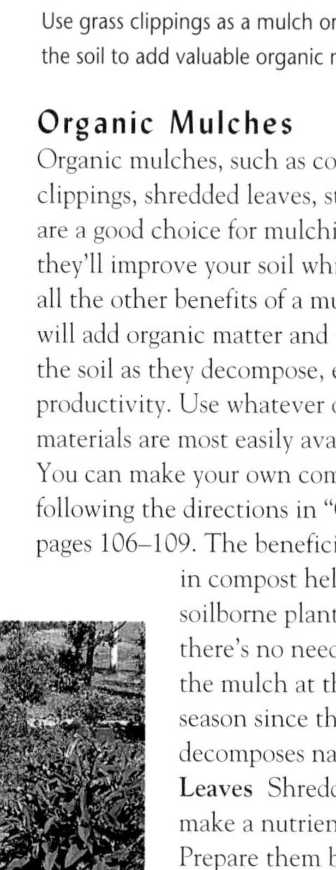

Organic mulches, such as compost, grass clippings, shredded leaves, straw and hay, are a good choice for mulching since they'll improve your soil while providing all the other benefits of a mulch. They will add organic matter and nutrients to the soil as they decompose, enhancing soil productivity. Use whatever organic materials are most easily available to you. You can make your own compost following the directions in "Compost" on pages 106–109. The beneficial organisms in compost help control soilborne plant disease, and there's no need to remove the mulch at the end of the season since the compost decomposes naturally.

Leaves Shredded leaves also make a nutrient-rich mulch. Prepare them by using a shredding machine, or run over leaves with a lawn mower. Don't use the leaves unshredded, as they can blow away when dry or create an impenetrable mat when wet, preventing moisture reaching the roots of the plants. If you're using leaves as a general mulch around perennials, trees or shrubs, dig them in half-rotted during the spring and let the soil warm up.

Hay and Straw Both hay and straw are loose mulches, so you will need to apply a thick layer of 6–10 inches (15–25 cm) for suitable weed control. Straw is preferable to hay, as hay tends to carry weed seeds and provide a habitat for rodents, snails and slugs.

Bark Chips Bark and wood chips are attractive, long-lasting mulches. They both work well to keep down weeds in plantings of perennial herbs but will dwarf smaller annuals and biennials. But be careful with what you buy. Bags labeled bark chips can contain wood other than bark, including leftovers from the timber industry that might have been treated with chemicals that could harm plants.

Newspaper and Cardboard These types of mulches aren't especially attractive, but they are cheap and effective in smothering weeds. They stop even the hardiest of weeds and at the same time still allow water to pass through. It's a good idea to cover them with another mulch that is more attractive and can anchor them.

Straw mulches are great for controlling weeds, but you need a thick application.

Rocks and pebbles are often overlooked as a mulch, but are a cheap and effective alternative.

Inorganic Mulches

Inorganic mulches include stones, marble chips and lava rock, as well as black plastic and various landscaping fabrics. Inorganic mulches don't decompose, so they won't need renewing like organic mulches. But they also don't improve soil as organic mulches do. The most common and practical inorganic mulching materials are black plastic and landscaping fabrics. Though you may find them expensive, if you purchase good-quality materials, you can remove and store them at the end of the growing season and can reuse them for several years.

Black plastic helps soil retain the warmth from the sun into the night. It also prevents weed growth and retains soil moisture. You can apply black plastic several weeks before planting to warm the soil. Buy sheets of plastic at least 1 foot (30 cm) wider than your row or bed. Lay out the plastic and anchor the sides with rocks or soil. Make holes for planting and to allow water to penetrate. Don't use black plastic as a general mulch; it can cause shrub roots to grow very close to the surface of the soil, and undermine the health of a plant. It can also cause overheating in hot weather.

Landscaping fabrics allow water and air to penetrate and can also be walked on. However, the roots of some shrubs may grow up into the fabric and make removal difficult. Some weeds may also survive and grow through the fabric. Some landscaping fabrics degrade in sunlight, so you will have to cover them with a second mulch, such as straw, hay or wood chips.

Choose Your Mulch

The following are some of the best mulches to consider for your garden.

Material	How to Apply
Chopped leaves	Apply in 3–inch (7.5–cm) layers; best if chopped or composted.
Compost	Spread as a topdressing 1 inch (2.5 cm) deep around plants.
Grass clippings	Apply a 1–4 inch (2.5–10 cm) layer around plantings. Make sure clippings are herbicide-free and not matted.
Newspaper	Anchor paper with soil or stones. Apply several layers but don't use colored newspaper as some inks are toxic. Cover with a more attractive mulch.
Pine needles	Apply in 2–inch (5–cm) layers. Needles make the soil more acid, so don't use around non acid-loving plants.
Straw	Lay down 8–inch (20–cm) layers around plants. Apply thickly to keep weeds at bay. Uses up soil nitrogen while decaying.
Shredded bark	Apply a 4–inch (10–cm) layer around established chips trees or perennials. Composted chips are best.

Caring for Container Herbs

Your container plants need to be cared for in the appropriate way if they are to look their best. Caring for container plants is much the same as for other plants in that they all need good soil, periodic fertilizing and regular watering. However, container plants will need more watering and feeding to remain healthy.

Potting your Herbs

Your herbs need to be planted in a good container mix to ensure healthy growth. As container plants have less soil for roots to grow in and to extract nutrients from, the soil must be carefully prepared. The container mix should be free from weeds and disease, be light enough to provide air space, and meet the nutritional needs of your plants. Some herbs prefer a slightly alkaline soil, so then your mix needs the addition of dolomite lime. While there are some quite good commercial container mixes available, the most economical approach is to make your own, which will specifically suit the requirements of your herbs. A good mix is: 2 parts good garden loam or well-rotted compost, 1 part leaf mold, 1 part well-rotted manure and 2 parts coarse sand.

Regular Watering

Unlike regular garden plants, which can search for moisture and nutrients in the soil with their roots, container plants require regular watering and feeding to remain healthy. Herbs in containers dry out quickly, so you may need to water every day during hot weather. Very small pots, small- and medium-sized terracotta containers, and hanging baskets dry out especially quickly; you may have to water these as often as twice a day.

If a pot or basket dries out completely, you still may be able to save the plants. Set the pot or basket in a larger container filled with water, let it sit there for an hour or two, and then set the pot or basket in a shady spot for a few hours until the plants perk up again. Then move the pot or basket back to its original spot, but be extra careful to keep those container plants well watered from then on.

One of the keys to lush-looking container plants is regular fertilizing. Give hanging baskets a boost by misting or watering them with a liquid fertilizer, such as fish emulsion.

Regular Fertilizing

Besides regular watering, the other key to lush-looking container plants is regular fertilizing. Give them a boost by watering them with fairly dilute fish emulsion or compost tea (made by soaking a shovelful of finished compost in a bucket of water for about a week, then straining out the soaked compost). Start in late spring by feeding once every two weeks, then assess

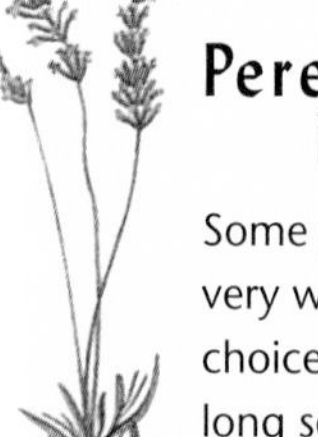

Perennial Herbs in Pots

Some perennial herbs work very well in containers. Good choices include those with a long season of bloom, such as lavender or yarrow. Other perennial herbs that look good in containers are those with showy flowers, such as purple echinacea, chamomile, bee balm (bergamot) and St John's wort.

Perennials need a little more care than annuals since you don't just pull them out at the end of the season. Because they are growing in containers, they are much more susceptible to winter damage than plants growing in the ground. In cold climates, you'll want to move container perennials to an unheated garage or cold basement to protect them from the alternate freezing and thawing cycles, which can damage or kill them. You will need to water the pots lightly during the winter months. In the spring, give them a good dose of compost to give them extra nutrients for the growing season ahead.

Potting and Repotting Herbs

Follow these easy steps to ensure problem-free potting and repotting.

- Water the herb in its original container. If repotting, choose a pot that is slightly larger than the old one.
- Ensure the new, fresh container mix is moist.
- Place small stones in the base of the new container to prevent container mix escaping through the drainage holes.
- Place some container mix on top of the stones and gently remove the herb from its original container. Place it in its new pot and fill with fresh container mix.
- Keep the plant out of direct sunlight for several days until it has recovered from the transplant.
- Water the container thoroughly.
- Top up with compost every spring.

Container herbs need regular water and feeding to remain healthy. For easy maintenance, group together plants that have similar needs.

the containers in midsummer. If plants look lush but aren't flowering well, change to fertilizing once every three weeks. If the plants look somewhat spindly, start fertilizing every week. If the plants seem to be growing and flowering well, stick with the two-week schedule.

Repotting Herbs

Your herbs will eventually need to be repotted, either because they grow too big for their pots or because they need to be moved into fresh container mix. Generally, you should repot your plants every year in the spring or summer, when plants are actively growing. If they get too big for their pot they can become root-bound, which means they have grown so many roots there isn't enough container mix left to support further growth.

Caring for Hanging Baskets

Hanging baskets dry out faster than other container plants, so it's a good idea to use a container mix that holds plenty of water. Adding extra vermiculite will also help. Try using larger baskets that will dry out more slowly.

The easiest way of watering hanging baskets that are out of reach is to get a long watering wand or extension nozzle for your garden hose. Alternatively, you can hang the basket on a rope that can be lowered. This way, you can water it as you would any other container, and carry out other necessary maintenance work at the same time. You won't need to water too much at first, when the plants are small, but as the plants grow, the basket may need watering at least once a day by the end of the season. If your baskets are drying out too quickly, consider using water-retaining granules to help you even out the moisture highs and lows in this miniature ecosystem.

Indoor Herbs

Some herbs adjust well to being grown indoors. For many gardeners, indoor cultivation is a convenient approach, particularly in areas which have cold, frosty winters. Growing indoors means you can have tender herbs all year round.

There are a few things to keep in mind when planning your indoor herb garden. Flowering herbs will require more light than herbs grown for their foliage. Glassed-in sunrooms and balconies are ideal for indoor herb cultivation because they create a hothouse environment. Bright, sunny window ledges are also suitable for growing some indoor herbs. But keep in mind that the intensity of light drops off very rapidly as it enters the room, so a plant even a short distance away from the window will get only half as much light as it would if it were right next to the window. If your plant isn't getting the right amount of light, it may show symptoms that tell you it needs a new location. It may become leggy and spindly, or its lower leaves may turn yellow and drop. Or it may stop putting out any new growth. If this is the case, move it to a new, sunnier location.

Next to getting the light levels right, watering is the most important aspect of indoor plant care. Most indoor plants need frequent watering, but always check moisture content first before watering. Watch the soil surface for clues. A lighter color usually indicates it is dry, while a dark color usually indicates the soil is damp and doesn't need watering. If the surface is dry, use your finger to check the soil an inch or two below the surface. If dry, water the plant. Another clue is to pick up the pot. If it feels light, you may need to water; if it feels heavy, wait a few days before watering.

A pebble tray will provide more humidity for your plants.

Herbs require good drainage and rich container mix, and should ideally be grown in terracotta herb pots or specially designed plastic herb trays. Only small quantities need to be grown at a time, so a wide variety of herbs can be grown in a relatively small area.

The Right Mix

As mentioned above, the container mix for indoor herbs needs to be rich, but it

Grow herbs on a sunny window sill in the kitchen so they will be in easy reach for cooking.

should also be light and friable. Add well-rotted animal or poultry manure or compost to the container mix. For light soil, add some sand to assist the drainage and prevent the soil from becoming hard-packed. The base of the container should be filled with a shallow layer of drainage material, such as gravel or crushed rocks, before the soil is added. When potting up new plants or repotting old ones, add one part compost for every three parts potting mix. If you remember that indoor herbs require plenty of sun and frequent watering along with feeding, success will be yours.

Herbs for Indoor Containers

You can grow the following herbs indoors in a sunny position with plenty of light. But don't be limited just to this list.

Basil Basil likes a rich container mix with good drainage. Pick the stems when the plant reaches 7 inches (18 cm) in height, before the flowers appear.

Chervil Plant in a large pot in a well-drained, moderately rich container mix enriched with compost. Chervil likes semi-shade in summer and full sun during winter. In summer, chervil goes to seed quickly. You can delay this process by pinching back to prevent flowering.

Chives Grow chives in a sunny position indoors in a rich and well-drained container mix. Cut the tops of the leaves with scissors as needed, or harvest a few leaves from the base. Frequent harvesting promotes growth.

Chives

Dill Plant in a fairly large pot in well-drained container mix. Harvest seeds by collecting the ripening flower heads in late summer and placing them in a dry place until the seeds can be easily rubbed off.

Marjoram

Marjoram Grow in rich, well-drained container mix with plenty of watering during summer. Can be picked and used fresh or dried and stored in an airtight container.

Mint Garden mint is ideal for growing in a pot because of its tendency to spread and take over the garden. Grow on a sunny window sill in a rich container mix with added peat. Water well and pick leaves as required.

Parsley Plant parsley in full sun or partial shade in a medium-sized pot. Use a rich container mix that has either animal or poultry manure added.

Sage Grow in a well-drained container mix. Fresh sage can be picked as required or dried before the flower stalks become too large.

Thyme Grow thyme in full sun or partial shade in a light, well-drained mix. Don't use artificial fertilizers, as they can kill the plant.

Parsley

Inside Out and Outside In

Just like people, many indoor plants appreciate a vacation. Moving your indoor plants outdoors for the summer months is a great way to keep them healthy and happy. Flowering herbs, which require bright light, will especially appreciate some time outdoors. If your plants have aphids, scales or other pests, moving them outdoors can give beneficial insects a chance to attack the unwanted insects, thus solving your pest problem. If you have a large number of indoor plants, you may want to move the bright-light lovers outside for the summer and shift some medium-light plants to the brighter spots vacated by the high-light lovers.

Before moving plants outside, wait until the weather is warm and settled. Introduce indoor plants to outside sunlight gradually. If you don't, their leaves can show brown or white scorched spots. To give your indoor plants time to adjust, always place them in full shade when you first move them outside. After a few weeks in the shade, you can move the kinds that enjoy brighter light out from the shade to partial- or full-sun locations.

Plants growing in the brighter, airier conditions of the great outdoors grow much faster than they do indoors, so they'll need more water and fertilizer than normal. Pay special attention to make sure they don't dry out; they may need daily watering when temperatures peak in summer.

A wick-watering setup is a handy way to water plants if you're going away on a long vacation.

Flower production takes a lot of energy, so blooming plants need all the light they can get.

Overwintering

If you live in a cold climate and want to grow plants that live for more than one year, you will need to plan carefully for winter. Tender perennials, such as bay and rosemary, won't survive when exposed to cold-climate winters. Herbs grow well indoors provided there is enough light and water, and tender perennials will keep growing if you protect them from freezing temperatures by moving them indoors for the winter months. Cuttings that you take in early autumn will be ready to move to the garden in spring if you nurture them indoors all winter. You can also pot up annuals and bring them indoors for winter use or start fresh ones from seed.

Perennials

You have several methods to choose from when raising a winter supply of herbs. Perennials can be grown in the garden soil in summer, then potted up for winter indoors. At the beginning and end of the season, leave the plants in their pots in a shady spot outdoors for at least one week before moving them to their new home. This helps them adjust to the change in light from bright to moderate and vice versa. When digging up the plant from the garden, cut all the way around it with a spade, then gently lift the whole root ball into a pot lined with fresh potting mix.

You can also start new plants for the winter from cuttings. To grow the largest winter plants, take 4-inch (10-cm) cuttings in midsummer and root them singly in pots of potting soil left in the shade. Keep them moist to encourage root formation. You can take cuttings from established plants outdoors well into autumn, as long as there is new growth to choose from and the plants have not become dormant.

Annuals

Annual herbs for winter growing are best started fresh from seed in autumn. Sow them the same way you start your spring seedlings indoors. Grow them in medium-sized pots so they will have room to grow all winter. Sow hard-to-transplant herbs, such as parsley, directly into deep pots.

Light and Temperature

Your indoor herbs will need plenty of light each day for strong, vigorous growth. A sunny window sill is ideal, but keep the pots away from cold windows and drafts. Most herbs appreciate daytime temperatures of 60 to 70°F (15 to 21°C), with cooler temperatures of 50 to 65°F

Some perennials can winter outdoors in cold climates, because snow is an excellent insulator.

Glass containers or plastic jugs can make handy individual plant protectors, but remember to remove these mini greenhouses on warm, sunny days to prevent the plant from overheating.

Many herbs will not survive a cold winter if left outdoors, but by being brought indoors in pots, annuals can have their growing season extended by a few months. Less hardy perennials also benefit.

(10 to 18°C) at night. Annual herbs, such as basil, prefer to be kept warm, while perennials and biennials do better if kept cool.

Moisture

Water thoroughly, then allow the soil to dry a little before watering again. Don't overwater. Evaporation may be less indoors, or more if your house is heated in winter. Excess moisture encourages fungal diseases and prevents roots from getting the oxygen they need. If humidity is low, spray plants several times a day with a light mist. Grouping plants together also helps to retain humidity.

Overwintering Outdoors

The success of overwintering your perennials outdoors in the garden depends on your climate. Hardy perennials, such as sage, will survive a cold winter in perfect condition, ready to grow again when temperatures rise in spring. Some of the less hardy herbs, such as oregano, may need help getting through a cold winter.

The best protection is a blanket of snow. If snowfall is minimal or absent, protect perennials from the drying effects of winter winds by covering them with evergreen boughs or surrounding them with sacking or plastic sheeting (especially bubble glaze). To overwinter small perennials, wait until the soil has frozen, then mulch heavily with straw, bark or leaves. Remove the mulch gradually in spring.

Cold Frames

For a permanent place to protect plants during winter, build a cold frame. They are called cold frames because they are not heated. The simplest type of cold frame is a bottomless, boxlike structure. Sides can be made out of wood or clear fiberglass, and the top out of clear plastic, glass or fiberglass so that good light can shine through. Build the back taller than the front, so the lid will sit at a 45-degree angle. At the lowest point, the frame should be tall enough so plants can grow without touching the roof.

Set the frame on a level, well-drained sunny site. On warm days, prop the lid open with a stick so the plants don't overheat. Set pots or trays in the frame, or plant directly in the soil on the floor of the frame.

Row covers made from fiberglass can be handy for protecting your plants if they are overwintering outdoors.

Frost Protectors

Frost protectors allow you to extend the growing season or to winter plants outdoors. Surround your plants with hay bales or trellising and drape burlap over them at night or during cold snaps. Or cover them with a floating row cover, which will help keep the air around the plants a few degrees warmer than the surrounding environment.

You can also cover plants with plastic jugs that have the bottom removed, plastic umbrellas or plastic tunnels stretched over wire hoops. These mini greenhouses can hold too much heat during a warm, sunny day, so be prepared to provide your plants with some ventilation.

Trellises help protect crops from cold breezes. For extra protection, drape row covers over crops during cold weather.

Preventing Pests

Having a garden offers many pleasures but a few challenges as well, such as pests and diseases. On the whole, herbs are not usually bothered by insect pests, especially when they are grown in an appropriate site with good soil and good care, which makes them more resistant to problems. Gardeners often notice that after several years of building up the soil, keeping the garden clean, and encouraging natural predators, insect and disease problems diminish. If your plants are kept healthy, they will attract fewer pests and will be less susceptible to diseases.

Prevention Control

Generally, pests and diseases are not a big problem for annual and perennial herbs. You may never have to spray if you seek out the most disease-resistant species and cultivars and then plant them where they will thrive. If you put a plant that prefers full sun into a lightly shaded nook, or interplant too tightly between taller plants, the plant will be weakened and unable to resist pest and disease attack. Strong, healthy plants do not make easy targets for pests or diseases. Just as we are constantly exposed to cold and flu germs, plant pests, fungi, viruses and bacteria are all around. They will infect weaker or stressed plants before harming vigorous ones, so you must be sure to keep sun-loving herbs, such as basil, in sunny locations.

To grow healthy, trouble-free plants, take good care of your soil—provide plenty of organic nutrients and make sure you keep the pH at an appropriate level. Give well-drained soil to plants that are prone to rot. Double check your various maintenance methods. Don't nick plants with your hoe or rake because wounds are an open invitation for pest and disease attack. Stay out of a planting when the foliage is wet, so you won't spread diseases as you brush past plants. Plant all your herbs with the proper recommended spacing to let air circulate freely through all the foliage and make conditions less hospitable for fungal diseases. Correct spacing also lessens the competition for water and nutrients. Remove and destroy any diseased leaves or insect-infested stalks as soon as you find them, and sterilize tools after dealing with infected plants to avoid spreading diseases. To check the individual requirements of each herb, refer to "A Guide to Popular Herbs", starting on page 172.

ABOVE: Attract beneficials to your garden with diverse plantings and a water source. LEFT: Praying mantids aren't picky—they'll eat any insects that cross their path, pest and beneficial species alike.

Pests and diseases are easiest to control if you catch them before they get out of hand. If you find a pest or disease problem, you'll need to properly identify it to be able to choose the best control. Only then can you decide how best to treat it: by handpicking, trapping, or by some other organically acceptable control.

Beneficial Insects

Almost none of the insects that you'll come across in your herb garden is harmful to you or your plants; in fact there are as many friends in the insect world as there are enemies. Some insects feed primarily on wild plants and will leave your garden alone. Other insect species directly benefit the garden. They survive by preying (feeding) on or parasitizing (living within) other insects. The species that attack other insects are especially significant to the gardener, since they're one of the tools you can rely on for pest control. Gardeners generally appreciate the presence of ladybugs (ladybirds) because their main diet is aphids, and some species eat mealybugs, scale insects, whiteflies and mites. An adult ladybug beetle can eat 50–60 aphids a day. Even the little dragon-like larvae of the ladybug can consume about 25 aphids a day. The praying mantid is also often a friend because it feeds on a great variety of insects, as do the green and

Provide shelter and food for hover flies and other beneficials, and they'll control pests in return.

brown lacewing flies. The larvae of hover flies prey on aphids, caterpillars, thrips and sawflies. And both wild and domestic bees perform vital functions, such as pollination of plants.

Predators

Predators eat other organisms. Most insect predators, such as ground beetles or rove beetles, aren't fussy eaters. They're called generalists, and they'll eat pest insects and mites, as well as fellow predators that are small enough to catch. Other predaceous insects are prey-specific. For example, some ladybug (ladybird) species prefer spider mites, some consume only mealybugs and others restrict their diet just to aphids. But not all predators are insects—spiders, centipedes and several species of mites, are also important pest controllers in your garden.

Parasites

Parasites are among the most important biological pest controls. They live on or in other organisms. Parasites steal nutrients from their host but usually don't kill it.

Parasitoids are a special kind of parasite. They make ideal biological pest controllers because they kill their host. Most parasitoids are tiny, aggressive wasps, such as braconid wasps, or bees that lay their eggs within the living host. Parasitoid larvae hatch and consume their host, then form a cocoon before emerging as adults that are eager to find more pests. Most parasitoids are species- and host-specific. Some may attack only a pest's larval stage, for example, while others will parasitize the adult form of the same pest.

Attracting Beneficials

Many of the small-flowered herbs, such as fennel, dill and thyme, attract beneficial insects. You can also entice beneficials to frequent your garden by providing them with the three basic necessities: water, food and shelter.

Water A water source will attract most kinds of beneficial insects (as well as insect-eating birds and frogs), especially during periods of dry weather. Fill shallow pans with water and set them in protected nooks and corners of your garden. Set rocks in the pans to serve as insect perches. You will have to change the water regularly to prevent mosquitoes breeding.

Bees are a vital part of a healthy garden. Without their pollination efforts, many plants could not set fruit or seed.

Food Access to suitable food is vital for beneficial insects. During various stages of their life, beneficials may need different types of food. Larvae, for instance, often prey on pests, while adults feed on pollen and nectar, so they may be killed if you spray flowering plants.

Small-flowered plants are ideal food sources for beneficials. Particularly good choices include members of the plant families Umbelliferae (such as dill, lovage, parsley and fennel) and Lamiaceae (including mint, hyssop, catnip and lemon balm). Plant these herbs around your garden especially if you are going to grow vegetables, and they will attract beneficial insects where pests are most likely to become a problem.

Weeds and flowering cover crops, such as buckwheat, clover and alfalfa, are also good food sources. Garden mail order companies sell special bug attractants. These flower seed mixtures encourage creatures, such as lacewings and ladybugs, to stay in your garden.

Shelter Once they have food and water, beneficials will look for a safe place to live and to lay their eggs. Provide shelter by adding organic mulches, such as straw, leaves or compost, to the soil surface around plants and along paths. Beneficials also appreciate the protection of trees, perennial plantings and cover crops that aren't frequently disturbed by harvest and tillage.

You can maintain a friendly environment for beneficials by avoiding broad-spectrum pesticides (those that kill a wide range of insects). Even organically acceptable chemicals, such as rotenone, will wipe out beneficials as readily as pests. Often, pest populations recover more quickly than the beneficials and multiply unchecked. This leads to a

Before spraying for pests, look around for ladybugs. They may control the problem for you.

Moth larvae

Signs of Damage

When you find signs of damage on your herbs, look for a description of the damage in the column on the left, then check the possible causes in the column on the right.

Damage	Possible Causes
Leaves with large, ragged holes	Adult or larval stages of beetles, such as Japanese beetles, Mexican bean beetles and others; grasshoppers; moth and butterfly larvae, such as caterpillars and armyworms or hornworms; slugs or snails; animal pests
Leaves curled, twisted, puckered, or distorted	Aphids; leafhoppers; tarnished plant bugs; nutrient deficiency; plant diseases
Leaves curled	Webworms; obliquebanded and other leafrollers; leafminers
Leaves with numerous small holes	Adult flea beetles; plant diseases
Leaves spotted or stippled	Tarnished plant bugs; spider mites; thrips; lace bugs; plant diseases
Leaves or stems with hardened bumps, scales, or cottony growths	Scale; mealybugs; plant diseases
Leaves with shallow tunnels under leaf surface	Larval leafminers; sawflies
Leaves with shiny, slimy, frothy or sticky coating	Aphids; mealybugs; slugs and snails; pear psyllas; scale; spittlebugs; whiteflies; plant diseases
Fruit with tunnels throughout	Apple maggots; moth larvae, such as codling moths or European corn borers
Fruit distorted, twisted	European corn borers; tarnished plant bugs
Fruit spotted, sticky	Aphids; leafhoppers; spittlebugs; plant diseases
Roots or bulbs with signs of feeding or dead spots	Wireworms; many kinds of beetle grubs; weevils (black vine or strawberry root weevils)
Roots or stem with galls, swellings	Gall wasps; nematodes; plant diseases
Roots with lumps and excessive branching	Nematodes
Stems hollowed, with larvae inside and leaves wilted	Borers (European corn, citrus, fruit borers)
Flowers eaten	Japanese beetles; rose chafers
Flowers fall before opening	Tarnished plant bugs
Seedlings chewed off at soil level	Cutworms; animal pests

Codling moth larvae

Wasps are valuable beneficials. Some species prey on aphids; others are important pollinators.

vicious circle—since you'll need to apply stronger control measures more frequently, the beneficial insects will not get a chance to recover.

Identifying Some Common Pests

Unfortunately, not all insects in your garden will be beneficial—occasionally, insect pests will attack your herbs. If pests stood up to be counted, gardeners would find pest identification and control an easier task. Unfortunately, pests often remain undetected until the harm is done. Even if you do spot damage, you may have difficulty identifying the culprit. Insects, disease, and even environmental problems, such as nutrient deficiencies or air pollution, can cause similar symptoms. But getting an accurate diagnosis is the only way to choose an appropriate and effective control measure.

Look for Signs

Fortunately, there are clues you can look for to help pin down plant problems. Give plants a thorough inspection at least once a week. Look at both sides of the leaves, around buds and flowers, and along the stem. If you find damage, jot down a few notes: the identity of the affected plant, the plant parts that are affected, and the

Having a healthy garden and encouraging natural predators is the first step in controlling insect pests. Crop rotation is also a good idea to help avoid pest problems. If you have a mixed garden, simply rotate your annual herbs with other garden plants to avoid planting them in the same position 2 years running.

kind of damage done, such as holes in leaves, discoloration and distorted fruit.

Check the undersides of plant leaves, and scratch the soil or mulch looking for likely culprits. Also search for clusters of eggs, webs or pellet- or sawdust-like insect droppings. See if neighboring plants show similar symptoms. If you find any insects, examine them with a magnifying lens and try to identify them. Don't assume that the insects must be pests—they could just as easily be beneficials that stopped by for a tasty insect meal.

If you can't find any suspects or can't identify the ones you have, try matching the damage symptoms with those in the "Signs of Damage" box on the opposite page. This approach may help you discover a possible cause.

Depending on where you live and the climate you live in, there will be a variety of insect pests in your garden. If you still aren't sure of the cause, consider other possible sources, such as wind damage, nutrient deficiency, animal pests, sunburn or frost damage. Use the following list to

Prune and destroy any insect-infected stems as soon as you discover them.

ABOVE: Adult snails have a single shell and a soft gray-black or brown body. They are about 3 inches (7.5 cm) long. They feed at night and can cause extensive damage to plants by eating large holes in leaves.
RIGHT: Marigolds suppress root-feeding nematodes and make wonderful companion plants for such fruits as tomatoes.

further identify the source of your problem. You can also identify insects by the appearance of the larvae or adults (you may need a magnifying glass) as well as the damage they do to the plants.

Aphids

Aphids are tiny, sap-sucking, soft-bodied, pear-shaped insects that feed on a variety of plants. They tend to cluster near the growing tips and on the undersides of leaves. Large groups of aphids can cause the foliage, flowers and shoots of plants to twist, pucker or drop, and they leave a trail of sugary excrement that is sticky and often harbors a black, sooty mold. Aphids can multiply rapidly when conditions are favorable.

Japanese Beetles

These shiny, metallic blue-green beetles with bronze wing covers feed on many different annuals, perennials and shrubs, including foxgloves, echinacea, basil and roses. They will eat the green part of leaves, so that only the leaf veins remain, and also chew on the flowers. The grubs are white with brown heads; they feed mainly on lawn grass roots.

Leafminers

Leafminers are the tiny larvae of small flies. The larvae tunnel inside leaves, leaving light-colored trails that you can see on the surface of the leaf.

Spider Mites

These tiny, spider-like pests will attack many plants, especially when the weather becomes hot and dry. The brown, pinkish-red or green mites make very fine webs on plants and suck the plant sap from the underside of a leaf, causing it to curl and its upper surface to turn speckled, pale and dull-looking.

Slugs and Snails

Slugs and snails can be a problem anywhere the soil stays damp, and this is especially a problem in shady gardens. They crawl up on annuals and perennials and chew ragged holes in the leaves, stems and flowers, and can eat the entire plant in this way. They can also ruin young seedlings or transplants. Snails and slugs are easy to identify as they are large and leave slimy trails behind them.

Thrips

Thrips are minute, quick-moving insects that feed on the flowers and leaves of many different kinds of plants. They give the affected plant tissue a pale, silvery look in damaged areas. Eventually the infected plant parts will wither and die.

Plant Bugs

Tarnished plant bugs are green or brown with yellow triangles on their forewings; four-lined plant bugs are yellowish green with four black stripes down their back. Both of these insects will leave irregular holes or sunken brown spots in the middle of leaves. They also cause distorted growth on the leaves or growing tips of many annuals and perennials.

Other Pests

You also may find mealybugs (slow-moving, soft-bodied insects hidden beneath a white, cottony shield) under leaves and along stems; leafhoppers (which look like tiny wedge-shaped grass-hoppers) on stems and leaves; borers (fat pink caterpillars or grubs), which tunnel down the leaves of bearded irises and eat large cavities in the rhizomes; and cutworms (fat, dark-colored brown or green caterpillars), which chew through the stems of many seedlings and young plants.

Garlic

Managing Insect Pests

Keeping insect pests under control doesn't mean you have to use a lot of chemical sprays. The aim in growing a herb garden is to use as little insecticide as possible. Once you have identified what pests you are dealing with, do a little research to find the most effective and least toxic cure. Learn more about the pest so you can target its weaknesses. There are many simple solutions that don't use toxic sprays; see "Simple Solutions to Pests and Diseases" on pages 130–131.

Get into the habit of checking your plants for pests at least once a week. Don't worry if you find a few. In most gardens, as in nature, the life cycles of beneficial predators and parasites are usually closely synchronized with those of the pests. When the pests increase, so do the predators, so leave pests to become food for insect predators and parasites. But keep an eye on pest population sizes so you'll see if they are getting out of hand. You'll know pests are a problem if their numbers are growing and their feeding is heavy enough to damage plants. Even small numbers of insect pests can be destructive if they carry diseases. Leafhoppers and aphids can spread plant viruses, while striped and spotted cucumber beetles spread bacterial diseases, including cucumber wilt.

Some herbs, such as pennyroyal, are planted in the garden for their ability to repel insect pests. They help to protect your herb crop by deterring insects from settling on neighboring plants. Other herbs, such as fennel, are useful because they attract beneficial insects.

Simple Controls

If nature's controls aren't doing their job quickly enough, handpick the pests from plants and crush them under your foot. This is effective for large, slow-moving pests, such as snails and slugs, Japanese beetles and cutworms, but not for small pests or large infestations. Alternatively, drop them into a can of soapy water. Or suck up insects from plants with a portable, hand-held vacuum cleaner. You can also use a forceful spray of water from

Mulch to Deter Pests

Mulching is a routine part of conserving soil moisture and preventing weeds, but it is also effective in controlling some pests and diseases. Materials such as newspaper, biodegradable paper mulch and black plastic mulch help to control thrips, leafminers and other pests that must reach the soil to complete their life cycle. Strips of aluminum foil repel aphids, leafhoppers and thrips on garden and greenhouse crops. (Leave the foil in place only as long as pests are a threat to avoid leaf damage from reflected heat.) Mulches also prevent raindrops from splashing soilborne disease spores onto plant leaves.

Fasten bands around tree trunks to trap pests, such as caterpillars, as they climb up and down.

If slugs or earwigs have damaged your plants in the past, try trapping them in inverted pots.

the hose to knock pests, such as aphids and mites, from foliage. If pests are limited to one plant or stem, prune away the infested parts and destroy them along with the invaders.

Insect-Repelling Plants

Many varieties of herbs can be planted in the garden specifically for their insect-repelling properties. Pennyroyal, rue and wormwood are just a few herbs that may be used to discourage insects from converging on neighboring plants. Garlic is also a natural repellent due to its pungent aroma. The roots of some marigolds secrete a substance that kills nematodes that feed on roots. For more examples see "Simple Solutions to Pests and Diseases" on pages 130–131.

Traps and Barriers

Avoid insects attacking your plants and young seedlings by catching them in traps or deterring them with barricades. Sticky traps are effective in attracting insects such as whiteflies. You can buy sticky traps from garden centers or make your own by painting wood or cardboard with an appropriate color and coating it with petroleum jelly. Hang the traps on stakes near where the insects are doing their damage, and clean and replace them as needed to keep them effective.

Creating a barrier around a plant will stop insects being able to reach the plant and eat it. You can protect individual seedlings by placing collars made from recycled cardboard around them. By the time the cardboard breaks down, your plants will be past the susceptible stage.

An alternative barrier for crawling pests, such as slugs and snails, is a wide band of abrasive material on the soil around plants. Try wood ash, seashells, broken eggshells or powders, such as diatomaceous earth. These only work well when dry, so renew the application after rain.

Sticky Trunk Bands

Some pests, such as ants, codling moth and gypsy moth caterpillars, leaf beetles, snails and slugs, will crawl up the trunks of your trees and attack them. A good way to stop them is by creating a barrier around the tree trunk. Wrap a 5 inch (12.5 cm) band of sacking or corrugated cardboard around the trunk and fasten the ends with tape. This will trap moth larvae. Or coat the trunk with a band or two of non-drying barrier glue, or use axle grease to which insects, such as weevils and leaf beetles, will stick. When the bands are filled with pests, remove and discard.

Collars made from recycled cardboard will protect your seedlings from a variety of insect pests.

Plant Covers

If insects are a serious problem, try covering your plants with a floating row-cover. These light gardening fabrics keep flying and crawling pests away from your plants. Remember to cover the rows as soon as you've planted seeds or transplants, anchoring the material with soil, stones or boards. As your plants grow, the lightweight fabric will rise with them. You can leave the covers on all summer as long as temperatures don't exceed 75°F (24°C). If you are growing herbs for their seeds, you'll need to remove the covers so that insects can pollinate the flowers.

Crop Rotation

Rotating your annual and biennial herb plants is a good idea, especially before you encounter any pest problems. Crop rotation, which means avoiding planting the same crop in the same place 2 years running, is common practice in organic gardening. If you usually grow several large annual crops, it makes sense to work out a rotation based on the same number of growing plots. The result will be that a given area will repeat a particular crop only every third or fourth year. There is no need to have an elaborate rotation scheme unless your herb garden is large.

Adult lacewings feed mostly on pollen and honeydew, but their larvae are voracious predators of many pest insects.

Some gardeners claim that nasturtiums can repel a variety of garden pests. They're worth growing not only for their insect-repelling properties, but also for their colorful flowers and culinary uses.

Simply avoid planting the same herbs in the same location each year, so that potential pests won't build up to the point of causing noticeable damage. Rotation also helps you make better use of soil nutrients, since different crops remove nutrients from the soil at different rates, thus avoiding the danger of exhausting the supply of nutrients especially favored by particular plants.

Organically Acceptable Insecticides

If the less extreme pest controls fail to stop the pests, you may have to use an organic insecticide as a last resort. If so, to avoid killing the beneficial insects that are also sure to be there, make sure you properly identify the pest, and then start with the most specific and least disruptive insecticide. Botanical insecticides break down quickly after use, so they don't linger long in the environment, but they can still harm beneficials.

When using any insecticide, carefully follow the label instructions. Apply it either early morning or late evening, when you're less likely to encounter helpful bees. Treat only attacked plants and direct the spray at the undersides of leaves where pests hide, as well as onto the upper surfaces. Try not to get spray on flowers, which may be visited by predatory insects. Wear protective clothing, including a suitable face mask and gloves. It's preferable never to spray botanical insecticides on herbs you plan to eat. However, if you must, check the recommended interval between spraying and harvesting and wait the full period. Wash well any herbs that have been sprayed, in case any residues remain.

To control aphids and mites, the most common pests found on herbs, use insecticidal soap products, whose active ingredients are of organic origin and break down quickly once applied. Aphids are soft-bodied insects with six legs and two thornlike projections on their backs. Mites usually look like dark dots on webbing. Through a magnifying glass you can see that mites are tiny, eight-legged creatures that resemble spiders. Both aphids and mites are often found on the undersides of leaves, or they may be clustered on unopened blossoms.

Microbial insecticides are naturally occurring insect diseases commercially available for use as pest-control agents. If caterpillars are your problem, consider using one of several brands of *Bacillus thuringiensis*, also known as "BT." This bacterial insecticide halts the process of digestion in caterpillars, permanently discouraging them from eating. It acts only against the immature stages of moths and butterflies.

If all of these means to control insects fail, you can select one of the several commercial brands of botanical insecticides that contain rotenone or pyrethrin. These naturally derived insecticides share with most synthetic poisons the disadvantage of killing the good insects along with the bad, so use them only as a last resort.

Butterflies are useful in your garden for pollination, but keep an eye out for hungry larvae.

Preventing Plant Diseases

Even the healthiest of gardens will occasionally fall prey to plant diseases. Before you can cope with such diseases, you need to understand what they actually are. Unfortunately, diseases are more difficult to define than insect problems. After all, insects are creatures with specific and predictable traits, while plant diseases can be anything that interferes with such normal growth functions as water uptake and photosynthesis.

To make this definition a little more useful, it's helpful to divide plant diseases into two main categories—infectious diseases and noninfectious diseases. Infectious diseases can spread from one plant to another. They're the problems we usually think of as plant diseases, such as rust, fireblight and powdery mildew. Noninfectious diseases cannot be transmitted from one plant to another. Nutrient imbalances, insufficient light and waterlogged soil are a few causes of noninfectious diseases.

Infectious Diseases

Infectious diseases are caused by microscopic living organisms called pathogens. Pathogens are commonly broken down into four groups: fungi, bacteria, viruses and nematodes.

Fungi Many kinds of molds, mildews and mushrooms play an important part in breaking down organic matter in soil and compost. There are, however, a number of fungi that also attack living plants. These fungal pathogens are one of the most common causes of plant disease. Powdery mildew, damping-off, anthracnose, late blight and black spot are all fungal. Some are host-specific but many will attack a variety of garden plants. Fungi produce spores that move with the wind, soil, water and animals to plant surfaces. Given the right environmental conditions and the right host plant, spores of these pathogenic fungi will germinate and infect plants.

Bacteria Like fungi, bacteria are specialized organisms with both beneficial and pathogenic species. Beneficial bacteria recycle organic matter and nutrients in the soil and they can help to control insect pests. Some pathogenic bacteria, however, can infect plants and cause such diseases as crown gall, bacterial wilt and blight. Bacterial cells travel to plants the same way as fungal spores. Once they reach a susceptible plant, bacteria move into and infect plants through wounds and natural openings in leaves, stems and roots.

Viruses These are the smallest disease agents. Once inside a living cell, they

Keeping your garden neat, well-maintained and free of debris helps remove sites where pests and diseases can survive.

multiply by making their host plant produce even more virus particles, upsetting the plant's normal metabolism and causing disease symptoms. Virus particles are carried to healthy plants by such pests as insects, mites and nematodes. They're also spread by taking cuttings, grafts, layers or division from infected plants. Compost that contains infected plants and is not properly decomposed can also spread viruses. Viral diseases can be the most difficult to diagnose. Some common indications of viral attack include mottled, discolored or distorted leaves.

Nematodes These are microscopic roundworms which are found free-living in soil and as parasites on plants and animals. Beneficial nematodes are important members of the soil community, since they feed on decaying material and such pests as cutworms and grubs. Pest nematodes damage plants by puncturing cell walls with their needle-like mouthparts and drawing out the cell content. This causes disease-like symptoms, including yellowing, wilting, stunting and reduced yields, which are difficult to distinguish from other causes.

Noninfectious Diseases

Changes to the environment and in your gardening techniques can also interfere with normal plant functions, so technically they are considered diseases. Unlike infectious diseases, though, these plant diseases or disorders cannot be transmitted from plant to plant. They can still be very serious when they occur, but some are fairly easy to prevent and correct with good gardening practices, such as regular soil improvement and adding organic material.

Diagnosing Disease Problems

Such symptoms as leaf wilting or leaf yellowing, stunted growth or misshapen leaves are often the only clues you'll have when trying to diagnose the problem. But like most garden problems, plant diseases are easiest to control if you catch them early. Unlike insect pests, pathogens are

Plant Disease Symptoms and Causes

What You See	Possible Causes
Leaves mottled or discolored	Mosaic virus; nutrient deficiency; ozone or sulfur dioxide injury; sooty mold; sunscald; yellows; insect pests
Leaves with yellow or brown spots	Anthracnose; bacterial spot; botrytis blight; leafspot; powdery mildew
Leaves with black or brown spots surrounded by yellow	Bacterial spot; black spot; leafspot
Leaves curled, cupped or blistered	Leaf gall; mosaic or other viral diseases; herbicide drift; insect pests
Leaves, shoots or fruit with white or gray spots or patches	Downy mildew; powdery mildew; salt injury
Leaves and stems wilted and dying	Bacterial wilt; verticillium wilt; waterlogged soil; lack of water
Leaves or stems with orange spots	Rust
Stems with irregular swellings	Black knot; crown gall
Stems oozing a sticky or gummy substance	Cytospora or other cankers
Stems condensed into short, bushy "rosettes"; plant stunted	Nematodes; peach rosette
Stems of seedlings rotted at the soil line; infected seedlings collapsed	Damping-off
Flowers or fruit with brown spots	Brown rot; botrytis blight or fruit rot; fireblight; frost damage
Fruit with small, dark, sunken spots	Anthracnose
Fruit with water-soaked spots that turn brown and leathery at the blossom end	Blossom end rot
Roots of young and old plants rotted; plants stunted or wilted	Root rot
Roots with irregular swellings	Club root; crown gall; nematodes

Mosaic virus produces yellow or white streaks or mottling.

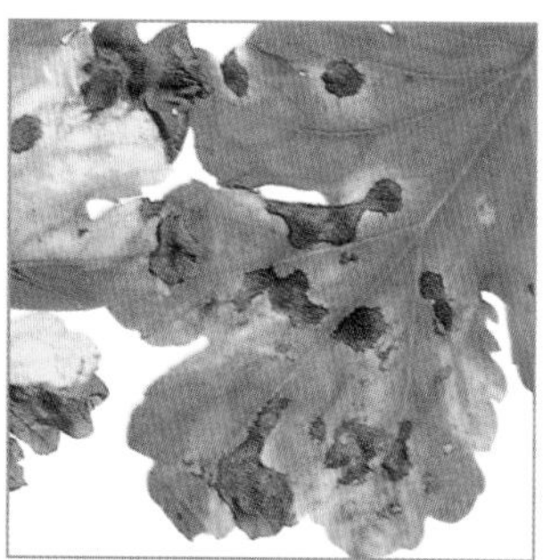
Fungal and bacterial leaf spots affect foliage.

Crown gall is a bacteria that forms knobbly tumors on plant tissue.

This leaf has signs of iron deficiency, not disease.

too small to see without magnification, so your best defense against disease organisms is prevention.

Preventing the Problem

When purchasing new herb plants, inspect them carefully for signs of disease and reject any that look suspiciously unhealthy. Remember that symptoms such as discolored leaves or stunted growth could be due to poor growing conditions, but they could also indicate another problem, such as disease. Good sanitation practices are essential in the garden or greenhouse. If it is likely that you've been handling soil or plants that may be sources of infection, clean your boots and hands with a 5-percent solution of household bleach in water, or wipe them with surgical spirit. If wet weather prevails, stay away from the garden until the weather is fine again. Many disease organisms require moisture for reproduction or mobility, and they're easily spread on films of water you may carry from plant to plant. These organisms can survive even the most extreme winters in bare soil or on garden rubbish, and will flourish as soon as they are transported to a plant.

Regularly inspect your plants for any signs of disease and remove unhealthy specimens. It's best to burn them, since a few pathogens that cause diseases are sufficiently hardy to survive the hottest compost piles. However, if burning rubbish is prohibited in your area, put the diseased plant materials in sealed bags for disposal with the household trash. Mulch your perennial herbs with regular applications of compost. Beneficial microbes in the compost suppress the development of some disease organisms.

When Problems Strike

Despite the best garden practices, there will be times when plant diseases will strike. The most important step is to diagnosis the problem correctly so you can take the appropriate prevention and control measures.

Unhealthy plants have special distress signals that let you know when pathogens have attacked. These can include a range of symptoms, such as leafspot, swellings, damaged fruit, stunted growth and even death. Check the following descriptions to see if any match the affected parts of your plants.

Blights Leaves, flowers, stems and branches that suddenly wilt, wither and die are common indications of blight. Common garden blights include botrytis (gray mold), early and late blight and fireblight.

Galls Swelling or overgrown patches of leaf or stem tissue are generally galls. They may be caused by fungi, such as leaf gall, bacteria, such as crown gall, or even insects, such as gall wasps.

Leaf Curl Deformed and discolored leaves may be caused by leaf curl. Viruses can also produce these symptoms.

Leaf Spots Rounded or irregular areas in various colors are common symptoms of leafspot. They are produced by many different pathogens.

Mildews Dusty white, gray or purplish patches on the surfaces or undersides of leaves are an easy clue to the fungal powdery and downy mildews.

Rots Soft or discolored and dying plant tissue generally indicates some kind of rot. Fungi and bacteria can cause rot on fruit, stems, flowers or roots.

Rusts Orange or yellowish spots, galls or coatings are caused by rust fungi. Rusts may affect leaves, stems, flowers or fruits.

Wilts Drooping leaves and stems indicate that the plant isn't getting enough water. This may be caused by improper watering or by fungi and bacteria that can clog the plant's water conducting system.

Disease Look-alikes

It's a good idea to be aware of the symptoms that are produced by non-infectious changes to the environment and gardening techniques so that when they do occur, you can deal with them effectively instead of mistaking them for an infectious disease.

Excess Water Too much water means that most or all of the tiny soil pores, which normally hold some oxygen, are filled with water. When roots don't get the oxygen they need, they can't function properly and are more prone to infectious diseases, such as root rot. Affected plants lack vigor and may wilt, and leaves may become yellow. Raised beds can help improve drainage.

Drought A shortage of soil water can stunt or slow plant growth and flower growth. Leaves either turn pale and wilt or develop brown, scorched areas. Shallow-rooted annual plants are most affected. Regular deep irrigation can help affected plants.

Cold Stress Sudden cold snaps can kill tender buds, growing tips and other plant parts. Leaves may turn yellow or drop, buds may drop, stems can crack and bark may split. Protect plants with row covers or other frost shields. Avoid fertilizing after midsummer, as fertilizing promotes soft growth that is more frost-prone.

Heat Stress Young plants exposed to high temperatures often wilt and may die. Shade and water may help plants recover.

Insufficient Light Plants become spindly when light is inadequate. Green leaves become pale, and variegated or colored leaves may turn evenly green. If this happens, move plants to a sunnier spot.

Deficient Nutrients When nutrients are lacking, plants become less vigorous and yield poorly. Common deficiency symptoms are abnormal leaf color, curled or stunted leaves and dead growing tips. Adding organic matter and compost regularly can help.

Excessive Nutrients High concentrations of nutrients may cause the same symptoms as nutrient deficiencies. Too much nitrogen will produce lush plants with few flowers or fruit.

Controlling Plant Diseases

As mentioned above, good garden hygiene and proper plant selection help prevent diseases. If you remove faded foliage and cut back flowers after they bloom, you'll remove common sites of disease attack.

If the leaves of your roses have dark, circular spots, you can be fairly sure that black spot fungi are at work.

Careful watering can help reduce disease outbreak. Whenever possible, avoid wetting plant leaves. If foliage stays wet overnight, fungal spores may have time to germinate and attack leaves. Overhead watering and even walking through wet foliage can transfer diseases from plant to plant. Use a ground-level irrigation system, such as drip irrigation or a trickle system, and don't work in the garden when plants are wet from recent rainfall.

If the weather is cold and wet, or hot and humid—conditions that encourage disease—and you do get an outbreak of disease in the garden, remove damaged plant parts promptly before the disease can spread and throw them away with the household rubbish. This can go a long way toward controlling disease.

Organically Acceptable Fungicides

If your herbs do fall prey to plant diseases, you can choose from several acceptable control options. Organically acceptable fungicides, such as sulfur and copper sprays, will protect your plants from fungal disease only if they're in place before infection. You can dust plants with copper or sulfur preparations if you suspect that fungal disease is a problem in your garden, but do it before or during bouts of wet weather, when plants are most likely to be infected, and before the organisms penetrate the leaf. Use low-toxic homemade fungicides on susceptible herbs before symptoms appear. See "Simple Solutions to Pests and Diseases" on pages 130–131.

Nature's Nursemaids

You can also use some of your own herbs to control disease problems and act as nature's nursemaids by helping ailing plants recover. Hyssop, for example, helps plants that are suffering from bacterial invasion. You can keep these helpful herbs in a pot and move them next to any diseased plants in your garden. Or, buy essential oils of these herbs, dilute a few drops in water, and spray on your diseased plants. For more ideas, see "Companion Planting" on pages 132–133.

Fungal wilts affect leaves and stems.

Rusts show as light-colored spots.

Powdery mildew is quite common.

Downy mildew has pale patches.

Simple Solutions to Pests and Diseases

There are many ways you can treat and control pests and diseases in your garden without resorting to harmful poisonous sprays. Picking off pests, trapping them, planting insect-repelling herbs nearby or using a homemade pest control remedy are all safe options that don't introduce hazardous chemicals into your garden. But be careful when mixing and using them, as some ingredients, such as chilies and garlic, can burn the skin.

Helpful Herbs

Many varieties of herbs are natural insect repellents. Plant these herbs among your other plants, such as vegetables, to keep pests at bay.

Tansy deters flying insects, so it is useful not only in the garden but also in a pot on a window sill or planted near an open door to keep flies out of the house. Tansy, rue, wormwood, lavender and elder are all good insect repellents.

Hyssop helps plants suffering from bacterial invasion, and chamomile helps sick plants to recover from a variety of ailments. You can either plant these herbs in individual pots and move them around the garden to act as nursemaids to your ailing plants, or you can make a spray using their essential oils. Use 5 drops to every 8 cups (2 l) of water and spray on troubled plants.

You can also use teas made from herbs to combat pests and diseases. Elderflower tea discourages molds on most plants. Chive tea is especially useful against gray mold (botrytis) on roses. Nettle tea combats mildew and horsetail tea helps to protect against all kinds of fungi. Use 1 cup of fresh herbs to 2 cups (500 ml) of water. Boil the water, pour it onto the herbs and leave it to stand for 6 hours. Then strain the liquid and store. Mix 2 tablespoons of this tea into 8 cups (2 l) of water in a watering can and water on ailing plants. A strong tea made from wormwood will deter against pests such as moth and butterfly caterpillars, flea beetles, slugs and snails. Brew the leaves in water, cool, then use at half strength on mature plants.

If you are troubled by aphids, use either basil leaves, rhubarb leaves or elder leaves. Take 8 oz (250 g) of leaves and simmer in 4 cups (1 liter) of water for 30 minutes. Cool, then strain. Separately, mix 1 teaspoon of dishwashing liquid or soapflakes in 2½ cups (625 ml) of cold water. Mix both solutions together and spray. Don't use food utensils when making sprays.

ABOVE: If your plants are invaded by aphids, don't despair. Spray them off with a jet of water from the hose.

RIGHT: Oils extracted from citrus peels will control many pests, including aphids and spider mites.

Handy Home Remedies

Despite your best efforts, pests and diseases can occasionally get out of hand. When things get to this stage you have several choices: Try a natural home remedy, resort to an organically acceptable chemical, or remove and dispose of the infected plant. Many gardeners have reported success with natural remedies, so why not try these first?

New Plants

Whenever you buy or are given new herbs, check to make sure no pests are lurking under the leaves or in the leaf axils. A good prevention is to mix a couple of drops of mild dishwashing liquid in a bucket of water. Hold your hand over the soil area or cover the soil with plastic to prevent it from falling out, invert the plant, plunge it into the water and swish it around gently.

Garlic

Garlic is a wonderful herb for the organic gardener. Not only does it taste great but it has a pungent aroma that is useful in deterring many flying pests. Garlic also has fungicidal as well as insecticidal properties and helps to clean up the soil and disinfect it. Also, rabbits do not like the aroma of garlic, so keep this in mind

LEFT: Handpicking large, slow-moving pests, such as snails, is an easy way to control damage.

RIGHT: Lure slugs with shallow dishes of beer. Sink the dish so that the top is level with the soil.

if they are a problem in your area.

Garlic works against some fungi and nematodes as well as many insect pests. If you're having problems in your garden, prepare an oil extract by mixing 3 oz (90 g) of finely minced garlic with 2 teaspoons of mineral oil. Allow it to stand for 24 hours, then add 2 cups (500 ml) of water. Mix and strain into a glass jar and store safely away from children. Combine 1–2 tablespoons of this concentrate with 2 cups (500 ml) of water before spraying on your plants. Adding a few drops of dishwashing liquid or soft soapflakes will help the solution stick to plant leaves.

Garlic

Earthworms

Start a compost bin with your kitchen vegetable and fruit scraps to encourage earthworms. Earthworms are invaluable in gardens as they not only burrow and create tiny tunnels that transport water to the plants' roots, but they aerate the soil as well. Worms also eat fungi and harmful insect eggs. A healthy compost will attract earthworms to your garden.

Baking Soda

For fungal problems, such as black spot and powdery mildew, try a baking soda (bicarbonate of soda) spray. Mix together 2 teaspoons of baking soda and 8 cups (2 l) of water. Use a clean spray bottle to drench your plants thoroughly with the mixture at the first sign of disease.

Natural Pest Controls

Snails
- Remove all debris from the garden.
- Pick them off by hand.
- Trap in a shallow container of beer set into the soil.
- Surround plants with sand or sawdust to discourage snails from reaching your plants.
- Spray with wormwood tea.
- Surround plants with copper strips.

Slugs
- Lure slugs by placing orange rind under flowerpots slightly raised on one side.
- Surround plants with sand or sawdust to discourage slugs from reaching your plants.
- Pick them off plants at night.
- Once collected, pour boiling water over the slugs. They will die instantly. Then, bury them in the garden.

Earwigs
- Trap them under inverted flowerpots on canes. Check traps daily and remove pests.

Ants
- Destroy ant nests by pouring boiling water over them.
- Encourage beneficial insects and small lizards into your garden.

Caterpillars
- Pick them off by hand.
- Spray with wormwood tea.

Aphids
- Spray with a hard jet of water from the hose.
- Encourage beneficial insects into your garden.
- Wipe them off by hand.
- Spray with a diluted solution of water and dishwashing liquid.
- Spray with a tea made from either basil, rhubarb or elder leaves.

Black spot, powdery mildew
- Spray with a baking soda mixture or nettle tea.

Mold
- Spray with elderflower tea or chive tea.

It's easy to handpick sawfly larvae as they rear up when disturbed.

Soap and Oil

To control a variety of insect pests, make up a soap and oil spray. Add 1 cup (250 ml) of soapy water to 1 cup (250 ml) of cooking oil. Mix 2 teaspoons of this per 1 cup (250 ml) of water for the spray. Neem oil is another botanical oil spray and is an excellent insect repellent.

Hot Dusts

To protect tender seedlings from root maggots, sprinkle hot seasonings, such as black pepper, chili pepper, dill, ginger, paprika and red pepper, over soil in a band on each side of the row after sowing. Make the bands several inches wide. Renew the application after heavy watering or rain.

Provide a water source in your garden to attract beneficial insects and insect-eating birds that will prey on pests.

Beer and Sawdust

Slugs and snails find beer irresistible. Sink a container into the soil so it is level with the soil surface and fill it with beer. Slugs and snails will be attracted to the beer and fall in and drown. You can also surround your herbs with a gritty substance, such as sawdust or sand. Slugs and snails will not walk over the surface so your herbs will be safe.

Companion Planting

Companion planting is the technique of growing together plants that will benefit each other. Companion planting uses ideas that gardeners have followed from earliest times to help them control pests and improve harvests. In past centuries, gardeners couldn't pop into their local garden center to pick up some insecticides or other pest deterrents—they had to rely on more natural means to control pests and make their gardens grow. Today, most gardeners have observed that certain herbs benefit the growth of nearby plants for a variety of reasons. Garlic and chives planted under roses deter greenfly, nasturtiums protect crops from aphids, while calendulas or pot marigolds attract hover flies whose larvae feed on aphids. If your crops of vegetables are regularly attacked by insects, you can use herb companion plants to hide, repel or trap pests. Repelling pests, however, is just one aspect of companion planting—attracting beneficial insects is another. Some herbs provide food and shelter to attract and protect beneficial insects.

Mixed plantings of flowers and herbs make it difficult for pests to track down their food. In addition, beneficial insects are attracted to mixed gardens because they can find food and shelter.

Fragrant herbs, such as lemon balm, scented geraniums and thyme, are popular and efficient repellents of insect and animal pests. Interplant them in your flower garden.

Repelling with Smells

Many insects use their sense of smell to find their way to favored crops. Onion maggots, for example, are lured to your onions by the sulfur compounds the crop releases. You can use herbs in companion planting to protect your plants by masking odors with other powerful smells. Garlic, for example, releases deterrent aromas into the air that may chase away insects, such as bean beetles and potato pests. Onions can prevent pests from attacking strawberries or tomatoes, while mint may keep cabbage loopers off cabbage plants. Basil is a popular companion plant as it discourages tomato hornworms or caterpillars, and is thought to improve growth and flavor. Try pungent herbs as an edging around garden beds, or mix them in among your crops of other herbs or vegetables. If you can't grow the repellent herbs close enough to your crops, you can spread clippings of these strong-smelling plants over garden beds for the same effect.

Luring Pests from Your Garden

Some plants have an almost irresistible appeal for certain pests. Nasturtiums, for instance, are an excellent attractant plant because they're a favorite of aphids. Attractant plants can protect your crops in two ways. First, they act as decoys to lure pests away from your crops. Second, they make it easier to control the pests because the insects are concentrated on a few plants. Once the pests are trapped, you can either pull the attractant plants and destroy them along with the pests, or apply some other type of control measure to the infested plants.

Beneficial Insects

Not all insects are enemies of your garden. Many help your garden grow by eating the plant pests. You can encourage these beneficial insects to make a home in your garden by planting their favorite flowering plants. Growing dill, for

Marigolds for Nematodes

Marigolds are probably the most widely grown companion plants. Many gardeners swear by their power to repel all kinds of pests. So far, scientists have only been able to show that marigolds can affect root knot nematodes and root lesion nematodes, which are microscopic soil-dwelling pests. The roots, and to a lesser extent the shoots, produce compounds called thiophenes. Researchers are not sure whether these chemical compounds kill nematodes outright or if the nematodes become trapped within marigold roots and the thiophenes keep them from reproducing. No matter how they work, you can use marigolds to clear nematodes out of the soil before or after planting susceptible crops. Plant any cultivar (but old-fashioned, strong-smelling types are best) and for good results, space the plants evenly over the bed and grow them through the whole season. Chop up the tall stems and turn everything under at the end of the season. As marigolds decay, they'll kill anything you plant. But by spring, the soil is safe for planting again.

Marigolds

The key to successful companion planting is to increase the diversity of your garden plants.

Good Companion Groupings

Combining plants with complementary growing habits makes good use of your garden's resources as well as the most efficient use of garden space.

Heavy Feeders

- Asparagus, celery, corn, parsley, bell peppers (capsicum), rhubarb, sunflowers.

Light Feeders

- Basil, cilantro (coriander), dill, fennel, garlic, leeks, onions, sage, thyme.

Height Groupings

- Cabbage (short, bushy) with thyme (sprawling).
- Corn (tall, upright) with squash (sprawling).
- Tomatoes (tall, bushy) with basil (short, bushy).

Herbs to Repel Insects

- Grow rosemary with cabbage, broccoli and cauliflower, to repel cabbage caterpillars and cabbage root maggots.
- Grow rue or garlic with roses to repel aphids.
- Grow tansy with roses to repel insects and improve vigor.
- Grow chives with carrots to deter carrot rust fly and improve growth and flavor.

Herbs for Beneficial Insects

- Hyssop flowers attract bees and other pollinating insects.
- Marjoram attracts bees.
- Sunflowers attract ladybugs and lacewings.
- Dill attracts many beneficial insects.
- Cilantro attracts tachinid flies and bees.
- Lemon balm attracts bees.
- Yarrow hosts hover flies and predatory wasps.

example, can attract pest-eating spiders, lacewings and parasitic wasps, which in turn will help to control caterpillars on cabbages, beetles on cucumbers and aphids on lettuces.

Complementary Crops

Some herbs make ideal vegetable garden companions because they don't compete, even when planted close together in small spaces. Deep-rooted plants, such as horseradish, and shallow-rooted plants, such as onions, occupy different soil zones so their roots can draw on different nutrient sources. Plants that need a lot of nutrients, such as heavy-feeding corn, combine well with light feeders, such as garlic. Taller plants, such as corn and sunflowers, can provide welcome light shade for ground-hugging cucumbers and lettuce. Besides making more efficient use of space, mixing plants with compatible growth habits also increases the diversity in your garden. Our gardens tend to contain plantings of just a few different plant species that are prime targets for insect and disease attack. Increasing the diversity of your plantings is a natural and effective way to minimize pest and disease problems.

Besides being colorful and easy to grow, nasturtiums may lure aphids from your crops.

Hostile Herbs

Just as some plants grow especially well together, a few are able to keep other plants from crowding in around them. This is called allelopathy. Allelopathic plants release inhibitory chemicals into the soil or air—a good trick for making sure nothing is going to compete with a plant for its share of rooting space, moisture and nutrients.

Fennel inhibits the growth of such vegetables as tomatoes and beans.

Chemical Release

Chemical compounds released by some living and decomposing plants—including legumes, grains, brassicas and marigolds—can lower the yields of existing crop plants, stunt growth, kill seedlings and limit seed germination. Chrysanthemums *Dendranthema* x *grandiflorum*, for instance, produce an allelopathic compound in their leaves. When the compound washes out of the leaves into the ground, it is said to prevent lettuce seeds from germinating. Red clover *Trifolium pratense* releases many different compounds that prevent new red clover seedlings from sprouting. Gray sage *Salvia leucophylla* releases a volatile compound that drifts to the earth nearby and stops the seedling growth of many species.

Chrysanthemum

Researchers and gardeners are continually learning more about the ways different plants can restrict the growth of others. Some more common examples are:

- Common wormwood can interfere with plant growth, especially when interplanted with other herbs.
- Fennel can inhibit the growth of vegetables and other herbs.
- Parsley is said to be a poor companion for lettuce and mint.
- Growing peas and beans near garlic, shallots or chives will produce a poor result, no matter what the soil and weather conditions.
- Corn, when young, releases water-soluble compounds that are allelopathic and fungicidal.
- Garlic is thought to be a hostile companion for a number of plants, including strawberries and cabbage.
- Evening primrose and peppergrass can stop the germination of other seeds, including crown vetch.
- Broccoli and cabbage are allelopathic.
- Cereal crop residues tend to be allelopathic and inhibit some fungal growth. Barley and oats can inhibit nutrient absorption in peas and hairy vetch (although the legumes encourage it in barley and oats). Rye seedlings are strongly allelopathic but grow more benign as they mature.
- Sunflowers are widely allelopathic and also inhibit nitrogen fixation. The seed hulls contain a compound similar to juglone, the allelopathic chemical released by black walnuts.

Red clover

Dealing with Difficult Plants

What does allelopathy mean for your garden? Whenever possible, keep strongly allelopathic plants, such as black walnuts and sunflower residues, away from planting areas to reduce the chance of crop damage. (Woven landscape fabrics or paving stones around the base of bird feeders make it easier to clean up seed hulls and avoid the patches of bare lawn under the feeder.)

In many cases, it's hard to identify when allelopathy is at work. The actual effect can be influenced by the soil, the amount of rainfall and by the plants themselves. If some of your crops are growing poorly and you've ruled out pests, diseases and nutrient imbalances, consider that allelopathy might be the cause and try growing those plants elsewhere or with different companion plants next year.

Allelopathy isn't always a problem in the garden. You may want to try using allelopathy to your advantage for keeping weeds and other vegetation under control. Annual rye is particularly useful for this in the vegetable garden. As it decomposes, it suppresses the growth of weeds, such as redroot pigweed, chickweed, ragweed and green foxtail. Grow it as a cover crop and turn it under while potent and young to choke out weeds. Or grow it separately in the garden and clip the growth regularly to use as a mulch.

Beware of Black Walnuts

Of all the plants with allelopathic properties, black walnut *Juglans nigra* is probably the most notorious. It was noted as far back as 50 AD that many plants grew poorly near this tree. We now know that black walnuts contain a compound called juglone. (Juglone is the material that will dye your hands brown if you handle ripe walnut husks.)

Black walnut

Rain dissolves juglone from the leaves and washes it down into the rooting area, killing or stunting many kinds of plants. Rhododendrons, blackberries, tomatoes, alfalfa and apple trees are some of the plants affected. A few plants that usually tolerate juglone include onions, corn, raspberries, grapes, forsythia and Kentucky bluegrass. Which plants survive under black walnuts and which ones don't can vary widely from place to place, depending on factors such as the soil conditions and the amount of rainfall. If you have black walnut trees, it's usually a trial and error process to see what plants will thrive or merely survive in your particular garden conditions.

When Companion Planting Doesn't Work

Experiment with companion planting and keep a record of your results. Even failures can be useful for future reference. You may find that a combination that was recommended by someone else simply doesn't work in your garden. If this occurs, try to figure out why the combination didn't work. Was there an allelopathic plant nearby? Was it due to an early hot spell that caused pests to emerge sooner than expected? Or did you forget to pull out the trap crop before pests spread to your good plants? If a particular combination performs poorly the first year, don't give up on it immediately; consider giving it another try a season or two later. Use your notes to compare the results for both years for the best results in your garden.

Beware of planting evening primrose among your other plants—it could suppress seed germination.

Wormwood *Artemisia absinthium* is a large perennial herb with gray-green leaves and a strong scent. Companion gardeners note that few plants thrive when planted near it. Glandular hairs on the surface of the leaves produce volatile oils and an inhibiting toxin called absinthin. Rain or watering washes these substances from the leaves and stunts nearby plants, such as mint or oregano.

Month by Month in the Herb Garden

Northern Hemisphere

When should you divide your perennials? What can you do in the garden on a cold, windy November day? Even experienced gardeners sometimes forget what needs to be done in the garden and when to do it. In this section, you'll find a month-by-month calendar for both the Northern and Southern hemispheres, with handy reminders of the garden jobs that are appropriate for each month of the year.

The calendar below for the Northern hemisphere is based on Zone 6, where the frost-free growing season is approximately late April to mid-October. If your garden is in a different zone, it is easy to adapt this calendar to fit your region. To find out which zone you are in, check the USDA Plant Hardiness Zone Maps on pages 270–272.

In warmer climates (Zones 7–9), spring comes sooner, so do the spring chores a month or two earlier and wait until the first frost to do your autumn cleanup. In Zone 10, you can still benefit from an autumn cleanup and mulching, depending on microclimates; but there will be less of a rest period during the cooler months and weeding, watering and dealing with pests will continue through more months of the year. In colder zones and at high elevations (where the frost-free season is short), this calendar will be about a month or more ahead of you in spring. Delay doing your spring tasks, and start your autumn jobs earlier before cold weather closes in.

When the weather begins to warm, clean up winter debris to eliminate sites for pests and diseases.

January

Review any notes that you made about last year's garden; transfer important reminders (such as plants to move or divide) to a list or calendar for the coming year. Start new garden plans or revise existing ones. Take stock of stored tender bulbs, and any seeds that you've collected and stored; toss out any that are damaged. Heavy snow kills garden pests, but its weight can break branches, so shake it off. Secure plants against strong winds and repair any heaving caused by frost.

February

Order summer-flowering bulbs and spring seeds, and consider what you can raise ahead indoors, or in a greenhouse if you have one. If weather conditions are good, do some winter digging and weeding, but don't work or walk on wet soil. Plant bare-rooted shrubs and trees, and prune existing deciduous ones. Sow caper seed indoors—germination will take about 3 months. Mend fences and trellises and do a winter cleanup.

March

In good weather, clean up any winter debris and enjoy early spring bulbs, such as aconites, snowdrops and narcissus. Pull some of the winter mulch off garden beds so the soil can begin to warm up for new plantings. Start early spring pruning of shrubs and trees, such as roses, before growth begins. You can begin to sow herbs under protection outdoors—most herbs are spring sown. Turn last year's compost pile so it will be ready to spread when the ground warms up. Take soil tests.

April

Spring is truly here, although the weather can be fickle. Growth is burgeoning, but still protect any vulnerable plants from frosty nights. Finish your garden cleanup, and continue weeding and digging beds for new plantings. Add plenty of compost, well-rotted manure and fertilizers as needed, according to your soil test results. Scout for pests. In dry climates, install a drip irrigation system for easy watering once the weather warms up. Plant garlic cloves.

Orris root

Remove spent bulb flowers but leave the foliage until it dies back so plants can store enough energy to flower well the following year. Divide summer- and autumn-flowering perennials. Plant annuals and biennials, such as anise, basil, borage and parsley, and perennials, such as salvia, rosemary, catmint and lemon balm, as soon as the ground warms up.

May

Plant mail order and container-grown perennials. You can still divide and replant spring-blooming perennials and crowded bulbs after they flower, but this is best done during dormancy. Sow annuals, and plant tender perennials and bulbs outside once danger of frost has passed. Replace and replenish mulches.

Pinch back perennials that tend to get leggy, such as oregano. Prune lavender and most spring flowering shrubs after flowering. Continue successive sowing of herbs, such as cress and mustard, and continue sowing other herb seeds, such as nasturtium, savory, dill and chervil. Pull or dig weed seedlings. If slugs or snails are a problem in your garden, set out shallow pans of beer to trap them.

June

Walk through your garden regularly, both to enjoy it and to scout for problems. Remove and destroy diseased foliage. Stake annuals and perennials that need support. Remove spent blossoms to prevent plants from self-seeding, unless you want to collect the seed. Water moisture-loving plants if rainfall is scarce. Potted herbs need regular watering in dry periods and sometimes daily watering in

Take semiripe cuttings of lavender in summer. Trim after flowering to keep bushes compact.

hot weather. You'll need a plantsitter or automatic irrigation if taking summer holidays. Sow or plant out parsley. Take cuttings from rosemary and sage. Harvest herbs for fresh use or for freezing or drying.

July

Water, weed and mulch and keep a watch for pests. If the weather is very dry, consider watering the compost pile, too; it breaks down faster when evenly moist. Deadhead herbs, particularly those where you want leaves rather than flowers. Sow perennial herb seeds, such as horehound, feverfew and lavender. Cut herbs for fresh and dried use regularly to maintain a supply of fresh young shoots. Harvest scented geranium leaves for drying, and take cuttings. Harvest flowers, such as nasturtiums, for decorative salads and for potpourris.

August

Feed and water leafy herbs if needed. Check for fungal diseases. Trim back plants which are getting leggy. Use trimmings for herbal teas, herb sachets and potpourris. Weed and prepare beds for autumn planting and dividing. Pot up strawberry runners.

Divide and plant bearded irises, and at the end of the month, divide peonies. Keep weeding and deadheading. Remove tattered, damaged or browning foliage, which may attract disease. Cut flowers before they open fully for using in floral arrangements, potpourris or drying. Cut leafy herbs for drying just when they start to bloom. Trim back flowered lavenders.

September

September is often a dry month, so keep deadheading, weeding and controlling pests. Autumn is a good time to divide and replant herbaceous perennials as they finish the season. Dig up and rearrange plants in beds, and plant new container-grown perennials and shrubs. Keep them regularly watered until they are established, to promote good root development. Now is the time to sow caraway, and to start new beds. Plant a cover crop, such as winter rye, to protect the soil over winter. Or dig in autumn leaves; they will decompose by spring. Now is a good time to get your soil tested if you didn't in March, and to correct pH imbalances.

October

Continue dividing plants and sow herb seeds, such as borage and lovage. Cover or protect tender plants on nights when frost is expected. Pull annuals after frost and toss them in the compost pile, or leave them if you want to collect seed. Cut back finished perennials. Remove and destroy any diseased foliage. Rake leaves for the compost pile or till them into new beds. Record where you planted any bulbs so you won't dig into them when you plant annuals in the spring. Water perennial beds (as well as new shrub and bulb plantings) thoroughly before they go dormant to help them survive the cold winter months as frozen ground locks up water. Lift parsley and mint and pot up for winter use. Harvest basil leaves for freezing. Harvest autumn roots and berries to enjoy through winter.

November

Continue harvesting seeds, roots and berries. Divide perennials and tidy beds. Drain and store hoses; shut off and drain outdoor water taps. Take stock of gardening tools, and clean and oil them. Sow angelica outdoors for spring germination. Sow strawberries. Divide lavender and replant in suitable areas. Bring pots of bay or citrus indoors or into shelter if you have not already done so.

December

Apply a winter mulch to protect plants from wind and frost heaving, if you don't get a regular blanket of snow. Lay branches over ground covers and low-growing plants to protect them. Make a wish list of garden supplies for Christmas presents. Buy a new calendar for next year's garden.

Order raspberries in May for winter planting. Enjoy the harvest in late summer or autumn.

Southern Hemisphere

The calender for the Southern hemisphere is based on Zone 10, but can be adapted to climates in other zones. If you live in a warmer climate, you will not be exposed to a cold winter, but remember to keep up the watering during the dry season. In colder zones and at high elevations, this calender will be a month ahead of you in spring, so delay some of your chores.

January

Summer is in full swing and you are now reaping the rewards of some of the hard work and preparation you did earlier in the season. Herbs are now growing quickly and it is important to care for them by watering, mulching, trimming and feeding when necessary. This will provide high returns in the form of healthy plants and abundant flowers. Harvest fresh leaves, shoots and flowers to encourage the production of more fresh, young shoots. Use leaves in cooking, and flowers to decorate salads or drinks, or use both in potpourris and other herbal crafts. If you don't want flowers in leafy herbs, snip them off and regularly deadhead all herbs. January is also a good time to cut leafy herbs for drying just before they start to flower. Collect in the cool of the morning after the dew has gone, tie in bunches and hang in a cool, dark, dry area. In this holiday period, make sure good watering arrangements are in place if you go away. Sow calendulas in mild climates from now until late autumn.

February

Usually the hottest month of the year. Remember to water the compost heap in dry weather—compost breaks down much faster when it is evenly wet. This is a good time to repair mulches, after rain or deep watering, to lock in the moisture. Not only does a compost mulch add vital nutrients to the soil, it also keeps plant roots cool and at an even temperature during hot weather. Mulching encourages earthworms, and helps to protect plants from the harsh effects of salt. You don't have to live near the ocean to be troubled with salty soils—salt is left as a residue after the application of some fertilizers and is also present in tap water. Good mulches include lucerne, straw, leaves, pine bark, composted grass clippings and even pebbles, newspapers or old pieces of carpet. Black plastic is not recommended because it does not allow moisture to penetrate or air to circulate.

March

Autumn is now here. Taking semi-hardwood cuttings of your favorite herbs. It is best to do this on dull, moist days and never in the heat of the day. To prolong the life of some annual herbs, cut off all flowering heads (once the plant flowers, all energy goes into seed production). If you want to save some seed for next year, select the healthiest plants and allow them to set seed. Tie small brown paper bags around the maturing seedpods to collect the seed as it falls. Clean, dry and store in a cool, dry place if planting in spring, but some seeds can be autumn planted, and some herbs, such as lemon balm, will self-seed. Make sure you label stored seeds with the herb name and date of harvest. Harvest berries, roots and rhizomes.

April

Harvest any remaining leaves then pull out finished annuals. Divide perennials that are dying back. This can be done through autumn and during a mild winter. You can also redesign the herb garden and transplant plants without stressing them too much. Autumn can be dry, so water when necessary, but too much moisture on leaves may encourage fungal diseases or root rot. Water at ground level or early in the day so leaves can dry out.

May

Plant spring bulbs this month and make a note of where you have planted them so that you won't dig them up during spring planting. Give the garden a good cleanup and remove all dead or damaged plant material, because good garden hygiene can help reduce overwintering diseases. Order asparagus, blackberries, elderberry, horseradish, raspberries, rhubarb and strawberries for winter planting.

June

Mulch in frost-prone areas. As in summer, mulching protects soil and roots from temperature extremes, and may make the difference between your plants surviving or not. Winter is a good time to do general garden maintenance that tends to be neglected in the flurry of activity in spring and summer. Repair paving and paths; mend fences or trellises. Take stock of your gardening tools—mend, repair or replace and clean in readiness for the new season. Pot up, divide or transplant dormant plants. Plant roses and other deciduous shrubs. Prune back straggly perennials and deciduous trees and shrubs.

July

Prune roses. Give a general winter clean-up and check what pest control measures are needed. Keep up with weeding. Catch up on all those gardening journals that have been piling up and get some new ideas for your herb garden design. Carry out any winter digging to be done. Check that your herbs are in the right areas. Are sun-loving herbs being relegated to shady areas and looking leggy or not thriving? Use this book to check on individual herbs' requirements in terms of sunlight and soil, and reposition if needed. Plants given the right conditions will reward you with vigorous growth and a good resistance to pests and diseases. Take root cuttings of herbs.

August

As spring is only a month away, days are starting to lengthen and warm up. If you mulched in winter, pull it back to allow the soil to begin to warm up. Prepare garden beds for planting by clearing all weeds and digging in well-rotted manure or good quality compost. Order the seeds and plants you want from mail order catalogs.

September

Spring is officially here and it's a wonderful time to be outdoors. In spring, you can sow many herb seeds, including angelica, basil, sweet woodruff, caraway, chervil, chamomile and dill. Sow your seeds in good-quality seed-raising mix in punnets, trays or pots, and place in a warm, sheltered, protected position. Cover seeds with a sheet of glass or plastic film to retain moisture and humidity during germination. Or sow direct—check seed packet instructions. Not only will herb seeds be starting to germinate, but so too will weed seeds that have been lying dormant over winter. One way to avoid an influx of weeds is to cover the surface of the garden bed with a thick covering of compost and mulch and plant seedlings into this. Protect your young plants from pests by using a cover. A cheap and effective cover is to cut plastic drink bottles in half and upend them over young plants. This will provide a warm, humid environment for the growing plant as well as preventing predators reaching vulnerable shoots. By the time the plant has grown too big for the container, it will be robust enough to withstand future pest attack.

Mustard

October

Bulbs planted in autumn should be blooming. It is important to fertilize well at this intense growing stage—not only will it determine the quality of foliage and flowers, but also the health of next year's crop. Maintain weed and pest control. Sow clary and other sages. Look for some of the perennial herbs available in pots at the nursery, and plant container-grown shrubs, such as gardenia or rosemary.

November

Days are getting hotter and the garden is responding. Keep the watering up to the plants and also to the compost heap. Snails can be a problem with young seedlings, so place saucers of beer around to tempt the snails and slugs. Replace regularly. Check for other pests, such as aphids, mites or scale. Continue sowing herbs, such as cress and mustard. Sow parsley. Take mint and other herb softwood cuttings.

December

This is a beautiful time of year to be in the garden. Keep scouting for pests and weeds and apply quality compost and organic fertilizers. Top up mulch and cut flower heads to prevent premature ripening of annual plants. Harvest fresh herbs regularly for the kitchen, crafts and potpourri. Cut herbs for drying at their peak, usually before flowering.

Sow echinacea seeds in spring for a colorful display of flowers in summer and early autumn.

SECTION SIX

Preserving, Storing and Using Herbs

For centuries, herbs were an essential part of everyday life. They played a significant role in everyone's diet, were made into cosmetics and beauty products and provided the main source of medical treatment. Today, herbs can be used in similar ways. Fresh herbs can be cut for culinary, medical or cosmetic use throughout their growing season, but for a year-round supply, you can dry or freeze herbs to preserve them for later use.

Harvesting Herbs

The best time to harvest your herbs depends on how you want to use them. If you plan to use fresh herbs immediately, you may pick and use them whenever you need them. For herbs that are to be dried or otherwise preserved, however, the best picking time is early morning, just after the dew has dried, but before the sun has had a chance to warm them. The reason is that essential oils, the components that give herbs their flavor and fragrance, lose their quality when exposed to heat.

There's nothing harmful about morning dew, but wet leaves require a longer drying period before you can store them. For the same reason, refrain from harvesting on rainy days. A cool, dry, sunny morning is best.

Your climate and the plant's maturity are other factors that influence the time of harvesting. Cold-climate gardeners will have fewer chances to harvest; they're happy to get their herbs up and growing before the frosts return. Gardeners in warmer climates have the advantage of a longer growing season, and the chance to harvest more often.

Saffron stigmas are harvested for their rich flavor and color. Each flower produces three stigmas which are collected by hand at dawn.

Bay, thyme, parsley, chives, mint and sage are all useful herbs in the kitchen and can be used fresh from the herb garden or dried.

Perennials

Avoid heavy harvests of perennial herbs during the first year of growth, to allow them to establish themselves in their new surroundings and to encourage root growth. You may trim them lightly to promote bushiness.

Once they're established, you can harvest up to two-thirds of the foliage of a hardy perennial at one time in the spring and again in summer. In colder climates, take only a third of the growth in autumn and stop cutting 40 to 60 days before you expect the first frost. During winter, perennials will subsist mainly on foods they have stored in their roots. Plenty of foliage and lots of autumn sun will let perennials manufacture and store adequate food for winter and the following spring's new growth. If food reserves are low, they are less likely to make it through a stressful winter. In warmer climates, plants will suffer little winter stress and the plants' dormant period may be relatively short. In these areas gardeners can harvest lightly right into late autumn.

Annuals

Since annuals are limited to one season of growth, your only concern in cold climates is harvesting as much as you can before the killing autumn frosts. The same is true if you are growing biennial herbs, such as parsley and clary, for their foliage. During the growing season, harvest annuals and biennials for foliage so that at least 4 to 5 inches (10 to 12.5 cm) of growth remains. A good rule is to harvest no more than the top half of the plant at one cutting. Most annuals and biennials may be harvested several times each season. Before the first frosts, you can cut annual plants to the ground, or pull them up for drying. If you are growing biennial plants, such as caraway, for their seeds, avoid harvesting the foliage the first year. The more energy the plants can make and store, the more seeds they can set the following year. Test for seed harvesting by tapping the stems of the herb. If seeds fall, then the stems are ready to be cut.

Harvesting for Crafts

Most of the fragrant herbs commonly used as wreath backing, or as the base of dried arrangements, should be cut when they're flowering. If you're collecting flowers such as yarrow for dried arrangements, wait until full bloom or just before. Cut them with plenty of stem. Southernwood may be cut back by a third after its first flush of spring growth, then again in late summer. Collect rose petals at full bloom, after the morning dew has dried. When cutting lavender, harvest the whole stem with the attached flower heads, just before the blooms are fully opened.

Southernwood

Nettles can be used to make a soothing tea, but wear gloves when harvesting them because they sting. However, they lose the sting if boiled.

How to Harvest

Use sharp scissors or a garden knife when harvesting your herbs. If you're collecting leaves, cut the whole stem, then strip away the foliage. With small-leaved perennials, such as rosemary and thyme, save only the leaves and discard the stems—or use them for potpourris or as kabob skewers. When harvesting herbs that spread from a central growing point, such as parsley and sorrel, harvest the outer stems or leaves first. If you're collecting leaves or flowers from bushy plants, do so from the top of the plant; new growth will come from below.

Of course, you can harvest foliage and flowers from both perennials and annuals continuously if you're just snipping a few leaves and blooms here and there to collect the ingredients for a recipe.

Herbs retain their best qualities if they're left unwashed until it's time to use them. Some growers advise sprinkling the plants the day before harvesting, to wash away the dirt and dust. If your plants are surrounded by a mulch that limits their contact with soil, you may not have to wash them. If they are gritty with soil, however, you can swish them through cold water and pat them dry, or hang them in the shade to drip.

If you plan to dry your herbs, bunching them as you collect them saves handling time later. Collect enough stems to make a 1-inch (2.5-cm) thick bundle, then wrap a rubber band over the cut ends. When harvesting annuals in autumn, simply pull and hang the whole plant, after first cutting away the roots and soil. For example, harvest plants of lemon balm, tie stems in a bunch, and hang indoors or outdoors in a dry, shady, airy place as soon as possible. Expose all herbs to minimum sun and light after harvesting.

Harvesting for the Kitchen

Rosemary

For the best flavor, harvest herbs just before the buds open, which is when the concentration of essential oils is greatest. It's especially important to follow this rule if you are harvesting a large quantity to dry or freeze for winter. See "Drying Herbs" on pages 144–145 and "Preserving and Storing Herbs" on pages 146–147.

Herbs grown for their seeds should be harvested after the seeds have turned from green to brown—but make sure you harvest them before they begin to fall from the plant. For garnish or flavor, harvest fresh blossoms such as chives, borage or calendula at full bloom or just before. If you're picking chamomile flowers (see picture below) for tea, pinch them off when they are fully open.

Harvest herbs grown for their roots when the roots are fully developed in autumn. Carefully scrape the soil away from the base of the plant, and use a sharp knife to harvest some of the largest roots. Or you could use a spading fork to lift the whole plant out of the ground for an easier harvest. Either way, make sure that you leave some roots on the plant so it can re-establish itself and provide future harvests. Replant or backfill with the soil you removed, and water the plant to settle it back into the soil. Scrub the harvested roots well before using or drying.

Drying Herbs

Some growers claim that dried, summer-grown herbs have better flavor than herbs grown indoors in winter. If you enjoy cooking with herbs, you may want to try preserving some of your summer garden's bounty for use in winter recipes. Most herbs dry easily, and under the proper conditions they will retain their characteristic aroma and flavor.

Dried herbs store best in cool, dark places. Store those that you plan to use for cooking in airtight containers. If you like the look of the bunches, hang some others around the house solely for decoration.

Where to Dry Herbs

The best place for drying herbs is somewhere dry and dark, with good ventilation. Depending on what the weather is like, you may find it necessary to speed up the process with fans, dehumidifiers, or an air conditioner. The best weather conditions for air-drying are low humidity and soft breezes.

Drying screens and bunches of herbs can be placed in a dry attic, around the hot-water heater, on top of the refrigerator, or in a gas oven with a pilot light. Barns make excellent drying sheds as long as they are shady and well ventilated. In summer, some gardeners dry their herbs on small drying screens placed inside the car. Just cover the herbs with a single layer of paper toweling and park the car in light shade.

If the weather hasn't cooperated and the drying process seems painfully slow, you can speed up the action in your oven. Place your herbs on baking sheets and set the oven temperature to its lowest setting. Monitor progress until leaves are crispy dry.

Drying in Bunches

Long-stemmed herbs such as lavender, mint and yarrow are easy to dry in bunches. Select only the highest-quality foliage and blossoms, removing any dead or wilted leaves. Make bunches about 1 inch (2.5 cm) in diameter for quick drying; the number of stems in each bunch will naturally vary. You can tie the bunches with string, leaving a loop for hanging, but small rubber bands are easier to use.

Fasten your bunches on wire clothes hangers. Hold the bunched stems along one side of the horizontal wire of the hanger, then pull a loop of the rubber band down and then up over the wire. Pull the band over the stems and release it. Hanging one full hanger in one spot is easier than hanging separate bunches all over the place. Have a separate hanger for each herb species or cultivar to make organization easy. You can label each bunch or each hanger. When you're ready to use the herbs, simply pull the bunch down to release it.

If dust is a problem, you can dry long-stemmed herbs in paper bags. Punch a hole in the bottom of the bag, secure the stems and hang to dry. Cut flaps in the bag to increase air circulation.

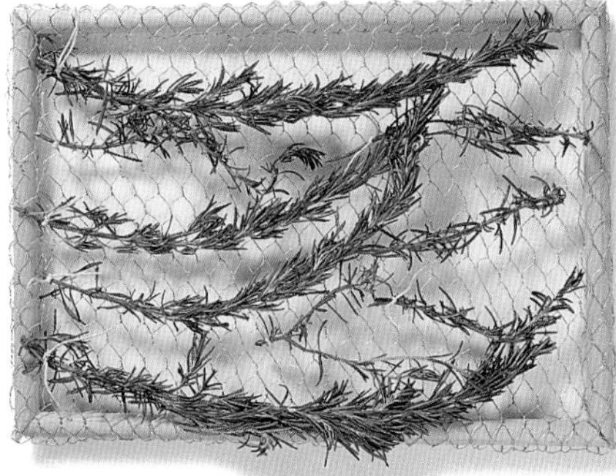

LEFT: You can construct your own screens with scrap lumber and window screening or wire.

RIGHT: For very simple storage, hang your herb bunches from clothes hangers. First, wrap each bunch with a rubber band. Then take one loop under the bottom of the hanger. Bring it up over the wire and the top of the stems to secure the bunch.

Hang your herbs where you have plenty of space, and where you can leave them undisturbed until they're dry. If your house has exposed ceiling rafters, arrange wooden dowels along them and hang the herbs from the dowels. Single bunches may be hung from conveniently placed hooks or nails. When the bunches are crispy dry, remove the leaves from the stems.

Brown Bag Method If dust is a problem, place the bunches inside paper bags. Punch a hole in the base of the bag, then pull the stems through the hole, and fasten them with string. Hang the bag in a cool, dry place. To increase air circulation, cut flaps in the side of the bag. After one week, look inside a few bags to make sure the herbs are drying and free of mold. They may take up to two weeks to become crisp and crumbly. (Seeds can be dried in the same way by placing seed heads, with stems up, in an unpunched paper bag.) When the herbs are dry, remove the stems and spread the leaves on a baking sheet. Place the baking sheet in an oven, set at about 100°F (40°C), for several minutes to complete the drying process.

Drying on Screens

Herbs with short stems and small leaves, such as thyme, are difficult to bunch. The best drying method is simply to snip off the foliage with scissors and spread it on a screen in a single layer. You can also dry herbs with large leaves on screens, but first strip the foliage from the stems. Hold the stems upside down in one hand while running the other hand down the stem. Loose herb blossoms and flower petals can also be dried on screens.

You can construct your own screens with scrap lumber and window screening, then set them on bricks so that air can circulate freely. If the herbs are fine, spread paper on the screen first. Your herbs should be dry in seven to ten days.

Drying in the Oven

Probably the best method for drying herbs is oven-drying, since the herbs dry quickly and retain their aromatic oils. In a conventional oven, spread the herbs one layer deep on paper toweling on baking sheets. It is best to start with the temperature set at around 80° to 100°F (25° to 38°C). If you smell the herbs, immediately lower the temperature to avoid losing essential oils. Stir once every half hour. Drying should be complete in three to six hours. Herbs with fleshy leaves will take longer to dry than those with tiny or thin leaves, so it is wise not to mix different leaf types in one batch. Remove the herbs when they are crispy dry, and before they turn brown. Food dehydrators are good for drying herbs, too. Follow the same instructions as for regular oven-drying.

Drying in the Microwave

You can also dry herbs in a microwave oven. Sandwich the herbs between sheets of microwave-safe paper towels. Put a cup of water in the microwave while drying the herbs. Leave the herbs in the oven for about one minute on a low setting then remove them and check for dryness. If they're still a little bit moist, repeat the process for a few seconds. Watch the herbs carefully during drying, and stop the process if any sparks appear. If your herbs turn brown or black, try heating for shorter periods.

Drying Herb Seeds

Many of the herbs you'll grow are used for their seeds. If you're collecting cilantro (coriander), dill, caraway or other herb seeds for the kitchen, snip off the seed heads when they have turned brown. Before drying seeds for culinary use, blanch them to destroy any minute insect pests that may hide inside. Gather the seeds in a piece of muslin or cheesecloth and dip them in boiling water. Alternatively, place the seeds in a sieve and pour boiling water over them. Shake well. Spread the seeds on paper or a fine mesh screen to dry in the sun. If you plan to sow the seeds, don't blanch. Just dry them in the sun for several days before transferring them to a cool, dry location.

To dry seeds, place seed heads inside a paper bag, stem up. After two weeks, the seeds will collect at the bottom of the bag.

Preserving and Storing Herbs

When your herbs have dried thoroughly, strip the leaves from their stems or remove them from the drying screens. Discard stems or save them to add to potpourris. If you're saving herbs for culinary use, crush them or push them through a coarse strainer. Leaves and blossoms saved for tea can be left whole. Crumble dried roots to sizes that will fit their use.

Store dried herb foliage, blossoms, roots or seeds in airtight containers away from bright light. Tins or canning jars with rubber seals work best. You can also pack the dried materials into resealable plastic bags, squeezing out the air before you seal them. Label your containers, since all dried herbs tend to look the same.

Bunches of herbs add a touch of summer to the kitchen and particularly suit the country-style kitchen. However, keep your culinary herbs in airtight containers in a cool, dry, dark place.

It's fine to dry your herbs on top of the refrigerator, but don't store them there. Ideally, dried herbs should be kept cool and dry. If you like the look of herb bunches strung about the kitchen, make them especially decorative with added ribbons or lace. Decorated jars of herbs can make attractive ornaments, but keep these separate from culinary herbs, which should be stored in airtight containers.

If your herbs are grown, harvested, dried and stored properly, they will remain green and fragrant for a long time. If you're in doubt, just crush a few leaves and sniff—scentless, brown herbs will have little flavor. Toss them away in your compost pile.

Freezing Herbs

1. Blanch herbs by holding the stems and dipping them in boiling water.

2. When the color brightens, remove from water and drain herbs on clean paper towel.

3. When dry and cool, lay the herbs in single layers on wax paper, then roll up and label.

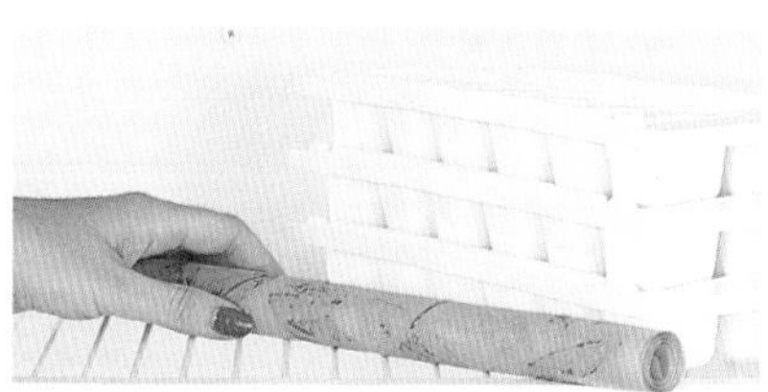

4. Store in the freezer for enjoyment through winter. Break off and use as needed.

Freezing Herbs

If you have more freezer space than cupboard space, you may want to freeze your herbs instead of drying them. Chervil, dill, fennel, marjoram, mint, parsley and tarragon freeze very well. Herb growers report mixed results with cilantro (coriander) and chives—it seems they freeze very well or very poorly. You'll have to experiment, and keep records of what works best for you.

Harvest the herbs at their peak and wash them gently but thoroughly, then pat dry. You can chop the herbs by hand, but the simplest method is to chop them in a food processor until the pieces are the right size to add to soups or other recipes. Pack them in freezer bags, squeezing out the air until you have a flat layer of herbs, and seal. Be sure to label the bags, since most frozen herbs look alike in the middle of winter. When you're ready to use them, simply break off a corner, or as much as you need, and return the bag to the freezer. Some people save fresh herbs by puréeing them with water or oil. Simply pour the purée into ice-cube trays and, when the cubes are solid, move them to labeled freezer bags. Herb cubes are easy to use—just toss them into soups or stews. Frozen basil retains the best quality when puréed in olive oil. It's easy to prepare winter pesto—mix in the cheese, pine nuts, and garlic as the basil thaws. Freeze some ready-made bouquets for soups, such as parsley, chives, chervil and tarragon.

Once your herbs have dried, strip the leaves from the stems and store in airtight containers.

Dried herbs and pot plants add fragrances and color to the kitchen.

Salting Herbs

Salting is an old method of culinary herb preservation, and it works especially well with basil, chives, garlic, marjoram, oregano, rosemary, savory, tarragon and thyme. Cooking with herb salt will add flavor to your meals and encourage you to reduce actual salt use. Harvest the herbs at their peak and wash and dry thoroughly. Then pack alternate layers of fresh leaves and salt in a glass jar. Make the first and last layers of salt thicker than the middle layers, which should be quite thin and just cover the herbs. Store the tightly sealed jar on a cool, dry shelf in the kitchen. Pick out the salted herbs for use in stews and sauces. Use the remaining flavored salt for salad dressings, roast meat, or wherever the flavor of herbs is needed.

Storing Herbs in Oil

Herbs keep well when stored in oil. Use only the very best olive oil. Place fresh, dry herb leaves in a glass jar and cover with oil. Seal and store in a dark place. Pick out the oiled herbs and use in cooking as needed. The oil takes on the flavor of the herbs and can be used in salad dressings and for cooking. For herb-flavored oil recipes see "Herbs in the Kitchen" on pages 148–155.

Herbs in the Kitchen

Herbs are a welcome addition to any kitchen. Your own herb garden, brimming with herbs that are useful for garnish, such as parsley and chives, and those that are important for flavor and aroma, such as basil and rosemary, lets you add a special touch to all your dishes. A pantry stocked with special herbal treats will also enable you to have something a little different for special meals or simply a treat. Sprinkle herbal vinegars and oils on salads all year round for a flavorsome alternative to bottled dressing. Herbal jellies and honeys are simple to prepare and can be used in a surprising number of ways, as well as making ideal gifts. And don't forget about candied flowers—these delicacies will last for months.

Cooking with Herbs

If you want to learn how to use culinary herbs, start simply by growing them. A bushy, fragrant herb plant just outside the kitchen door is the best inspiration for culinary success. If you've never used fresh herbs, start by following simple recipes that appeal to you. Most cookbooks offer a variety of dishes that require herbs for flavoring. Try something you've enjoyed in a restaurant but never made at home.

Another way to become familiar with herbs is to add them to foods you already make. Add snipped fresh herbs to scrambled eggs or omelets, trying a new herb each time. Or add them to bland foods, such as cottage cheese, cream cheese or rice. Once you've developed preferences for certain herbs, try combining them with other herbs in the same foods.

When using herbs, a little bit goes a long way. Culinary herbs should be used sparingly, to enhance the natural flavors of other ingredients in your recipes. Most herbs should be added at the end of the recipe. Their flavors are released with gentle heat, but are lost if cooked for longer than 30 minutes. An exception is bay, which stands up to a long stewing time.

Herbs go just as well in cold foods. Add them to butter or sour cream and refrigerate for several hours or overnight. The addition of lemon juice or vinegar speeds up the development of the flavors.

It's very important to wash and dry herbs thoroughly before using them in cooking. When using fresh herbs in recipes, save the leaves, flowers, stems or seeds. Snip the leaves with kitchen shears, or if you need larger quantities, bunch the leaves on a cutting board and mince the pile with a sharp knife. Food processors are useful for chopping large batches of herbs for recipes such as pesto or tabbouleh.

Many cooks rub fresh and dried herbs between their hands before adding them to the pot, because crushing the herbs releases their essential oils. If your recipe calls for a fine powder, grind dried herbs with a pestle and mortar, or purchase a special spice grinder. A coffee grinder works well, but be sure to wipe it clean carefully after use. Ground herbs should be used immediately for the best flavor. You can freeze the leftovers in airtight containers or plastic bags.

Using Fresh Herbs

You can substitute fresh for dried herbs in most recipes. Since fresh herbs contain more water than dried ones, use two to three times more fresh herbs than the dried measurement to get the same amount of essential oil.

Fresh herbs are great salad additions. Add chopped or whole sprigs of basil, chervil, chives, dill, oregano, thyme, tarragon or whatever flavors or blends you enjoy. Use herb blossoms from chives, borage and nasturtium to garnish the finished salad. Or use fresh herb leaves, such as nasturtiums, as a wrapping for pâté or softened cream cheese, rolled into bundles.

Culinary Terms

The following terms describe different culinary uses for herbs.

Bouquet Garni Add this "herb bouquet" to soups, stews and sauces, but remove it before serving. The essential oils provide a subtle flavor and aroma. Traditional bouquet garni includes a bay leaf, thyme, and parsley or chervil, all bunched together with string, or in a muslin bag. Tie the string to the pot handle to make removal easy. You may add other seasonings to suit your taste.

Fines Herbes Unlike bouquet garni, fines herbes are left in the food to add color as well as flavor. Mince together fresh herbs, such as basil, chervil, chives, marjoram, tarragon and thyme, and add them to sauces and omelets at the end of cooking.

Garnish A decoration or trim added to improve the appearance or flavor of food.

Infusion An infusion is made in the same way as a tea, but it is used as an ingredient in recipes. For instructions on making infusions, see "Medicinal Herbs" on pages 156–158.

Marinade A marinade tenderizes and flavors the foods that soak in it. Refrigerate pieces of meat or poultry in a marinade containing wine, vinegar and herbs for several hours or overnight, turning the pieces several times.

Ravigote Ravigote is a sauce of mixed and chopped herbs, such as tarragon, chives and parsley, with shallots, oil and wine vinegar.

Tisane This term usually refers to a tea made from fresh or dried herbs.

Herbs such as chili, bay, rosemary and garlic can transform a routine meal into a gourmet treat.

Herbal Vinegars

You can use herbal vinegars in most recipes that call for vinegar, including sauces, marinades and stews. Follow the simple instructions in the recipe below or experiment with your own. With experience, you'll learn how much of each herb to use for the best flavor. Some herb growers simply pack the jar with fresh herbs, then fill with vinegar (no need to measure); heat the vinegar almost to boiling—warm vinegar releases the essential oils faster.

Wine-based vinegars are ideal as a base for herbal vinegars, since their flavor is mild and blends well with that of herbs. Use white-wine vinegar with chive blossoms, lavender, marjoram, nasturtium flowers and leaves, dark opal and lemon basil, tarragon and thyme. Use red-wine vinegar with bay leaves, dill, fennel, garlic, lovage, mint, sweet basil and thyme.

Try combining several herbs to create your own special vinegars. Garlic and chives combine well with most of the strongly flavored herbs, such as basil, dill and thyme. Mix equal parts of parsley, thyme and rosemary for a special blend.

After two weeks, transfer the herb vinegar to sterilized decorative bottles that you can buy from cooking-supply stores or through catalogs. Or you can use recycled bottles from salad dressing, ketchup, sauce and wine.

For a special effect, seal the bottle caps with scented wax. Melt 1 cup (250 ml) of paraffin or candle wax with 1/4 cup of mixed spices (try cinnamon, nutmeg, cloves or allspice) in a tall can placed in 1 inch (2.5 cm) of water in a saucepan. Melt the mixture slowly (paraffin wax ignites easily). Make sure the vinegar bottles are capped tightly, then turn them over and dip the top of each bottle (just past the cap) into the melted wax. Dip them several times, allowing the wax to dry (less than 30 seconds) between dips. Add more wax and spices as needed. You can store any leftover wax in the same can. Let the bottles cool before handling them. To open, lightly score the wax just under the end of the cap.

Herb-flavored oils can be as varied and distinct in taste as wine. Try different combinations of herbs to add a unique flavor to salads, sauces and marinades.

Herb-flavored Oils

Herb-flavored oils can be used in marinades or vinaigrettes, brushed over meat or chicken prior to cooking or drizzled over Italian bread for a tasty snack. Flavored oils go well with herbal vinegars in salads and are far superior to the commercial versions. Extra-virgin olive oil (made from the first pressing of the olives) or sesame oil are best to use, but other oils such as safflower, macadamia or walnut work well, too. Don't forget to label your oils so you know what each of the bottles contains. Add a fresh herb sprig to the oil before sealing to intensify the flavor and for a special touch.

Herbal Oil Ingredients

6 tablespoons of one of the following combinations:
basil, lemon thyme, rosemary
bay, thyme, rosemary, oregano
basil, lemon thyme, chives, garlic
dill leaves, dill seeds, burnet, garlic
1 pint (600 ml) of extra-virgin olive oil or an oil of your choice

Place the herbs in the bottom of a hot, sterilized jar. Heat the oil in a saucepan until just warm, then pour it into the jar. Let the flavored oil cool, then cover tightly and store in the refrigerator.

Salad Dressings

Homemade salad dressings are far superior to the commercial versions, and you can adjust the ratio of ingredients to suit your palate. Shake the ingredients together 30 minutes before serving. Use any single herb or combination that suits your menu.

French Dressing

2 tablespoons minced fresh herbs, washed and dried well
3/4 cup (180 ml) olive oil
1/4 cup (60 ml) vinegar

Shake all ingredients together.

Herb and Yogurt Dressing

2 tablespoons minced fresh herbs, washed and dried well
1 cup (250 g) plain yogurt

Stir the herbs through the yogurt.

Dried Herb Dressing

1 cup dried parsley
1/2 cup each dried basil, thyme, savory and marjoram
3/4 cup (180 ml) olive oil
1/4 cup (60 ml) vinegar

Mix together the dry ingredients and store in an airtight container. Each time you need a dressing, mix one tablespoon of the dry herb mix with the oil and vinegar and shake to combine.

Herb-flavored vinegars can be used to replace ordinary vinegars in recipes and salad dressings.

Herb Butters

Aromatic herb butters, with the scents of a summer garden, are colorful and fragrant spreads for warm cookies, vegetables, poultry, fish or meat. Add a dab to pasta or rice, or use a herb butter to baste grilled or baked fish. Make it up when your herbs are plentiful and use it when needed.

Parsley is the herb most commonly used in herb butters, but there are plenty of alternatives. Experiment with basil, mint, tarragon or a combination of different herbs. Choose herbs that will complement the food with which the butter is being served. Mint butter melting over hot potatoes is an excellent choice. Most herb butter recipes call for unsalted butter, but this is not essential. Let the butter soften at room temperature, then beat in the herbs and other seasonings by hand or with an electric mixer.

For the best flavor, chill for at least 3 hours before serving. Pack the flavored butter into molds or basins; form balls with a melon-baller; or shave curls from chilled butter with a sharp knife. Wrap tightly in plastic warp and store for up to 1 month in the refrigerator, or keep frozen for up to 3 months. Create your own herb butters to suit your menu or follow the ones below.

Before you begin, remember to wash the herbs carefully before using them; soil and grit can be concealed in the small folds of leaves. Dry them thoroughly because even small amounts of water will affect the texture of the butter. For 1 tablespoon of fresh herbs, you may substitute 1½ teaspoons of dried herbs or, if you prefer, ½ teaspoon of lightly bruised seeds. (Dried, ground herbs are unsuitable.)

Simple Herb Butter

1 tablespoon washed and dried fresh herbs, minced
4 oz (125 g) unsalted butter, softened

Mix ingredients together. Use herbs singly or in different combinations. Try mint with dill, garlic with dill, chives with lovage, or marjoram with garlic.

Parsley Butter

⅓ cup washed and dried fresh curled parsley, minced
1 tablespoon lemon juice
1 teaspoon Worcestershire sauce
8 oz (250 g) unsalted butter, softened

Mix all ingredients together.

Garlic Butter

4–6 cloves garlic, finely minced
8 oz (250 g) unsalted butter, softened

Mix all ingredients together.

Mixed Herb Butter 1

1 teaspoon each of washed and dried fresh marjoram, thyme and rosemary, minced
¼ teaspoon each of washed and dried fresh garlic, basil and sage, minced
4 oz (125 g) unsalted butter, softened

Mix all ingredients together.

Mixed Herb Butter 2

½ cup each washed and dried fresh parsley and lovage, minced
1½ teaspoons washed and dried fresh thyme, minced
½ teaspoon each washed and dried fresh sage, marjoram and garlic, minced
¼ teaspoon freshly ground pepper

Herbal Vinegar

Herb vinegar is easy to make and if prepared in advance, can make a beautiful Christmas gift.

Ingredients

2 sprigs fresh sage, rosemary, thyme or other pungent herb
2 long spirals of lemon zest (rind)
4 teaspoons white peppercorns
4 cups (1 liter) white wine vinegar

1. Place the herbs of your choice, lemon zest and peppercorns in a sterilized bottle. Add the vinegar.
2. Place on a sunny window sill for two weeks. After this time the vinegar is ready for use.
3. For long-term use, pour the mixture through coffee filter papers, discarding the herbs, peppercorns and lemon zest.
4. Rebottle into a hot sterilized jar or decorative bottle adding a few sprigs of fresh herbs.

Spread herb butter on fresh, crusty bread for a tasty treat. Or use it to baste fish, meat or poultry.

8 oz (250 g) unsalted butter, softened

Mix all ingredients together.

Garlic and Lemon Butter

2 teaspoons minced fresh garlic

2 tablespoons lemon juice

4 oz (125 g) unsalted butter, softened

Mix all ingredients together.

Herbal Jellies

Herbal jellies are simple to prepare and make attractive and useful gifts. You can use herbal jellies just like fruit jellies, but that is only the beginning. Glaze roast or grilled meat, fish and chicken with herb jellies. Spread them on sandwiches or with cream cheese on savory crackers, or on herbal rolls hot from the oven. Good herbs to use are mint, tarragon and rosemary.

While most jelly recipes require large quantities of sugar, it is also possible to create attractive, great-tasting jellies with honey as a healthier alternative. Honey-sweetened herb jellies do require longer cooking times than traditional jellies. If you are used to making sugar-based jellies, be sure to follow the instructions in the following recipe closely for best results.

As you prepare your jelly, you'll want to boil it until it is ready to set properly. Skim off any foam that forms during the cooking process. When you are ready to test, put a spoonful of boiling syrup on a cold plate and chill it in the freezer compartment of your refrigerator for a few minutes. If the mixture gels, it is done. If not, keep cooking for a few more minutes, then test again.

Once your jelly is done, pour it into sterilized glass bottling jars. If you plan to use the jelly immediately, unsealed, covered jars will keep in the refrigerator. Try pouring hot jelly into lightly buttered molds and place them in the refrigerator, then invert them on a decorative plate garnished with fresh herbs for a special meal. If you want to store your jelly for any length of time, you'll need to process the jars in a boiling-water bath to inhibit the growth of micro-organisms. Follow the instructions that come with your preserving equipment.

Apple and Mint Jelly

4½ pounds (2.25 kg) apples

water

honey

fresh mint leaves, washed and dried well

Wash the apples, and remove the stems and dark spots. Quarter the fruit, but don't core it. Place the pieces in a medium-sized stainless steel or enamel pot and add just enough water to half cover the fruit. Cook over a low heat until the fruit is soft (this will take about 1 hour). Place the cooked apples in a jelly bag and drain out the liquid. (You'll get more juice if you squeeze the bag, but it will make a cloudy jelly.)

Bay, thyme, parsley, chives, mint and sage are all useful herbs in the kitchen.

Measure the juice and add ½ cup (125 ml) of honey for every 1 cup (250 ml) of juice. Boil until syrupy, then test to see if it has gelled. Just before removing the apple jelly from the heat, add ¼ cup packed mint leaves for every quart (liter) of juice. Stir, strain to remove the leaves, and ladle the jelly into hot, sterilized jars.

Herb-flavored Honeys

Herb-flavored honey makes a comforting addition to hot tea, as well as an attractive gift. Use it to sweeten hot and cold drinks, substitute it for sugar in recipes or combine it with an equal part of butter or margarine for a sweet spread. Use any herb singly or combine a few. Good herbs to use include aniseed, cilantro (coriander), fennel seed, lavender, lemon verbena, marjoram, mint, rose-scented geranium, rosemary, sage and thyme. Both sweet and savory herbs will work, depending on your taste and the intended use of the honey.

Herbal Honey

1 tablespoon fresh herbs, washed and dried well, or 1½ teaspoons dried herbs, or ½ teaspoon herb seeds

2 cups (500 ml) honey

Bruise the herbs lightly and place them in a muslin bag or directly into a saucepan. Pour the honey into the pan and heat until just warm; high heat will spoil the honey. Pour the mixture into hot, sterilized glass jars and seal tightly. Store at room temperature for about 1 week, then rewarm the flavored honey and strain out the herbs. Alternatively, you can leave the fresh chopped herb leaves in the honey, for texture and color. Return the honey to hot, sterilized jars and seal.

Candied Flowers

Edible herb blossoms are a treat usually limited to the growing season. You can preserve blossoms, such as borage and violets, with sugar, and they'll last for 4–6 months if stored under the right conditions. Only use flowers

Candied Flowers

Follow these simple steps to turn your edible flower petals into a tasty herbal treat.

Assemble the ingredients and utensils you'll need and wash and dry the fresh blossoms. Beat an egg white until it is frothy. Using a soft brush, thoroughly coat the petals with egg white, being sure you cover them completely. Sprinkle them well with caster sugar. Shake off excess.

Let them dry for 2 days, then place the candied blossoms between layers of waxed paper in a tightly sealed glass jar.

that haven't been sprayed. Pick them after they've opened, and leave enough stem attached to the flower to hold as you work. Try using rose petals, mint leaves, lavender flowers or scented geranium leaves.

Crystallized Flowers and Leaves

2 cups sugar
fresh leaves and/or flowers of your choice, washed and drained well
1 cup (250 ml) water

Boil the leaves and flowers in a little water until tender. Drain and place in a shallow dish. Sprinkle with sugar, cover and leave for 2 days until thoroughly dry. Transfer to a saucepan with the water and bring to the boil, stirring all the time. Simmer until the syrup is absorbed. Drain and cool. Sprinkle with sugar to coat and spread on a wire rack to dry. Use to decorate cakes, desserts and summer drinks.

Herb Bread and Cookies

When baking bread or cookies at home, knead in about 1 teaspoon of fresh minced herbs per loaf or dozen cookies. Use parsley, dill, oregano, chives or rosemary fresh from your garden. For an added treat, top off with garlic-flavored butter before serving.

Salt Substitutes

If you're trying to cut down on salt, use dried herbs to make salt substitutes. Grind the dry ingredients together and fill the salt shaker. Experiment with combinations of dried herb leaves and seeds, orange peel and spices, such as ground cloves or ginger. Add ground pepper if you like.

Herb Salt for the Table

Herb salt can add instant flavor to your oils and dressings and encourage you to reduce actual salt use.

1 cup rock or sea salt
1 cup packed fresh herbs, washed, dried and minced, or 2 tablespoons dried herbs (basil, chives, marjoram, garlic, oregano, rosemary, savory, tarragon and thyme work well)

Grind the salt and herbs together. Place the mixture in a shaker and use it to add flavor to your meals.

Herb Seasoning

Herb seasonings can be used instead of salt to flavor meat and vegetable dishes.

1/4 cup each of dried parsley, savory and thyme
2 tablespoons dried marjoram

Grind ingredients together.

Spicy Herb Seasoning

3 tablespoons each dried basil, marjoram, parsley and thyme
4 1/2 teaspoons dried chives
2 1/2 teaspoons each dried onion powder, paprika and rosemary

Grind ingredients together.

Pick fresh herbs when they are in season for use in the kitchen, or freeze and dry for winter use.

Herbal Teas

Tea made from aromatic leaves, flowers or roots steeped in boiling water is one of the most ancient drinks. Herbal teas don't have to be medicinal for you to enjoy them. After a stressful day, a soothing cup of herbal tea is relaxing and satisfying. Use 1/2 to 1 teaspoon fresh herb leaves for each 1 cup (250 ml) of boiling water. Make herbal tea by pouring boiling water over the herb in a china or glass pot. (Metals, including stainless steel, can change the flavor of some herbs.) Herbal tea should be lightly colored and mild. Steep for 4–6 minutes for the best flavor. A strong tea will be bitter and might cause unexpected side effects if the herb has medicinal properties.

Leaves and blossoms that will be used for tea should be left whole and stored.

Culinary Uses of Herbs

Herb	Baking	Dairy	Fish	Garnish	Jam	Meat	Oil	Poultry	Salad	Seasoning	Tea	Vegetable	Vinegar	Wine/Liqueur
Allium spp. Onions, shallots, leeks	✖	✖	✖	✖		✖		✖	✖	✖		✖	✖	
Allium sativum Garlic	✖	✖	✖	✖		✖	✖	✖	✖	✖		✖	✖	
Allium schoenoprasum Chives	✖	✖	✖	✖		✖	✖	✖	✖	✖		✖	✖	
Alpinia galanga Galangal			✖			✖	✖	✖	✖			✖	✖	
Anethum graveolens Dill	✖	✖	✖	✖		✖		✖	✖	✖		✖	✖	
Angelica archangelica Angelica	✖	✖		✖	✖								✖	✖
Anthriscus cerefolium Chervil			✖	✖		✖		✖	✖	✖		✖		
Apium graveolens Celery (cultivars)	✖		✖	✖		✖		✖	✖	✖		✖	✖	
Armoracia rusticana Horseradish			✖	✖		✖		✖	✖	✖		✖	✖	
Asparagus officinalis Asparagus			✖	✖		✖		✖	✖			✖		
Avena sativa Oats	✖	✖										✖		
Borago officinalis Borage				✖					✖		✖	✖	✖	✖
Brassica spp. Mustard			✖	✖		✖	✖	✖	✖	✖		✖	✖	
Capparis spinosa Caper			✖	✖		✖	✖	✖	✖	✖		✖	✖	
Capsicum annuum Pepper	✖		✖	✖		✖		✖	✖	✖		✖	✖	
Carum carvi Caraway	✖	✖				✖			✖	✖		✖	✖	✖
Cichorium intybus Chicory				✖		✖		✖	✖	✖	✖	✖	✖	
Citrus spp. Lemon, orange, lime	✖	✖	✖	✖	✖	✖	✖	✖	✖	✖	✖	✖	✖	✖
Coriandum sativum Cilantro (coriander)	✖		✖	✖		✖	✖	✖	✖	✖		✖	✖	
Crocus sativus Saffron	✖	✖	✖			✖		✖	✖	✖	✖	✖	✖	✖
Cuminum cyminum Cumin	✖		✖	✖		✖		✖	✖	✖		✖	✖	✖
Curcuma longa Turmeric			✖			✖		✖	✖	✖		✖	✖	
Cymbopogon citratus Lemongrass			✖	✖	✖	✖		✖		✖	✖	✖	✖	✖
Ferula assa-foetida Asafetida			✖			✖		✖	✖	✖		✖	✖	

Herbs	Baking	Dairy	Fish	Garnish	Jam	Meat	Oil	Poultry	Salad	Seasoning	Tea	Vegetable	Vinegar	Wine/Liqueur
Fragaria spp. Strawberry	✖	✖			✖		✖		✖		✖		✖	✖
Helianthus annuus Sunflower	✖						✖	✖	✖			✖	✖	
Juglans regla Walnut	✖		✖	✖		✖	✖	✖	✖	✖	✖	✖	✖	✖
Juniperus communis Juniper			✖			✖	✖	✖		✖		✖	✖	✖
Laurus nobilis Bay, sweet	✖	✖	✖	✖		✖	✖	✖	✖	✖		✖	✖	
Melissa officinalis Lemon balm		✖	✖	✖	✖	✖		✖	✖	✖	✖	✖	✖	✖
Mentha spp. Mint	✖	✖	✖	✖	✖	✖	✖		✖	✖	✖	✖	✖	✖
Murraya koenigii Curry leaf	✖		✖	✖		✖	✖	✖	✖	✖		✖	✖	
Myristica fragrans Nutmeg	✖	✖		✖	✖	✖			✖	✖	✖	✖	✖	✖
Nasturtium officinale Watercress			✖	✖		✖		✖	✖	✖		✖		
Ocimum basilicum Basil, sweet	✖		✖	✖		✖	✖	✖	✖	✖		✖	✖	
Origanum majorana Marjoram, sweet	✖	✖	✖	✖		✖	✖	✖	✖	✖		✖	✖	
Origanum vulgare Oregano	✖		✖	✖		✖	✖	✖	✖	✖	✖	✖	✖	
Petroselinum crispum Parsley	✖	✖	✖	✖		✖		✖	✖	✖		✖	✖	
Pimpinella anisum Anise	✖	✖	✖		✖			✖	✖	✖	✖	✖	✖	✖
Piper nigrum Black pepper	✖		✖	✖		✖	✖	✖	✖	✖		✖	✖	
Rheum palmatum Chinese rhubarb	✖	✖			✖						✖		✖	✖
Rosmarinus officinalis Rosemary	✖	✖	✖			✖	✖	✖		✖	✖	✖	✖	✖
Salvia officinalis Sage	✖	✖	✖			✖		✖	✖	✖	✖	✖	✖	
Tamarindus indica Tamarind	✖		✖			✖		✖		✖		✖	✖	
Thymus vulgaris Thyme	✖	✖	✖	✖		✖	✖	✖	✖	✖		✖	✖	
Trigonella foenum-graecum Fenugreek	✖		✖			✖		✖	✖			✖	✖	
Vanilla planifolia Vanilla	✖	✖			✖					✖	✖		✖	✖
Zingiber officinale Ginger	✖	✖	✖		✖	✖		✖	✖	✖	✖	✖	✖	✖

Medicinal Herbs

Compared with the precision of modern diagnosis and prescription medicine, herbal remedies can seem out of place today. But herbal preparations were once the only medications available. Modern physicians argue that synthetic medicines are superior because they are free of impurities, are of known strength and effects, and are more stable. Herbal practitioners believe that when used appropriately, herbal remedies have an important role today. In many countries, herbal remedies remain the only readily available treatment. And, of course, many of today's medicines are derived from naturally occurring plants.

The History of Medicinal Herbs

In most cultures around the world, the earliest forms of healing were based on herbs. People built up a wealth of knowledge based on experimentation within their environments, and they handed that knowledge on to the next generation. The arrival of written language provided us with records of the use of herbs as medicine as early as 3000 BC in Egypt, Babylon, China and India.

Ginseng

Examples abound of the importance herbs played in the health and well-being of ancient peoples. In 300 BC, a medical school was set up in Alexandria, where research was conducted into the uses of herbs in treating illnesses. This led to the creation of a document listing more than 600 herbs, with a prescription for how to prepare each as a treatment for specific diseases. This book was considered the most important source of information on herbal medicine for the next 1,500 years.

Native Americans used many different herbal medicines. From willow bark they extracted a pain-relieving ingredient used in today's aspirin. Iris roots ground with suet, lard and beeswax made an ointment for cuts and grazes. Coca leaves were used as a local anesthetic. Juice of lady's slipper roots eased pain, soothed hysterics and relieved cold and flu stymptoms.

Honey is used as a base in medicinal herbal syrup. Beeswax is used in herbal ointments.

Traditional Chinese medicine attaches a great deal of importance to the harmony of the human body and the relationship of the body with nature. Chinese people have been using natural herbs to treat a wide variety of diseases for over 3,000 years.

While much has been added to the basic philosophy of this ancient healing system, very little has been taken out. Herbal medicines comprise roots, bark, flowers, seeds, fruits, leaves and branches. In China today, there are up to 5,000 different herbs in use in traditional medicine. It is wise to use only Chinese herbs that have been prescribed by a professional.

Herbal Remedies

Prepare your own herbal remedies, such as infusions, decoctions, compresses, poultices and tinctures, from herbs you have harvested, to treat a number of common ailments. Refer to the "Quick Guide to Medicinal Herbs" on pages 158–159 for the appropriate herb to use.

Herbal Infusions

Infusions are made by pouring boiling water over herb leaves or flowers and steeping them for up to 15 minutes to release the aromatic oils. They are a good way of making herbal remedies at home and are best drunk fresh, while still hot, although they can be stored in the refrigerator for a day or two. If you find them too bitter, dilute them to your taste or try sweetening them with honey or apple juice. Use a glass or ceramic pot, and bottled water or rainwater if possible.

1 teaspoons dried herbs or 1–2 teaspoons of fresh herb leaves or flowers, washed and dried well
1 cup (250 ml) boiling water

Herbs are the oldest form of medicine in the world and have been used for centuries. Many herbs, however, have poisonous properties and should be used only under professional supervision.

Herbal Remedy Precautions

Use all herbal remedies cautiously and follow these guidelines:

- Always consult a doctor if you have painful or chronic symptoms.
- Don't mix herbal medicines with medical prescriptions.
- Take care to identify wild plants accurately and be aware of their properties and dangers.
- Avoid large doses of any herb.
- Grow your own herbal medications for the best purity and quality.
- Follow the instructions for harvesting and storing herbs properly.
- Stop using any herbal medicine if you notice any side effects, such as headaches, dizziness or nausea.
- Avoid using herbal medicines if you are pregnant or breastfeeding, unless you have the consent of an obstetrician.
- With children, always consult a doctor first before giving herbal medications. Do not give herbal medicines to children younger than two years old.

Pour the boiling water over the herbs, and allow it to brew for 10–15 minutes. Strain. For infusions for external use, triple the herb quantities and steep for several hours.

Herbal Teas

An herbal tea is an infusion of aromatic herbs that is steeped for a short period of time in water. Herbal teas should be lightly colored and mild. Steep for only 5–10 minutes for the best flavor. A strong tea will be bitter and might cause unexpected side effects if the herb has medicinal properties. Herbal teas don't have to be medicinal for you to enjoy them. Drink them after a stressful day to help you relax. Use about 1 teaspoon of fresh herb leaves to 1 cup (250 ml) of boiling water. Use a china or glass pot, as metal can change the flavor of some herbs.

Herbal Decoctions

Decoctions are made from the roots, bark, and sometimes twigs, berries or seeds of herbs and need to be simmered in order to extract their active ingredients.

2 tablespoons dried herbs, or 1½ cups fresh bark, roots or stems, washed and dried well
2 cups (500 ml) boiling water

Add the herbs to the boiling water and simmer gently for up to 30 minutes. Strain. Decoctions are used fresh.

Herbal Compress

Follow the instructions for preparing an infusion or decoction, then soak a towel in the warm liquid. Wring it out and lay it upon the affected area, covering it with a dry towel. As the compress cools, replace it with a warm one. Continue treatment for 30 minutes or until the skin is flushed or tingly. A hot compress made with mustard, cayenne, garlic or ginger will improve circulation and is good for treating nasal and chest congestion. Compresses prepared with such herbs as comfrey or aloe are good for sprains and bruises.

Herbal Poultice

A poultice is similar to a compress except that plant parts are used rather than liquid extracts. They are generally more active than compresses and are used to stimulate circulation and draw impurities out through the skin.

¼ cup dried herbs or 3 cups fresh herbs, washed, dried and minced
4 cups oatmeal

Mix the herbs and oatmeal with hot water to form a paste. Place some paste directly on the skin and cover with a towel. As it cools, replace with more warm paste. Continue treatment for 30 minutes. Don't use hot, spicy herbs, such as mustard, that may burn the skin. Poultices are used to draw out infection and relieve muscle aches.

Herbal Plaster

Place dried or fresh herbs, or a freshly mixed paste (see the poultice recipe) in the fold of a towel, then lay it on the injured area. Since the herbs don't have direct contact with the skin, plasters are useful for particularly sensitive wounds, such as minor burns. Flush with cold water, then apply a plaster of echinacea paste.

Herbal Tincture

Tinctures are made from alcohol and powdered herbs. The alcohol extracts the herbs' active ingredients.

½ cup powdered dried herbs
2 cups (500 ml) brandy, vodka or gin

Mix the ingredients together in a glass bottle and allow to steep in a warm place for several weeks, shaking occasionally. Strain, then store in a cool, dark place. Use approximately 10 drops either straight or mixed in 1 cup (250 ml) of hot water. Tinctures will keep for a long time due to their alcohol content.

Herbal Ointment

Mix 5 tablespoons of crushed fresh herbs with 18 oz (500 g) of lard or petroleum jelly in a bowl. Place over boiling water. Stir thoroughly. Strain while hot and pour into sterilized glass storage jars.

Herbal teas are made by infusing leaves, flowers or roots of herbs in boiling water.

Quick Guide to Medicinal Herbs

Use the following as a quick reference to some of the more common and beneficial medicinal herbs and their soothing and healing properties.

Aloe Apply the fresh transparent gel from the leaves externally to scalds, sunburn, blisters, cuts and acne to promote healing and prevent infection. Do not take internally.

Angelica To ease painful arthritic joints, make a compress by soaking a towel in a hot diluted tincture made from the roots.

Arnica Make a tincture from the flower heads and apply as a compress to soothe sore muscles and sprains. Do not take this herb internally.

Barberry Prepare a decoction from the roots and drink 1 cup (250 ml) daily for its antibacterial and laxative properties.

Basil Make an infusion from the dried leaves and apply to the skin to treat acne and skin problems.

Bee balm (bergamot) Prepare an inhalation using the leaves and boiling water; inhale twice a day for the relief of blocked nasal passages and catarrh.

Burdock Prepare a poultice from the roots and apply to the skin to help soothe skin sores and ulcers. Make a poultice from the leaves and apply to ease bruises and skin inflammations.

Calendula Make a compress from the flowers and apply to stings, bruises, scrapes and minor burns. Prepare an ointment and apply to the skin to reduce inflammation and speed healing.

Catnip Make an infusion from the leaves and drink 1 cup (250 ml) for a calming effect and to aid digestion.

Celery Dried leaves of celery in a thin soup will supply vitamins and mineral salts to combat arthritis and rheumatism.

Chamomile Make an infusion from the flowers and drink 1 cup (250 ml) up to three times a day to relieve stress and insomnia, ease cramps and help an upset stomach. Also use to aid digestion.

Comfrey Make a compress or poultice from the leaves and apply to bruises and sprains. Or make an ointment to treat minor burns and abrasions.

Dandelion Prepare an infusion from the leaves or a decoction from the roots. Drink 1 cup (250 ml) once or twice a day as a diuretic and laxative.

Echinacea Make a tea of fresh roots and drink 1 cup (250 ml) up to three times a day to relieve respiratory infections such as colds or bronchitis.

Elder Prepare an ointment using 1 part of leaves to 2 parts petroleum jelly to improve blood circulation and relieve chilblains.

Eucalyptus Make an infusion from the leaves, add to the bath, or inhale the vapors to relieve congestion and other cold and bronchial symptoms.

Fennel Make an infusion from the seeds or leaves and drink 1 cup (250 ml) up to three times a day to soothe an upset stomach and to relieve flatulence.

Feverfew An infusion made from the leaves can relieve headaches, menstrual pain, arthritis and rheumatism. Must not be taken by pregnant women.

Echinacea

Garlic Use raw cloves to prepare antibiotic and antiseptic infusions, syrups and plasters. (If you ingest raw garlic, chew a sprig of parsley afterward to freshen your breath.) A garlic ointment applied around the anus at night can help treat worms in children.

Ginger Make an infusion from the dried root and take in small doses to relieve nausea, morning sickness, travel sickness and to aid digestion.

Ginseng An infusion or tea made from the root and drunk half an hour before a meal will help stimulate the appetite.

Goldenrod An infusion made from the leaves and drunk as a tea is said to relieve hay fever and other allergies.

Hops Make an infusion from the fresh "cones" and drink 1 cup (250 ml) a day to calm nerves, help depression and settle an upset stomach. A cup before bed is a useful sedative for insomnia.

Garlic

Aloe

Dandelion

Horehound

Marsh mallow

Ginseng

Horehound Make an infusion from the leaves and drink 1 cup (250 ml) three times a day as an expectorant. Make a syrup from the leaves and take ½ to 1 teaspoon up to three times a day for colds, sore throats and bronchitis.

Hyssop Make an infusion from the leaves and drink 2 cups (500 ml) per day as a cold and flu remedy. Add honey to mask hyssop's bitter taste.

Lemon balm Make an infusion from the leaves and drink 1 cup (250 ml) up to three times a day to help soothe stomach aches, fight infection, ease menstrual pain, relieve stress and help depression.

Licorice Chew the roots or make an infusion and take up to three times a day to act as a mild laxative.

Marigold Make a salve from fresh flowers, boiled water and aqueous cream (available from pharmacists) or petroleum jelly to provide relief from scratches, cuts and abrasions.

Marsh mallow Make a decoction from the roots and drink 1 cup (250 ml) up to three times a day to soothe sore throats and calm upset stomachs.

Meadowsweet Make an infusion from the leaves and drink 2 cups (500 ml) a day to relieve arthritis, rheumatism, indigestion and diarrhea.

Mint Place a drop or two of essential oil directly onto minor burns and scalds. Make an inhalation from fresh leaves and inhale to relieve nasal congestion.

Onion To encourage boils to come to a head, place half a warm baked onion over the boil with the center layer removed to create a small dome.

Orange A tea made with 1 cup (250 ml) of boiling water poured over 2 tablespoons of blossoms helps to calm nervous tension.

Parsley Make an infusion from the leaves or seeds and drink 1 cup (250 ml) three times a day as a diuretic and mild laxative.

Passionflower Make an infusion from the leaves and drink 1 cup (250 ml) three times a day to relieve nervous tension, aid digestion and ease menstrual discomfort.

Peppermint Make an infusion from the leaves and drink 1 cup (250 ml) three times a day as a decongestant, for an upset stomach and to relieve menstrual cramps.

Raspberry Prepare a tea from the leaves and drink freely during the last months of pregnancy to tone the muscles of the uterus. Check with your doctor first.

Rose Make an infusion from the hips and drink 1 cup (250 ml) up to three times a day to treat cold and flu symptoms.

Rosemary Make an infusion from the leaves and flowers and drink 1–2 cups (250–500 ml) a day as an antiseptic, or for stomach upsets or nausea. Use the infusion as a hair rinse to combat dandruff.

Sage Make a gargle from the leaves and white wine vinegar and gargle three times a day to relieve ulcers, and mouth and throat infections. Make a hot compress to relieve sore throats.

Sorrel Infuse the leaves to make a tea to help relieve sunstroke and exhaustion. A sorrel compress has a cooling effect, so place on minor burns.

St John's wort An infusion made from the whole plant is said to relieve anxiety-related conditions, tension and irritability.

Thyme Prepare an infusion from the leaves and stems and drink up to 3 cups (750 ml) a day for cold and flu symptoms.

Valerian Make an infusion from the roots and drink about ½ cup (125 ml) once or twice a day to calm the nerves and treat insomnia, ease headaches and relieve menstrual discomfort.

Vervain Make an ointment from the dried leaves, flowers and roots and use for eczema and weeping sores.

Witch hazel Make a decoction from the leaves or the bark and use it as a compress for aching joints, sore eyes, sore muscles, cuts, bruises and insect bites.

Parsley

Yarrow Make an infusion from the flowers and leaves and drink 1 cup (250 ml) up to three times a day for indigestion and to relieve menstrual cramps. Yarrow also helps to eliminate toxins from the body.

Licorice

Peppermint

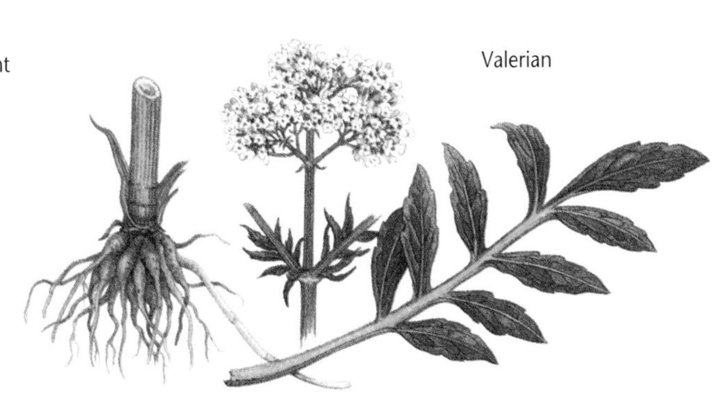
Valerian

Medicinal Uses of Herbs

	Antiseptic	Asthma	Burns	Colds	Constipation	Coughs	Cuts & wounds	Diarrhea	Eczema	Headaches	Indigestion	Inflammation	Insect bites	Insomnia	Nausea	Sedative	Sore joints	Sore throats	Vomiting
Achillea millefolium Yarrow				✖		✖		✖		✖							✖	✖	
Agave americana Agave			✖		✖						✖								
Agrimonia eupatoria Agrimony								✖	✖								✖	✖	
Allium sativum Garlic	✖			✖		✖			✖										
Aloe vera syn. *A. barbadensis* Aloe			✖		✖				✖										
Aloysia triphylla Lemon verbena				✖							✖								
Alpinia galanga Galangal									✖		✖				✖		✖		
Althaea officinalis Marsh mallow		✖				✖						✖	✖		✖			✖	
Anethum graveolens Dill											✖								
Angelica archangelica Angelica						✖					✖						✖		
Anthriscus cerefolium Chervil									✖								✖		
Arctium lappa Burdock			✖	✖					✖								✖		
Artemisia absinthium Wormwood											✖		✖						✖
Artemisia dracunculus Tarragon, French											✖						✖		
Avena sativa Oats									✖			✖				✖			
Azadirachta indica Neem									✖								✖		
Betula spp. Birch									✖								✖		
Borago officinalis Borage				✖	✖				✖	✖								✖	
Brassica spp. Mustard				✖		✖				✖							✖		
Calendula officinalis Calendula	✖						✖		✖			✖							
Camellia sinensis Tea							✖	✖					✖						
Cannabis sativa Hemp					✖										✖	✖			✖
Capparis spinosa Caper						✖		✖									✖		
Capsicum annuum Pepper		✖		✖							✖								
Carum carvi Caraway								✖			✖				✖				
Ceanothus americanus New Jersey tea				✖		✖												✖	
Centaurea cyanus Cornflower							✖												
Centella asiatica Gotu kola							✖										✖		
Chaenomeles speciosa Flowering quince								✖			✖						✖		✖
Chamaemelum nobile Chamomile, Roman		✖							✖	✖	✖			✖					✖
Chrysanthemum parthenium (Tanacetum parthenium) Feverfew										✖	✖		✖				✖		
Citrus aurantiifolia Lime				✖		✖		✖		✖						✖		✖	
Citrus limon Lemon				✖		✖			✖	✖							✖	✖	
Coffea arabica Coffee			✖												✖				✖
Coriandrum sativum Cilantro (coriander)											✖						✖		
Cuminum cyminum Cumin										✖	✖								
Curcuma longa Turmeric							✖				✖								
Cymbopogon citratus Lemongrass				✖			✖				✖								
Dendranthema x *grandiflorum* Chrysanthemum				✖		✖				✖									
Echinacea purpurea Echinacea	✖			✖		✖	✖		✖										
Elettaria cardamomum Cardamom											✖				✖				✖
Eucalyptus spp. Eucalyptus	✖			✖		✖	✖	✖									✖	✖	
Eupatorium perfoliatum Boneset				✖		✖			✖									✖	
Ferula assa-foetida Asafetida		✖				✖					✖						✖		

Herb	Antiseptic	Asthma	Burns	Colds	Constipation	Coughs	Cuts & wounds	Diarrhea	Eczema	Headaches	Indigestion	Inflammation	Insect bites	Insomnia	Nausea	Sedative	Sore joints	Sore throats	Vomiting
Filipendula ulmaria Meadowsweet				✖				✖									✖		
Foeniculum vulgare Fennel					✖						✖							✖	✖
Fragaria vesca Wild strawberry			✖					✖	✖		✖								
Galium odoratum Sweet woodruff												✖		✖					
Gardenia augusta Gardenia							✖		✖			✖							
Gentiana lutea Great yellow gentian											✖				✖				
Geranium robertianum Herb Robert							✖	✖	✖			✖						✖	
Ginkgo biloba Ginkgo		✖				✖													
Glycyrrhiza glabra Licorice		✖		✖	✖	✖			✖								✖		
Hamamelis virginiana Witch hazel			✖					✖				✖	✖					✖	
Humulus lupulus Hop									✖	✖				✖		✖			
Hypericum perforatum St John's wort			✖				✖							✖					
Hyssopus officinalis Hyssop			✖	✖		✖	✖									✖			
Iris 'Florentina' Orris				✖			✖	✖											
Juglans regia Walnut		✖			✖	✖			✖										
Laurus nobilis Bay, sweet	✖										✖						✖		
Leptospermum scoparium New Zealand tea tree	✖					✖	✖	✖	✖				✖						
Levisticum officinale Lovage											✖							✖	
Magnolia officinalis Magnolia		✖				✖		✖											✖
Marrubium vulgare Horehound		✖		✖		✖									✖				✖
Melissa officinalis Lemon balm				✖						✖	✖		✖	✖	✖	✖	✖		✖
Mentha spp. Mint			✖	✖		✖			✖	✖	✖				✖			✖	✖
Monarda didyma Bee balm (bergamot)				✖					✖	✖	✖							✖	
Murraya koenigii Curry leaf					✖			✖											
Myristica fragrans Nutmeg								✖			✖			✖					✖
Nasturtium officinale Watercress						✖			✖								✖		
Nepeta cataria Catnip				✖		✖		✖		✖				✖					
Ocimum basilicum Basil, sweet				✖					✖	✖			✖	✖	✖	✖	✖		
Oenothera biennis Evening primrose		✖							✖								✖		
Origanum majorana Marjoram, sweet										✖	✖			✖			✖		
Origanum vulgare Oregano		✖		✖		✖											✖		
Paeonia lactiflora Peony									✖										
Panax ginseng Ginseng														✖					
Passiflora incarnata Passionflower		✖								✖				✖					
Piper longum Long pepper		✖				✖				✖	✖						✖		✖
Portulaca oleracea Purslane			✖						✖				✖						
Rosmarinus officinalis Rosemary	✖			✖			✖			✖	✖						✖		
Ruta graveolens Rue	✖								✖								✖		
Sanguinaria canadensis Bloodroot						✖				✖								✖	
Santolina chamaecyparissus Santolina							✖		✖		✖		✖						
Symphytum officinale Comfrey			✖			✖	✖		✖								✖		
Thymus vulgaris Thyme	✖	✖				✖		✖									✖	✖	
Trigonella foenum-graecum Fenugreek						✖			✖		✖						✖		
Urtica dioica Stinging nettle			✖						✖				✖				✖		
Zingiber officinale Ginger				✖		✖		✖			✖				✖		✖		✖

Aromatherapy

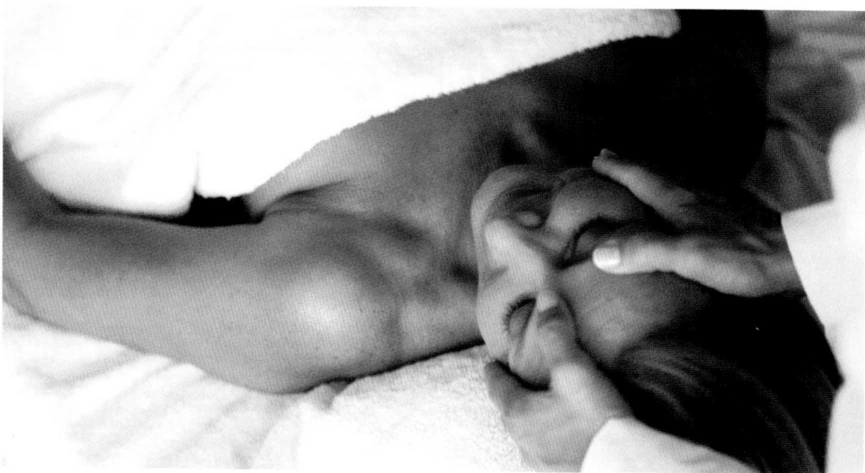

Essential oils need to be diluted before applying them to the skin as they are highly concentrated. Choose a base oil that is pure, has no scent and is cold-pressed, so that the properties of the essential oil remain.

Aromatherapy is a way of healing the body through massage, inhalation or bathing, and uses essential oils extracted from certain plants and plant parts. Aromatherapy literally means "therapy by smell". The fragrant, natural essential oils of herbs and flowers have a beneficial effect on the body.

Essential oils are found in small glands in various parts of aromatic plants. They can be extracted from leaves, flowers, fruits, berries, seeds, wood, resin, roots and bark. Each herb releases different scent molecules, which are detected by the olfactory nerves in the nose. These nerves are directly linked with the areas of the brain that deal with emotions, memory and creativity. The messages picked up by these nerves travel quickly to the brain and can have an immediate effect on particular chemicals being injected into the body; in turn this can affect the workings of bodily functions. The job of an aromatherapist is to work out how the body can benefit from this chemical reaction to scents. Since the aroma of a plant is contained in its oil, extracting the oil produces a very concentrated scent that should be used carefully. Of course the effects of a herb's aroma can be enjoyed just by smelling the plant itself.

By mixing two or more essential oils, you can create an aroma that has added therapeutic properties. It is important, however, to get the ratio right. You will need to refer to a specialist publication or a professional for recommended quantities and combinations.

It's easy to enjoy the benefits of aromatherapy at home. The three main ways of doing this are by massage, adding oils to the bath or by inhalation.

Massage

Essential oils are highly concentrated and should not be used directly on the skin. In massage they need to be diluted with a lubricating oil to allow the hands to glide smoothly over the skin. Mix up 15 drops of your favorite essential oil to 2 fl oz (50 ml) of a base oil such as almond, apricot kernel or evening primrose oil. Only use vegetable oils, as they do not evaporate when warmed.

Adding Oils to the Bath

Fill a warm bath and add 8 drops of either a single oil or a combination of oils. Swish the water around so that the oil rises and

Bee balm

Popular Essential Oils

Here are some popular essential oils to use in aromatherapy and a list of the conditions they help to alleviate.

Basil anxiety, stress, headaches, respiratory problems
Bee balm (bergamot) cold sores, ulcers, depression
Black pepper stimulates circulation, muscular aches, colds
Chamomile skin problems, depression, insomnia
Cilantro (coriander) rheumatic pain, digestion problems
Clary menstrual problems, insect bites, high blood pressure
Clove toothache, infections, fatigue, respiratory problems
Eucalyptus colds, viruses, cuts, insect bites, laryngitis
Juniper eczema, water retention, fatigue
Lavender insomnia, infections, indigestion
Lemon water retention, acne, stomachache
Rose stress, circulation problems, headaches, nausea
Rosemary fatigue, bronchitis, memory problems
Sage low blood pressure, fatigue, menopause problems
Tea tree respiratory problems, skin infections and wounds
Thyme indigestion, depression, muscular pain

Diffusers are especially made to heat essential oils in order to release their aroma. A few drops of the oil are added to water in a bowl; the bowl is then heated from below. When buying an oil labeled "aromatherapy", check whether it is an essential oil mixed in a base oil. If so, it is meant for massage.

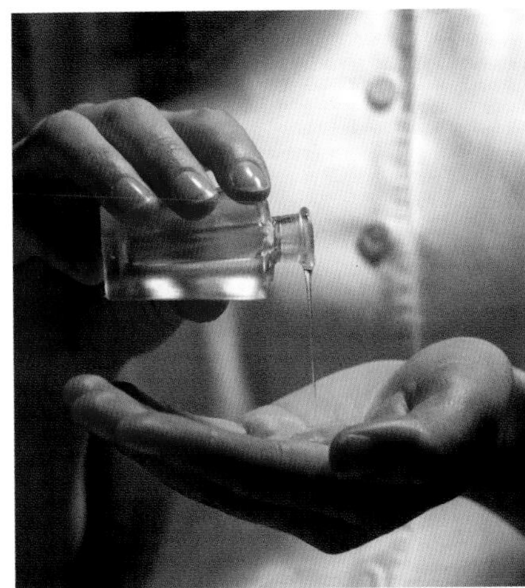

Essential oil does not go off but the carrier oil will, so only make up what you can use for five weeks.

mixes with the steam. You will notice that the oil forms a scented film on the top. It's important not to add the oils to a running bath or they will evaporate. Soak in the bath for 10–15 minutes, lightly splashing the oil over your body and inhaling the steam.

Inhalation

Vaporization is the easiest method of releasing the aroma of essential oils; the aroma is absorbed by the body through inhalation. The idea behind this process is that heating the oils allows their molecules to be released into the air. Add 6 drops of the selected essential oil to 4 cups (1 l) of steaming water in a bowl or sink. Cover your head with a towel and lean over the bowl with your face well away, keeping your eyes closed. Breathe deeply through your nose for about 1 minute. This is particularly helpful if you have a cold.

There are other ways to enjoy aromatherapy. Try using a diffuser, which is a small burner that heats essential oils in order to release their aroma. Some are heated by a candle, others by electricity. It's important that the bowl isn't porous, so it can be cleaned and used for a different oil; otherwise you may be mixing scents.

You can add a few drops of essential oil to the water in a humidifier or place a drop on a log half an hour before you put it on the fire. If you want to enjoy the aroma of your garden herbs, try using stove simmers. These mixtures are especially good if you plan to spend the day in the kitchen. Just set them in a saucepan at the back of the stove where the gentle heat will release the oils. Add 1/2 cup of dried herbs to 2 cups (500 ml) of water. Keep an eye on the mixture to make sure all of the water doesn't simmer away. To create a spicier scent, mix your herbs with equal parts of allspice, cinnamon sticks, fresh ginger, whole cloves and citrus peel. You can also add a drop of commercially produced essential oils to accent the aroma.

When buying products containing essential oils, go to health-food stores rather than stores that sell cosmetics. Essential oils are expensive, but cheaper synthetic oils don't have the healing properties of natural ones.

Herbal Beauty

For thousands of years, people have been relying for their beauty treatments on natural preparations made from the leaves, flowers, roots, bark and berries of herbs. Hippocrates recommended scented baths and massages for improving health and beauty, while the Romans developed recipes for stopping wrinkles and body odors. Many of today's commercially available beauty treatments are based on herbal ingredients, so why not make your own from herbs grown in your garden? However, when making herbal beauty preparations, it's important to keep aside special equipment and not to use utensils from your kitchen, so that the taste and scent of herbs, soaps and essential oils won't contaminate food.

After a hard day's work, try a herbal foot bath to ease aching feet. Choose from bay, lavender, sage or thyme, and add a large handful to hot water. To soothe itchy feet, add cider vinegar to the water. To deodorize feet, soak them in a decoction of sage or lovage. To warm feet, add black mustard seed.

Herbal Soaps and Cleansers

Once you learn how simple it is to make your own scented soaps and cleansers, you'll want to make plenty to keep for yourself and to give as gifts. For the strongest aroma, use herbs such as rosemary, lavender and thyme—their oils seem to linger on the skin the longest.

Soft Herbal Soap

- 1½ cups dried herbs
- 1½ quarts (1.5 l) water
- 2 cups shredded pure soap
- ½ cup borax

In an enamel saucepan, combine the herbs and water and bring to the boil. Simmer for 30 minutes to release the oils. Reheat slowly and add the shredded soap and borax while stirring. Boil gently for 3 minutes, then cool. Strain the soft soap into clean containers and seal.

Hard Herbal Soap

- 2 teaspoons dried herbs or 2 tablespoons fresh herbs
- ¼ cup (60 ml) water
- several drops essential oil
- 2 cups shredded pure soap

In an enamel saucepan, combine the herbs, water and oil and bring to the boil. Simmer for 30 minutes, and then add the shredded soap, mixing thoroughly. Allow to cool for 15 minutes, then mix with your hands. Divide into six parts and roll each into a ball. Place the soaps on waxed paper to dry and harden for at least several days before using.

Lemon Cleansing Cream

- 1 tablespoon strained lemon juice
- 1 tablespoon beeswax
- 1 tablespoon petroleum jelly
- 3 tablespoons almond oil
- 1 tablespoon witch hazel
- pinch of borax
- 5 drops essential oil of lemon

Over a low heat, melt the beeswax and petroleum jelly. Gradually add the almond oil, stirring for 5 minutes. In another pan, combine witch hazel and lemon juice and warm gently. Stir in borax until dissolved. Gradually add to the wax mixture and beat until creamy. Cool, then add the lemon oil. Pour into clean bottles. Store in the refrigerator.

Elderflower Cleansing Cream

- 5 tablespoons fresh elderflowers (or you may substitute chamomile, sweet violets or lime blossoms)
- ½ pint (300 ml) buttermilk
- 2 tablespoons honey

Heat the buttermilk gently in a saucepan and immerse the elderflowers in it. Simmer for 30 minutes, or until the blossoms have softened. Remove from heat and leave to infuse for 2 hours. Reheat briefly, then strain and add the honey. Bottle and store in the refrigerator for up to 10 days.

Herbal Baths

The soothing relaxation of herbal baths is hard to beat. Warm water slowly releases the fragrant oils, which rise with the steam. For the most soothing bath, keep the water temperature around 98°F (36°C). A hotter bath will dry your skin and make you feel sleepy. To soften your skin, use chamomile or calendula blossoms, lemon balm leaves or marsh mallow root. The most relaxing herbal baths are made with

If you have sensitive skin, avoid using violets in herbal beauty preparations, as they can cause allergic reactions in some people.

catmint, hyssop, scented geranium or valerian root. To soothe dry skin, common during cold weather, use your own scented bath oil (see instructions below). Or to relieve strained and tired muscles, try making herbal bath bags.

Herbal Bath Oil

½ teaspoon essential oil
½ cup (125 ml) almond oil

Shake the ingredients together and store in a glass bottle away from light. Use a small amount in your bath.

Herbal Bath Bag

½ cup dried herbs or 3 cups packed fresh herbs
8 inch (20 cm) square of muslin or cheesecloth

Center the herbs in the fabric, bring the edges together and secure tightly with string. To soften the water, you can add a tablespoon of dried milk powder or a few teaspoons of oatmeal. Allow the bag to float in the water as the bath fills.

Facial Steams

Facial steams are a great way to clean your face. The heat of the steam makes the face perspire, which helps eliminate toxins and increase circulation. The steam also softens the skin and opens the pores, which helps the skin absorb the beneficial properties of the herbs.

Select a handful of fresh or dried herbs and place in a bowl. Pour boiling water over the herbs and place a towel over your head to make a steam tent. Close your eyes and allow the aromatic steam to refresh your face for 10–15 minutes. Rinse with cold water to close the pores, or use lavender toner (see recipe below).

Herbal Toners

Now that you have cleaned your face, the next step is to tone the skin. Toners remove any trace of cleansing cream and oil from the face and help firm the skin and make it feel refreshed. For a simple lavender toner, add two handfuls of lavender flowers to 1 pint (600 ml) of cider vinegar. Leave to infuse for two weeks. Strain, then add 2 pints (1.2 l) of water, bottle and seal.

Herbal Face Masks

A face mask helps draw impurities out of the skin, aids circulation and tightens the skin. Apply it after a facial steam, before the pores on the face have closed.

An ancient beauty treatment for refreshing and cleaning the face was to apply a mask of fresh strawberries. After washing your face thoroughly or after a facial steam, mash to a pulp a handful of strawberries and spread all over the face, leaving the eyes clear. Leave for about 30 minutes, then wipe off.

Make a fragrant bath oil by mixing essential oils from herbs such as hyssop, marigold and catmint.

Powdered orris root combined with powdered arrowroot makes an excellent dry shampoo.

Oatmeal is also an excellent ingredient for face masks. Mix 2 tablespoons of oats with the juice of your favorite aromatic herbs (extract the juice using a juicer). Apply to your face, avoiding the eye area. Leave for 30 minutes, then wipe off.

Hair Care

Herbs can be used to enhance all aspects of your hair, from restoring color and treating dandruff to preventing baldness. Rub catmint into your hair to relieve scalp irritation. Or massage parsley or rosemary into the hair to eliminate dandruff.

For a herbal hair rinse to improve hair shine, boil 4 cups (1 liter) of water and pour over a handful of fresh chamomile and mullein flowers. Leave to infuse for one hour. Strain and add 2 tablespoons of lemon juice before using.

Dry Shampoo

If you're ever travelling and can't wash your hair with water, try this dry shampoo. Mix together 2 tablespoons powdered orris root and powdered arrowroot. Rub into the hair and leave for 10 minutes to absorb any grease. Brush out vigorously.

Nettle Dandruff Tonic

4 tablespoons nettle leaves
1 pint (600 ml) boiling water
2 fl oz (50 ml) cider vinegar
2 fl oz (50 ml) eau de cologne

Steep the nettle leaves in the water for several hours. Strain and add the remaining ingredients. Massage into the scalp nightly.

Herbal Gifts

Don't just limit the use of your herbs to the kitchen or medicine chest. You can make wonderful gifts and crafts using the fragrant herbs and flowers from your garden.

Potpourris

Potpourris are long-lasting and fragrant mixtures of dried herbs and other crushed plant material. They have been made for centuries and were originally used to freshen the air and scent rooms. Making a potpourri preserves your favorite summer fragrances in a jar—just lift the lid and remember your garden's perfume.

Good potpourris use a variety of flowers, scented leaves and spices. Use the recipe below or create your own custom blends using plants you've grown yourself. Roses and lavender flowers have always been popular as the base of potpourri, but other good choices include lemon verbena, woodruff, pennyroyal, marigolds, cornflowers, scented geraniums, borage, mint, rosemary and magnolia. Use contrasting colors and add some pine needles, ground cedarwood, or orange and lemon rind for added fragrance.

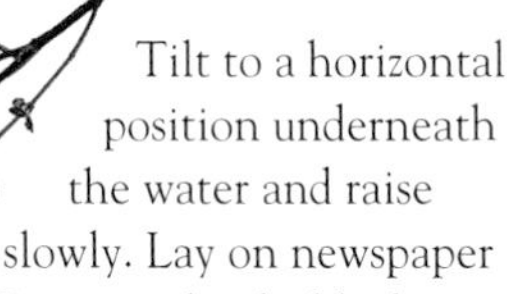

Pick the flowers and leaves during a sunny period and dry them in a dark, well-ventilated room for several days. This will preserve their color. Make sure all the ingredients are thoroughly dry before using or the potpourri will go moldy.

Fragrant Potpourri

- 4 handfuls of thoroughly dried flowers and leaves
- Dried orange peel
- 6 cinnamon sticks
- 4 nutmegs
- 3 teaspoons of essential oil, such as orange, lemon or mint
- 1 tablespoon of fixative (orris root, rose attar, dried rosemary or musk)

Mix all ingredients except the fixative together in a glass bowl. When the oils have been absorbed, tip the mixture into a plastic bag, add the fixative, seal and leave for 2 weeks. Shake from time to time. Place in decorative jars or bowls.

Herbal Paper

Paper can be scented or decorated with herbs or have herbs in the fibers. The easiest way to make herbal paper is by recycling old paper, such as newspaper, computer paper, wallpaper or writing paper. Soak small pieces overnight in warm water. Mix 2½ tablespoons of paper with 3 cups water, then add ⅕ teaspoon laundry starch mixed with a little water to the pulp. Place the pulp into a large plastic bucket. Place a small wooden frame (the deckle) over another frame covered with fine netting or mesh (the mold), and dip vertically into the bucket.

Potpourris are usually on show, so choose plant material for its appearance as well as its scent.

Tilt to a horizontal position underneath the water and raise slowly. Lay on newspaper to dry. Remove the deckle frame. Scatter petals, leaves and stems on top of the paper in the mold and leave to dry. Flowers that work well are rose, lavender, cornflower, sunflower and dandelion. Try onion skins, lavender seeds or sunflower stems for a special effect. When the paper is completely dry, slide a knife under the sheet to loosen it from the frame.

For scented paper, store your special writing paper in a box with aromatic herbs. Or place a muslin bag filled with potpourri between layers of drawer-lining paper for a fresh scent every time you open your drawers.

Herb-scented Candles

Scented candles can help to create a refreshing or a tranquil atmosphere, and they are easy to make at home. Make them as strongly scented as you like and leave in the plant materials—they will add extra color and texture and make your candle prettier and more interesting. You can use any of the herbal scents you'd like to evoke indoors. Lavender is a favorite, along with rosemary and southernwood. Mix your own blends using materials you've grown in your herb garden.

- 2 lb (1 kg) paraffin wax, broken into small pieces
- 2 wax crayons, or candle colorant
- 2 cups dried herbs, or 4 cups packed fresh herb leaves, blossoms or woody stems, or 1 fl oz (30 ml) essential oil
- Petroleum jelly
- Sufficient candle wicking to reach the lengths of your candle molds
- Several candle molds or recycled tin cans or other heatproof molds
- Pencils

Melt the wax in a bowl placed over a saucepan of hot water, then stir in the crayons or coloring. Remove from heat. As the wax cools, add the plant materials or oil. Coat the molds with petroleum

You can make attractive gifts using dried herbs and flowers, such as lavender, from your garden.

jelly. Drop a length of wicking to the bottom of each mold, wrapping the top around a pencil resting across the top of the mold to keep the wick centered while you pour in wax. When the wax resembles a gel, pour it into the molds. Allow the candles to set overnight, then remove.

Herb Pillows and Bags

Herb pillows and bags make wonderful gifts and add a unique touch to your home. Choose fabrics and colors to match your furnishings or those of a special friend.

Herb-scented pillows were originally a medical treatment for inducing sleep when stress prevented a restful night. It was thought that the fragrance of such herbs as hyssop would send you to sleep quickly. You can fill herbal pillows with whatever herbal blend suits you. Cut two pieces of fabric 8 inches (20 cm) square and stitch them, right sides together, along three sides. Turn them right side out, and stuff the pocket loosely with potpourri or any mixture of dried herbs (remove the stems), then stitch closed. Slip the pillow inside your pillowcase for a soothing sleep.

Herb bags are useful to scent drawers, closets, linen chests or luggage, or toss them in the tumble dryer to scent your clothing. Place several tablespoons of crushed potpourri in the center of a fabric square, gather together the edges, and tie with a length of ribbon; you can also add lace and other special effects. When bags begin to lose their scent, gather several in a glass jar and sprinkle them lightly with essential oils. Cover and let them sit for a week before reusing them.

Pressed Herb Notebooks

Notebooks are always handy and make attractive gifts, especially when decorated with pressed herbs, flowers and petals. You can buy special flower presses or use an old pile of books. Pick flowers when they are at their brightest and press until completely dry. Arrange into an attractive design on the front cover and glue the flowers and leaves into position. Cover with a self-adhesive plastic film.

Pressed Herb Cards

You can make your own greeting, birthday and Christmas cards using the same method. They are time-consuming, but the finished cards are very attractive and well worth the effort. Attach them to special gifts you have made.

Herbal Wreaths

Herbs can be used to make attractive wreaths to greet guests to your home on special occasions or to give as gifts to friends. They are a pretty and fragrant way to use your own home-grown herbs and flowers.

Start with a wreath frame of straw or wire, and sufficient quantities of a base herb, such as southernwood or wormwood, to cover the frame. Make small bunches of the base herb and wrap the cut end of each with florist's wire, then insert them into the frame or wrap them onto the frame with more wire. Continue adding the base herb until the entire wreath form is covered. Hang the wreath to dry in a dark place for several weeks. You can attach contrasting herb bunches, dried flowers, or ribbon-wrapped bundles of spices with more wire, or use a glue gun. Add small packets of herb seeds for your gardening friends. Or, for your friends who love cooking, design a wreath for the kitchen covered with bunches of their favorite culinary herbs.

Herbal candles offer a variety of colors and scents. Float small herb candles in clear or colored water and use as a dinner table ornament. Herbal candles in containers are perfect for outdoor use on windy evenings.

Herbal Insect Repellents

Herbs were one of the first pest controls used by our earliest ancestors. We enjoy the distinctive aroma of such herbs as eucalyptus, tansy and rosemary, but many insects find them repellent and tend to keep away from them. Herbs work safely to control these pests, and are more pleasant in keeping moths away from your clothes than are conventional mothballs, the pungent odor of which lingers for a long time. Herbs are also easily recycled through the compost pile, so when they have finished their job, put them in the compost bin to add further benefit to your garden later on.

Use herbs to help control pests on clothing, people and pets with the following remedies.

Lemon-scented eucalypts produce the volatile oil citronella, which is used widely in insect repellents.

Insect Repellent for Clothing

- 1/2 cup cedar shavings
- 1/4 cup each of at least four of: dried lemon verbena, lavender, pennyroyal, mint, rue, rosemary, tansy, santolina, southernwood, or wormwood
- 2 tablespoons each of at least two of: whole cloves, cinnamon, nutmeg, lemon peel, peppercorns or bay
- 5–10 drops essential oil of cedar, lemon, lavender or pine
- 2 tablespoons orris root

Mix the ingredients together and allow to stand in a covered jar for one week. Cut scraps of fabric 8 inches (20 cm) square. Place 1/2 cup of the mix in the center of the fabric, gather the edges together, and tie securely with string or ribbon. You can hang the repellent sachets in closets, or place them in stored luggage or linen cupboards to chase away the moths that enjoy a meal of cotton or wool. Replace the sachets each season.

Insect Repellent for Skin

- 1 teaspoon each of: essential oils of pennyroyal, citronella, eucalyptus, rosemary and tansy
- 1 cup (250 ml) vegetable oil

Shake the ingredients together in an airtight jar and store away from light. To repel outdoor insect pests, rub a small amount between the palms of your hands, then apply to any exposed skin. Avoid applications to the face to prevent contact with your eyes. Reapply as necessary. If a rash develops, discontinue use.

Moth Balls

You can make your own moth balls rather than using the commercial ones. Use equal quantities of dried cotton lavender, tansy and costmary leaves. Process in a grinder or pound in a mortar, place in circles of fabric, gather up, and tie off with ribbon or string. Make only as much mixture as required, as its effectiveness will only last

Simple Home Remedies

- Mosquito bites can be alleviated by rubbing hyssop, lavender or calendula oil onto the bite.
- Insect bites can be relieved by rubbing fresh sage leaves onto the skin.
- To lessen the pain of a bee sting, first remove the sting then rub fresh winter or summer savory onto the sting.
- A bunch of rue, tansy, wormwood and elder leaves hung near an open door will keep flies away.
- Lavender oil sprinkled around the house or bunches of fresh lavender in vases will keep house flies away.
- If your cats and dogs are bothered by fleas, rub fresh pennyroyal sprigs or pennyroyal oil into their fur.
- To control fleas in the house, place pennyroyal sprigs under rugs or mattresses. Use pennyroyal oil if you don't have fresh sprigs.
- Cinnamon bark, dried tansy, mint and wormwood leaves mixed together and placed in muslin bags will keep moths and silverfish away from clothes for months.
- Place sprigs of pennyroyal, rue or tansy on shelves or in cupboards to deter ants.
- Fleas and lice on animal coats can be treated with a solution of walnut leaves and water.
- Sandfly and other insect bites can be eased by rubbing fresh fennel, parsley, feverfew, costmary or marigold leaves onto the skin.
- Keep rats away by spreading catmint wherever you suspect their presence.
- If mice are a problem, hang sprigs of mint and tansy.
- Burn citronella in an oil burner to keep mosquitoes and other biting insects away when you are sitting outside at night.

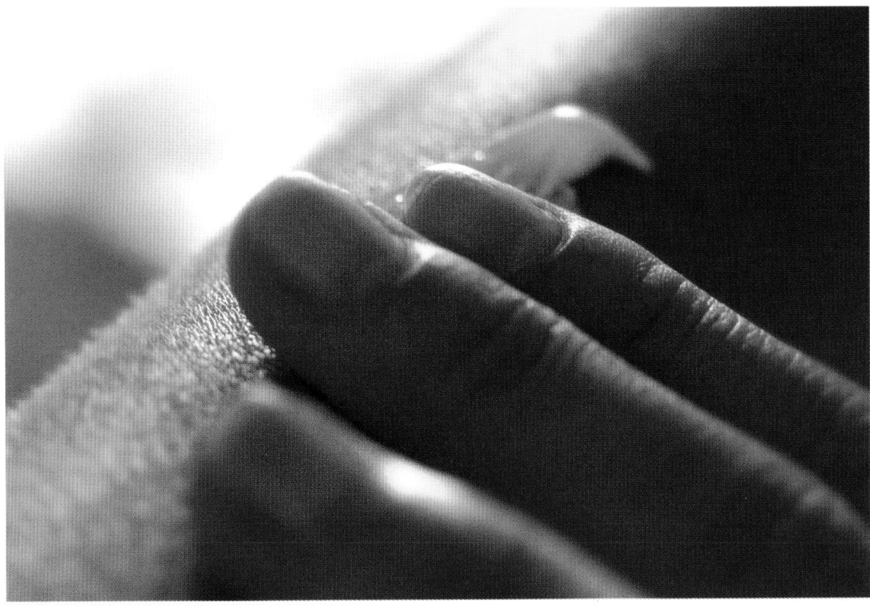

If you have been bitten by an insect, rub in chamomile cream to soothe the bite and take away the itch.

for about 3–6 months. To increase the strength of the moth balls, add a little pyrethrum powder or pyrethrum flowers.

Cotton Lavender Moth Repellent

A useful moth repellent can be made from a mixture of cotton lavender and other herbs. Mix together equal parts of cotton lavender leaves, lavender flowers, rosemary leaves and dried rue. Place into squares of fabric. Tie off with ribbon or string, then hang in cupboards or place in drawers to keep moths away.

Southernwood is a well-known insect repellent. Combine with cinnamon to keep insects away.

Southernwood Insect Repellent

Southernwood is a strongly scented herb with the reputation of being an excellent insect repellent. Grow it well away from other plants, as it even repels bees. To repel moths from clothes and linen, combine 1 oz (25 g) dried southernwood and 1 teaspoon crushed cinnamon stick. Place the mixture into small bags made of cheesecloth (muslin), sew up, and hang in cupboards or place in drawers or between stored garments.

Soothing Herbs

An infusion of chamomile flowers rubbed onto exposed parts of the body will repel insects. If insects still bite, try dabbing on eucalyptus oil for relief. Alternatively, soak in a bath that has chamomile oil or leaves infused in the water. This will soothe the bites and take away some of the itch.

Pennyroyal

Insect Repellents for Pets

Use one or both of the following herbal insect repellents for your pets, depending on the extent of the problem. You may apply these repellents when your pet already has fleas, or as a preventative measure at the start of the flea season.

Herbal Pet Dip

2 cups packed fresh peppermint, pennyroyal or rosemary
1 quart (1 l) boiling water
4 quarts (4 l) warm water

Prepare an infusion by pouring the boiling water over the herbs, and allow it to steep for 30 minutes. Strain the liquid and dilute it with the warm water. Saturate the animal's coat thoroughly with the solution, allowing it to air-dry. Use at the first sign of flea activity.

Herbal Bedding

If your pet has a flea problem, then it is also important to treat their bedding. Sew together small pillows of cheesecloth (muslin) or other cotton fabric. Stuff loosely with dried pennyroyal, cedar, rue, tansy, pine shavings or rosemary. Seal the bags and place in the folds of your pet's bedding. Refresh the dried materials weekly. Use at the first sign of flea activity.

Catmint has a scent that cats love, and it will also keep mice and rats away.

Herbal Dyes

Hyssop

Herbs have been used to dye cloth for thousands of years. Until the 19th century, when the chemical industry was developed, all dyes were natural. Today, chemical dyes offer a wider range of colors, but plant dyes are unsurpassed for richness and subtlety of color. They are created by simply boiling fresh or dried plant parts in water, then adding fabric.

Natural fibers such as cotton, linen, silk and wool are simple to dye at home using your own herbs, vegetables, flowers, and wild plant materials. You can create unique, subtle, earthy tones.

The following instructions are for dyeing wool, since it is the easiest material for beginners to work with. Before you begin, read through the procedure and assemble the tools and supplies you'll need.

Fiber You can dye 1 pound (500 g) of wool yarn with the instructions below. Tie the skeins loosely with cotton thread to hold them together while you work. Before dyeing, gently wash the wool with mild soap to clean any traces of soil or oil that may cause the fiber to color unevenly.

Water Use "soft" water for dyeing. Collect rainwater in a clean bucket, or add 1 tablespoon of washing soda or water softener if your water is hard.

Pots and Utensils Use stainless steel or enamel pots that won't react with the chemicals, and that will hold at least 4 gallons (18 liters) of water, plus the wool. Aluminum pots will brighten the color, copper pots add a greenish shade, and iron kettles tend to darken the colors. Some dyeing chemicals are poisonous. Do not prepare food in any pot that has been used for dyeing. For stirring, use glass rods or enamel or wooden spoons. You'll also need glass or enamel measuring spoons and cups, a scale that registers ounces (grams), a thermometer that goes up to 212°F (100°C), either muslin, cheesecloth or an enamel colander, several buckets for rinsing, and rubber gloves.

Plant Materials Harvest leaves, flowers, stems, bark, roots, seeds or nuts at their peak color. You'll need about 8 quarts (8 l) of light plant materials (leaves, blossoms and small seeds) for 1 pound (500 g) of wool, or about 1 pound (500 g) of heavy materials (nuts, large seeds, roots, stems and bark). Getting the right hue will take some experimenting, since parts of the same plant combined with different mordants (see below) will create different colors.

Mordants Color is influenced by your choice of mordant. Mordants help to set the dyes and prevent fading and running. Remember to wear rubber gloves when

What Herbs to Use

Hyssop

Herbs for brown dye
Walnut husks and shells, juniper berries, tea leaves

Herbs for orange dye
Onion skins, turmeric root, bloodroot root, lily of the valley leaves

Herbs for yellow dye
Safflower flowers, tansy flowers, chamomile flowers, agrimony flowers

Agrimony

Herbs for beige dye
St Johns' wort flowers, blackberry shoots

Herbs for red dye
Madder roots, lady's bedstraw roots, oregano

Herbs for pink dye
Sorrel roots, lady's bedstraw roots

Herbs for blue dye
Elder berries, cornflowers

Herbs for green dye
Nettle plant, hyssop leaves, elder leaves

Oregano

Directions

1. Add the mordant and cream of tartar to a small amount of water, mixing well, then add 4 gallons (16 l) of water. Heat to lukewarm and add the dry or freshly washed wool. Heat to boiling, then lower the temperature and allow to simmer for 1 hour. Let the bath cool slowly, then remove the wool. Squeeze it dry and roll in towels to absorb excess moisture. (You can pause here if you like, and continue the dyeing process another day. Just tag the skeins with the type of mordant and date, and allow them to dry.)
2. Chop or break apart the plant materials you've collected. Soak heavier materials in water overnight. Mix plant materials with 4 gallons (16 l) of water, allow to simmer for 1 hour, then strain. This solution is the dye bath. Make it as light or dark as you like.
3. Place the prepared wool in the dye bath and slowly raise the temperature to simmer, poking the wool occasionally for a uniform color, for 1 hour. You can continue simmering for up to 2 hours if you want a stronger color. Check the wool occasionally. When you've finished, remove the wool. You can add another pound (500 g) of wool to the bath, but this second lot will have a lighter shade than the first.
4. Rinse the wool in water of the same temperature, and continue rinsing with fresh water that is progressively cooler until the water is clear. Rinse once more in a mixture of 1/4 cup (60 ml) vinegar in 1 gallon (4 l) water to set the color. Squeeze the water out of the wool, then hang to dry.

Chamomile

Use herbal dyes to make your own uniquely colored garments. Natural fibers are simple to dye at home, and wool is the easiest material for beginners to try first. Use enamel or stainless steel pots when making dyes.

Dried turmeric root gives a gold to orange dye. Use it with an alum mordant.

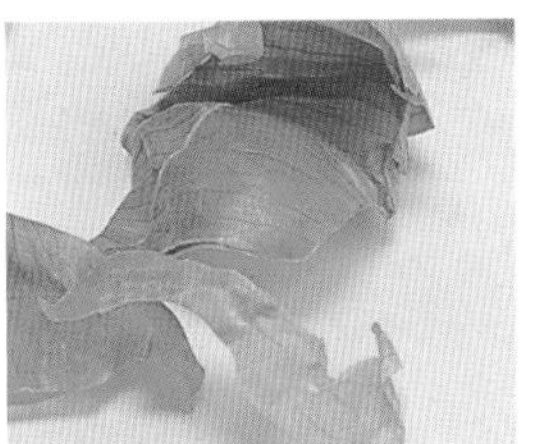

Onion skins give a rich orange to brown dye. Use with a mordant of copper.

handling mordants, in particular chrome copper, and tin, as these materials can harm your skin.

Alum The most common mordant. For 1 pound (500 g) of wool, use 4 ounces (125 g) alum and 1 ounce (30 g) cream of tartar to 4 gallons (16 l) of water.

Chrome (potassium dichromate) Use for deepening yellows and golds. It's light sensitive, so keep the lid on the pot while dyeing. It is also very poisonous. For 1 pound (500 g) of wool, use ½ ounce (15 g) of chrome and ½ ounce (15 g) cream of tartar to 4 gallons (16 l) of water.

Copper (cupric sulfate) Helps rid greens of yellowness. For 1 pound (500 g) of wool, use ½ ounce (15 g) copper and 1 ounce (30 g) cream of tartar to 4 gallons (16 l) of water. Or use a copper pot.

Iron (ferrous sulfate) Dulls and deepens most colors. For 1 pound (500 g) of wool, use ½ ounce (15 g) iron and 1 ounce (30 g) cream of tartar to 4 gallons (16 l) of water. Or use an iron pot.

Tin (stannous chloride) Brightens and gives depth to most colors. For 1 pound (500 g) of wool, use ½ ounce (15 g) tin and 1 ounce (30 g) cream of tartar to 4 gallons (16 l) of water.

SECTION SEVEN

A Guide to Popular Herbs

This section tells you all about the herbs you want to grow. It describes ideal growing conditions, when to sow seed, at what stage to transplant herbs into the garden, the ideal soil conditions and the climatic zones best suited to each plant. There is additional information on what pests and diseases could cause problems for your plants, and advice on what part of the herb to harvest and the various ways in which each herb can be used.

Herbs are listed alphabetically by their botanical names, with their most generally used common name also prominently displayed. Each plant is photographed in color to make identification easy.

Acacia farnesiana
MIMOSACEAE

WATTLE (MIMOSA)

Wattle is grown extensively throughout southern France as a crop for the perfume industry. Wattle trees are popular as ornamentals for gardens in warmer regions and are fast growing and quick to flower when young.

Best climate and site Zones 7–9. Full sun. Occurs throughout dry tropical to warmer temperate regions.
Ideal soil conditions Well-drained soil; pH 4.5–7.0.
Growing guidelines Propagate by scarifying seed (soaking in boiling water until seed swells or rubbing the coat of the seed with sandpaper until coating is thin enough to let water in). Also by semiripe cuttings of lateral shoots in late summer.
Growing habit Straggly, many-branched tree; height to 23 feet (7 m). Sparse, feathery leaves are divided into four to eight pairs of leaflets. Light pruning after flowering will maintain shape.
Flowering time Masses of golden, strongly perfumed ball flowers are produced in summer.
Pests and disease prevention Prone to leaf miner, borer, acacia scale and galls.
Harvesting and storing Flowers are picked as they open and dried for infusions and baths, or distilled for oil. Seeds and pods are collected when ripe and pressed for oil.
Parts used Bark, flowers, pods, seeds.
Culinary uses Ripe seeds are pressed for cooking oil and also used in cakes and cookies.
Medicinal uses Internally for skin complaints, diarrhea and gastric disorders.
Externally in baths to relieve dry skin (flowers).
Other uses Oil is distilled from the flowers and used in insecticides. The bark and pods are used for a black dye. Used in some countries as a screen to keep out animals.

Achillea millefolium
ASTERACEAE

YARROW

Yarrow displays light, delicate ferny foliage and attractive, long-lasting flowers. It is frost hardy and very easy to grow from seed and division. Plant in ornamental beds, borders and the herb garden.

Best climate and site Zones 2–9. Full sun, but tolerates shade.
Ideal soil conditions Fertile, well-drained soil; pH 6.0–6.7.
Growing guidelines Sow seed shallowly indoors in early spring, or outdoors in late spring. Divide large clumps in spring and autumn to extend the planting.
Growing habit Perennial with fernlike, finely divided, aromatic leaves that are rich in vitamins and minerals; height to 3 feet (90 cm).
Flowering time Summer to autumn; numerous tiny white, pink or red florets in dense, flat clusters; has a pungent scent.
Pest and disease prevention Flowers attract beneficial insects that prey on aphids. Prone to powdery mildew.
Harvesting and storing Pick flowers with plenty of stem and strip foliage before drying; holds color well.
Special tips Add a finely chopped leaf to a wheelbarrow load of compost to speed the process of decomposition. Yarrow bears flat flower clusters that attract insects, including many beneficials. It is an attractive plant for borders with long-lived flowers that last well in water.
Precautions Internal use may cause allergic skin reactions.
Parts used Whole plant.
Medicinal uses Internally for colds, influenza, diarrhea, arthritis, measles and to protect against clotting after a stroke or heart attack.
Other uses Use in dried arrangements and to make a yellow or olive dye.
Other common names Milfoil, soldier's woundwort.

Aconitum carmichaelii
RANUNCULACEAE

MONKSHOOD

Named after the characteristic hood shape of its flowers, monkshood is extremely toxic and has been used in the past to make arrow poisons. It is a frost-hardy, attractive perennial with unusual foliage and colorful flowers.

Best climate and site Zones 3–8. Full sun to light shade. Prefers climate with cool summer nights and warm days with low humidity.
Ideal soil conditions Fertile, humus-rich, moist but well-drained soil; pH 4.2–6.5.
Growing guidelines Propagate by seed sown in spring or by division in autumn and winter. Dislikes disturbance once established, so plant or sow seed where plant is to grow.
Growing habit Perennial plant; height 3 feet (90 cm). Leaves are glossy and deeply cut and can reach 6 inches (15 cm) across. May need to be staked if growing position is windy.
Flowering time Spikes or racemes of deep blue, hoodlike flowers appear in summer and autumn. Removal of dead flower heads will encourage a second crop of flowers.
Pest and disease prevention Usually not bothered by pests.
Harvesting and storing Young roots are removed from the mother plant in autumn or winter.
Precautions Monkshood contains the chemical aconitine, which is one of the most toxic plant compounds known. Should only be used by qualified practitioners as all parts are extremely toxic. It is illegal to grow in some countries.
Parts used Roots.
Medicinal uses Internally for sedation, painkilling and stimulation of the heart and kidneys. Recent research has found it to be effective in congestive heart failure. Externally for rheumatism, arthritis and as an anesthetic.
Other common names Azure monkshood.

Aesculus hippocastanum
HIPPOCASTANACEAE

HORSE CHESTNUT

Horse chestnut is an ornamental tree that has long been used as a fodder and medicinal plant for cattle and horses. It has foliage that turns rich brown in autumn and edible seeds that resemble chestnuts.

Best climate and site Zones 3–8. Full sun to partial shade.
Ideal soil conditions Tolerates a variety of soil conditions but prefers deep, moist, well-drained, rich soil; pH 6–7.5.
Growing guidelines Propagate by seed sown in summer, or cuttings taken in winter. Keep well watered until established. Growth is rapid.
Growing habit Large, deciduous tree; height to 83 feet (25 m). Bright green, palm-shaped leaves that turn a rich brown in autumn. Pruning is not necessary.
Flowering time Upright, pyramidal clusters of small, white flowers occur in spring, followed by round, spiny fruits containing large shiny seeds sometimes called conkers.
Pest and disease prevention Clean up leaves to remove overwintering sites for disease spores. Keep well watered. Prone to Japanese beetles, fungal leaf blotch and canker.
Harvesting and storing Bark and seeds are collected in autumn and treated for medicinal use. Seeds are roasted before use.
Precautions Horse chestnut is harmful if eaten.
Parts used Seeds, bark.
Medicinal uses Internally for hardening of the arteries, stroke, chilblains, circulatory disorders and fever. Contains a chemical which has a potent anti-inflammatory effect. Horse chestnut has to be processed commercially.
Other uses Ingredient in cosmetics and hair products.
Other common names Buckeye, due to the resemblance of the seeds to the eyes of deer.

Agastache foeniculum
LAMIACEAE

ANISE HYSSOP

Anise hyssop has the appearance of a mint with square stems and attractive lavender blossoms, but the leaves have a distinctive licorice scent and flavor. Use them to flavor meat dishes, in salads and as a tea.

Best climate and site Zones 6–10. Prefers full sun but tolerates partial shade.
Ideal soil conditions Rich, well-drained garden soil; pH 6.0–7.0.
Growing guidelines Sow seed shallowly in spring indoors or outdoors, thinning to 1 foot (30 cm); transplants very well. The tall plants occasionally require staking.
Growing habit Perennial; height to 3 feet (90 cm); tall and branched at the top.
Flowering time Late summer to autumn; topped with spikes of lavender flowers.
Pest and disease prevention Usually free from pests and diseases.
Harvesting and storing Harvest fresh leaves as necessary throughout the summer. The best time to collect foliage for drying is just before blooming; hang bunches to dry. Or cut whole plants after blooming, and hang them to dry for both foliage and dried flowers.
Parts used Leaves, flowers.
Culinary uses Used in salads, as a flavoring of meat and as a tea.
Medicinal uses Internally for coughs, nausea and colds. Also helps to improve appetite and can lower a fever by increasing perspiration.
Other common names Licorice mint, anise mint, fennel giant hyssop.

Agave americana
AGAVACEAE

AGAVE (CENTURY PLANT)

The gigantic leaf rosettes of this succulent make agave among the most striking feature plants for gardens. Pharmaceutically, agave is an important plant as it contains a chemical used in the manufacture of steroid drugs.

Best climate and site Zones 9–10. Requires full sun. Drought resistant.
Ideal soil conditions Well-drained soil. Responds well to an application of animal manure; pH 4.6–7.9.
Growing guidelines Propagate with offshoots taken from the parent plant in spring and left to dry for some days before potting. Seeds slow to germinate.
Growing habit Long-living perennial with a spread of 6 feet (2 m) or more. Leaves are gray, smooth and broadly linear with spiny, serrated edges. Water only in summer.
Flowering time Takes at least 10 years before sending up a 20-foot (6-m) flower spike of greenish-yellow petals.
Pest and disease prevention Prone to attack by mealybugs and to rot if watered in winter.
Harvesting and storing Parts are harvested as required.
Precautions Fresh sap has been known to cause skin irritation and dermatitis.
Parts used Whole plant, leaves, roots, sap.
Culinary uses Tender plant core is cooked as a vegetable. Sap is used to make alcoholic drinks.
Medicinal uses Internally for indigestion, constipation, jaundice and dysentery.
Other uses Roots are used in the manufacture of soap.
Other common names Foxtail plant, spiked aloe.
Other varieties *A. americana* 'Marginata' has dramatic pale, yellow-margined leaves.

Agrimonia eupatoria
ROSACEAE

AGRIMONY

Beginning herb growers will appreciate this easy-to-grow, aromatic perennial herb with dark green, hairy foliage and yellow blossoms. Its most common use is as a tea, but it is also used as a gargle for sore throats.

Best climate and site Zones 5–9. Full sun, but tolerates partial shade.
Ideal soil conditions Light garden soil with good drainage; pH 6.0–7.0.
Growing guidelines Sow seed outdoors in early spring and thin to 6 inches (15 cm). Agrimony can self-sow each year. Or divide older plants in spring. Thrives with little attention.
Growing habit Perennial with upright, hairy stems and downy leaves; height to 2–3 feet (60–90 cm).
Flowering time Summer; tall spikes with small, lightly scented yellow flowers followed by bristly fruits.
Pest and disease prevention Keep foliage dry to prevent powdery mildew.
Harvesting and storing Collect and dry foliage just before blooming. Strip the leaves and spread them to dry, or hang in bunches.
Special tips Adds height to rock gardens.
Precautions Not given to people with stress-related constipation.
Parts used Whole plant.
Culinary uses As a tea.
Medicinal uses Internally for food allergies, diarrhea, cystitis and rheumatism. Also used to help control bleeding. Has anti-inflammatory properties.
Externally for sore throats, hemorrhoids, cuts, skin wounds and acne.
Other common names Sticklewort, cocklebur.

Allium ampeloprasum
ALLIACEAE

LEEK

Leeks are the national emblem of Wales. They are grown for their stout, flavorful bulb and stem. They are popular ingredients in French cooking. These onion relatives hold well in the ground for late harvest.

Best climate and site Zones 6 and warmer; grow as a winter vegetable in mild areas. Full sun.
Ideal soil conditions Loose, very rich, well-drained soil; pH 6.0–7.5.
Growing guidelines By seed planted in spring or autumn or by division. Transplant to small, individual pots when large enough to handle. This produces better leeks. Set out after frost, in a 6-inch (15-cm) deep trench covering all but 1 inch (2 cm) of leaves. Keep well weeded. As leeks grow, fill in the trench gradually or, if planted on level soil, "hill" them by drawing soil up around the stems. This produces a longer white stem, which is the edible part. Keep soil moist.
Growing habit Perennial with cylindrical bulb; height 3 feet (90 cm).
Pest and disease prevention To avoid root maggot damage, do not plant where other onion family members have grown the previous year.
Harvesting and storing Dig or pull when large enough for use. Harvest wintered leeks before spring growth begins.
Parts used Stems, bulbs.
Culinary uses Cooked in soups, stir-fries and meat dishes.
Medicinal uses Internally for colds, earache, respiratory tract infections and bronchitis.
Other species Garlic chives, Chinese chives, Asian leek *A. tuberosum* is a hardy perennial grown for its mildly garlic-flavored leaves, which are used in stir-fries and soups. The spring flowers are also edible.

Allium cepa
ALLIACEAE

ONION

A staple since before the Pharaohs, the bulb of the versatile onion provides plenty of good eating in little garden space. Its characteristic smell is caused by sulfur compounds, which have beneficial medicinal properties.

Best climate and site Zones 4 and warmer. Full sun.
Ideal soil conditions Rich, well-drained soil; pH 6.0–7.5.
Growing guidelines Sow seed in autumn or spring, or by "sets" (small bulbs). Plant 3–4 inches (8–10 cm) apart a month before last frost. Keep well weeded; young onions have slender, grasslike leaves and are easily shaded out. Fertilize with fish emulsion or compost tea to encourage good early growth, which will determine eventual bulb size.
Growing habit Robust biennial with a large bulb up to 4 inches (10 cm) across and hollow leaves; height 4 feet (1.2 m).
Flowering time Star-shaped, green-white flowers in summer.
Pest and disease prevention Onion fly and maggots can cause problems. Downy mildew is prevalent in wet conditions and will rot growing bulbs. Onion thrips can be a problem.
Harvesting and storing Pull onions for fresh use as needed.
Parts used Bulbs.
Culinary uses Onions are an indispensable vegetable and add flavor to most meat and vegetable dishes. Also eaten raw in salads or pickled.
Medicinal uses Internally for coughs, colds, bronchitis and gastric infections.
Externally for boils and acne.
Other varieties and species Red (Spanish) onion *A. cepa* 'Noordhollandse Bloedrode' is a red-skinned cultivar; sweeter than brown and white onions.
Scallion, Welsh onion *A. fistulosum* is a biennial or perennial with elongated bulbs.

Allium cepa, Aggregatum group
LILIACEAE

SHALLOT

An onion relative, shallots produce small, firm bulbs in clusters that keep like garlic but are much milder in flavor. They are sometimes used as green onions or spring onions, and are used medicinally as a diuretic.

Best climate and site Zones 4 and warmer; may be planted in autumn in Zones 6 and warmer. Full sun.
Ideal soil conditions Deep, humus-rich, well-drained soil; pH 6.0–7.5. Will tolerate all but the most acid soil.
Growing guidelines Shallots do not grow from seed but from bulblets or "sets." In cold climates, plant 2–4 weeks before last spring frost, 1 inch (2.5 cm) deep and 4–6 inches (10–15 cm) apart. Keep cultivated, or mulch and water regularly to encourage strong early growth. Each set will divide and produce 8–10 shallots. Where climate permits, autumn planting will produce larger shallots the following summer.
Growing habit Small, firm bulbs produced in sets; height 8 inches (20 cm).
Pest and disease prevention To avoid root maggots, do not plant where shallots or their relatives, such as onions or leeks, have grown the previous year.
Harvesting and storing Harvest in spring, summer or late autumn. When the tops are nearly dry, pull plants and dry the bulbs in a well-ventilated, sunny area by hanging in a cool, dry place, or clip the stems and store the bulbs in mesh bags.
Parts used Bulbs, young leaves.
Culinary uses As a vegetable to flavor meat, chicken and vegetable dishes.
Medicinal uses Internally as a diuretic, antibiotic and expectorant. Also for coughs, colds, laryngitis and bronchitis. Can reduce blood pressure and blood sugar level.
Externally for cuts, acne and to promote hair growth.

Allium sativum
LILIACEAE

GARLIC

Garlic is one of the most familiar herbs. The strongly scented bulb is used to flavor dishes from almost every ethnic cuisine. It is also recommended as an insect-repelling plant.

Best climate and site Zones 7–10. Ideally in full sun.
Ideal soil conditions Rich, well-drained soil; pH 4.5–8.3.
Growing guidelines Separate individual cloves from the bulb immediately before planting, then plant in late autumn in mild areas for harvesting the following summer; space 6 inches (15 cm) apart and 2 inches (5 cm) deep. For largest bulbs, prune away flowering stems that shoot up in early summer; side-dress with compost in early spring. In severe winter areas, plant in early spring.
Growing habit Perennial bulb; height to 2 feet (60 cm); foliage resembles onions, iris, or tulips, depending on variety.
Flowering time Early summer; small, white to pinkish blooms atop a tall, central stalk.
Pest and disease prevention Avoid over-watering the soil to prevent bulb diseases.
Harvesting and storing Dig bulbs after tops begin to fall over, and before bulb skins begin to decay underground; place in a single layer in a shaded spot to dry, then cut away tops or plait together the tops of freshly dug plants.
Parts used Bulbs.
Culinary uses Adds flavor to most meats, seafood and vegetables. Raw garlic used in sauces and added as a condiment to butter, vinegar and salt.
Medicinal uses Internally to prevent infection and treat colds, whooping cough and dysentery.
Externally for skin problems such as acne, rashes and fungal infections.

Allium schoenoprasum
LILIACEAE

CHIVES

The graceful leaves and blossoms of chives have a mild onion flavor, especially when used fresh. Use the leaves in cooking and toss the flowers in salads or use them as a garnish.

Best climate and site Zones 5–10. Full sun.
Ideal soil conditions Rich, well-drained soil; pH 6.0–7.0.
Growing guidelines Sow seed indoors in late winter, covering seeds lightly and keeping the soil moist; transplant in clumps in early spring spacing 5–8 inches (12–20 cm) apart. Sow outside in spring. Every three years, divide older clumps in the early spring and freshen with compost or rotted manure.
Growing habit Perennial bulb with green, tubular leaves; height 6–12 inches (15–30 cm).
Flowering time Summer; pink or lavender to purple globular flower heads.
Pest and disease prevention Avoid wet areas that encourage stem and bulb diseases.
Harvesting and storing Use fresh leaf tips all summer once plants are 6 inches (15 cm) tall; leave at least 2 inches (5 cm) remaining. Chives are best used fresh, or chop and dry.
Special tips Chives are recommended companion plants for carrots, grapes, roses and tomatoes as they ward off pests.
Parts used Leaves, flowers, bulbs.
Culinary uses Chives are used in egg and potato dishes. Leaves and bulbs are added to soups, salads, omelets, sauces and soft cheeses. Flowers have a mild onion flavor and are added to salads.
Other species Garlic chives *A. tuberosum* is somewhat similar, but flowers are white and leaves are flat and broader. They have a garlicky aroma and flavor. Also known as Chinese chives.

This clump-forming herb is a stemless rosette of spiny, tapered leaves. The yellow to red flowers are drooping and tubular and appear on top of a tall, leafless stalk.

Aloe vera syn. *A. barbadensis*
ALOACEAE

ALOE

There are more than 300 perennial species of succulent aloe. The long, tapering leaves are ornamented with soft spines, and contain a medicinal as well as a cosmetic gel. It is an extremely bitter herb.

Best climate and site Zones 9–10, or greenhouse not below 41°F (5°C). Prefers full sun but tolerates light shade. If growing indoors, plant in a well-drained, regular container mix and keep in a sunny position.
Ideal soil conditions Gritty, well-drained soil low in organic matter; pH 6.7–7.3.
Growing guidelines Sow seed in spring. Separate new shoots from established plants then dry for 2 days before planting. In cool climates, plant in pots and move indoors in winter. Aloes thrive with little attention. Indoors, avoid excess water around roots and mix coarse sand with potting soil to facilitate good drainage.
Growing habit Clump-forming perennial with dense rosettes of thick, spiky, tapered green-gray leaves; height 2–3 feet (60–90 cm).
Flowering time Rarely flowers in cool climates; in warmer climates, produces drooping, tubular, yellow to red flowers in summer on top of a tall stalk. *A. vera* rarely forms seed.
Pest and disease prevention Spray with insecticidal soap to control mealybugs. Control insect pests before bringing pots indoors.
Harvesting and storing Inside each leaf is clear, gelatinous sap which has a soothing effect when rubbed on burns, chapped skin or skin wounds. Cut leaves for gel as needed from 2- and 3-year-old plants; remove outer leaves first. Sap can be used fresh or evaporated to be made into creams and tinctures.
Special tips Grow on sunny windowsills in the kitchen and bathroom.
Precautions Not given to pregnant women or to people with hemorrhoids. Also not recommended for people with irritable bowel syndrome. This herb is subject to legal restrictions in some countries.
Parts used Leaves from 2- to 3-year-old plants, sap.
Medicinal uses Internally for constipation, poor appetite, digestive problems and colonic irrigation but unsafe for home use.
Externally for burns, sunburn, eczema, cuts and to help stop nail biting. It also has anti-inflammatory properties and aids healing.
Other uses Used in pharmaceutical preparations, facial creams and cosmetics.
Other common names First-aid herb, healing herb, medicine plant.
Other species Zanzibar aloe *A. perryi* produces a rich violet-blue dye.
A. variegata is popular as an ornamental pot plant.
Gardener's trivia This plant is important historically. It was used for embalming and records of Christianity show that the body of Jesus was wrapped in a cloth that had been impregnated with aloe and myrrh. It has also been identified in wall paintings from ancient Egypt, where it was used to treat excess mucus. *Aloe vera* was also one of Cleopatra's secret beauty ingredients.

Aloysia triphylla
VERBENACEAE

LEMON VERBENA

Grown for its strong lemon aroma and flavor, lemon verbena is well worth the extra care required. It was once used in perfumery but evidence showed that it may sensitize the skin to sunlight, so its popularity declined.

Best climate and site Zones 9–10. Full sun; frost-free greenhouse in cooler areas.
Ideal soil conditions Fertile, light, well-drained soil; tolerates most soils; pH 6.0–6.7.
Growing guidelines In cold climates, grow in pots placed outdoors in summer and indoors in winter. Keep the soil moist but never soggy; feed with compost tea regularly. Pinch tips to encourage bushy growth. In autumn, prune away long branches before bringing pots indoors; overwinter in a greenhouse kept at 45°F (7°C).
Growing habit Perennial, deciduous, woody shrub with light green, lancelike leaves in whorls; height 5–10 feet (1.5–3 m).
Flowering time Late summer to autumn; tiny white to lavender blossoms on spikes from leaf axils.
Pest and disease prevention Wash mites from foliage with a spray of water directed at the undersides of leaves. For stubborn infestations, wipe infected areas with cotton soaked in alcohol, or spray with a botanical insecticide, such as citrus oil, pyrethrum or rotenone.
Harvesting and storing Snip sprigs of leaves or cut foliage back halfway in midsummer and again in autumn. Dry foliage in a shady spot. Use in potpourri.
Special tips Will train as a mop-headed standard.
Parts used Leaves, oil.
Culinary uses Fresh leaves are used to flavor stuffing and added to salads. Also used in herbal teas.
Medicinal uses Internally for colds and indigestion.

Alpinia galanga
ZINGIBERACEAE

GALANGAL

The tropical galangals are members of the same family as ginger, with which they have much in common both in form and flavor. Galangal is a popular ingredient in many Indonesian, Thai and Malaysian dishes.

Best climate and site Zone 10. Partial shade; drought and frost tender. Minimum temperatures 59–64°F (15–18°C).
Ideal soil conditions Well-drained but moist, humus-rich soil; pH 4.5–6.8.
Growing guidelines Propagate by rhizome division as new growth becomes apparent.
Growing habit Perennial, upright plant; height 6 feet (1.8 m). Leaves are long and narrow. Rhizome is creeping, cylindrical and branched with a reddish exterior marked with circular bands of lighter color and a grayish white interior.
Flowering time Small, pale green flowers with a white lip, which resemble orchids, are produced all year.
Pest and disease prevention Prone to attack by red spider mite.
Harvesting and storing Roots of plants 3–6 years old are lifted and used raw, dried or distilled for oil. Store fresh root galangal in an airtight container.
Parts used Rhizomes, oil.
Culinary uses Rhizomes used in cooking for their ginger-like flavor. Oil is used in liqueurs, soft drinks and bitters.
Medicinal uses Lesser galangal A. *officinarum* is used internally for digestive disorders, rheumatic pain, catarrh and respiratory problems. A drink made from grated galangal and lime juice is taken as a tonic in Southeast Asia. Externally for skin infections and gum disease.
Other common names Greater galangal, Siamese ginger.
Gardener's trivia In some countries, galangal is worn as a charm to protect children and animals from evil spirits.

Althaea officinalis
MALVACEAE

MARSH MALLOW

Use marsh mallow leaves to add a fresh flavor to salads, or slice and cook the roots like potatoes. The roots were originally used to produce the consistency typical of the confection marshmallow.

Best climate and site Zones 6–9. Full sun.
Ideal soil conditions Light soil that stays damp; pH 6.0–8.0.
Growing guidelines Sow seed in shallow beds outdoors in spring, thinning to 2 feet (60 cm). Divide clumps or take basal cuttings from foliage or roots in autumn.
Growing habit Robust perennial with soft, gray, velvety foliage that dies down in autumn; height to about 4 feet (1.2 m).
Flowering time Summer; pink or bluish white mallow-like blossoms are followed by circular downy seedpods called "cheeses"; each holds one seed.
Pest and disease prevention Usually free from pests and diseases.
Harvesting and storing Harvest leaves in autumn, just before flowering. Collect and dry flowers at their peak. If you plan to use the tap roots, dig them in autumn from plants at least 2 years old; scrub them, and cook them like potatoes or slice before drying.
Parts used Leaves, roots.
Culinary uses Use the leaves to add a fresh flavor to salads. Cook the roots and eat like potatoes.
Medicinal uses Internally for bronchitis, asthma, hiatus hernia, cystitis and excess mucus.
Externally for insect bites, mastitis, boils and gangrene.
Other uses Peeled root traditionally given to young children to chew as a teething aid.
Other common names White mallow, sweet weed, mortification root.

Anethum graveolens
APIACEAE

DILL

Dill is an aromatic annual. Select varieties for either seed or foliage and use in cooking with seafood or potatoes. Dill's tall, graceful habit makes it an attractive background in flowerbeds.

Best climate and site Zones 6–10. Full sun.
Ideal soil conditions Rich, well-drained soil; pH 5.0–7.
Growing guidelines In spring, sow seed in shallow soil about 10 inches (25 cm) apart in prepared beds. Firm down the soil. Keep seedlings moist and weed diligently. The soft, delicate seedlings do not transplant well and are easily blown over by strong winds. The plants do best in a sunny, sheltered area.
Growing habit Hardy annual resembling fennel; height 2–3 feet (60–90 cm).
Flowering time Summer; yellow flowers in umbels.
Pest and disease prevention Usually free from pests and diseases.
Harvesting and storing Clip fresh leaves at the stem as needed. Freeze whole leaves, or chop first; or dry foliage on nonmetallic screens. Collect flower heads before the seeds mature and fall; hang in paper bags or dry on paper. Store dried foliage and seeds in an airtight container. Fresh leaves can be refrigerated for 1 week. Seeds will retain their flavor for at least 1 year.
Special tips Sow seed every 2 to 3 weeks for a continuous leaf harvest through to autumn.
Parts used Leaves, seeds, oil.
Culinary uses Both seeds and leaves are used in Scandinavian cooking, with potatoes, fish, seafood and eggs. Also added to vinegar.
Medicinal uses Internally for flatulence, colic, indigestion and hiatus hernia.

Angelica archangelica
APIACEAE

American angelica grows wild in North America in wet areas such as damp meadows, around ponds and along riverbanks. It is similar in appearance to European angelica, except that it has a purple root.

ANGELICA, EUROPEAN

This tall, sweet-scented herb resembles its close relatives parsley and cilantro (coriander). Leaf stems can be candied, or the seeds and root can be infused and drunk as a tea. The seeds are also used to flavor drinks.

Best climate and site Zones 6–9. Full sun or partial shade. Thrives with little attention but needs moist conditions.
Ideal soil conditions Rich, cool, damp garden soil; pH 6.0–6.7.
Growing guidelines Angelica seeds need light to germinate. When sowing, just press them into the soil surface and leave uncovered. Indoors, sow seed in early spring in peat pots placed in plastic bags in the refrigerator; in 6–8 weeks, place in bright, indirect light at 60° F (15°C). Or sow seed outdoors in spring or summer, preferably where plants will grow, as angelica transplants poorly. Ideally, sow three to four seeds in a cluster about 3 feet (90 cm) apart and thin to the strongest seedling. Angelica will self-seed. Angelica can also be grown to maturity in a container. Ideally, plant it in a 10-inch (25-cm) pot filled with rich compost and either sow direct or set one young plant in the middle. Water regularly and apply a liquid manure at 10- to 14-day intervals as soon as roots show at the drainage hole.
Growing habit Herbaceous or monocarpic perennial often grown as a hardy biennial. It has stout, hollow stems and broad, lobed leaves; height 5–8 ft (1.5–2.4 m).
Flowering time Angelica blooms the second or third year in summer, then dies; has honey-scented, yellow-green flowers resembling those of fennel.
Pest and disease prevention Prone to aphids and crown rot. Wash aphids from seed heads with a spray of water or an organic spray. Avoid growing angelica in hot climates to prevent crown rot.

Harvesting and storing Collect small stems the first summer, then harvest roots in autumn. Pick stems and leaves in spring of the second year. Harvest the ripe seeds before they fall, dry them and store in airtight containers in the refrigerator.
Special tips In potpourris, seeds act as a fixative.
Precautions Some scientists say that angelica is a suspected carcinogen, while others say it contains an anticancer compound. Research is continuing. Angelica can also cause skin allergies. Not to be used during pregnancy or by diabetics. Those using it for medicinal purposes should seek professional advice.
Parts used Leaves, stems, seeds, roots.
Culinary uses Leaves eaten as a vegetable; leaf stems candied for cake decorations; stewed for jam. The dry roots can be used for a tea.
Medicinal uses Internally for digestive problems, anorexia and migraines.
Externally for pleurisy and rheumatism.
Other uses Seeds used to flavor drinks, especially gin. Also in potpourris.
Other common names Wild celery, wild parsnip.
Other species American Angelica *A. atropurpurea* has tiny white flowers in umbels 10 inches (25 cm) in diameter; height to 6 feet (1.8 m).

Anthriscus cerefolium
APIACEAE

CHERVIL

Chervil grows best and retains more flavor when temperatures are cool in spring and autumn. Grow this lacy, delicate-looking plant for medicinal, culinary and craft uses. It is reputed to improve poor memory and depression.

Best climate and site Zones 6–10. Cool sun to partial shade.
Ideal soil conditions Moist but well-drained garden soil rich with humus; pH 6.0–6.7.
Growing guidelines Sow fresh seed shallowly outdoors in early spring or autumn; thin to 9–12 inches (23–30 cm). Keep seedlings moist. Sow again at 2-week intervals until midsummer for continuous harvest. Transplants poorly. Mulch to protect autumn-sown seed. Chervil can seed itself each year if flowers are left to mature in the garden.
Growing habit Annual with fernlike leaves; height 1–2 feet (30–60 cm).
Flowering time Summer; small, umbrella-like, white clusters.
Pest and disease prevention Usually free from pests and diseases.
Harvesting and storing Snip leaves continuously after 6–8 weeks; best used fresh.
Special tips Loses flavor quickly when heated, so add to recipes at the end. Chervil grows well below taller plants that offer some shade.
Parts used Leaves.
Culinary uses Chervil has a warm pungency like anise and parsley combined and is used in soups and salads. Also added to potatoes, eggs and fish dishes, especially in French cooking.
Medicinal uses Internally for fluid retention and rheumatism. Externally for hemorrhoids and conjunctivitis.
Other uses In floral arrangements.
Other common names Garden chervil.

Apium graveolens
APIACEAE

WILD CELERY

Wild celery has been used as a food and medicinal plant since earliest times. It was even found in the tomb of Tutankhamun. Cultivated celery is used in salads, soups and stews and has all the flavor of wild celery.

Best climate and site Zones 5 and warmer. Full sun but needs protection from strong winds.
Ideal soil conditions Rich, moisture-retentive soil, with adequate calcium and plenty of well-rotted manure or compost worked in; pH 5.5–7.5.
Growing guidelines Sow seed in early spring. Wild celery germinates slowly and can be overtaken by weeds. In colder climates, start indoors 6–8 weeks before last spring frost. Set out 10–12 inches (25–30 cm) apart. Keep bed well weeded and watered. Apply compost tea or fish emulsion at least once a month.
Growing habit Aromatic perennial with bulbous, fleshy roots; height 1–3 feet (30–90 cm). Ridged, branching, green stem and light green divided leaves.
Flowering time Tiny green-white flowers produced in late summer of second year followed by small, oval, aromatic, gray-brown ridged seeds.
Pest and disease prevention Rotate plantings of celery to avoid blights to which it is vulnerable. Also prone to slugs, celery-fly maggots and celery leafspot. If troubled, spray with an insecticidal soap or recommended fungicide.
Harvesting and storing Harvest the roots in autumn and use fresh or dried in tinctures. Collect seeds as they ripen in autumn. Cut stems close to the roots and store like turnips in damp sawdust or sand in a cool place.
Special tips Water and feed cultivated celery regularly as inadequate water and fertility produce small, fibrous plants.

Cultivated celery was developed during the 17th century in Italy and became popular all over the world. It isn't easy to grow, but with a little attention and plenty of water and food, it will thrive in the backyard.

Precautions Can be toxic if used in large quantities. Not given to pregnant women.
Parts used Whole plant, roots, seeds, oil.
Culinary uses Wild celery is rarely used in cooking as it is extremely bitter and toxic in large amounts. The seeds are used in small quantities to flavor soups, curries and pickles. Also mixed with salt as a condiment. Can be used as a salt substitute in a salt-free diet.
Medicinal uses Internally for rheumatoid arthritis, gout and osteoarthritis. Also used to relieve indigestion and stimulate the uterus. Used in Ayurvedic medicine for flatulence, hiccups, bronchitis and asthma. Seeds also used as a sedative and to calm nerves.
Oil used externally to treat tumors and fungal infections.
Other common names Marsh parsley, knob celery, turnip celery, German celery, smallage.
Other varieties Cultivated celery A. *graveolens* var. *dulce* needs full sun and plenty of moisture. Excessive heat, inadequate moisture or lack of fertility will result in tough or stringy celery. Prone to being overtaken by weeds, so plant celery in well-manured beds, 10 inches (25 cm) apart. Dense growth will shade out weeds and automatically blanch the celery. Use the stalks for cooking or in salads. Extract juice for a refreshing drink.
Celeriac A. *graveolens* var. *rapacium* is a variety of celery in which the taproot is grossly swollen. It is a useful vegetable for flavoring.

Arctium lappa
COMPOSITAE

BURDOCK

This biennial or short-lived perennial has large, woolly leaves, purplish red thistle-like daisy flowers, and a long, edible root. The seeds have been shown to lower blood sugar levels.

Best climate and site Zones 3–10. Full sun but tolerates partial shade.
Ideal soil conditions Deep, loose, moist, fertile soil; pH 5.0–8.5.
Growing guidelines Sow seed shallowly in early spring or autumn outdoors or indoors. Burdock's deep taproot makes transplanting difficult. Thrives despite neglect; self-seeds.
Growing habit A biennial grown as an annual, burdock is stocky but branched at the top; height 5 feet (1.5 m).
Flowering time Summer, but only if plants are not harvested; individual purple to red thistle-like flowers mature to burr-like seed heads that cling to passersby.
Pest and disease prevention Usually free from pests and diseases.
Harvesting and storing At the end of the season, dig up roots, scrub them, and slice to dry on paper in the sun. Store dried roots in airtight containers and use for tea. Harvest young leaf stalks in spring and summer and use as a vegetable.
Parts used Stems, roots, seeds.
Culinary uses Stalks cooked like celery; roots eaten raw in salads, added to stir-fries and cooked like carrots.
Medicinal uses Internally for skin problems, eczema, psoriasis and rheumatism. Seeds used to treat colds and pneumonia. Seed extracts lower blood sugar levels.
Other common names Great burdock, gobo, cuckold, harlock, lappa, beggar's buttons.

Arctostaphylos uva-ursi
ERICACEAE

BEARBERRY

Bearberry is a prostrate, creeping, evergreen shrub with long shiny leaves, pink or white flowers and red berries that are said to appeal to bears. It is a useful plant to grow on banks to control erosion.

Best climate and site Zones 4–9. Full sun, but tolerates partial shade.
Ideal soil conditions Acid, well-drained soil with plenty of organic matter; pH 4.5–5.5.
Growing guidelines Sow seed outdoors in spring or autumn into a mixture of peat and sand, or take cuttings from new growth in autumn. Stems may be layered in pots set close to the mother plant. Bearberry needs little care except for pinching away stem tips to encourage sideshoots.
Growing habit Mat-forming perennial shrub with leathery, shiny leaves; height to 6 inches (15 cm) or more.
Flowering time Spring to early summer; flowers white or pink, waxy and drooping.
Pest and disease prevention Usually free from pests and diseases.
Harvesting and storing Gather fresh green leaves during sunny autumn weather, in the morning; dry thoroughly in the sun and store in airtight containers. Use the leaves to make a medicinal, diuretic tea to treat bladder infections.
Precautions Contains irritant substance, so not safe to use without professional advice. Not given to pregnant or breastfeeding women, or people with kidney disease.
Parts used Leaves.
Medicinal uses Internally for urinary infections such as cystitis and vaginitis.
Other common names Bear's grape, hog cranberry, uva ursi, mountain box.

Armoracia rusticana
BRASSICACEAE

HORSERADISH

Horseradish is a weedy herb with a white perennial root. Originally it was cultivated as a medicinal herb but today it is considered a flavoring herb. Its sharp, pungent taste adds flavor to roast beef.

Best climate and site Zones 5–10. Full sun.
Ideal soil conditions Fertile, moist but well-drained garden soil; pH 6.0–7.0.
Growing guidelines Plant straight, young roots that are about 9 inches (23 cm) long and ½ inch (1 cm) wide so that the crown or growing point is 3–5 inches (7.5–12.5 cm) below the soil surface, and plants are 12–18 inches (30–45 cm) apart. Plant at a horizontal angle.
Growing habit Upright perennial with a thick taproot. Leaves are stalked and oblong; height 1–4 feet (30–120 cm).
Flowering time Early summer; small, white blossoms that do not produce viable seed.
Pest and disease prevention Usually free from pests and diseases.
Harvesting and storing Horseradish is grown mainly for its large, white, pungently spicy roots. Harvest roots in autumn and winter, and scrub them before storing in the refrigerator, or pack in dry sand in the cellar for spring planting. Can also leave roots in the soil and harvest as required.
Special tips Harvest early for the most tender roots.
Parts used Leaves, roots.
Culinary uses Leaves can be used in salads and sandwiches. Fresh roots are grated and added to fish, vinegar or added to cream for roast beef.
Medicinal uses Internally for arthritis, gout, sciatica and urinary infections. Excess can cause vomiting or allergies. Externally as a poultice for wounds, arthritis and pleurisy.

Arnica montana
ASTERACEAE

ARNICA

Arnica is a hardy perennial with several flower stalks, which attract bees to the garden. An ointment to soothe sprains, bruises and aching muscles can be made using the flowers.

Best climate and site Zones 5–9. Full sun to partial shade.
Ideal soil conditions Dry, sandy, acidic soil rich in humus; pH 4.0–6.5.
Growing guidelines Sow seed indoors in early spring; once the danger of frost has passed, transplant outdoors. Propagate by dividing the whole plant in spring.
Growing habit Perennial with bright green leaves that form a flat rosette, from the center of which rises a flower stalk; height 2 feet (60 cm).
Flowering time Midsummer; yellow-orange, daisy-like blossoms 2–3 inches (5–7.5 cm) across.
Pest and disease prevention Occasionally bothered by aphids. To control, spray leaves with water. Dust or spray severe infestations with a botanical insecticide, such as pyrethrin.
Harvesting and storing Cut flowers from the stalk after they have dried. In autumn, dig roots after the leaves have died. Mix flowers with some vegetable oil or lard to make an ointment for aching muscles.
Precautions Only use internally under the supervision of a qualified practitioner. External use can cause dermatitis in allergy-prone individuals.
Parts used Flowers.
Medicinal uses Internally for coronary disease but only under the supervision of a qualified practitioner.
Externally in creams and liniments for sprains, bruises, dislocations and aching muscles.
Other common names Leopard's bane, mountain tobacco.

Artemisia abrotanum
ASTERACEAE

SOUTHERNWOOD

This ornamental and drought-tolerant perennial was once used as an aphrodisiac and to stimulate the growth of men's beards. These days it is considered more useful as an ornamental.

Best climate and site Zones 5–9. Full sun.
Ideal soil conditions Well-drained garden soil. Don't fertilize; southernwood prefers a lean diet.
Growing guidelines Propagate by cuttings, or divide older plants in spring or autumn. Space 2–4 feet (60–120 cm) apart. Southernwood is very difficult to grow from seed, but cuttings root easily. In early spring, prune to shape.
Growing habit Semi-evergreen subshrub; height 3–6 feet (90–180 cm); finely divided, gray-green leaves.
Flowering time Summer; small, inconspicuous, button-like yellow-white blossoms (rarely blooms in cool summers).
Pest and disease prevention Usually trouble free.
Harvesting and storing Collect foliage anytime in summer and dry thoroughly. Use dried foliage to repel moths in stored clothing, or as an aromatic backing for herbal wreaths.
Special tips Plant southernwood in the back of borders to give height or grow as a light hedge. Plant as a living insect repellent; its essential oils keep moths and other pests away. Its sharp, acid scent has a reputation as a general stimulant; if you're tired, hang a sprig at work or in the car.
Precautions Not given to pregnant women.
Parts used Leaves.
Medicinal uses Internally for painful menstruation, worms in children and hair loss. Seek professional advice before use. Externally for frostbite, extracting splinters and hair loss.
Other uses As an insect repellent.
Other common names The lover's plant, old man, lad's love.

Artemisia absinthium
ASTERACEAE

WORMWOOD

Wormwood is a common member of sand-dune communities. The gray-green foliage and bushy growth make it an attractive garden plant. Try a wormwood spray on flea beetles and other pests.

Best climate and site Zones 4–9. Full sun to partial shade.
Ideal soil conditions Ordinary, well-drained soil; pH 6.0–6.7.
Growing guidelines Sow seed outdoors in autumn; or sow seed indoors in late winter, planting outdoors in spring. Thin first-year plants to 15 inches (38 cm), then to 3 feet (90 cm) the second year. Divide established plants in early spring or early autumn, or take cuttings in late summer. Most plants last several years, with peak production during the second and third years.
Growing habit Hardy, woody-based perennial with gray-green, finely dissected foliage; height to 4 feet (1.2m).
Flowering time Summer; green-yellow flowers in panicles.
Pest and disease prevention Few pests. Wormwood is said to repel most insect and mammal pests.
Harvesting and storing Restrict harvests to the tops of plants when they flower in summer. Hang in bunches to dry, then store in airtight containers. Withstands two harvests.
Special tips Wormwood is a pretty plant, despite its name, but keep other plants away; few plants thrive when planted nearby.
Precautions Take only in small doses; unsafe for home use. Subject to legal restrictions in some countries.
Parts used Whole plant, leaves.
Medicinal uses Internally for worms, gall bladder problems and indigestion.
Externally for bites and bruises.
Other uses In sachets to repel insects, or make a wormwood tea to repel aphids in the garden.

Artemisia dracunculus
ASTERACEAE

TARRAGON, FRENCH

Tarragon's heavy licorice flavor holds well in cooking, making it an extremely useful herb in the kitchen. It used to be known as a dragon herb, hence the species name, and was used as a cure for poisonous stings and bites.

Best climate and site Zones 4–9. Full sun but tolerates partial shade.
Ideal soil conditions Well-drained garden soil; pH 6.0–7.3.
Growing guidelines Seldom sets seed. Take cuttings of new growth in spring or autumn. Divide older plants in late winter to spring every 3 years; space 1–2 feet (30–60 cm) apart. Prune away flower stems each year, for most vigorous growth and best flavor. To grow indoors in winter, cut foliage in summer to just above the soil and pot up and place in the refrigerator to mimic winter. In autumn, unwrap and place on a sunny windowsill for winter harvests.
Growing habit Hardy perennial with long, branched green stems; height to 2–4 feet (60–120 cm).
Flowering time Late summer; small, greenish yellow flowers. Will only flower in warm summers.
Pest and disease prevention Usually trouble free.
Harvesting and storing Clip foliage as needed all summer, or indoors in winter. Foliage may be harvested entirely twice each summer. Fresh foliage lasts several weeks in the refrigerator when wrapped in paper towels, then placed in a plastic bag. Bunch and hang to dry away from sunlight.
Precautions Not given to pregnant women.
Parts used Leaves, oil.
Culinary uses Leaves used to flavor sauces, chicken and egg dishes. Also used to flavor vinegar and mustard.
Medicinal uses Internally for indigestion and worms.
Externally for toothache and rheumatism.

Artemisia vulgaris
ASTERACEAE

MUGWORT

Mugwort is an attractive ornamental both in the garden and as part of dried arrangements or for making floral wreaths. The leaves have a sage-like smell and are said to repel insects.

Best climate and site Zones 5–9. Full sun.
Ideal soil conditions Light, well-drained garden soil enriched with organic matter; pH 6.0–7.0.
Growing guidelines Sow seed shallowly indoors then transfer outdoors after danger of frost. In spring or autumn, divide older plants. May be invasive.
Growing habit Perennial with upright, purple stems and deeply cut, dark green leaves that have soft and downy white undersides; height 3–6 feet (90–180 cm).
Flowering time Late summer; reddish brown or yellow ball-shaped flower heads in panicles.
Pest and disease prevention Usually trouble free.
Harvesting and storing Collect leaves just before flowering in summer. Dry in the shade and store in airtight containers.
Precautions Unsafe when given internally to pregnant or breastfeeding women; may be generally unsafe.
Parts used Leaves.
Culinary uses Used in English, German and Spanish cooking. Added to fish dishes; used in stuffing for meat and game dishes.
Medicinal uses Internally for depression, loss of appetite, worms and menstrual problems. Stimulates the uterus and controls uterine bleeding.
Externally in traditional Chinese medicine where the leaf is dried and burned on the skin at acupuncture points. Also used as a wash for fungal infections.
Other uses In flower arrangements and wreaths.
Other common names St John's plant, felon herb.

Asparagus officinalis
ASPARAGACEAE

ASPARAGUS

This classic spring vegetable requires well-prepared soil with high fertility. A well-maintained patch may yield for decades. Asparagus has been cultivated for over 2,000 years.

Best climate and site Zones 3 and warmer, but asparagus grows best in areas where the soil freezes in winter. Avoid low-lying areas subject to heavy dew and morning fogs, to reduce the possibility of rust. Prefers full sun, but will tolerate some shade.
Ideal soil conditions Deep, fertile, well-drained, moist soil; will tolerate slightly alkaline and saline soils; pH 6.5–7.5.
Growing guidelines Grow from seed started indoors or in an outdoor seedbed; or hasten the first harvest by using 1-year-old crowns. Dig a trench 8 inches (20 cm) deep in well-composted and limed soil. Place the crowns in the trench 15 inches (38 cm) apart, fanning the roots in all directions. Cover with soil to half the depth of the trench. When foliage peeks above ground level, finish filling the trench with soil. Mulch or cultivate shallowly and irrigate in dry spells. Keeping the foliage healthy and lush after harvest is critical to the next year's crop. Each autumn, cut back dead foliage and mulch heavily with compost or manure. Early each spring, rake off all but 1–2 inches (2.5–5 cm) of mulch to let spears emerge.
Growing habit Perennial with creeping rhizomes and upright stems that appear in the spring as shoots; height 3–5 feet (90–150 cm). Soft, feather-like foliage.
Flowering time Green-white, bell-shaped flowers in summer followed by red berries.
Pest and disease prevention Asparagus rust can be a serious problem in damp locations; use rust-resistant cultivars.

When the harvest is finished, the graceful fronds of asparagus add an ornamental touch to the garden. Asparagus contains asparagin, a diuretic that gives urine a characteristic odor.

Reduce damage from asparagus beetles, which overwinter in garden debris and emerge in spring to feed on young spears, by burning or hot-composting the old asparagus foliage and cultivating the asparagus patch shallowly before applying autumn mulch. Cover young spears with a row cover.
Harvesting and storing Young shoots are cut in late spring at ground level, leaving woody stems behind. Harvest while tips of spears are still tightly closed; in warm spring weather, this may require daily harvesting. Roots are lifted when plant is dormant and boiled before drying.
Special tips Perennial weeds and grasses can be troublesome in the asparagus patch. Be sure the area is free of weeds before planting, and mulch or cultivate to stay ahead of them. In heavy soils, plant asparagus in raised beds to improve the drainage. Lay crowns at ground level, rather than in trenches, and mound soil over them.
Parts used Young shoots, rhizomes.
Culinary uses Young shoots are steamed and served as a vegetable. Also used in soups. They are a popular canned vegetable.
Medicinal uses Internally for kidney disease, gout, cystitis and rheumatism. Also as a diuretic.
Other species Chinese asparagus *A. cochinchinensis* is a hardy perennial with pale yellow-green flowers in summer; height 5 feet (1.5 m). Used to control coughs, reduce inflammation and as a diuretic.

Astragalus gummifer
PAPILIONACEAE

GUM TRAGACANTH

This native of the Middle East is one of the species of milk vetches, which have been used as medicines, food and fodder crops in many parts of the world for countless centuries.

Best climate and site Zones 9–10. Full sun; needs hot, dry conditions. Drought resistant and can tolerate light frost.
Ideal soil conditions Well-drained, sandy and slightly alkaline soil; pH 5.6–7.9.
Growing guidelines Propagate by scarified seed; rub seed with sandpaper or place in a cup of boiling water and wait for seed to swell. Germinates slowly.
Growing habit Perennial, evergreen, umbrella-shaped shrub; height 12 inches (30 cm). Stems are erect, branching and cushion forming, leaves spiny and egg shaped.
Flowering time Flowers are small, white and pea-shaped and occur in clusters in spring and summer.
Pest and disease prevention Usually trouble free.
Harvesting and storing Gum is collected from 2-year-old plants by making an incision in the stem base. Once collected, the gum is dried.
Parts used Gum.
Medicinal uses Stimulates the immune system and suppresses tumor growth.
Other uses As the thickening agent in toothpastes, processed cheese and confectionery; also to bind the ingredients of pills.
Other species *A. membranaceus* and *A. complanatus* are both important in Chinese medicine as tonics to stimulate and rejuvenate the immune system. Some species of this large group of herbs accumulate minerals in their leaves from the soil and have been used as indicators in prospecting because of this.

Avena sativa
POACEAE

OATS

This popular cereal is cultivated around the world, where its food value has been known since earliest times. It is a powerful stimulant and rich in bodybuilding materials, making it a first-class food for humans and animals.

Best climate and site Zones 3–9. Full sun. Grown widely in northern and southern temperate regions. Needs water and humidity and dislikes dry summer weather.
Ideal soil conditions Well-drained, fertile soil; pH 4.5–7.3.
Growing guidelines Propagate by seeds sown in spring.
Growing habit Erect, annual grass with flat leaves, smooth stems and spreading panicles of large, pendulous seed-heads; height 1–3 feet (30–90 cm).
Flowering time Nondescript flowers occur in summer followed by seed heads. Seeds are spindle shaped and pale gold.
Pest and disease prevention Can be prone to grasshoppers and other flying insects.
Harvesting and storing Plants are cut in summer and threshed to separate the grains, which are then dehusked and rolled.
Parts used Seeds.
Culinary uses Important ingredient of breakfast cereals, breads, cakes and muesli snacks.
Medicinal uses Internally for depression, herpes, shingles and for strengthening the body after a debilitating illness. Regular consumption of oat germ reduces blood cholesterol levels. Oats are rich in copper, cobalt, zinc and iron. They are an important source of vitamins and contain protein, starch, minerals and oils.
Externally as a soothing skin wash for dry skin. Stimulates the central nervous system (responsible for excitability in horses).
Other uses Dried stalks are included in tonics.

Azadirachta indica
MELIACEAE

NEEM

Neem is a fast-growing, long-living tree that is popular as an ornamental feature in the tropics. The timber is highly valued for its insecticidal properties and is grown in hedges in Africa to combat insect-borne diseases.

Best climate and site Zones 4–9. Full sun; native to the tropics of Eurasia and Africa. Drought tolerant.
Ideal soil conditions Tolerates poor soil, but must be well drained; pH 4.5–7.0.
Growing guidelines Propagate from ripe, fresh seed.
Growing habit Fast-growing, evergreen tree; height 40–50 feet (12–15 m), pinnate leaves to 1 foot (30 cm) long.
Flowering time Small, yellow-white, fragrant flowers appear from spring to late autumn, followed by yellow to red-brown berry-like fruit.
Pest and disease prevention Due to the insecticidal and repellent properties of this tree, it has very few natural pests.
Harvesting and storing Seeds are harvested when ripe for oil extraction. Leaves, bark and resin are collected when required and dried or used fresh.
Precautions Not given to the old or very young.
Parts used Leaves, bark, seeds, oil, resin.
Medicinal uses Internally for malaria, intestinal worms, tuberculosis, arthritis, jaundice and skin diseases. Important in Ayurvedic medicine as a detoxicant and has long been used to lower fevers.
Externally for lice, eczema, ringworm, fungal infections and sore muscles.
Other uses Resin is added to soap, toothpaste and skin creams. Oil is used in hairdressing products and insecticides. Leaves are used in libraries to protect against insect damage.
Other common names Nimba, margosa.

Berberis vulgaris
BERBERIDACEAE

BARBERRY

This woody ornamental shrub makes an excellent hedge, and is easily trained to twist and turn in knot gardens. Recently, barberry has been shown to have anticancer properties.

Best climate and site Zones 3–9. Full sun to partial shade.
Ideal soil conditions Moist, fertile, well-drained soil; pH 6.0–7.0.
Growing guidelines Sow seed indoors or outdoors in spring, or plant fresh seed outdoors in autumn. Take cuttings in late summer and root suckers in autumn. Prune and thin branches after flowering, or in late winter. If barberry becomes overgrown, cut growth to 1 foot (30 cm). Provide wind shelter in winter.
Growing habit Height up to 8 feet (2.4 m); deciduous, ornamental shrub with spiny stems.
Flowering time Spring; hanging yellow flowers are followed by orange-red berries.
Pest and disease prevention Provide well-drained soil to prevent weakening of the shrub.
Harvesting and storing Collect berries in autumn and use fresh. Dig roots in summer or autumn and shave into slices. Strip bark from stems anytime, then dry thoroughly. Use roots and bark for yellow dye and berries for culinary or medicinal purposes.
Special tips Barberry quickly becomes overgrown if neglected.
Precautions All parts except ripe berries are harmful if eaten.
Parts used Leaves, bark, roots, fruits.
Culinary uses Fruits once used in jelly for meat dishes.
Medicinal uses Internally for gallstones, dysentery, cancer chemotherapy and as a gargle for sore throats. Valued as a liver tonic and detoxicant in Ayurvedic medicine.

Betula spp.
BETULACEAE

BIRCH

Birches are regarded as excellent medicinal plants, especially in the treatment of arthritis. The twigs, inner bark and fermented sap of birch trees have been used as the main ingredients in birch beer.

Best climate and site Zones 3–8. Full sun but tolerates partial shade.
Ideal soil conditions Fertile, ideally neutral to acid soil with good drainage; pH 5.0–6.0.
Growing guidelines Sow seed when ripe in late summer or autumn. Indoors, sow thickly in trays, cover only lightly and keep moist. Transplant seedlings when 1 year old. Staking may be necessary to maintain upright growth.
Growing habit Deciduous trees that live for 50–100 years, sometimes more; height 40–90 feet (12–27 m).
Flowering time Spring; both female catkins, which are small and cylindrical, and male catkins, which are longer, yellowish and pendulous, are produced on the same tree.
Pest and disease prevention Provide ample water during the summer months to keep birch trees vigorous and healthy. Check for cankers, leaf pests and borers on young, sappy limbs.
Harvesting and storing In spring, collect the sap by boring holes in the tree trunk, inserting a tube and collecting the liquid in a container. Collect leaves in spring and use them fresh, or dry and store them in an airtight container. Collect bark as it peels off the tree; dry the bark and twigs in a cool, dry area; store in airtight containers. Keeps well.
Parts used Leaves, bark, oil, sap.
Medicinal uses Internally for arthritis, rheumatism, kidney stones and water retention. Use with professional advice. Externally in preparations for psoriasis and eczema.
Other uses Sap used in beer; wood used for smoking.

Borago officinalis
BORAGINACEAE

BORAGE

This green, robust and bristly plant attracts honeybees to the garden. The leaves have a cucumber flavor. Historically, borage had the reputation of making people happy and giving them courage.

Best climate and site Zones 6–10. Full sun to partial shade.
Ideal soil conditions Fairly rich, moist soil with good drainage; pH 6.0–7.0.
Growing guidelines Sow seed outdoors after danger of hard frost. Indoors, plant in peat pots to avoid disturbing the sensitive taproot when transplanting. Control weeds to reduce competition for moisture. To promote blooming, go easy on the nitrogen. Self-sows well. Tall plants may need support.
Growing habit Annual; height 1½–2 feet (45–60 cm) with broad, hairy leaves arising from a central stalk.
Flowering time From midsummer until frost; star-shaped blooms in pink, purple, lavender, or blue, with black centers.
Pest and disease prevention Mulch with light materials, such as straw, to keep foliage off soil and prevent rotting.
Harvesting and storing Harvest foliage anytime for culinary use. Snip blossoms just after they open and candy, toss fresh in a salad, or dry with silica gel for flower arrangements.
Precautions May be harmful in excess; subject to legal restrictions in some countries.
Parts used Leaves, flowers, seeds, oil.
Culinary uses Leaves chopped in salads and used in cream cheese. Flowers used as a garnish and candied for cake decorations. Leaves also added to flavor drinks.
Medicinal uses Internally for bronchial infections, throat infections and as an alternative to evening primrose oil for skin problems.
Externally for mouthwashes, eyewashes and poultices.

Boswellia sacra
BURSERACEAE

FRANKINCENSE

In Christianity, frankincense was given to baby Jesus by one of the Three Kings. It is an aromatic gum resin highly valued since ancient times for its medicinal and cosmetic properties.

Best climate and site Zones 8–10. Full sun.
Ideal soil conditions Well-drained to dry soil; pH 5.0–7.9.
Growing guidelines Propagate by semi-hardwood cuttings in summer.
Growing habit Evergreen, resinous tree; height 15 feet (5 m). Small, divided leaves and papery, peeling bark.
Flowering time Late spring and summer. Dense heads of small, white or occasionally blue flowers, followed by red-brown seed capsules.
Pest and disease prevention Usually free from pests and diseases.
Harvesting and storing Gum is collected all year. Collection time and season will determine quality of harvest. The best-quality resin is collected when the plant is growing during the hottest months in the driest season. Either used fresh or dried for powders.
Precautions Use under medical supervision.
Parts used Gum resin.
Medicinal uses Internally for urinary and bronchial infections and to treat menstrual pain.
Externally as an exhalant for congested chests and as a wash for gum, mouth and throat infections.
Other uses In cosmetics, incense and perfumery.
Other common names Olibanum, mastic tree.
Gardener's trivia Four-thousand-year-old stone carvings found in Egypt show frankincense trees being grown and used to make rejuvenating facemasks for the royal family.

Brassica spp.
BRASSICACEAE

MUSTARD

Most mustards are annuals or biennials. Some are "winter annuals" that remain green even when buried in snow. The cultivated species can benefit most crops by deterring pests.

Best climate and site Zones 6–10. Full sun.
Ideal soil conditions Rich, well-drained soil; pH 4.2–6.0.
Growing guidelines Easily grows from seed sown in shallow beds outdoors from early spring until autumn; thin to 9 inches (23 cm). Can self-sow if allowed to. Prepare beds with compost or well-rotted manure, but avoid excessive applications of manure, as this can damage the roots.
Growing habit Very frost-hardy annual or biennial with leaves of various shapes; height 4–6 feet (1.2–1.8 m).
Flowering time Summer; four-petaled yellow flowers in terminal racemes.
Pest and disease prevention Can attract the same pests as its close relatives in the cabbage family, but usually trouble-free.
Harvesting and storing Collect and dry seeds when ripe.
Parts used Leaves, seeds, flowers, oil.
Culinary uses Young leaves can be cooked as a vegetable. Seedlings can be added to salads. Seeds are blended and ground for mustard; also used in curries and pickles.
Medicinal uses Externally in poultices and in baths for rheumatism, muscular pain and respiratory tract infections.
Other species Black mustard *B. nigra* is a much-branched annual; height to 6 feet (1.8 m); cultivated as the main source of pungent table mustard.
White mustard *B. hirta* is an annual; height up to 4 feet (1.2 m); cultivated for greens, and its mustard- and oil-producing seeds.

Calendula officinalis
ASTERACEAE

CALENDULA

Calendula is a cheery, dependable bloomer in the garden and is one of the most versatile herbs. Plant enough to make long-lasting fresh and dried bouquets or use it as a substitute for saffron.

Best climate and site Zones 6–10. Full sun to partial shade.
Ideal soil conditions Average garden soil with good drainage; pH 6.0–7.0.
Growing guidelines Sow seed outdoors in autumn or spring; thin to 10–18 inches (25–45 cm). Work in compost or aged manure before planting. Deadhead old blooms for continuous flowering.
Growing habit Annual; branched, succulent stem with fine hairs and aromatic, hairy leaves; height 1–2 feet (30–60 cm).
Flowering time Spring or summer; golden yellow to orange daisy-like flowers, 2–3 inches (5–7.5 cm) across.
Pest and disease prevention Check for aphids, powdery mildew and rust.
Harvesting and storing Dry petals in shade on paper to prevent sticking; store in moisture-proof jars. Preserve whole flowers in salad vinegar. Dried, ground calendula flowers can be used as a substitute for saffron.
Special tips Plant calendula seeds in pots in summer for indoor autumn color.
Parts used Flower petals.
Culinary uses As a substitute for saffron in rice and soups; infused to color butter and cakes. Flowers added to salads.
Medicinal uses Internally for ulcers, gastric problems, hepatitis and swollen glands, but not during pregnancy. Externally for eczema, conjunctivitis, herpes and athlete's foot. Used also as a general antiseptic.
Other common names Pot marigold.

Camellia sinensis
THEACEAE

TEA

Tea has been drunk in China for over 3,000 years and was introduced to Europe in the 17th century. Tea contains beneficial antioxidants, which help protect against heart disease, strokes and cancer.

Best climate and site Zones 6–8. Prefers open, sunny position with high humidity. Tolerates some shade.
Ideal soil conditions Light, humus-rich soil; pH 4.5–6.2.
Growing guidelines Propagate by semiripe cuttings in summer or by layering.
Growing habit Evergreen shrub; height 3–20 feet (1–6 m). Slender stems, with yellowish gray bark. Leaves are dark green and glossy, leathery and elliptical in shape.
Flowering time White flowers with yellow stamens in autumn or winter followed by capsules of large, oily seeds.
Pest and disease prevention Usually trouble free.
Harvesting and storing Leaves are picked during the year from bushes over 3 years old and used dried for green tea or dried and fermented for black tea.
Special tips Tea contains high concentrations of tannins, which are a possible cause of esophageal cancer. Drinking tea with milk eliminates this risk because the milk neutralizes the tannins.
Parts used Leaves (shoot tips only), oil.
Culinary uses Used worldwide as a refreshing beverage. Also used in cooking to flavor foods.
Medicinal uses Internally for hepatitis and diarrhea. Externally for tired eyes, insect bites and minor injuries.
Other uses Oil used in perfumes, hair oil and food flavoring.
Other species There are more than 250 different species in the Camellia genus, most notably the distinctive flowering camellias that are a favorite in temperate gardens.

Cannabis sativa
CANNABIDACEAE

HEMP

Hemp has been grown in Asia for over 4,000 years, both as a drug and a fiber plant. Today, its possession and use in most Western countries is illegal, but not in some parts of Asia, where the dried plant is eaten or smoked.

Best climate and site Zones 9–10. Full sun.
Ideal soil conditions Most soil conditions as long as there is sufficient water; pH 4.5–8.8.
Growing guidelines Grown from seeds and cuttings in summer.
Growing habit Strong-smelling annual with a long taproot. Stem is erect, rough, angular, hairy and branched. Leaves are dark green and palmlike with a lighter green, downy underside; height 3–15 feet (0.9–5 m).
Flowering time Small green flowers appear in summer. Plants are either male or female. Female plants have green flowers in spikelike clusters while males have small, rounded, nondescript blooms. Fruit is small, ash-colored and filled with seeds.
Pest and disease prevention Usually trouble free.
Harvesting and storing Only female flower heads are harvested in summer and air-dried before extraction of volatile oils. For hemp fiber, stems are collected and chemically treated.
Precautions This herb is subject to legal restrictions in most countries.
Parts used Whole plant, flowering tops, seeds.
Medicinal uses Internally for nausea associated with cancer chemotherapy, to reduce eyeball pressure in glaucoma and to help AIDS patients gain weight.
Externally for skin disorders.
Other uses Source of fiber for rope and clothing manufacture.

Capparis spinosa
CAPPARIDACEAE

CAPER

Capers are tiny, unopened, green flower buds of a spiny shrub native to the drier regions of southern Europe and North Africa. Capers have an aromatic pungency, and have been used in regional cooking for centuries.

Best climate and site Zones 8–10. Full sun.
Ideal soil conditions Well-drained sandy soil; pH 5.6–8.0.
Growing guidelines Propagate by ripe wood cuttings in summer.
Growing habit A prostrate shrub with long, trailing stems; height 3–6 feet (90–180 cm). Leaves are oval and noticeably ribbed.
Flowering time Flowers occur in summer to early autumn and are white to pink with four petals and long and numerous stamens.
Pest and disease prevention A drought-hardy perennial bush usually free from pests and diseases.
Harvesting and storing Pick flower buds early in the morning and pickle in salt or white vinegar. Strip bark from roots harvested in autumn and dry.
Parts used Root bark, flower buds.
Culinary uses Pickled or dry-salted capers feature strongly in Mediterranean cooking, especially in dishes from Provence. They are often described as having a "goaty" taste. The finest capers are known as *non-pareilles* and are round and hard. They are of value in reducing oiliness in food, and have an affinity with garlic, lemon, anchovies and olives.
Medicinal uses Root bark is used internally for gastrointestinal infections, diarrhea, gout, rheumatism and as a diuretic. The flower buds are used to treat coughs. Externally for eye infections, skin abrasions and as a renal disinfectant and tonic.

Capsicum annuum
SOLANACEAE

PEPPER

Cultivated bell peppers (capsicums) are rich in vitamin C. They are crisp and juicy when green, but sweeter when allowed to ripen to red, yellow or orange. The fruit is used medicinally to treat asthma, coughs and fevers.

Best climate and site Perennial in Zone 10. Greenhouse or very sheltered sites out of doors in full sun in cooler areas.
Ideal soil conditions Light, well-drained soil, not overly rich but with even moisture; pH 6.0–7.0.
Growing guidelines Sow seed in warmth and light; set young plants outdoors several weeks after last frost. Plant 1–1½ feet (30–45 cm) apart. Do not overwater seedlings as they are vulnerable to root rot. Young peppers will tolerate cool spells but will not thrive until warmer weather arrives. Do not mulch until the soil is thoroughly warm. Too much nitrogen will produce lush foliage and few peppers, but an application of fish emulsion or compost tea when plants are in flower can help increase yield. Water in dry spells as peppers are prone to blossom-end rot if drought-stressed.
Growing habit Height 1–2 feet (30–60 cm); shrubby tropical perennial, grown as an annual in cool areas.
Flowering time Summer; flowers followed by red, orange, brown or yellow fruit.
Pest and disease prevention Generally, pests tend to avoid spicy pepper plants. Check for powdery mildew or leafspot.
Harvesting and storing Pick immature or green peppers when they are large enough to use. Leave some fruit on the plant to mature. Fully ripe peppers will be yellow, orange, brown or red, depending on the cultivar. Pick mature peppers when they are 75 percent colored; they will finish ripening at room temperature. Fresh peppers will keep for 2 weeks or more, or freeze them for winter cooking. Freeze or pickle thick-fleshed

The soul of many Asian and Mexican dishes, hot peppers come in many sizes, shapes, and degrees of heat. The thinner-fleshed, elongated peppers tend to hold their flavor better in cooked dishes.

hot peppers, such as jalapeño, and dry, thin-fleshed ones, such as cayenne.
Special tips Hot peppers and bell peppers may cross-pollinate. Plant them well away from each other, especially if you intend to save the seeds.
Precautions Accidental contact can cause eye irritation.
Parts used Fruits.
Culinary uses As a vegetable, in pickles and chutneys, and in salads. Ripe fruits dried to make cayenne pepper, chili powder and paprika.
Medicinal uses Internally for fevers and digestive problems. Externally for sprains, chilblains, pleurisy and laryngitis.
Other varieties Hot peppers C. *annuum* Longum Group, also called chili peppers. Hot peppers come in a wide variety of shapes, sizes and degrees of "heat." A medium cultivar, 'Poblano', is often served stuffed. Medium–hot peppers include jalapeño and Hungarian wax. Fiery peppers include cayenne and Thai types. Hot weather intensifies the flavor.
Sweet (bell) peppers C. *annuum* Grossum Group are blocky in shape and thick-fleshed. They are most often used fresh in salads, relish or for stuffing. Most cultivars turn red or yellow when fully ripe.
Sweet peppers (others) C. *annuum* Grossum Group, also called sweet Italian or banana peppers. Banana peppers can be sweet or hot. They have elongated fruit up to 1 foot (30 cm) long. They are generally thinner fleshed and hold their shape and flavor better in cooked dishes.

Carthamus tinctorius
ASTERACEAE

SAFFLOWER

The orange-yellow flowers of safflower are used to produce yellow and red dyes, which when mixed together with powdered talc form the facial makeup rouge. A popular cooking oil is manufactured from the seeds.

Best climate and site Zones 6–10. Full sun.
Ideal soil conditions Well-drained soil enriched with organic matter; pH 6.0–7.0.
Growing guidelines Sow seed in shallow beds outdoors in spring; thin to 6 inches (15 cm). Safflower transplants poorly.
Growing habit Tall annual with upright stems and spiny oval leaves; height 2–3 feet (60–90 cm).
Flowering time Summer; orange to yellow thistle-like flowers followed by small, shiny, white fruit.
Pest and disease prevention Handpick snails and slugs from seedlings.
Harvesting and storing Collect flowers in the morning, before they are fully open, and use fresh or dried for infusions. To dry, hang upside-down in a shaded, airy spot. Flowers keep for 1 year only.
Special tips The seed of the safflower plant is high in linoleic acid, an essential fatty acid which can help to lower cholesterol in the blood and prevent heart disease. Infuse the flowers for a tea that will soothe skin problems.
Precautions Not given to pregnant women.
Parts used Flowers, seeds, oil.
Culinary uses Oil is used in cooking and in cholesterol-reducing diets.
Medicinal uses Internally for coronary artery disease, measles, jaundice and as a laxative.
Externally for skin problems, bruises and painful joints.
Other uses As a food coloring. Flowers used in natural dyes.

Carum carvi
APIACEAE

CARAWAY

The seeds of this biennial have been used for over 5,000 years. Caraway was thought to give protection from witches and was also believed to be able to prevent departures, so was used in love potions.

Best climate and site Zones 6–10. Ideally in full sun.
Ideal soil conditions Fertile, light garden soil; pH 6.0–7.0.
Growing guidelines Sow seed outdoors in spring or early autumn or indoors in pots; thin to 6–12 inches (15–30 cm). Don't allow seedlings to dry out. A thick, long taproot makes transplanting difficult. Self-seeds in the right conditions.
Growing habit Biennial with glossy, finely dissected foliage resembling the carrot plant and slender branching stems; height 1–2 feet (30–60 cm).
Flowering time Spring or summer of the second year, depending when seed is sown. White to pink flowers in umbels on stalks are followed by a ribbed fruits containing the licorice-flavored seeds.
Pest and disease prevention Watch for pests in dried seeds.
Harvesting and storing Snip tender leaves in spring and use fresh in salads, soups and stews. After blooming, cut plants when seeds are brown and almost loose, then hang seedheads upside down in paper bags to dry. Collect seed heads and dry a few more days in the sun; store in a tightly sealed container.
Special tips Excessive pruning during the first year weakens the plant.
Parts used Leaves, roots, seeds, oil.
Culinary uses Leaves added to soups and salads; roots cooked as a vegetable; seeds used to flavor bread, cakes, cheese and liqueur.
Medicinal uses Internally for flatulence, indigestion, bronchitis and diarrhea.

Catharanthus roseus
APOCYNACEAE

MADAGASCAR PERIWINKLE

This tender perennial, which can be grown as an annual, is used in the treatment of cancer as it has properties that can reduce the number of white blood cells. It has been used to treat leukemia in children.

Best climate and site Zones 9–10. Full sun but tolerates partial shade.
Ideal soil conditions Moist, well-drained soil; pH 6.0–7.0.
Growing guidelines Propagate by seed sown shallowly indoors several months before last frost date; plant outdoors after danger of frost has passed. Space at 10–12 inches (25–30 cm). Can be propagated by cuttings of non-flowering shoots in spring. In cool climates, bring potted plants indoors to overwinter. Pinch tops for best growth and shape.
Growing habit Tender perennial with glossy evergreen leaves on a compact plant; height to 1–2 feet (30–60 cm). Cut back in spring to shape. Is weedy in warm areas.
Flowering time Late spring to autumn; rosy pink to white blossoms, up to 2 inches (5 cm) across with darker centers.
Pest and disease prevention Usually free from pests and diseases, but low temperatures may cause fungal diseases.
Harvesting and storing Leaves are picked before or during flowering and dried for infusions.
Precautions Madagascar periwinkle is poisonous if eaten. It should be used by a qualified practitioner only.
Parts used Leaves.
Medicinal uses Madagascar periwinkle reduces blood sugar levels, stimulates the uterus and increases perspiration. It is used internally for diabetes, constipation, asthma and menstrual regulation. Is used to treat cancer and leukemia in children.
Other common names Rosy periwinkle, cayenne jasmine.

Ceanothus americanus
RHAMNACEAE

NEW JERSEY TEA

This plant has small, sparse leaves, small white flowers, and seedpods resembling acorns with horns. An astringent tea made from the leaves can be used as a gargle for sore throats.

Best climate and site Zones 4–9. Best in full sun; tolerates partial shade.
Ideal soil conditions Light, well-drained soil; pH 6.0–7.0.
Growing guidelines Take cuttings from new growth in spring or autumn. Roots are tough and difficult to divide. Plants tend to be short-lived and may need replacement every few years. Prune severely in winter to control growth.
Growing habit Straggly, deciduous shrub with downy, dark green, oval-shaped leaves up to 4 inches (10 cm) long; height 2–3 feet (60–90 cm).
Flowering time Late summer; panicles of small white blossoms on long stalks followed by triangular seedpods.
Pest and disease prevention Usually free from pests and diseases. Check for scale.
Harvesting and storing Collect leaves anytime; use fresh or dried for tea. Roots are dug up and dried in late autumn or early spring when the red color is at its deepest.
Parts used Leaves, roots.
Culinary uses Used as a substitute for tea during the American War of Independence.
Medicinal uses Roots used in preparations taken internally for colds, coughs, sore throats, bronchitis, tonsillitis, whooping cough and nosebleeds. Was used externally by Native Americans to treat skin cancer and venereal sores.
Other common names Redroot, mountain-sweet, wild snowball.

Centaurea cyanus
ASTERACEAE

CORNFLOWER

Cornflowers were common in cornfields throughout Europe. Its botanical name comes from the legendary centaur Chiron, who was famed for his knowledge of herbs and first revealed the cornflower's healing properties.

Best climate and site Zones 3–8. Full sun.
Ideal soil conditions Well-drained soil; pH 4.2–7.2.
Growing guidelines Grows easily from seed sown directly into the garden in spring or autumn. To extend the flowering season from an early spring planting, sow again every 2–4 weeks until midsummer. Cornflowers will self-sow if you leave a few flowers to set seed.
Growing habit Dependable, easy-care, frost-hardy annual; height 8–36 inches (20–90 cm). These bushy plants have narrow, lance-shaped, silvery green leaves and thin stems topped with fluffy flower heads.
Flowering time Bright blue, thistle-like flowers in late spring and summer. Flower color can vary from white to shades of bright blue, purple, pink or red.
Pest and disease prevention Leaves can be affected by rust, and flowers can be attacked by petal blight.
Harvesting and storing Flowers are harvested when young.
Parts used Flowers.
Culinary uses Flowers can be used fresh in salads and as garnishes.
Medicinal uses Externally for minor wounds and ulcers of the mouth. Also used as an eyewash for eye inflammation.
Other uses Extracts of cornflower are added to cosmetic and hair preparations. Also used in natural dyes. Flowers used in potpourris.
Other common names Bluebottle, knapweed, bachelor's button.

Centella asiatica
APIACEAE

Gotu Kola

This herb was traditionally used to treat leprosy in India and Africa. It is an important medicinal plant for clearing toxins, reducing inflammation and fever and improving healing and immunity.

Best climate and site Zones 9–10 or more. Sun to partial shade.
Ideal soil conditions Well-composted, moist soil; pH 5.5–7.8.
Growing guidelines Propagate from cuttings or seed in spring.
Growing habit Low-growing, creeping perennial; height 6–8 inches (15–20 cm). Clusters of bright green, kidney-shaped leaves. Thrives in humid, wet places such as those adjacent to waterways and ponds.
Flowering time Tiny pink flower clusters in summer.
Pest and disease prevention Not usually bothered by pests.
Harvesting and storing Whole plant or leaves are collected whenever required and used fresh or dried.
Precautions Can be a skin irritant and cause headaches. Excess can be dangerous. Subject to legal restrictions in some countries.
Parts used Whole plant, leaves.
Culinary uses Leaves are picked fresh and added to curries and salads in Asia.
Medicinal uses Internally for wounds, varicose veins and ulcers. Externally for reducing scarring from wounds and to quicken healing. Sap of leaves has been used to treat prickly heat.
Other uses Added to face masks and creams to increase collagen and firm skin.
Other common names Indian pennywort, tiger grass.
Gardener's trivia Extracts added to cosmetic formulations to firm the skin. Highly valued in Ayurvedic medicine, where it is known as *brahmi*, meaning "bringing knowledge of supreme reality," and has been used for centuries to aid meditation.

Chaenomeles speciosa
ROSACEAE

Flowering quince

Flowering quinces are deciduous shrubs and small trees that are native to China. They are among the loveliest of early spring-flowering plants with the added bonus of edible fruits.

Best climate and site Zone 5–10. Prefers full sun in an open position but can be trained to grow along a wall or fence.
Ideal soil conditions Well-drained soil, slightly acid to neutral; pH 6.0–7.0.
Growing guidelines Propagate by seed sown in autumn and placed in a cold frame, by semiripe cuttings in summer or by layering shoots in early autumn. For plants grown in the open, thin out and prune after flowering or when cutting blossoms for vases. For wall-trained species, cut back after flowering to reduce the previous year's growth to two or three buds and cut back any outward-growing shoots.
Growing habit Deciduous shrub or small tree with dense, spiny twigs and ovate leaves; height 6–20 feet (2–6 m).
Flowering time Scarlet, five-petaled flowers appear in late winter followed by aromatic, greenish yellow, speckled fruits.
Pest and disease prevention Prone to fireblight. Plants grown in alkaline soil may suffer from chlorosis.
Harvesting and storing Fruits are collected when ripe in autumn and either eaten fresh or dried for used in decoctions.
Parts used Fruits.
Culinary uses Fruits can be eaten fresh or are used as a substitute for quince *Cydonia oblonga* in jams.
Medicinal uses Internally for arthritis, rheumatism, swollen lower limbs, leg cramps and stomach cramps due to diarrhea, indigestion and vomiting.
Other cultivars *C. speciosa* 'Moerloosei' has small, pinkish white flowers that resemble apple blossoms.

Chamaemelum nobile
ASTERACEAE

CHAMOMILE, ROMAN

Herb gardens of yesteryear often included a lush lawn of chamomile that released a sweet, apple-like scent when walked upon. Chamomile tea is relaxing after a stressful day.

Best climate and site Zones 4–10. Full sun to partial shade.
Ideal soil conditions Moist, well-drained soil; pH 6.7–7.3.
Growing guidelines Sow seed and thin to 6 inches (15 cm). Once established, it will self-sow. Divide older plants in early spring. In the first year, clip to prevent flowering and encourage vegetative growth while it becomes established. Creeping runners spread the plant, creating a carpet-like surface. Chamomile is a poor competitor, so weed often. Established lawns can be mowed like grass.
Growing habit Height 6–9 inches (15–23 cm); low-growing perennial with aromatic, lacy foliage.
Flowering time Summer; small white daisy-like flowers with yellow centers.
Pest and disease prevention Usually not bothered by pests.
Harvesting and storing Collect flowers at full bloom and dry on screens or paper. Store in tightly sealed containers.
Parts used Flowers, oil.
Culinary uses As an herbal tea.
Medicinal uses Internally for digestive problems, insomnia, hyperactivity and stress-related illnesses. Used in inhalations for asthma and bronchitis.
Externally for irritated skin and caffeine-induced stress.
Other uses Oil is used in beauty cosmetics.
Other common names Garden chamomile, ground apple and Russian chamomile.
Other species German chamomile *Matricaria recutita* has a similar herbal effect and is an annual.

Chimaphila umbellata
PYROLACEAE

PIPSISSEWA

Pipsissewa is an ingredient in root beer, and has been used medicinally for hundreds of years. It is one of the wintergreen family. Its species name comes from the Greek cheima, *meaning winter, as it remains green in winter.*

Best climate and site Zones 5–8. Partial shade.
Ideal soil conditions Humus-rich, well-drained but moist acid soil; pH 4.8–6.7.
Growing guidelines Propagate by division of older plants, or take root cuttings in spring or autumn. Mulch plants with pine needles to maintain acid pH and soil moisture. Not easy to grow.
Growing habit Low-growing, evergreen, shrubby perennial; height to 10 inches (25 cm). Shoots from a creeping underground rootstock; slightly crooked stems trail along the ground. Thick, glossy, obovate leaves to 2 inches (5 cm) long.
Flowering time Spring to late summer; long stalks topped by white or pink blossoms with five rounded petals, in small terminal clusters. Followed by egg-shaped seed capsules.
Pest and disease prevention Not usually bothered by pests.
Harvesting and storing Harvest leaves for medicinal and culinary uses in late summer or early autumn; store in an airtight container.
Special tips Grow pipsissewa in a rock garden with partial shade. Thrives in woodland conditions.
Parts used Whole plant, leaves.
Culinary uses A traditional ingredient of root beer.
Medicinal uses Internally for arthritis and rheumatism. Tea made with pipsissewa leaves has a good reputation as a tonic for kidney problems, urethritis and urinary infections. Used by early American settlers to treat typhus.
Other common names Prince's pine, waxflower, ground holly.

Chrysanthemum parthenium (Tanacetum parthenium)
ASTERACEAE

FEVERFEW

Double-flowered feverfew makes an attractive border plant. Folklore states that it repels undesirable insects from the garden. Scientific research has proved it effective in the treatment of migraine and rheumatism.

Best climate and site Zones 6–10. Full sun to partial shade.
Ideal soil conditions Well-drained garden soil; pH 6.0–6.7.
Growing guidelines Sow seed shallowly in late winter indoors, then transplant outdoors 9–12 inches (23–30 cm) apart 2 weeks after danger of frost has passed. In mild areas, sow directly outdoors when danger of frost has passed. Divide mature plants or take cuttings in spring or autumn, but best plants are grown from seed. Avoid planting in wet areas. For vigorous plants, pinch blossoms before seeds set; side-dress with compost or rotted manure in early spring.
Growing habit Aromatic perennial with erect stems and foliage that resembles chamomile; height 8–24 inches (20–60 cm).
Flowering time Summer to autumn; daisy-like white rays with yellow center.
Pest and disease prevention Usually free from pests and diseases.
Harvesting and storing Cut and dry stems at full bloom for arrangements.
Precautions Fresh leaves may cause dermatitis and other skin allergies if eaten. Not given to pregnant and breastfeeding women.
Parts used Whole plant, flowers, leaves.
Medicinal uses Internally for migraine caused by heat stress, and for arthritis and digestive problems. Also relieves pain and muscle spasms. This herb is available in tablet form. Externally for insect bites and bruising.
Other uses Flowers used for crafts and floral arrangements.

Cichorium intybus
ASTERACEAE

CHICORY

Look for chicory's bright blue, dandelion-shaped flowers along roadsides and field edges. This frost-hardy wild plant thrives under a variety of harsh conditions; it dislikes the cozy warmth of indoors.

Best climate and site Zones 3–9. Full sun.
Ideal soil conditions Neutral to alkaline, deeply tilled, well-drained soil; pH 6.0–8.0.
Growing guidelines Sow seed outdoors in spring, thinning to 1 foot (30 cm). Side-dress in midsummer with compost or rotted manure, but avoid heavy nitrogen applications. Keep weeded and moist. In the autumn, witloof types can be "forced" indoors away from light to produce chicons. To do this, plant roots trimmed to 8–9 inches (20–23 cm) long in deep containers and keep away from light. Within about 3 weeks, cone-shaped heads of leaves, or chicons, are ready to be sliced off and used. Discard the root and start again with a new one. Loose-leaved chicory is boiled as a vegetable; radicchio kinds are cooked or eaten raw.
Growing habit Deep-rooted perennial with bristly, branched stem; height of 1–5 feet (30–150 cm).
Flowering time Early spring to autumn; bright blue, dandelion-shaped flowers open and close each morning and evening, even when cut for arrangements.
Pest and disease prevention Few pests bother this fast-grower.
Harvesting and storing Chicory leaves do not freeze well. Collect the roots in spring or autumn, and dry them before grinding.
Parts used Leaves, roots.
Culinary uses Use leaves fresh in salads or cook like spinach. Sliced roots are roasted and used as a coffee substitute.
Medicinal uses Internally for gout and liver complaints.

Citrus aurantiifolia
RUTACEAE

LIME

There are 16 species of tree and shrub in the citrus genus, all closely related. Aromatic, tart limes are native to the West Indies. They have valuable culinary and medicinal properties.

Best climate and site Zones 9 and warmer; prefers humid, tropical and warm temperate climates with full sun and wind protection. Frost and drought sensitive.
Ideal soil conditions Prefers light, well-drained, fertile soil; pH 4.6–7.0.
Growing guidelines The Tahitian lime will take cooler conditions than the Mexican lime. Keep well watered during spring and summer. Propagate from seed or by grafting.
Growing habit Small, evergreen tree with short, spiny branches and light green, glossy leaves; height 10–15 feet (3–5 m). Native to humid tropics, mainly the West Indies.
Flowering time Clusters of 2–7 small, white flowers appear in spring and summer, followed by small, round green fruit.
Pest and disease prevention Scale insects, mealybugs, leaf miners and caterpillars.
Harvesting and storing Harvest fruit when ripe and use fresh. Peel can be used fresh or dried and distilled for oil. Harvest leaves as required for infusions.
Parts used Leaves, fruits, peel, oil.
Culinary uses Fruits used in marmalade, savory and sweet dishes; also in drinks. Peel used to flavor confectionery and cakes; used in similar ways to lemon peel. Juice used in South Pacific countries to "cook" fish.
Medicinal uses Internally for treatment of diarrhea and headaches. Juice used to soothe coughs and sore throats.
Other uses Oil used in perfumes. Also used in potpourri and as an astringent and skin tonic.

Citrus bergamia
RUTACEAE

BERGAMOT ORANGE

High in vitamin C, acids and volatile oils, the orange has been valued for centuries for its sweet, refreshing flavor. The highly aromatic rind of the bergamot provides an oil that gives Earl Grey tea its characteristic flavor.

Best climate and site Zones 9–10. Full sun.
Ideal soil conditions Prefers light, well-drained, fertile soil; pH 4.7–7.2.
Growing guidelines Propagate from seed or by grafting.
Growing habit Rounded tree with slender, spined branches and glossy, oval green leaves; height to 30 feet (9 m).
Flowering time Fragrant, small, white flowers occur in spring and summer. Fruits are round to pear-shaped, pale to bright yellow, with an aromatic pulp. The thin peel yields oil.
Pest and disease prevention Scale insects, mealybugs, leaf miners, caterpillars and possibly root rot.
Harvesting and storing Pick fruit when ripe and use fresh. Peel can be used fresh or dried and distilled for oil.
Parts used Flowers, ripe fruits, peel.
Culinary uses Eaten fresh and in fruit salads. Juice and rind used in sweet dishes and cakes. Orange-flower water is used in pastries and desserts.
Medicinal uses Orange-flower water used internally for colic. Oil used externally for douches and skin conditions.
Other uses Bergamot oil is used to flavor Earl Grey tea.
Other species Seville orange *C. aurantium* is a rounded tree with slender, spined branches; height 30 feet (9 m). Fragrant, large, white flowers occur in spring. Fruits have aromatic rind.
Mandarin *C. reticulata* is an evergreen shrub or small tree; height 6–25 feet (2–8 m). White flowers occur in spring, followed by yellow to red-orange fruit.

Citrus limon
RUTACEAE

LEMON

Citrus trees are valued for their culinary and medicinal uses. Unknown in Europe until the 12th century, they are now appreciated worldwide for their bitter and aromatic properties. The lemon is a popular ornamental tree.

Best climate and site Zones 9–10. Prefers full sun with wind protection.
Ideal soil conditions Prefers light, well-drained, fertile soil; pH 5.0–8.0.
Growing guidelines Choose container-grown grafted cultivars. Propagate by cuttings or grafting. Ample moisture must be available during spring and summer.
Growing habit Evergreen, subtropical tree with gray bark and glossy, dark green, elliptical leaves; height 10–20 feet (3–6 m).
Flowering time Clusters of small, simple, white flowers occur at all times of the year but main flush is in spring and summer; followed by sour-tasting, bright yellow oval fruits.
Pest and disease prevention Scale insects, mealybugs, leaf miners, caterpillars or fruit flies may attack.
Harvesting and storing Fruit harvested when ripe for juicing. Rind used either fresh or candied; also dried for potpourri.
Parts used Fruits, juice, rind, flowers, leaves, oil.
Culinary uses Lemon juice is used extensively throughout the world as a souring agent in cooking. Its fresh, natural sharpness is used in savory and sweet dishes, and in drinks.
Medicinal uses Lemon fruit, juice and peel are rich in vitamins and minerals and are valued for their antioxidant properties. Internally for varicose veins, colds, coughs, sore throats, headaches, rheumatism and fevers; also as a diuretic. Externally for eczema and stings.
Other uses Oil from fruit used in perfumes and soaps. Also as a skin tonic and astringent.

Coffea arabica
RUBIACEAE

COFFEE

Coffee beans are actually the seeds inside a pulpy fruit. To produce the seeds, the plant requires a hot, moist climate and rich soil. Coffee contains caffeine, which is used in many commercial painkillers.

Best climate and site Zone 10 with full sun to semishade, or greenhouse with a minimum winter temperature of 55–60°F (13–16°C).
Ideal soil conditions Well-drained soil rich in humus; pH 6.0–7.0.
Growing guidelines Sow seed shallowly in spring in a temperature of not less than 65°F (18°C). Germinates quickly. Does well indoors in pots, but benefits from regular misting with water to maintain humidity.
Growing habit Evergreen large shrub with glossy leaves; height 15–20 feet (4.5–7 m).
Flowering time Late spring; white, star-shaped blooms in clusters, followed by deep red berries which contain large seeds or beans.
Pest and disease prevention For healthy plants, keep coffee plants well watered during periods of dry weather.
Harvesting and storing Collect the berries when they are deep red, and extract the seeds. Sun dry for 7–10 days, then roast them.
Precautions Coffee contains caffeine, which is a stimulant that can cause irritability. It also contains a known allergen.
Parts used Seeds.
Culinary uses As a beverage and flavoring. Can be combined with chocolate to give a mocha flavor.
Medicinal uses Internally for nausea, vomiting and narcotic poisoning.
Powdered seeds are used externally to treat burns and scalds.

Convallaria majalis
CONVALLARIACEAE

LILY-OF-THE-VALLEY

Established clumps of this plant compete well with weeds and can thrive in the same spot for decades with little or no care. The fragrant, poisonous flowers are used in potpourri and the oil in perfumery.

Best climate and site Zones 3–9. Prefers partial shade.
Ideal soil conditions Fertile, moist soil; pH 4.2–7.0.
Growing guidelines Plants need a winter with frost. Propagate by seed sown in spring, or by division in autumn.
Growing habit Frost-hardy perennial that grows from creeping, horizontal rhizomes. Leaves are in pairs and are large and oval in shape and deep green in color; height 9–12 inches (23–30 cm). Deciduous leaves turn brown in late summer. Benefits from an application of compost in autumn. Divide crowded plantings if they stop flowering.
Flowering time Spikes of small, white, bell-shaped flowers appear in spring. They are waxy in texture and are sweetly perfumed; followed by poisonous, small, round, red berries.
Pest and disease prevention Botrytis (gray mold) affects the leaves in wet conditions. Some caterpillars attack roots.
Harvesting and storing All parts are collected in spring and used fresh or dried.
Special tips Grows well in moist soil in the dappled shade of deciduous trees.
Precautions All parts of the plant are poisonous if eaten. Subject to legal restrictions in some countries.
Parts used Whole plant, oil, leaves, flowers.
Medicinal uses For use by qualified practitioners only. Internally for cardiac failure, hypertension and angina.
Other uses Oil from the flowers is used for perfumery and for tobacco manufacture.
Other common names May lily.

Coriandrum sativum
APIACEAE

CILANTRO (CORIANDER)

Cilantro (coriander) is an annual with finely divided leaves that are both strong-smelling and tasty. The seeds, which are also used, become more fragrant with age. This is one of the oldest known herbs.

Best climate and site Zones 6–10. Full sun for seed production but some shade for best leaves.
Ideal soil conditions Fertile, well-drained soil; pH 6.0–7.0.
Growing guidelines Sow seed ½ inch (1 cm) deep outdoors in spring after danger of frost; thin to 4 inches (10 cm). Can self-sow. Weed diligently to prevent delicate seedlings from being overcome by more vigorous weeds. To prevent sprawling, avoid heavy applications of nitrogen.
Growing habit Annual with graceful, glossy, finely dissected foliage; height 1–3 feet (30–90 cm).
Flowering time Early to late summer, depending on when sown; tiny white flowers in umbels.
Pest and disease prevention Usually trouble free.
Harvesting and storing Harvest foliage before seeds form and use fresh. Dried foliage is of lesser quality. Freezes poorly. Gather seeds as they ripen in midsummer.
Special tips Sow every 2–3 weeks for a continuous supply of fresh leaves. Honeybees are attracted to the flowers. The seeds remain viable for 5–7 years.
Parts used Leaves, seeds, roots, oil.
Culinary uses Leaves used to flavor Middle Eastern and Southeast Asian food. Seeds added to curries, stews, pastries and some wines. Oil is used in liqueur.
Medicinal uses Internally for digestive problems. Externally for joint problems and hemorrhoids.
Other uses Seeds used in laxatives and in potpourri.
Other common names Chinese parsley.

Crataegus laevigata
ROSACEAE

HAWTHORN

In pagan times, hawthorn was both a symbol of hope and an omen of death. Because it flowers in the Northern spring, it is also know as May or Mayblossom.

Best climate and site Zones 5–9. Frost hardy and drought resistant; prefers an open sunny position.
Ideal soil conditions Clay or loamy soils; pH 4.5–8.2.
Growing guidelines Hawthorn grows easily from seed or by grafting. Sow ripe seeds outdoors in early spring, or plant young trees from autumn to early spring.
Growing habit Deciduous tree with erect trunk, reddish-brown bark and thorny branches; height 15–20 feet (5–6 m). Leaves are dark green, lobed and toothed.
Flowering time In spring; white scented flowers with pink or purple anthers appear followed by dark red, egg-shaped fruit.
Pest and disease prevention Leaves attacked by caterpillars or affected by leafspot, powdery mildew or rust. Honey fungus causes death of tree.
Harvesting and storing Fruit collected when ripe and used raw, cooked or dried.
Special tips For a hedge, plant shrubs 12 inches (30 cm) apart and prune to shape.
Precautions For use by qualified practitioners only.
Parts used Fruit.
Medicinal uses Internally for circulatory disorders and heart disease.
Other names May, quickset, midland hawthorn.
Other species Chinese haw *C. pinnatifida* is a hsardy small tree; white flowers with pink anthers followed by red fruit. Used to treat irritable bowel syndrome. Fruits baked for digestive problems.

Crocus sativus
IRIDACEAE

SAFFRON

The fragrant pink, mauve and purple blooms of saffron with their red stigmas and long, yellow anthers are a striking and valuable addition to the garden. Saffron is the source of a yellow dye and a unique culinary flavoring.

Best climate and site Zones 6–9. Best in full sun, sheltered from winds and frost.
Ideal soil conditions Light, fertile, well-drained soil; pH 6.5–7.5.
Growing guidelines Plant saffron crocus corms 3–4 inches (7.5–10 cm) deep, with the rooting side down, in early autumn at 4-inch (10-cm) intervals. Lift and divide corms every two to three years, after the foliage has died down in spring or autumn. Self-propagates. Mulch in severe winters.
Growing habit Perennial with grasslike leaves; height 3½–6 inches (8–15 cm).
Flowering time Autumn; flowers appear with or before leaves.
Pest and disease prevention Usually free from pests and diseases, but after cool wet summers may flower poorly.
Harvesting and storing Collect individual dark yellow stigmas and dry on paper away from breezes. Store in an airtight glass container in a cool, dry place away from direct light. The flowers can be dried whole.
Parts used Flower stigmas.
Culinary uses Used as a flavoring and color agent for cakes, paella, risotto and bouillabaisse.
Medicinal uses Internally for liver problems and depression.
Other uses To flavor and color liqueurs. Also in perfumery.
Gardener's trivia Good quality saffron is expensive because the crops yield very little product; there is a short blooming period of only about 20 days. From 160,000 flowers only about 2 pounds (1 kg) of saffron is produced.

Cryptotaenia canadensis
APIACEAE

MITSUBA

Mitsuba is one of the few culinary herbs to flourish in shade and as such is a welcome addition to the herb garden. Plant between taller, sun-loving herbs whose foliage can provide shade.

Best climate and site Zones 3–7. Temperate and shady.
Ideal soil conditions Rich, moist soil; pH 4.3–6.7.
Growing guidelines Grow from seed in early spring through to midsummer or by division in spring.
Growing habit Attractive, hardy succulent perennial with creeping roots, hollow stalks and leaves comprising of three leaflets with serrated edges; height 3 feet (1 m) and spread 12–36 inches (30–90 cm). Responds very well to fertilizing with fish emulsion. Often grown as an annual.
Flowering time Small, white flowers appear in clusters in the summer and quickly turn to seed.
Pest and disease prevention Usually trouble free.
Harvesting and storing Young leaves picked as required and used fresh. Plants are ready to harvest in about 7–8 weeks after germination.
Parts used Leaves.
Culinary uses In Japan, mitsuba is added fresh or cooked to soups, salads, sukiyaki, sashimi, tempura batter, custards and rice. Young leaves are cooked as a green vegetable. Leaf stalks are added to stews and soups instead of celery. Mitsuba turns bitter if overcooked.
Other common names Honewort, Japanese wild chervil.
Gardener's trivia Mitsuba is celery-flavored and found in woodland ravines and riverbanks throughout northern temperate and mountainous regions of Japan and China. It is widely cultivated as a pot herb both in Japan and by Japanese communities in other parts of the world.

Cuminum cyminum
APIACEAE

CUMIN

Cumin is a small and delicate annual of the parsley family. Cumin seeds have been used for centuries as a pungent and aromatic addition to curries and spicy dishes. Cumin grows in Mediterranean and warm climates.

Best climate and site Zones 8–10. Full sun with wind protection.
Ideal soil conditions Light, well-drained soil; pH 5.6–8.2.
Growing guidelines Propagate by seed sown in spring in a sheltered, sunny site. Seeds may not ripen in cold climates.
Growing habit Small, tender annual with dark green leaves which are slightly fragrant and threadlike; height 10 inches (25 cm).
Flowering time White or pinkish flowers appear in summer and are followed by aromatic seeds. These are similar in appearance to caraway seeds except they are bristly.
Pest and disease prevention Usually trouble free.
Harvesting and storing Seeds are collected when ripe and stored whole. They are used whole or ground for culinary use.
Parts used Seeds.
Culinary uses Powerfully flavored seeds are either roasted or crushed and added to many Middle Eastern and Indian dishes, especially to lamb, curries and yogurt. Also used for pickling and flavoring liqueurs and cordials.
Medicinal uses Internally for minor digestive problems, flatulence, colic and migraine. Used to improve liver function. The oil of the cumin plant is antibacterial.
Other uses Cumin oil is used in perfumery and veterinary medicine.
Gardener's trivia The Romans used ground cumin seeds in the same way as we use pepper. They also believed it stimulated sexual organs.

Curcuma longa
ZINGIBERACEAE

TURMERIC

A member of the ginger family, turmeric is known for its pungent, musky taste and its aromatic and peppery fragrance. Its characteristic orange color has been used for centuries to dye the robes of Buddhist monks.

Best climate and site Zones 8–9. Prefers full sun and high humidity. Native to Southeast Asia.
Ideal soil conditions Rich, well-drained soil; pH 4.0–7.5.
Growing guidelines Propagate by root division when dormant or by seed sown in autumn.
Growing habit Tall, perennial plant with large, lily-like leaves; height 3 feet (90 cm). Rhizome is large, oval shaped, aromatic and tuberous.
Flowering time Flowers appear late spring to mid-summer; pale yellow in color and clustered in dense spikes 4–6 inches long (10–15 cm) with pale green and pink bracts.
Pest and disease prevention Usually trouble free.
Harvesting and storing The rhizomes are lifted during the dormant period. These are then boiled or steamed, then dried and ground.
Parts used Rhizomes.
Culinary uses An essential ingredient in curry powder and as a flavoring ingredient in Asian dishes. Used commercially in processed foods and sauces as a natural coloring agent. Often used as a substitute for saffron; however, although its color is similar, its taste is quite different.
Medicinal uses Used fresh or dried as a tonic and remedy for liver problems. Internally to improve digestion and stimulate the circulatory system.
Externally to treat skin disorders.
Other uses As a food coloring; also as a source of yellow and orange dye.

Cymbopogon citratus
POACEAE

LEMONGRASS

This clump-forming perennial has slim, grassy foliage and provides a contrast to broad-leaved garden herbs. Use lemongrass in cooking or infuse the leaves for a soothing tea. Add dried foliage to potpourri.

Best climate and site Zones 9–10 or greenhouse in colder climates. Prefers full sun to partial shade.
Ideal soil conditions Well-drained garden soil enriched with organic matter; pH 6.5–7.3.
Growing guidelines Propagate by division of older plants. Trim the leaves to 3–4 inches (7.5–10 cm) before dividing.
Growing habit Tender perennial; forms dense clumps of typical grass leaves; height 6 feet (1.8 m).
Flowering time Seldom flowers.
Pest and disease prevention Usually trouble free.
Harvesting and storing Snip fresh foliage as needed. Harvest larger amounts anytime in summer and dry quickly for best flavor. Use the white base in cooking.
Special tips Lemongrass oil blends well with the oils of basil, geranium, jasmine and lavender; use in oil burners and mixed into a base oil for massage.
Parts used Leaves, stems, oil.
Culinary uses Base of leaves used in Southeast Asian cooking, especially meat and fish. The leaves can be infused for a tea. Also used as a food flavoring.
Medicinal uses Internally for digestive problems in children and for minor feverishness.
Externally for athlete's foot, scabies, ringworm and lice.
Other uses Lemongrass oil is used in soaps, hair oil, herbal baths and cosmetics.
Other common names Oilgrass, West Indian lemon.

Dendranthema x grandiflorum
ASTERACEAE

CHRYSANTHEMUM

These attractive, easily grown perennials were introduced to the West from China in the 18th century. Also known as florists' chryanthemum, they have been valued for medicinal purposes since the first century.

Best climate and site Zones 4 and warmer; prefers a sunny, sheltered position.
Ideal soil conditions Rich, well-drained soil; pH 6.0–6.7.
Growing guidelines Grow from root divisions or cuttings in early spring or by seed in late winter or early spring. Sow seed ½ inch (12 mm) deep and thin to 4–6 inches (10–15 cm). Pinching out plants encourages sideshoots.
Growing habit Perennial with spreading stems and strongly scented leaves; height 1–7 feet (0.3–2.2 m).
Flowering time Clusters of single or double red, yellow, bronze, pink or white flowers appear in late summer.
Pest and disease prevention Prone to aphids, slugs, snails, mildew and virus diseases.
Harvesting and storing Flowers are harvested in late autumn and dried for used in tinctures and infusions.
Precautions Can cause skin allergies.
Parts used Flowers.
Culinary uses Flowers can be blanched and the petals sprinkled on salads.
Medicinal uses Internally for coronary artery disease, angina, colds and liver disorders. Also increases blood flow to the heart and inhibits pathogens.
Other common names Florists' chrysanthemum, mulberry-leaved chrysanthemum.
Gardener's trivia The edible chrysanthemum leaves, featured in Asian cooking, come from *Chrysanthemum coronarium*, an annual with spicy foliage and yellow flowers.

Dianthus caryophyllus
CARYOPHYLLACEAE

CLOVE PINK

Always a favorite addition to any garden because of its colorful flowers and wonderful fragrance, clove pink is one of the few flowers that tolerates dry, alkaline conditions. It is also known as the carnation.

Best climate and site Zone 8. Full sun to partial shade. Best where summers are cool and winters are not very cold. Drought resistant.
Ideal soil conditions Well-drained slightly alkaline soil; pH 8–9.0.
Growing guidelines Propagate by softwood cuttings in spring, layering in summer or by seed sown in spring.
Growing habit Small, upright, hardy perennial; height 10–20 inches (20–50 cm). Leaves are very slender and grayish green in color. Benefits from a protective light mulch in autumn and winter.
Flowering time Flowers appear in summer and have a clove-scented fragrance. Color usually pink but can vary from pearly white to purple. Snipping off the dead flowers can promote further flowering in the season.
Pest and disease prevention Affected by botrytis (gray mold), powdery mildew, and leaf and stem rot.
Harvesting and storing Flowers are cut in the early morning after a few hours of sun and used fresh or dried.
Parts used Flowers, oil.
Culinary uses Flowers sometimes added to salads and as garnish. Flowers used as flavoring for liqueurs, syrups, jams and vinegars.
Medicinal uses Historically has been used to reduce fevers but its medicinal uses are now restricted to oriental medicine.
Other uses Oil used in perfumery and flowers in potpourri.
Other common names Carnation, gillyflower.

Digitalis purpurea
SCROPHULARIACEAE

Foxglove

Foxglove is grown commercially by the pharmaceutical industry as it is a source of digitalis, an important heart stimulant. Its Latin name of Digitalis *means "finger," referring to the way the flower caps fit over the finger.*

Best climate and site Zones 5–9. Prefers partial shade. Native of Western Europe.
Ideal soil conditions Well-drained, acid soil; pH 4.5–7.0.
Growing guidelines Sow seed in spring or autumn.
Growing habit Biennial or short-lived perennial; height 5 feet (1.5 m). Usually only one stem, with narrow, lancelike leaves growing directly off this stem. Leaves are downy and can have a reddish tint. Benefits from an application of organic matter.
Flowering time Tubular, bell-like flowers, often spotted internally, are produced on one side of a single spike in summer, followed by numerous seed capsules. Colors range from purple to rose, pink and white. To promote rebloom, remove spent flower stalks. Leave one stalk to self-sow.
Pest and disease prevention Is susceptible to crown and root rot in wet conditions.
Harvesting and storing Leaves are picked before flowering and dried for their active components.
Precautions This plant is poisonous if eaten. Can cause nausea, vomiting and visual impairment. In some countries, the growing of this plant is restricted.
Parts used Leaves.
Medicinal uses For over 200 years, *D. purpurea* was the main drug source for treating heart failure. Today, a synthetic form of the drug has been developed, but this plant is still grown commercially for the drug industry. Used internally for irregular heartbeat and heart failure.
Externally as a poultice to aid healing of wounds.

Echinacea purpurea
ASTERACEAE

Echinacea

The name Echinacea *comes from the Greek word* echinos, *meaning hedgehog, and refers to the prickly scales on the flower cone. This plant was highly valued by Native Americans, who regarded it as a universal cure-all.*

Best climate and site Zones 3–8. Full sun. Drought tolerant once established. Native to eastern North America.
Ideal soil conditions Average to humus-rich, moist but well-drained soil; pH 4.2–7.0.
Growing guidelines Propagate by division in autumn and winter, seed sown in spring, or by root cuttings in winter.
Growing habit Tall, rhizomatous perennial; height 4 feet (1.2 m). Leaves are lance-shaped and thick skinned, stems are stout and hairy. Plants grow from thick rootstocks with short rhizomes.
Flowering time Pinkish purple daisy-like flowers are produced in summer and early autumn. Flowers are honey scented and have a conical, orange-brown center. Echinacea gives a wonderful display of color in the garden during summer and autumn and makes a superb cut flower.
Pest and disease prevention Usually trouble free.
Harvesting and storing Plants are lifted in autumn and the roots and rhizomes are dried for use in powders, tablets and infusions.
Parts used Roots, rhizomes.
Medicinal uses Research has recently shown that echinacea stimulates the immune system, promotes rapid healing of wounds, and has antiviral and antibacterial properties. Internally for coughs, colds, venereal diseases, gangrene, septicemia, boils and other skin diseases.
Externally for acne, herpes and infected wounds.
Other names Purple coneflower, purple echinacea.

Elettaria cardamomum
ZINGIBERACEAE

CARDAMOM

Cardamom is one of the most ancient spices in the world and also one of the most highly valued. Only saffron and vanilla are more expensive. The cardamom plant is a large perennial related to ginger.

Best climate and site Zone 10 or warmer. Does best in partial shade. Needs tropical conditions to fruit well.
Ideal soil conditions Moist, humus-rich soil; pH 4.8–6.7.
Growing guidelines Propagate by division of rhizomes in spring or summer and by seed in autumn.
Growing habit Tender perennial of the ginger family; height 6–10 feet (2–3 m).
Flowering time In spring to early summer, spikes of white and pink flowers appear, followed by small oval fruits.
Pest and disease prevention A perennial usually free from pests and diseases. Watch for thrip infestation.
Harvesting and storing The first harvest occurs 3 years after planting and from then on the plants bear for another 10–15 years. The fruits are harvested every few weeks just before they ripen during the dry season. After picking, dry the capsules on open platforms in the sun. Store in airtight containers.
Parts used Seeds, oil.
Culinary uses Cardamom is one of the main ingredients in curry powder. Also used in sweetmeats, pastries, bakery products, ice cream and mulled wine.
Medicinal uses Internally for flatulence, indigestion and stomach disorders. Chewing the seeds cleanses the breath. Also used to detoxify caffeine and to counteract mucus-forming foods. There are legal restrictions in some countries for tinctures.
Other uses Oil used in perfumes.

Equisetum spp.
EQUISETACEAE

HORSETAIL

A primitive, spore-bearing, grasslike plant containing silica, horsetail has often been used as a pot-scrubber and for sanding wood. The silica can be used by the body to accelerate the healing of broken bones.

Best climate and site Zones 5–9. Full sun to partial shade.
Ideal soil conditions Humus-rich, moist soil; acid to neutral pH.
Growing guidelines Rarely cultivated, since it is difficult to eradicate once established. Plant in buckets to prevent spreading. Propagate in autumn by division of mature plants.
Growing habit Primitive, spore-bearing perennial with hollow stems impregnated with silica; height 4–18 inches (10–45 cm). A green stalk and a flesh-colored leafless stalk crowned with a spore-producing cone are produced from the rhizomes. The plant is a declared noxious weed in some areas.
Flowering time Spring; spikes form at the top of the stalks and terminal conelike structures release spores.
Pest and disease prevention Usually trouble free.
Harvesting and storing Cut stems just above the root, dry in the sun and tie in bundles.
Special tips Dried stems are said to act as a garden fungicide. Steep the stems in hot water, strain and spray on plants.
Precautions Horsetail is toxic when large doses are taken. For use by qualified practitioners only.
Parts used Stems.
Medicinal uses The stems contain large amounts of silica, which is used by the body in the production and repair of connective tissues and accelerates the healing of broken bones. Internally for incontinence, cystitis and conjunctivitis. Externally for hemorrhage.
Other common names Bottle brush, scouring rush.

The young leaves of the blue gum are oval and silvery blue; when mature they are long, glossy, green and narrow. The trunk is bluish white with bark that peels off in strips. The flowers are pale yellow with a darker yellow center.

Eucalyptus spp.
MYRTACEAE

EUCALYPTUS

Eucalyptus are evergreen trees well known for their pungent scent and silvery leaves. They are among the world's fastest growing and tallest trees. Eucalyptus are rich in volatile oils, such as citronella and eucalyptol.

Best climate and site Zones 8–10. Full sun or a frost-free greenhouse in cooler zones. Trees grow in a wide range of conditions; drought tolerant.
Ideal soil conditions Light loamy soils; tolerate a wide range of soil pH.
Growing guidelines Best to purchase container-grown trees, but can easily be grown from seed under cover in spring or autumn. Cut back in spring only to restrict size or to retain the juvenile foliage.
Growing habit Over 500 species ranging from 5-foot (1.5-m) shrubs to 300-foot (90-m) trees. Hardiness varies with species. Some species are susceptible to frost but usually survive.
The lemon-scented gum *E. citriodora* is a slender tree with smooth, pale bark and lancelike leaves. Height ranges from 80–160 feet (25–50 m). All parts have a strong lemon scent. The river red gum *E. camaldulensis* is a spreading riverside tree with smooth red-brown bark and small cream flowers. Height ranges from 70–150 feet (20–45 m). The broad-leaved peppermint *E. dives* is a short-trunked tree with shiny, thick leaves and small white flowers. Height ranges from 50–70 feet (15–20 m).
Flowering time Depends on species; most with umbels of white, cream, pink, yellow, orange or red flowers.
Pest and disease prevention Few severe pest problems. Can be injured by strong, cold winds.
Harvesting and storing Leaves are harvested as required and dried; oil distilled for medicinal and industrial use. Branches and seedpods are harvested throughout the year and dried for use in crafts. All parts retain their scent.
Special tips A spray made from blended eucalyptus foliage may deter garden pests.
Precautions Can cause skin irritations. Volatile oils are toxic.
Parts used Leaves, oil, resin, branches, bark, seedpods.
Medicinal uses Most eucalyptus have antiseptic and anti-inflammatory properties. Internally for diarrhea.
Externally in inhalations for fevers, influenza and bronchitis; in liniments for bruises and sprains; in ointments for cuts and wounds; and in vapor rubs. Also for athlete's foot and arthritis.
Other uses The lemon-scented gum is the richest known source of citronella, which is used in insect repellents, perfumery and detergents. Oil used as a flavoring in pharmaceutical products such as throat lozenges; also in oil and grease removers. Seedpods used in crafts.
Other species Red-flowering gum *E. ficifolia* syn. *Corymbia ficifolia* is a fast-growing tree with rough bark and lance-shaped leaves and pink or red flowers that occur in summer; height 40 feet (12 m).
White ironbark *E. leucoxylon* is a large gum with pendulous branches, grayish narrow leaves and flaking gray bark. It bears white, pink or red flowers from winter to spring; height 50–70 feet (15–20 m).
Tasmanian blue gum *E. globulus* is a large, spreading tree with smooth, creamy white to blue peeling bark and creamy flowers; height 100–160 feet (30–50 m).

Eupatorium perfoliatum
ASTERACEAE

BONESET

This plant's genus name comes from the ancient King of Persia, Eupator, who was famed for his herbal skills. This reflects the importance this herb has had throughout the ages for its health-giving properties.

Best climate and site Zones 3–9. Partial shade or full sun.
Ideal soil conditions Rich, marshy soil; pH 4.5–7.
Growing guidelines Sow on the surface of seed trays in autumn or spring; divide mature plants in spring and autumn, and grow in damp or marshy soil in sun or light shade. Cut stems almost down to ground level in autumn after flowering. Semi-hardwood cuttings can also be taken in summer.
Growing habit Rhizomatous perennial with long, narrow, pointed leaves that are dark green and shiny above and white and downy underneath; height 5 feet (1.5 m).
Flowering time Summer and autumn; dense heads of small white or occasionally purple flowers, followed by feathery seed heads.
Pest and disease prevention Usually trouble free.
Harvesting and storing Plants are cut when in bud, and dried for use in infusions, liquid extracts and tinctures. Rhizomes and roots are lifted in autumn and dried for use in decoctions and tinctures. Leaves have been used in an immune-boosting tea.
Parts used Whole plant, roots, leaves.
Medicinal uses Internally for influenza, colds, acute bronchitis, excess mucus and skin diseases.
Other common names Thoroughwort, feverwort.
Other species Joe-Pye weed *E. purpureum* is a tall, frost-hardy perennial with leaves that have a vanilla scent when crushed.
Gardener's trivia Boneset can often be mistaken for ageratum, as they are both very similar in appearance.

Ferula assa-foetida
APIACEAE

ASAFETIDA

This plant has the dubious reputation of being the most foul-smelling of all herbs. It has a "rotten-egg" odor, but, if used in small quantities, adds a pleasant oniony flavor to many foods. It is also an effective medicinal herb.

Best climate and site Zones 8–9. Full sun. Native to Iran. Frost hardy but not fully hardy.
Ideal soil conditions Rich, well-drained soil; pH 4.3–7.3.
Growing guidelines Propagate by ripe seed sown in late summer.
Growing habit Large, lacy perennial; height 6 feet (2 m). Big, finely divided leaves, light green in color, that emit an unpleasant smell when crushed.
Flowering time Tiny, yellow flowers appear in summer after 5 years, followed by small seeds, after which the plant dies.
Pest and disease prevention Usually free from pests and diseases. Check occasionally.
Harvesting and storing Stems and roots are shallowly cut during the growing season so that the resin will exude and can be collected. Whole plants are cut as soon as flowering begins and gum resin is scraped from the top of the root. The resin is formed into lumps that are then processed into pastes, pills and powders.
Special tips When storing asafetida, store in an airtight container to avoid contamination of surrounding food.
Parts used Gum resin.
Culinary uses Used in Indian cuisine. Also to flavor vegetables, sauces and pickles.
Medicinal uses Internally for asthma, minor digestive complaints and coughs.
Externally for sore joints.
Other common names Giant fennel, devil's dung.

Filipendula ulmaria
ROSACEAE

MEADOWSWEET

This plant has an impressive place in the history of plant pharmacology. It was from meadowsweet that the compound of salicylic acid, later to be known as aspirin, was first isolated in 1838.

Best climate and site Zones 2–7. Full sun to partial shade. Native to boggy soils throughout North America, Europe and temperate Asia.
Ideal soil conditions Rich, wet soil with low acidity; pH 6.3–8.1.
Growing guidelines Propagate by division of rootstock in autumn or spring, or by seed sown in early spring.
Growing habit Hardy, woody perennial with bright green oval leaves that emit a smell of wintergreen when crushed. Rootstock is aromatic when cut; height 4 feet (1.2 m).
Flowering time Big clusters of creamy-white, almond-scented flowers occur from mid-summer through to autumn.
Pest and disease prevention Usually free from pests and diseases. Check occasionally.
Harvesting and storing Plant is harvested as flowering begins and is dried for use in tablets, liquid extracts and other uses. Flowers are picked when open and dried for infusions.
Precautions Some people are sensitive to salicylates.
Parts used Whole plant, flowers.
Medicinal uses Internally for peptic ulcers, heartburn, digestive disorders, rheumatic and joint pain, dysentery and colds. Also has been used for diarrhea in children.
Other uses Used in potpourri. Also as a natural dye; the plant produces a greenish dye and the roots produce a black dye. Meadowsweet was also an important strewing herb in the Middle Ages due to its perfume and its ability to repel skin parasites. It was used to fill mattresses and cover floors.

Foeniculum vulgare
APIACEAE

FENNEL

Grow licorice-scented fennel as a tall ornamental in the flower garden and for its culinary properties in the kitchen. The seeds were used in medieval times as a flavoring and were also eaten during Lent to keep hunger at bay.

Best climate and site Zones 6–9. Full sun.
Ideal soil conditions Humus, well-drained soil, pH 6.0–6.7.
Growing guidelines Sow seeds shallowly outdoors in spring or autumn and keep moist; thin to 6 inches (15 cm); transplants poorly.
Growing habit Semi-hardy perennial usually grown as an annual; height to 4 feet (1.2 m). The leaves are feathery and blue-green in color. Can be weedy.
Flowering time Summer to early autumn; small yellow flowers in umbels.
Pest and disease prevention Usually trouble free.
Harvesting and storing Snip leaves before blooming for fresh use; leaves can also be frozen. Collect seeds when dry but before they shatter by snipping the ripe seed heads into a paper bag; dry them on paper.
Special tips The delicate flavor of the leaves is destroyed by heat, so add them at the end of the cooking time.
Parts used Leaves, stems, roots, seeds, oil.
Culinary uses Leaves and seeds used in fish dishes; the anise-flavored leaf bases and stems can be eaten raw in salads and cooked as a vegetable.
Medicinal uses Internally for indigestion, colic, to aid lactation, and for urinary problems.
Externally as a gargle for sore throats and gum diseases.
Gardener's trivia Try the bronze-colored variety for foliage contrast outdoors, and on the dinner plate as a garnish. Flowers attract beneficial insects.

Fragaria vesca
ROSACEAE

WILD STRAWBERRY

This tasty perennial is found naturally in northern temperate regions. It is the parent plant of the popular cultivated strawberry that is loved throughout the world for its delicious flavor and sweetness.

Best climate and site Zones 5–10. Full sun to partial shade.
Ideal soil conditions Well-drained, rich soil; pH 4.2–6.2.
Growing guidelines Sow from seed in spring by scattering seed on the surface of potting soil in a container. Transplant the seedlings when they are large enough to handle. To divide older plants, separate rooted runners or plantlets from the outside of the clump; replant divisions immediately. Replace plants every few years.
Growing habit Perennial, low growing plant with long runners and shiny bright green leaves, toothed on the edges; height 10 inches (25 cm).
Flowering time Five-petaled, white flowers with yellow centers occur throughout spring and summer; followed by bright red, conical fruit with tiny seeds.
Pest and disease prevention Keep birds at bay with netting, or grow yellow-fruited cultivars, which birds may leave alone.
Harvesting and storing Harvest the fruits when they are soft and aromatic. They do not store well. Leaves are picked in summer and dried. Roots are lifted in autumn and dried.
Parts used Leaves, roots, fruits.
Culinary uses Used in herb teas. Fruit eaten fresh or cooked in jams and desserts. Also used to flavor wines, vinegars and confectionery.
Medicinal uses Internally for digestive problems, gout and diarrhea.
Externally for skin inflammations, burns, sunburn and for discolored teeth.

Galium odoratum
RUBIACEAE

SWEET WOODRUFF

Sweet woodruff is a hardy perennial groundcover that grows well in full shade and smells like vanilla when dried. In the past, garlands of woodruff were hung in homes and churches.

Best climate and site Zones 5–9. Prefers shade; grows well under trees. The color of the leaf will fade in full sun.
Ideal soil conditions Moist, well-drained soil rich in humus; pH 5.0–8.0.
Growing guidelines Sow ripe seed shallowly in summer to autumn outdoors; germination may take as long as 200 days. Purchase plants from nurseries and plant 6–9 inches (15–23 cm) apart; divide the creeping rootstock of established plants in spring or autumn. Sweet woodruff is suitable to be brought indoors.
Growing habit Rhizomatous perennial with whorls of lance-shaped leaves; height 8–18 inches (20–45 cm).
Flowering time Late spring to early summer; small, star-shaped, scented white blossoms.
Pest and disease prevention Usually free from pests and diseases; has insect-repellent properties.
Harvesting and storing Gather foliage and flowering stems anytime in summer, hang in bunches to dry.
Special tips The leaves only develop their sweet, distinctive scent of vanilla or hay when dried.
Precautions Can cause dizziness and vomiting and may be carcinogenic.
Parts used Whole plant.
Culinary uses Used in wines and other alcoholic beverages.
Medicinal uses Internally for varicose veins, hepatitis, jaundice and insomnia in children.
Other uses In potpourris; also as a tan-colored dye.

Galium verum
RUBIACEAE

LADY'S BEDSTRAW

Lady's bedstraw needs little attention and readily spreads by seed. It is often grown as an ornamental. Herbalists seal the dried foliage in pillows that release a sleep-inducing scent when rested upon.

Best climate and site Zones 3–9. Full sun, but tolerates light shade.
Ideal soil conditions Deep, light, fertile to average well-drained soil; favors neutral to alkaline soil; pH 6.7–7.3.
Growing guidelines Sow seed shallowly in spring or divide roots of mature plants; plant 2 feet (60 cm) apart. Self-sows; requires little attention.
Growing habit Frost-hardy perennial with creeping rootstock and slightly branched, square stems with whorls of linear leaves; height to 3 feet (90 cm).
Flowering time Throughout summer; sizeable clusters of small, bright yellow, honey-scented flowers are produced in panicles.
Pest and disease prevention Usually free from pests and diseases.
Harvesting and storing Harvest foliage and hang in small bunches for quick drying.
Parts used Whole plant.
Medicinal uses Internally for kidney and bladder complaints. Used as a diuretic and to relax spasms.
Other uses Foliage was once used as stuffing for mattresses. Foliage used as a yellow food dye for cheese and butter. The roots provide a red dye.
Other common names Our Lady's bedstraw, yellow bedstraw, maid's hair, cheese rennet.

Gardenia augusta
RUBIACEAE

GARDENIA

A beautiful and highly fragrant, ornamental shrub, gardenia is known as the "happiness herb" as it is said to improve general well-being. Gardenia is named after a Scottish physician, Alexander Garden (1730–1791).

Best climate and site Zones 8–10. Full sun to partial shade, but must be kept moist. Prefers warm to tropical conditions.
Ideal soil conditions Well-drained, acid soil with high humus content; pH 4.2–5.6.
Growing guidelines Plants like humid conditions. Propagate by semiripe cuttings in summer or greenwood cuttings in spring. Young plants will flower the best.
Growing habit Tender evergreen shrub with dark green, glossy leaves; height 5 feet (1.5 m). Plants respond well to pruning in early spring or during flowering.
Flowering time Very fragrant single, semidouble or double, white, waxy flowers occur in summer, followed by oval fruit.
Pest and disease prevention Avoid damaging plants with gardening tools, because such wounds are a common entry point for pests and diseases, such as mealybugs. Check for mealybugs. If mealybugs, aphids or whiteflies attack, spray with insecticidal soap.
Harvesting and storing Fruits are picked when ripe and dried.
Parts used Fruits, flowers.
Culinary uses Fruits used in China to flavor tea.
Medicinal uses Fruits have been used internally for jaundice, hemorrhage and hepatitis.
Externally for toothache, wounds, sprains and skin infections.
Other uses The gardenia holds a valued position in the perfumery industry, as the volatile oil extracted from its flowers is one of the most highly valued for its fragrance.
Other common names Cape jasmine.

Gentiana lutea
GENTIANACEAE

GREAT YELLOW GENTIAN

Gentian contains one of the most bitter chemicals known and as such forms the benchmark for grading other bitter agents. It is highly valued for its stimulating, tonic effect on the liver, gall bladder and digestive system.

Best climate and site Zones 5–7. Sun to partial shade. Needs shade from afternoon sun to avoid leaf browning.
Ideal soil conditions Moist, well-drained, alkaline soil; pH 5.5–8.9.
Growing guidelines Propagate by offshoots in spring, seed sown in autumn, or by division in autumn.
Growing habit Herbacious perennial that thrives with little care; height 3–6 feet (90–180 cm). Has been known to survive for as long as 50 years. Stems are simple, erect and hollow and bear oval, strongly veined, shiny leaves; roots are large, thick and fleshy.
Flowering time Small, tubelike flowers with five starry lobes occur in clusters in summer. Color is usually yellow. Flowers only appear on mature (10 years and older) plants.
Pest and disease prevention Root rot may be a problem in wet conditions.
Harvesting and storing Roots are lifted in autumn and dried for use. This is the main commercial source of gentian root.
Precautions Not given to people with stomach ulcers.
Parts used Roots, rhizomes.
Medicinal uses Internally for liver disorders and gastric infections. Particularly useful in anorexia associated with indigestion as it stimulates the appetite.
Externally for cleaning wounds.
Other uses Due to its bitter taste, gentian is used in commercial tonics, bitters, vermouth and schnapps.

Geranium robertianum
GERANIACEAE

HERB ROBERT

An old medicinal plant of the Middle Ages, its name comes from St Robert or Pope Robert, and reflects the importance this plant had as a cure-all. It is still used in many parts of the world today in folk medicine.

Best climate and site Zones 5–9. Full sun to partial shade. Thrives on rocky soils and walls. Native to North America, Europe and Africa.
Ideal soil conditions Well-drained, sandy soil; pH 4.3–7.0.
Growing guidelines Propagate with seed sown in spring or summer. Grows well. Benefits from an application of nitrogenous fertilizer.
Growing habit Either annual or biennial plant; height 20 inches (50 cm). Stems are hairy and can be reddish; leaves are palm-shaped and large. Has an unpleasant smell.
Flowering time Simple, pink flowers are produced in summer through to autumn. Petals have longitudinal, white stripes.
Pest and disease prevention Prone to attack from slugs, snails and caterpillars.
Harvesting and storing Plants are harvested as soon as flowering begins and used fresh or dried.
Parts used Whole plant.
Medicinal uses Internally for diarrhea, ulcers, gastrointestinal infections and bleeding.
Externally for skin infections, wounds and inflamed gums. Leaves can be chewed to treat inflammation in the throat and mouth. Also has been used externally as an eyewash.
Other common names Red Robin.
Other species American cranesbill G. *maculatum* is a perennial with pink, round flowers followed by beaked fruits. Used to control bleeding and gum inflammations.

Ginkgo biloba
GINKGOACEAE

GINKGO

An ancient species of plant that is often referred to as a "living fossil," ginkgo contains a unique chemical that is important in blocking allergic responses and improving the circulation. It is important in Chinese medicine.

Best climate and site Zones 4–8. Full sun. Native of China.
Ideal soil conditions Deep, moist, humus-rich, well-drained soil; pH 5.3–6.9.
Growing guidelines Plants are either male or female. Take cuttings of male trees in summer. Female trees bear evil-smelling fruit and are therefore not desirable as a garden tree. Seed can be sown when ripe in autumn.
Growing habit Deciduous, pyramidal-shaped tree; height 80–120 feet (24–36 m). Beautiful, fan-shaped leaves up to 5 inches (12 cm) across. Leaves turn yellow in autumn. Likes a good organic mulch especially when plant is young.
Flowering time Inconspicuous, greenish flowers occur in early spring on female plants, followed by small, yellow, unpleasant-smelling seeds. Fruiting only occurs when male and female plants are grown together and if conditions are warm enough.
Pest and disease prevention Usually trouble free.
Harvesting and storing Leaves are picked in autumn as they change color and are dried. Seed kernels are cooked for use in medicinal preparations.
Precautions Excess can cause vomiting and diarrhea. The seed pulp can cause dermatitis.
Parts used Leaves, seeds.
Culinary uses Nuts or inner kernels are roasted and eaten.
Medicinal uses Internally for allergic inflammatory responses, asthma and urinary incontinence. Helps to improve circulation by dilating blood vessels.
Other common names Maidenhair tree.

Glycyrrhiza glabra
PAPILIONACEAE

LICORICE

The bittersweet licorice root has been enjoyed as a natural confection for thousands of years. The licorice plant is a perennial legume and is native to south-western Asia and the Mediterranean.

Best climate and site Zones 8–10. Full sun.
Ideal soil conditions Deep, rich, moist soil; pH 6.5–7.8.
Growing guidelines Divide rootstocks or take stolon cuttings in autumn and spring or propagate by seed in spring or autumn. Slow to grow from seed. Remove flower heads to encourage stronger roots and stolons, unless seed is required.
Growing habit Hardy stoloniferous perennial with long, narrow, dark green leaflets; height 2–5 feet (60–150 cm). Its taproot can be up to 3 feet (90 cm) in length and has several long branches, which are wrinkled and brown with yellow flesh.
Flowering time Pale blue or purplish flowers appear in summer followed by reddish-brown pods.
Pest and disease prevention Usually trouble free.
Harvesting and storing Roots and stolons are lifted in early autumn 3–4 years after planting and dried for decoctions, liquid extracts, lozenges and powder.
Parts used Roots, stolons.
Culinary uses Used as a flavoring in confectionery, ice cream and beverages. Roots are boiled to extract the familiar black substance used in licorice candy.
Medicinal uses Internally for constipation, asthma, bronchitis and coughs but not for people with high blood pressure. Externally for eczema, herpes and shingles.
Other uses Licorice is a basis for most commercial laxatives. Licorice extracts are used to flavor tobacco, beer, soft drinks and pharmaceutical products; used as a foaming agent in beers.

Hamamelis virginiana
HAMAMELIDACEAE

WITCH HAZEL

Witch hazel is a frost-hardy, small tree with scented yellow autumn flowers and black fruits. Its forked branches are used as water divining rods and an extract from its bark has been a popular astringent for centuries.

Best climate and site Zones 5–9. Full sun to partial shade.
Ideal soil conditions Moist, humus-rich garden soil; pH 6.0–7.0.
Growing guidelines Propagate by seed planted outdoors in early autumn. Prevent seeds from drying. Germination is slow and erratic and can take 2 years. You can take cuttings or layerings from established plants. Cut back untidy growth after flowering.
Growing habit Deciduous shrub or small tree with smooth, gray to brown bark; height 8–15 feet (2.5–4.5 m).
Flowering time Autumn; yellow, threadlike petals followed by black seed capsules.
Pest and disease prevention Usually trouble free.
Harvesting and storing Leaves are collected in summer; branches, twigs and bark in spring.
Parts used Leaves, branches, twigs, bark.
Medicinal uses Internally for dysentery, diarrhea and excessive menstruation.
Externally for burns, sore throats and eye inflammations. An infusion of the young, flower-bearing twigs can be used on a compress for bruises, sprains, muscle aches and insect bites.
Other uses Witch hazel is an important ingredient of commercial eye drops, skin tonics and skin creams. Also used as an astringent.
Other common names American or Virginiana witch hazel.
Gardener's trivia The twigs of witch hazel are often used for water divining.

Helianthus annuus
ASTERACEAE

SUNFLOWER

All parts of the sunflower are usable. Each flower contains over 1,000 seeds, which can be used fresh or pressed for oil. The plants have been used medicinally for over 3,000 years and were used as a treatment for malaria.

Best climate and site Zones 5 and warmer. Full sun.
Ideal soil conditions Rich, well-drained soil; pH 6.0–7.5.
Growing guidelines Propagate by seed sown in spring. Sow ½ inch (12 mm) deep and 6 inches (15 cm) apart. Thin to stand 18–24 inches (45–60 cm) apart. Cultivate or mulch. Drought-tolerant, but regular watering will produce larger seed heads.
Growing habit Giant annual with erect stems and large flower heads; height 3–10 feet (90–300 cm).
Flowering time Yellow-petaled flowers in summer with heads up to 12 inches (30 cm) across; disc flowers red or brown.
Pest and disease prevention Provide good air circulation to avoid mildew. Flowers attract beneficial insects that eat pests such as aphids.
Harvesting and storing Whole plants are cut as flowering begins. Seeds are collected in autumn. Rub the seed heads to dislodge the seeds and store them in airtight containers.
Special tips Sunflowers bloom relatively quickly but take a long time to ripen their seeds. Very heavy heads may need support.
Parts used Whole plant, seeds, oil.
Culinary uses Oil is used for cooking and salads. Seeds are used in cereals and breads, either roasted or fresh.
Medicinal uses Internally for malaria, tuberculosis and bronchial infections.
Externally as a massage oil and to treat arthritis in China.
Other uses Oil is used in the manufacture of margarine.

Humulus lupulus
CANNABACEAE

HOP

A pillow stuffed with hops is said to be soporific and relaxing, and will calm nervous conditions. Hop is an attractive vining perennial for arbors and screens, as well as an essential ingredient in beer.

Best climate and site Zones 5–9, however may stand temperatures that are lower. Full sun.
Ideal soil conditions Moist and rich soil; pH 6.0–7.0.
Growing guidelines Take basal cuttings in spring and grow singly in pots for 1 year before planting out, then plant in clumps of up to five plants spaced 6 inches (15 cm) apart. Place poles for the twining stems at the base of plants. In autumn, remove both poles and old growth. Mulch with compost or rotted manure each spring. Seeds are slow to germinate and grow, so are not good for propagation.
Growing habit Prickly, herbaceous climbing vine with dark green, lobed, grapelike leaves; height 20–30 feet (6–9 m) in one season.
Flowering time Late summer; bears male and female flowers on separate plants the third year; female flowers resemble papery cones.
Pest and disease prevention Usually free from pests and diseases, but check for aphids and mites.
Harvesting and storing Flowers are picked in autumn and used fresh or dried. Young shoots are harvested in spring for culinary use.
Parts used Leaves, shoots, flowers, oil.
Culinary uses Hops are the main flavoring in beer. Oil is used in soft drinks and food flavoring. Young shoots can be eaten.
Medicinal uses Internally for insomnia, nervous tension, irritable bowel syndrome and anxiety.
Externally for eczema, herpes and ulcers.

Hydrangea arborescens
HYDRANGEACEAE

HYDRANGEA

Hydrangea's cup-shaped fruits are described in its botanical name, which is adapted from the Greek for "water vessel." There are twenty-three species of hydrangea, ranging from small shrubs and trees through to climbers.

Best climate and site Zones 5–9. Sun to partial shade; frost resistant but drought tender.
Ideal soil conditions Prefers rich, moist soils; pH 4.5–8.0. The pH determines color of flowers.
Growing guidelines Propagate by softwood cuttings taken in summer and autumn. Prune back to pairs of plump buds in early spring. Remove dead flower heads.
Growing habit Deciduous shrub with large, glossy, toothed leaves; height 3–10 feet (90–300 cm). Stems are numerous and covered with rough, layered bark.
Flowering time In summer, small white flowers sometimes tinged pink or purple occur in rounded or globular clusters.
Pest and disease prevention As long as hydrangeas receive regular watering, they are generally healthy. Plants can be attacked by aphids, red spider mite and scale.
Harvesting and storing Roots are lifted in autumn and dried for use in extracts and tinctures.
Special tips Color of flower can be determined by the pH of the soil. Colored hydrangeas will be blue in acid soil and pink in alkaline soil. White varieties are not affected by pH.
Parts used Roots.
Medicinal uses Internally for kidney and bladder stones, rheumatoid arthritis and gout. Excess causes dizziness.
Other common names Sevenbark, hills of snow.
Other varieties *H. arborescens* 'Annabelle' is a cultivar with even larger flower heads, reaching up to 12 inches (30 cm) in diameter.

Hypericum perforatum
CLUSIACEAE

ST JOHN'S WORT

This herb has been valued for centuries for its reputed ability to protect from evil. When crushed or soaked in oil, the flowers exude a bright red pigment resembling blood, which was one reason for this plant's significance.

Best climate and site Zones 5–8. Full sun to partial shade.
Ideal soil conditions Well-drained to dry soil; pH 4.5–8.0.
Growing guidelines Set plants 2 feet (60 cm) apart in spring or autumn. Prune stems back in early spring. Propagate by cuttings after flowering, or by seed in spring and division in autumn.
Growing habit Weedy perennial; height 10–36 inches (25–90 cm). Stem is very branched near the base of the plant and has two raised lines throughout its length. The leaves are small and oval-shaped with numerous, transparent, round oil glands on the surface and small, black dots on the edges.
Flowering time Flowers occur in summer and early autumn and are golden-yellow with glandular, black dots that exude brown oil when pressed.
Pest and disease prevention Hardy to most pests but has been known to be attacked by rust.
Harvesting and storing Plants are harvested as flowering begins and either used fresh or dried for use in liquid extracts or medicated oils.
Precautions Only used under professional supervision. Harmful if eaten; is a known skin allergen.
Parts used Whole plant.
Medicinal uses Internally for depression, premenstrual tension and shingles. Used recently in drug trials for AIDS. Externally for wounds, bruising and burns.
Other uses As a red dye and in cosmetics. Also used traditionally in anointing oil.

Hyssopus officinalis
LAMIACEAE

HYSSOP

The blossoms of this evergreen, shrubby plant attract honeybees and other beneficial insects. The leaves add a minty aroma and flavor to salads, soups and meat dishes. The oil is used in liqueurs.

Best climate and site Zones 3–9. Full sun to partial shade.
Ideal soil conditions Light, well-drained soil; pH 7.0–8.5.
Growing guidelines Sow seed about ¼ inch (5 mm) deep in early spring, thinning to 1 foot (30 cm). Take cuttings or divide mature plants in spring or autumn. Prune to 6 inches (15 cm) in spring and lightly mulch with compost. Replace every 4–5 years.
Growing habit Semi-evergreen perennial with woody base and narrow, aromatic leaves; height 1–2 feet (30–60 cm).
Flowering time Summer; blue or violet flowers in whorls along the stem tops.
Pest and disease prevention Usually trouble free.
Harvesting and storing For medicinal use, harvest only green material. Cut stems just before flowers open and hang in bunches to dry; store in an airtight container.
Special tips Excellent border plant in knot gardens.
Precautions The essential oil is toxic and may cause convulsions.
Parts used Whole plant, leaves.
Culinary uses Leaves are bitter and have a sage-mint flavor. Used sparingly in meat dishes and with legumes.
Medicinal uses A tea of the leaves and flowers can be drunk at the early stages of colds and flu to promote sweating, or when there is chest congestion or coughing to promote expectoration. Also used for bronchitis and flatulence. Externally for cuts, burns and bruises.
Other uses Oil used in liqueurs and perfumes.

Inula helenium
ASTERACEAE

ELECAMPANE

Otherwise known as wild sunflower, elecampane is a tall perennial with hairy stems and bright yellow daisy flowers. The Latin word helenium *is named after Helen of Troy.*

Best climate and site Zones 5–9. Full sun to light shade.
Ideal soil conditions Moderately fertile, moist soil; pH 6.5–7.0.
Growing guidelines Sow seed outdoors in spring, or collect root cuttings from mature plants in autumn; winter them in frame pots, setting plants out in the garden the following spring.
Growing habit Branched perennial with large, elliptical basal leaves and smaller, oblong top leaves; height 4–6 feet (1.2–1.8 m). Has a thick, aromatic rootstock.
Flowering time Summer months; daisy-like yellow flowers.
Pest and disease prevention Usually trouble free, but can be vulnerable to pests that suck juices from leaves. Control with a botanical insecticide such as pyrethrin.
Harvesting and storing Collect roots for medicinal and culinary use in autumn of the plant's second season, after several hard frosts. Dry them thoroughly before storing.
Special tips It is best propagated by offsets taken in autumn from the old root, with a bud or eye to each.
Parts used Roots, flowers, oil.
Culinary uses Used as a flavoring for desserts and sweets. Is still used today in some wines and cordials.
Medicinal uses Internally as a remedy for chest ailments, hay fever, asthma, stomach aches and excess mucus. Externally as a skin wash for varicose ulcers.
Other uses Root used to make a blue dye.
Other common names Wild sunflower, scabwort, velvet dock.

Iris 'Florentina'
IRIDACEAE

ORRIS

A fanlike spray of green, bladelike leaves sprouts from an aromatic root. The dried root of orris is used as a fixative in perfumery and potpourri and has a strong violet fragrance.

Best climate and site Zones 4–9. Full sun.
Ideal soil conditions Deep, rich, well-drained soil; pH 6.7–7.3.
Growing guidelines Plant after flowering, leaving the top surface of the rhizome above soil. Divide the roots every 2–3 years in early autumn to promote vigorous flowering. Half the divided root should be left above the soil so that it doesn't rot.
Growing habit Perennial with sword-shaped leaves, overlapping at the base; height to 2½ feet (75 cm).
Flowering time Spring or early summer; blossoms are large, white and tinged with blue or purple with yellow beards.
Pest and disease prevention Usually free from pests and diseases.
Harvesting and storing Harvest orris at maturity. If using the roots for their aroma, dig them up in autumn. Wash and split them, then cut them into small pieces before drying the pieces on paper or on a screen. Grind them to a powder in an old blender, or use the fine mesh of a food grater (it's easier to do it while the pieces are still slightly moist). Store the powder in a dark glass container for at least 2 years; the violet fragrance needs this time to mature.
Parts used Rhizomes.
Medicinal uses Internally for coughs, excess mucus and diarrhea but can have adverse reactions. Harmful if eaten. Externally for deep cuts.
Other uses Added to breath fresheners and dental products. Used as a fixative in perfumery and potpourris.

Jasminum officinale
OLEACEAE

COMMON JASMINE

Native to China and other parts of Asia, common jasmine is a vigorous, semi-evergreen vine or loose shrub. Its white flowers are delightfully fragrant and it is an excellent plant for growing on trellises and arbors.

Best climate and site Zones 7–10. Fun sun to partial shade.
Ideal soil conditions Moist, well-drained soil; pH 4.2–6.5.
Growing guidelines Take cuttings during active growth in spring or autumn or by layering in autumn. Thin out shoots and cut back after flowering. Keep soil moist in summer.
Growing habit Vigorous, deciduous climber with twining green stems and soft, pointed leaflets; height 30 feet (9 m).
Flowering time Very fragrant white flowers occur in summer and early autumn. Prune after flowering to keep vigorous growth under control.
Pest and disease prevention Prone to red spider mites (two-spotted mites), aphids, whiteflies and mealybugs.
Harvesting and storing Flowers are picked early in the morning and used fresh for oil extraction or dried for teas and powders.
Parts used Flowers, oil.
Culinary uses Essential oil used to flavor Maraschino cherries. Jasmine flowers used to flavor tea and other beverages.
Medicinal uses Mainly used in aromatherapy for depression, nervous tension and menstrual disorders. Also thought to have aphrodisiac and antiseptic effects.
Other uses Essential oil used in perfumes.
Other species Arabian jasmine *J. sambac* is an evergreen rambler with white to purple-pink flowers. Used mainly as a flavoring for Chinese green tea.
Royal jasmine *J. grandiflorum* is an evergreen rambler with white to pink flowers. Used mainly to treat cancer and bacterial infections.

Juglans regia
JUGLANDACEAE

WALNUT

Cultivated since Roman times for its nuts and oil, walnut is thought to have anticancer properties and the ability to control certain disease-causing organisms. It was the most widely used laxative in the 19th century.

Best climate and site Zones 4–8. Full sun.
Ideal soil conditions Deep, well-drained, fertile soil; pH 4.3–6.7.
Growing guidelines Propagate by grafting or by seed sown in autumn.
Growing habit Frost-hardy, deciduous tree up to 100 feet (30 m) high. Bark is silver-gray and leaves are dark green, divided and aromatic. Young leaflets are bronze-purple.
Flowering time A tree has flowers of both sexes; male flowers are dark yellow catkins; female flowers are upright spikes. Flowers appear in late spring to summer and are followed by dark green fruits, which contain a woody nut.
Pest and disease prevention Prone to bacterial walnut blight and leaf spot.
Harvesting and storing Fruits are collected both ripe and unripe. The kernels, or nuts, are pressed for oil and eaten fresh. Leaves are picked anytime throughout the growing season. Bark is stripped anytime.
Parts used Leaves, bark, fruits.
Culinary uses Nuts are popular as a snack food and in baking, cakes, bread and regional dishes. Oil is used as a salad dressing and for frying. Unripe fruits are pickled and used in liqueur.
Medicinal uses Internally for menstrual problems, constipation, coughs and asthma.
Externally for skin disorders, eye problems and hair loss.
Other uses The wood is highly valued in furniture making. Oil is used in paint manufacture and cosmetics.

Juniperus communis
CUPRESSACEAE

COMMON JUNIPER

Juniper is an evergreen, coniferous shrub that has been used for centuries for its medicinal properties. It is a bitter, aromatic herb that has antiseptic and diuretic properties, as well as the ability to reduce inflammation.

Best climate and site Zones 3–9. Full sun to light shade. Drought tolerant.
Ideal soil conditions Tolerates different soil conditions, wet and dry, acid and alkaline; pH 4.2–8.2.
Growing guidelines Take heel cuttings in late summer, autumn or winter. Remove seed from its fleshy covering and sow in autumn.
Growing habit Upright or prostrate shrub with papery, red-brown bark and spiky, needle-like foliage; height to 20 feet (6 m). Due to its wide distribution and adaptability, this plant can vary greatly in size, habit and color.
Flowering time Inconspicuous spring flowers, yellow on the male, greenish on the female, followed by small fruit on the female. Fruits are green at first, turning dark blue when ripe.
Pest and disease prevention Prone to juniper scale, mites and blight.
Harvesting and storing Berries are harvested by shaking the branches and are used fresh for oil distillation or dried.
Precautions May cause skin allergies.
Parts used Berries, oil.
Culinary uses Berries added to game dishes, pickles, pork and ham. Also used as a tea.
Medicinal uses Internally for poor digestion, kidney inflammation, rheumatism and gout.
Externally for rheumatic pain.
Other uses Oil distilled from the berries is used to flavor the alcoholic drink gin. Oil is also used in spicy fragrances.

Laurus nobilis
LAURACEAE

BAY, SWEET

Bay is the only laurel that is not poisonous. Bay leaf garlands represent victory. Use leaves for flavor in soups and stews, and as an aromatic addition to potpourri and herbal wreaths.

Best climate and site Zones 8–10, but needs a sheltered site in colder areas. Full sun to partial shade.
Ideal soil conditions Rich, well-drained soil; pH 6.0–7.0.
Growing guidelines Take cuttings from fresh green shoots in autumn and keep the soil in which you plant them moist, since rooting may take 3–9 months. In warm climates, sow seed outdoors; germination may require 6–12 months. Grows well in pots in cold areas if moved indoors during winter; survives moderate frost in the garden. Trim away roots from large, potbound plants and add fresh compost to stimulate new growth.
Growing habit Evergreen tree; height 10–50 feet (3–15 m) but easily kept to any desired size with pruning. Slow growing.
Flowering time Spring; inconspicuous, yellowish flowers; rarely flowers in pots.
Pest and disease prevention Mainly trouble free. Dried leaves sprinkled throughout kitchen cupboards help repel pests.
Harvesting and storing Best used fresh, but the leathery leaves can be dried and stored in airtight containers.
Special tips Add whole leaves to soups and stews at the beginning of recipes, since bay holds its flavor a long time in cooking. Remove before serving.
Parts used Leaves.
Culinary uses Added to sauces, soups, stews; in bouquet garni.
Medicinal uses Internally for indigestion, colic and flatulence. Externally for dandruff, sprains, rheumatism and scabies.
Other common names True laurel.

Lavandula angustifolia
LAMIACEAE

LAVENDER, ENGLISH

Most herb growers never have enough lavender, since this aromatic garden ornamental is also useful for crafts and cosmetics. The silvery foliage and purple blossoms are stunning in borders and the blossoms attract bees.

Best climate and site Zones 5–9. Prefers an open, sunny position.
Ideal soil conditions Light, well-drained, ideally limey soil. Neutral or slightly alkaline is best; pH 6.7–8.0.
Growing guidelines As seeds do not always produce plants identical to the original, the best way to propagate is by cuttings 2–3 inches (5–7 cm) long, taken from sideshoots in spring or autumn; space 1–2½ feet (30–75 cm) apart. Place cuttings in a well-drained medium; transplant them as soon as they root to avoid rot. Pinch away flowers on first-year plants to encourage vigorous growth. Provide shelter from winter winds; in areas with cold, wet winters, loose, well-drained soil is the secret to success. Some growers find that plants weaken with age, requiring replacement every 5 years. Remove old plants each spring, and lightly mulch with compost or well-aged manure before planting new, young plants. The hardiness of lavender varies with each species, but generally plants are extremely drought tolerant. Let the soil dry well between waterings. Excess fertility will make the silver-gray foliage fade to green. Prune immediately after flowering.
Growing habit Small shrubits downy, slender leaves are white at first then turn gray-green; height 2–3 feet (60–90 cm).
Flowering time Summer; lavender-blue blossoms on tall spikes.
Pest and disease prevention Usually free from pests and diseases. Humidity may cause fungal diseases.

Italian or spike lavender produces more oil than English lavender. The oil is distilled from glands on the flowers and leaves. It is sometimes mixed with higher-quality lavender oil to add bulk.

Harvesting and storing For the most intense scent in fresh and dried arrangements, gather the flower stems just as the flowers are opening, during dry weather. The leaves, which are bitter and sometimes used in European cooking, can be harvested after the first year of growth and then picked at anytime. Hang bunches of lavender upside-down, away from sunlight, to dry. When using the dried flowers in potpourris or herbal sachets, keep the stems; they can be burned in the same way as incense, or in a log fire to scent the smoke.
Special tips Plant lavender as a hedge or border or to configure knot gardens. In borders, combine lavender with other plants that need excellent drainage, such as yarrows and rosemary. Incorporate it into vegetable and ornamental gardens to increase populations of visiting beneficial insects. Used in a spray, lavender is reputed to control pests of cotton. It has also shown some repellent effect toward clothes moths; dry a sprig and slip it in a pocket or pin it to a sleeve in drawers or closets. Oil of lavender is said to rejuvenate the skin of the face and hands so that they look younger.
Parts used Flowers, oil.
Culinary uses Fresh flowers are crystallized; can be added to jam, ice cream and vinegar.
Medicinal uses Internally for depression, anxiety, indigestion, migraines and bronchitis.
Externally for sunburn, muscular pain, cold sores, halitosis and vaginal discharge.

French lavender has attractive, fernlike leaves with a rosemary-like scent. It is less hardy than English lavender and makes an interesting and fragrant pot plant.

Other uses Oil is used in perfumes, toiletries and cleaning products. Also added to baths for people suffering nervous tension and insomnia. Dried flowers are used in potpourris and herbal crafts.

Other species French lavender *L. dentata* is less hardy than English lavender, with a rosemary-like scent and dark purple flowers. Mainly grown as an ornamental but the flowers can be dried for potpourris.

Lavandin *L.* x *intermedia* is an aromatic herb with a camphoraceous lavender scent and dark violet to white flowers. Fresh flowers are crystallized; dried flowers added to herb pillows. The oil is used in perfumes and cleaning products.

Italian lavender *L. latifolia* produces more oil of a lesser quality than English lavender. The oil is distilled from glands around tiny hairs on the flowers, leaves and stems.

Spanish lavender *L. stoechas* is an antiseptic herb with a balsam-like scent and dark purple flowers. It helps digestion, relaxes muscle spasms, repels insects and has a mild sedative property that can help the nervous system.

Giant lavender *L.* x *allardii* is a hybrid with broad, gray-green leaves and violet-purple flowers. Used mainly in the perfume industry. Flowers are dried for potpourris.

English or common lavender *L. angustifolia* 'Hidcote' is a compact plant with strongly scented, deep purple flowers. Popular cultivar for hedges.

Leptospermum scoparium
MYRTACEAE

NEW ZEALAND TEA TREE

The tea tree gets its name from the habit early New Zealand settlers had of steeping this plant's leaves in boiling water as a substitute for tea. It is now grown worldwide as an ornamental. It is also native to Australia.

Best climate and site Zones 8–10. Prefers a warm temperate climate with full sun; can resist drought, wind and salt winds. Thrives in coastal gardens without full exposure.

Ideal soil conditions Tolerates most soils; pH 4.5–7.8.

Growing guidelines Propagate from seed or semihardwood cuttings struck in a sandy mix in summer.

Growing habit A compact evergreen shrub; height 6–10 feet (2–3 m). Slow growing. Leaves variable in shape and size; usually needle-like and tapering, 3–8 inches (7–20 cm) in length. Bark is shaggy and brown-gray in color.

Flowering time Profusion of small, scented, white to pale pink or purplish blooms from spring to summer.

Pest and disease prevention Prone to scales with associated black smut and webbing caterpillars.

Harvesting and storing Leaves are picked at any time of year; oil extracted by steam distillation.

Special tips Prone to transplant shock; do not allow to dry out when becoming established.

Parts used Leaves.

Medicinal uses Used by New Zealand and Australian settlers to combat scurvy. Maoris used it for diarrhea, dysentery, coughs and fevers. Also used to relieve aches and pains and to relax tight muscles. The oil can be used neat on the skin for rashes and wounds. Also used externally for acne, athlete's foot, candida, cold sores, insect bites, ringworm, warts and whooping cough.

Other common names Manuka.

Levisticum officinale
APIACEAE

LOVAGE

If you are unsuccessful growing celery, try this easy and flavorful substitute. Used medicinally for indigestion and kidney stones, lovage can also improve the growth and flavor of vegetable crops.

Best climate and site Zones 5–9. Full sun to partial shade.
Ideal soil conditions Fertile, moist but well-drained soil; pH 6.0–7.0.
Growing guidelines Sow ripe seed shallowly in late summer or early autumn; thin to 2–3 feet (60–90 cm) apart. Prune away flowers to encourage vegetative growth. Each spring, mulch with compost or well-rotted manure. Replace plants every 4–5 years.
Growing habit Perennial; height to 6 feet (1.8 m) or more; hollow, ribbed stems and toothed, divided green leaves.
Flowering time Summer; tiny green-yellow flowers in umbels.
Pest and disease prevention Usually trouble free.
Harvesting and storing Once established, harvest leaves as needed for fresh use. In autumn, bunch foliage and stems and hang to dry. Or blanch small bunches before freezing for winter use. Seeds are ripe and ready to harvest when the fruits begin to split open. Dig roots in late autumn, wash and slice into ½-inch (1-cm) pieces and dry before storing.
Special tips The leaves, stems and seeds have a savory, celery-like flavor.
Parts used Leaves, stems, roots, seeds, oil.
Culinary uses Blanch young shoots and eat as a vegetable. Stalks can be candied. Leaves added to soup, salads and savory dishes. Oil is used in commercial food flavoring.
Medicinal uses Internally for indigestion, flatulence, kidney stones, colic and cystitis.
Externally for sore throats.

Magnolia officinalis
MAGNOLIACEAE

MAGNOLIA

This hardy, ornamental tree has been used in Chinese medicine for over 2,000 years. Its beautiful, waterlily-like blooms and sweet fragrance make it an excellent feature plant. It is among the most exotic of flowering trees.

Best climate and site Zones 8–10. Full sun to partial shade with shelter from cold winds.
Ideal soil conditions Moist, humus-rich, well-drained soil; pH 4.2–7.0.
Growing guidelines Remove seed from its covering and sow in autumn or take cuttings in summer. Graft in winter.
Growing habit Deciduous tree with gray, peeling bark and long, tongue-shaped leaves that have a pale, downy underside; height to 75 feet (22 m).
Flowering time Strongly scented, creamy white flowers appear in late spring and early summer followed by red-seeded, strawberry-like fruit. Prune after flowering only if necessary to shape the tree.
Pest and disease prevention Prone to scales and root rot. If scales attack, causing yellow leaves, prune out badly affected growth and spray the remaining stems with horticultural oil.
Harvesting and storing Flower buds are picked in spring; flowers are collected in summer when open. Bark is collected in autumn and dried. The aromatic properties don't keep well, so parts need to be collected on a regular basis.
Parts used Bark, flowers.
Medicinal uses Internally for asthma, coughs, stomach pains, diarrhea and vomiting. Magnolia contains a compound that has important muscle-relaxant properties.
Other uses The Chinese used the fibers from the wood of the magnolia as a source of paper centuries ago.

Marrubium vulgare
LAMIACEAE

HOREHOUND

Plant this ornamental, aromatic perennial to attract bees to your garden. The menthol-flavored leaves are said to soothe coughs when taken as a syrup. Horehound flourishes on roadsides.

Best climate and site Zones 4–9. Full sun to partial shade.
Ideal soil conditions Average, well-drained, fairly neutral to alkaline garden soil on the dry side; pH 6.7–7.5.
Growing guidelines Sow seed 1/8 inch (3 mm) deep in early spring, thinning to 10–20 inches (25–50 cm). Germinates slowly, then grows easily. Divide mature plants in spring. Plant in a well-drained location, since horehound will die in winter in wet soil. In good conditions it becomes weedy.
Growing habit Perennial; height 2–3 feet (60–90 cm); branching, square stems with round to oval, wrinkled, woolly leaves.
Flowering time Summer; first blooms are fairly insignificant white flowers arranged in whorls around the upper part of the stems; small, white, tubular blooms in dense whorls are produced in the upper leaf axils. The flowers die off, leaving a spiny burr containing four small brown or black seeds.
Pest and disease prevention Not usually bothered by pests.
Harvesting and storing The first year, cut foliage sparingly. The second year, harvest leaves when flower buds appear, chop and dry them, then store in airtight containers.
Precautions Causes irregular heartbeat if overused internally. Can increase perspiration rate and stimulates bile flow.
Parts used Whole plant.
Medicinal uses Internally for bronchitis, asthma, coughs, colds and sore throats.
Externally for skin problems and minor cuts.
Other common names White horehound.

Melissa officinalis
LAMIACEAE

LEMON BALM

Lemon balm has lemon-scented leaves and is a popular tea for its calming properties. Both foliage and flowers are attractive in herb gardens. The small white flowers attract honeybees and other beneficial insects.

Best climate and site Zones 4–10. Full sun to partial shade.
Ideal soil conditions Any well-drained soil; pH 6.7–7.3.
Growing guidelines Sow shallowly in spring, thinning to 1½–2 feet (45–60 cm); readily self-sows. Take cuttings or divide older plants in spring or autumn. Each autumn, cut away old stalks.
Growing habit Perennial; height 1–2 feet (30–60 cm); stems square and branching, with oval, toothed, very fragrant leaves. Keep the soil around lemon balm moist, and keep the weeds away with a layer of organic mulch.
Flowering time Summer; small green to white tubular blossoms in bunches in the leaf axils.
Pest and disease prevention Thin dense plantings for best air circulation, to prevent powdery mildew.
Harvesting and storing Collect leaves in late summer, use fresh, or dry quickly to prevent them from turning black. Cut the entire plant, leaving about 2 inches (5 cm) of stem.
Parts used Whole plant, leaves, oil.
Culinary uses Fresh leaves with a lemon flavor can be added to salads, soup, herb vinegar, game and fish. Also used in wine and liqueurs.
Medicinal uses Internally for indigestion, depression, feverish colds and headaches. Also as a sedative.
Externally for herpes, insect bites and gout.
Other common names Sweet balm.
Gardener's trivia The leaves lowest on the plant are the highest in essential oils. Lemon balm is said to repel pests.

Mentha pulegium
LAMIACEAE

PENNYROYAL

This attractive and low-maintenance groundcover has a pleasant, mintlike fragrance and repels insects. It can be grown between paving stones in courtyards, in rockeries or as a lawn.

Best climate and site Zones 7–9. Full sun to partial shade.
Ideal soil conditions Moist, loamy garden soil; pH 6.0–7.0.
Growing guidelines Sow seed shallowly and thickly in early spring; thin to 6 inches (15 cm). Or take cuttings from stems, which easily root at joints. Divide in spring or autumn.
Growing habit Creeping perennial; mat-forming with flowering, square stems, 6–12 inches (15–30 cm) tall. Slightly hairy, grayish green, oval leaves, sometimes serrated. Spreads rapidly.
Flowering time Summer, early autumn; reddish purple to lilac blossoms in whorls.
Pest and disease prevention Reported to repel insects.
Harvesting and storing Harvest foliage just before blooming, then hang in bunches to dry; store in an airtight container.
Special tips A powder made from the dried leaves keeps pets free from fleas. Crush the leaves and rub on your skin to repel insects while you work in the garden.
Precautions Not given to pregnant women.
Parts used Whole plant, leaves, oil.
Culinary uses Leaves are added to blood sausage (black pudding) in England and sausages in Spain.
Medicinal uses Internally for indigestion, colic, colds and menstrual problems. Also used to stimulate the uterus and increase perspiration. For professional use only.
Externally for skin rashes and irritations.
Other uses Traditionally used to repel mice and insects. Leaves added to potpourris. Oil used in soaps and detergents.

Mentha spp.
LAMIACEAE

MINT

The mints are herbaceous perennials that thrive in most locations. The fresh and dried foliage provides flavoring for both sweet and savory dishes. The flowers attract beneficial insects.

Best climate and site Zones 3–10; varies with species. Full sun, though some shade is tolerated.
Ideal soil conditions Rich, moist, well-drained garden soil; pH 6.0–7.0.
Growing guidelines Propagate from new plants that spring up along the roots, or by cuttings in spring or autumn. Allow 1–1½ feet (30–45 cm) between plants. Mint is a rampant spreader. To control, plant in bottomless cans 10 inches (25 cm) deep, or in large pots. Cut frequently and severely or the plant will become woody after several years. Large areas can be mowed frequently like lawns. Top-dress with compost or well-rotted manure in autumn.
Growing habit Aromatic, mainly perennial; height up to 2½ feet (75 cm) or more. Square stems with smooth, lancelike leaves.
Flowering time Summer; tiny purple or pink blossoms in whorls on spikes.
Pest and disease prevention Thin crowded clumps for good air circulation to prevent root and foliage disease. Watch for aphids, which damage leaves; control them with a strong spray of water or with a botanical insecticide, such as pyrethrin or rotenone.
Harvesting and storing Harvest fresh leaves as needed. Just before blooming, cut the stalks and hang in bunches to dry; store in airtight containers.
Special tips Mints are said to do well when planted where water drips, such as near outdoor taps that are used often in

One of the many varieties of the mint genus, the chocmint is a delightful addition to any garden. Its leaves, when crushed, emit a wonderful chocolatey-mint odor very reminiscent of an after-dinner chocolate. Add it to sweet dishes or use it in potpourri.

Famous worldwide for its distinctive flavor, peppermint is cropped on a large scale in Europe, the USA, the Middle East and Asia. Its leaves and extracted oil are used to flavor sweet foods as well as toothpastes and medicines.

summer. Mint oil has many medicinal uses and may have fungicidal or pest-repellent uses; try a homemade spray using the fresh leaves. Any of the mints makes a refreshing addition to ice-cold water in summer and chewing on the leaves will relieve bad breath or a foul taste in the mouth.

Parts used Whole plant, leaves, oil.

Culinary uses Leaves used to accompany lamb, added to salads, used to flavor sausages, meat dishes, tomatoes and fruit salads. Important in Middle Eastern cooking. Also used in teas and iced drinks.

Medicinal uses Peppermint used internally for indigestion, colic, colds, excess mucus and nausea.

Externally for skin irritations, upper respiratory tract infections, burns, ringworm and sinusitis.

Other uses Peppermint and eau-de-cologne mint oils are used in oral hygiene preparations, antacids, toiletries, candy, chewing gum, ice cream and liqueurs.

Other species Apple mint M. *suaveolens* is apple-scented and has broader, hairy leaves. A variegated cultivar is sometimes called pineapple mint.

Corsican mint M. *requienii* has a creeping growth habit. It is good as a groundcover but is less frost-hardy than most mints. Bears tiny, bright green leaves with a strong peppermint flavor; also called crème-de-menthe plant. Hardy in Zone 6.

Eau-de-cologne mint M. x *piperita* f. *citrata* has leaves which, when crushed, give off a lemony aroma. It is also called bergamot mint.

Japanese mint M. *arvensis* var. *piperascens* has large, green leaves with hairy stems and strong peppermint flavor; it is a major source of menthol in Japan.

Peppermint M. x *piperita* has smooth, lancelike leaves and purple stems; height 2–4 feet (60–120 cm). Rampant grower with a strong peppermint flavor. Spreads quickly and likes lots of water but rarely bears fertile seeds. Must be started by cuttings or division.

Spearmint M. *spicata* is a creeping, aromatic perennial with bright green, lance-shaped, serrated leaves with a strong, sweet spearmint flavor; height 1–3 feet (30–90 cm).

Pennyroyal mint M. *pulegium* is a pungent, low-growing, creeping perennial with ovate, sparsely toothed, light green leaves and lilac to pink flowers in distinct whorls (see page 229).

Watermint M. *aquatica* is a marginal water plant or semi-aquatic perennial with long, thin rhizomes. It has red-purple stems and toothed, hairy leaves which have a peppermint aroma. Lilac flowers bloom on a rounded terminal head with smaller heads on side branches; height 6–36 inches (15–90 cm).

Gingermint M. x *gracilis* is an erect, sweetly scented perennial with reddish stems and smooth, oval leaves. Lilac to purple flowers are produced in summer. Has a fruity aroma and is used fresh to flavor fruit. Also used to aid digestion and to relieve muscle spasms. Also called redmint.

Monarda didyma
LAMIACEAE

This plant gets its name from its aroma, which resembles that of the bergamot orange *Citrus bergamia*. It is a hardy perennial that thrives in dry and rocky positions. Its brightly colored flowers are a great attractant to birds and beneficial insects such as butterflies.

BEE BALM (BERGAMOT)

This North American native has a citrusy fragrance and brilliant blooms in a range of colors. A tea of infused bee balm was a popular drink in New England after the Boston Tea Party in 1773.

Best climate and site Zones 4–9. Likes full sun but tolerates partial shade.
Ideal soil conditions Rich, moist, light garden soil; pH 5.0–7.0.
Growing guidelines Grow from seed, cuttings or division in spring. Plants grown from seed flower in the second year. Divide established plants every 3 years and discard old growth. For autumn blooms, prune stems back after first flowering. Grows in quickly spreading clumps.
Growing habit Aromatic perennial with erect stems and oval shaped, serrated leaves; height 3–4 feet (90–120 cm).
Flowering time Summer for several weeks; tubular flowers clustered together with bracts that range in color from red and pink to lavender and white.
Pest and disease prevention Plant away from mint, since it attracts the same insect pests. Prune after flowering to discourage foliage diseases.
Harvesting and storing Harvest leaves for tea just before blooming and dry them quickly for best flavor. Pull individual flowers for a fresh salad garnish. Bee balm flowers make a colorful bouquet. Dry flowers with stems in bunches of five or six, then add to wreaths and arrangements. The dried flowers and leaves retain their color well, so they are a good addition to potpourris.
Special tips Plant near tomatoes or peppers (capsicums) to enhance their growth. The bright bee balm flowers attract butterflies and nectar-eating birds. Also attracts solitary bees such as bumblebees, but not honeybees, which cannot reach the nectar unless holes have been made in the flower by other insects.
Parts used Whole plant, leaves, flowers.
Culinary uses Leaves infused as a tea and to flavor iced drinks. Also added sparingly to salads, fruit salads and stuffing. Flowers eaten fresh and added to salads.
Medicinal uses Internally for minor digestive problems and flatulence. Native Americans used various monardas as teas to treat colds, headaches, sore throats and excess mucus. Steam was inhaled to relieve sinus congestion.
Externally for skin complaints.
Other uses In flower arrangements and potpourri.
Other common names Oswego tea.
Other species Wild bergamot M. *fistulosa* is a hairy perennial with lavender flowers that are produced in summer through to autumn. The leaves are used to flavor meat and vegetable dishes and infused to make a herbal tea. Also used for sore throats, colds and skin lesions. Was used by Native Americans to make a hair oil.
Dotted mint M. *punctata* is an annual, biennial, or perennial; height to 3 feet (90 cm); also called horsemint. Used medicinally for vomiting, diarrhea and indigestion.
Lemon mint M. *citriodora* is an annual or biennial with long, lance-shaped leaves; height to 2 feet (60 cm); white to pink and purple flowers from spring to summer.

Murraya koenigii
RUTACEAE

CURRY LEAF

Curry leaves come from a small, ornamental tree that grows wild in southern India and Sri Lanka. The small leaves of this plant give off a distinct curry-like odor when bruised. Use fresh; dried leaves lose their aroma and flavor.

Best climate and site Zone 10. Full sun. Although a tropical plant, it will grow in warm temperate areas if protected in a pot, but can be deciduous in these conditions.
Ideal soil conditions Well-drained, moist soil rich in organic matter; pH 5.2–7.8.
Growing guidelines Grows easily from seed in tropical conditions, or propagate by semiripe cuttings in summer. Prune back excess growth in late winter.
Growing habit The curry leaf tree is an evergreen tropical tree. Leaves are large and pinnate. The leaflets have a pungent, spicy aroma when fresh; height 20 feet (6 m).
Flowering time Clusters of tiny, white flowers appear in summer, followed by small, blue-black, peppery-tasting, edible berries.
Pest and disease prevention Usually free from pests and diseases.
Harvesting and storing Leaves are picked all year and used fresh. Dried curry leaves lose flavor, and are a poor substitute for the fresh leaves. Bark and roots are collected when required and used either fresh or dried. Oil is extracted from the seeds.
Parts used Leaves, bark, roots, seeds, oil.
Culinary uses Leaves are used in curries.
Medicinal uses Internally for digestive problems, colic, constipation and diarrhea.
Other species Orange jessamine M. *paniculata* blooms on and off all year round, producing white flowers that smell strongly of orange blossoms.

Myristica fragrans
MYRISTICACEAE

NUTMEG

This unassuming, aromatic spice was responsible for the fierce competition in the 16th century surrounding the ownership of the Moluccas, the islands where this tree grew naturally.

Best climate and site Zone 10. Full sun and high humidity. Native to the Moluccas and Banda islands.
Ideal soil conditions Rich, well-drained soil; pH 4.6–7.0.
Growing guidelines Propagate by hardwood cuttings in autumn, or by seed sown when ripe.
Growing habit Bushy, large, evergreen tree with long, shiny leaves which can be covered in silvery, pungent scales when young; height 30–50 feet (9–15 m).
Flowering time Yellow flowers occur in spring, followed by yellow, round to pear-shaped fruits containing an aromatic, brown seed (nutmeg) surrounded by a red starchy material (mace).
Pest and disease prevention Dried seed prone to attack by insects.
Harvesting and storing Nutmeg fruit is picked and left to dry. When dry, the seed coat is removed and the whole nutmeg is then ground for use as a spice. It is best to grate nutmeg when needed, as the ground spice loses flavor with storage.
Parts used Seeds, oil.
Culinary uses Widely used in both savory and sweet dishes, bakery products, puddings and drinks. Nutmeg is often used in combination with other spices and blends well with a wide variety of flavors. Mace is also ground as a spice.
Medicinal uses Externally for abdominal and labor pains, rheumatism and toothache.
Internally for indigestion, vomiting and diarrhea.
Other uses Oil used in perfume, soap and candles.

Myrrhis odorata
APIACEAE

SWEET CICELY

Sweet cicely has a scent like lovage and a sweet licorice taste. The leaves can be used fresh in salads and the roots cooked like a vegetable. It is an ornamental and frost-hardy perennial.

Best climate and site Zones 5–9. Partial shade.
Ideal soil conditions Rich, moist, well-drained soil with humus; pH 6.0–6.7.
Growing guidelines Sow seed shallowly outdoors in autumn or spring, thinning to 2 feet (60 cm); germination is slow; self-sows. Divide older plants in spring or autumn, leaving each new piece with a bud. Mulch each spring with compost or well-rotted manure.
Growing habit Large perennial with aromatic, fernlike leaves that are finely divided, whitish and spotted underneath; height up to 3 feet (90 cm).
Flowering time Spring to early summer; numerous white blossoms in umbels, followed by shiny, chocolate-colored fruit 1 inch (2.5 cm) long with ridged seeds that have a licorice flavor.
Pest and disease prevention Usually trouble free.
Harvesting and storing Use fresh leaves as needed all summer in salads and cooking. Collect seed heads and dry on paper in a shady spot; store in airtight containers. Dig roots after the first year, scrub them, and dry until brittle or use them fresh like parsnips.
Parts used Leaves, roots, seeds.
Culinary uses Leaves added to soups and stews; used as a low-calorie sweetener for desserts. Roots are cooked as a vegetable and added to salads. Seeds used in salads and desserts.
Medicinal uses For minor digestive problems and anemia.
Other common names Myrrh, anise, sweet chervil.

Nasturtium officinale
BRASSICACEAE

WATERCRESS

A dark green herb whose ideal habitat is shallow, free-flowing water. Watercress is rich in vitamins and minerals, including iron, iodine and calcium, making it a valuable medicinal plant.

Best climate and site Zones 6–10. Grow in shallow, flowing water in full sun. Water temperature should not go below 50°F (10°C).
Ideal soil conditions Thrives in water that is slightly alkaline; pH 6.5–7.9.
Growing guidelines Propagate by root cuttings in water during the growing season. Can be grown in pots in a rich potting mix; pots must stand in water that is changed daily.
Growing habit Aquatic perennial with rooting stems and glossy, dark green, pinnate leaves that grow from the branch-like stems. Pinch out to delay flowering.
Flowering time Small, white flowers occur in late summer.
Pest and disease prevention Prone to aphid attack.
Harvesting and storing Leaves cut as required.
Precautions Watercress should not be harvested from the wild due to the frequent occurrence of pollutants and bacteria in watercourses.
Parts used Leaves.
Culinary uses Leaves add a sharp, peppery zest to salads and sandwiches. Also used in soups, juices and as a garnish.
Medicinal uses Watercress is a bitter, pungent herb that is valued for its stimulating tonic effects on the body and is traditionally taken as a spring tonic. Internally for catarrh, bronchitis, skin disorders, rheumatism and debility associated with chronic disease.
Gardener's trivia Watercress leaves contain a volatile mustard oil, giving the taste a characteristic burning tang.

Nepeta cataria
LAMIACEAE

CATMINT

Catmint is closely related to mint and is similarly hardy. Look out for it growing wild among the weeds near homes or in fields. Cats find its scent irresistible and will lie in the center of the plant rubbing its leaves.

Best climate and site Zones 3–10. Full sun to partial shade.
Ideal soil conditions Dry, sandy garden soil; pH 7.0–8.0.
Growing guidelines Sow seed outdoors when ripe or in early spring; thin to 1½ feet (45 cm). Take softwood cuttings in spring or early summer.
Growing habit Height 1–3 feet (30–90 cm); new stems each season from a perennial root; heart-shaped, toothed, grayish green leaves. Self-sows but transplants poorly.
Flowering time Summer to early autumn bloomer; white-spotted, blue-violet flowers in branching spikes.
Pest and disease prevention Usually trouble free. Planting near vegetables, such as eggplant (aubergine) and turnips, may reduce infestations of flea beetles.
Harvesting and storing In late summer, strip topmost leaves from stems and spread them to dry on a screen in the shade, or hang bunches upside down. Store in tightly sealed containers.
Special tips Grow enough catmint to share with your cat, since the bruised foliage releases a scent that turns cats into playful kittens.
Parts used Whole plant, leaves.
Culinary uses Leaves can be added to salads, sauces and stews. Also used to infuse tea with a mintlike flavor.
Medicinal uses Internally for insomnia, colds, influenza, palpitations and colic. Tea used to calm nerves and as a tonic.
Other uses The dried leaves can be used to stuff cat toys.
Other common names Catnip.

Ocimum basilicum
LAMIACEAE

BASIL, SWEET

Sweet basil is one of the most popular herbs in home gardens, mainly due to its strong flavor (with hints of licorice and pepper), which is so useful in the kitchen. Grow it in pots on a sunny window sill for easy picking.

Best climate and site Zone 10. Needs a warm, sheltered site in colder areas. Thrives in hot, sunny conditions protected from wind, frost and scorching midday sun.
Ideal soil conditions Accepts a wide range of soil textures; likes rich, moist soil; pH 5.5–7.5.
Growing guidelines Sow seed outdoors, after all danger of frost has passed, to a depth of ⅛ inch (3 mm), then thin to 6 inches (15 cm). Or sow indoors in seed trays in a warm place 6 weeks before last frost, then transplant to small pots before setting outdoors. Mulch with compost to retain soil moisture, and prune away flowers to maintain best foliage flavor. Side-dress with compost in midseason to enhance production. Basil is easily damaged by low temperatures. In autumn, cover with plastic to prolong the season and protect from the earliest frosts.
Growing habit Aromatic annual or short-lived perennial with bright green, oval-shaped leaves and erect, branched stems; height 6 inches–2 feet (15–60 cm).
Flowering time Continuous beginning in midsummer; white blooms, carried on green spikes at terminal buds.
Pest and disease prevention Plant away from mint to prevent damage from common pests. Basil is a good companion plant because it repels aphids, mites and other pests.
Harvesting and storing Harvest leaves every week, pinching terminal buds first to encourage branching. Leaves can be used fresh or dried. Dried foliage loses color and flavor but can be used as a tea to aid digestion; use about one teaspoon of

Thai basil is a variation on the popular and common sweet basil. It is a tropical plant with lancelike leaves, some purplish, and small mauve flowers. Its intense fragrance and flavor are perfect for Asian cooking.

Dark opal basil has a gingery aroma and adds an exotic flavor and decorative air to any salad. Grow it near silver foliage in the flower garden as a contrast plant.

leaf per 1 cup (250 ml) water. Best preserved chopped and frozen, or as pesto. If freezing pesto, leave out the garlic until you're ready to use it, as garlic has a tendency to become bitter after a few months. Basil keeps well in a glass jar covered with olive oil.

Special tips Plant near tomatoes and peppers (capsicums) to enhance their growth. Some gardeners plant a second crop to ensure a plentiful supply when older plants become woody.

Parts used Whole plant, leaves, stems, seeds, oil.

Culinary uses Leaves are used in salads, with tomatoes, in pasta sauces, with vegetables, in soups and in meat and poultry stuffing.

Medicinal uses Internally for colds and influenza, nausea, abdominal cramps, insomnia and migraine.

Externally for acne, insect stings, skin infections and non-venomous snakebites.

Other uses Oil is used in perfumes and aromatherapy. Also used in dental preparations.

Other common names Basil, St. Josephwort, common basil.

Other species and cultivars There are many different species and cultivars of basil that range widely in foliage size, color, aroma and plant habit.

Thai basil O. *basilicum* 'Horapha' grows to 1½ feet (45 cm); leaves have a sweet licorice scent; has purple-flushed foliage and pale pink flowers.

Tree basil O. *gratissimum* is a large, shrubby annual or perennial with a strong clove scent. Toothed leaves and pale green flowers appear in summer. The leaves are used to make a tea and the oil used in perfumery. The plant is grown to repel insects.

Holy basil O. *tenuiflorum*, syn. O. *sanctum* is a shrubby perennial with a spicy aroma. Violet to white flowers are produced in summer. The leaves are used fresh in salads but not cooked. It is used medicinally for arthritis, cramps and to lower temperatures, especially in children. The stems are used in rosaries, hence the name holy basil. The oil is used as an antibiotic and as an insect repellent.

Bush basil O. *basilicum* var. *minimum* is a dwarf, bushy, compact plant with tiny white flowers and small green leaves. Grows well in pots. Also called Greek basil.

Dark purple basil O. *basilicum* var. *purpurascens* has lavender blossoms with deep purple, shiny foliage. Germinates slowly.

Lemon basil O. *basilicum* x *citriodorum* has flowers and foliage with a strong lemony fragrance. The whole plant and leaves are smaller and more compact than sweet basil. Unlike sweet basil, lemon basil successfully reseeds itself each season if left in the garden to flower and produce seed.

Purple ruffles basil O. *basilicum* 'Purple Ruffles' has slow-growing, delicate seedlings. Plant early indoors in peat pots to minimize disturbance; do not overwater seedlings. Best preserved in salad vinegars. Several types of purple basil offer a range of color and leaf texture.

Oenothera biennis
ONAGRACEAE

EVENING PRIMROSE

Oil from the evening primrose plant has been found to contain chemicals that assist the body in producing hormone-like substances and is used to regulate hormonal systems, especially in women.

Best climate and site Zones 4–10. Prefers full sun. Often found on wastelands; can tolerate coastal conditions.
Ideal soil conditions Dry, sandy soil; pH 5.7–8.9.
Growing guidelines Propagate by seed in spring and autumn. Self-seeds readily.
Growing habit Tall biennial (sometimes annual) plant; height 5 feet (1.5 m). Erect stems and varying leaf shape and size. Roots are thick, yellowish and conical in shape.
Flowering time Bright yellow, fragrant flowers occur in summer and scent the air heavily at night. Downy seed capsules contain many tiny seeds.
Pest and disease prevention In suitable conditions, plants can be susceptible to root rot and powdery mildew.
Harvesting and storing Seeds are collected when ripe and processed for oil. Roots are dug up in the second year.
Parts used Oil from seeds, roots.
Culinary uses Young roots can be either boiled or pickled and eaten as a vegetable. Used as an aperitif in some parts of Europe. All parts of the plant are thought to be edible.
Medicinal uses Internally for premenstrual and menopausal disorders, acne, skin problems, asthma, hyperactivity, coronary artery disease and other degenerative diseases.
Externally for dry skin.
Other uses Oil is added to cosmetic preparations.
Gardener's trivia The petals of the evening primrose flower emit a phosphorescent light at night, giving rise to the lesser-known common name of "evening star."

Origanum majorana
LAMIACEAE

MARJORAM, SWEET

Sweet marjoram is a bushy, aromatic perennial with lush foliage and a mild oregano taste. Its flowers attract beneficial insects to the garden. It is traditionally used in Italian and Greek cooking.

Best climate and site Zones 7–10. Full sun.
Ideal soil conditions Light, well-drained soil; pH 6.7–7.0.
Growing guidelines The small seeds are slow to germinate; sow shallowly indoors in spring. Set plants out after danger of frost has passed, spacing clumps of several plants 6–12 inches (15–30 cm) apart. Cut back by half just before blooming, to maintain vegetative growth. In autumn, divide roots and bring pots indoors or into a frost-free greenhouse. Replant outdoors in spring.
Growing habit Bushy, tender perennial with square stems covered with fine hairs; height to 2 feet (60 cm). It has a dense, shallow root system.
Flowering time Summer; white or pink blossoms. The flowers have knotlike shapes before blossoming.
Pest and disease prevention Usually trouble free.
Harvesting and storing Cut fresh leaves for cooking; hang small bunches to dry, then store in airtight containers.
Precautions Not recommended for pregnant women.
Parts used Whole plant, leaves, seeds, oil.
Culinary uses Leaves and flowers are used in Italian and Greek cooking in soups, tomato sauces, and meat, cheese and bean dishes. Used to flavor vinegar and oil.
Medicinal uses Internally for insomnia, headaches, anxiety and painful menstruation. Tea was used as an aid to digestion. Externally for bronchitis, arthritis, sprains and stiff joints.
Other uses Oil used in liqueurs, perfumes and soap.
Other common names Knotted marjoram.

Origanum vulgare
LAMIACEAE

OREGANO

Interplant oregano at permanent spots in the vegetable garden, or use it as a border. Oregano can also be attractive in flower beds. The sprigs, with their small leaves and miniature blossoms, make an attractive garnish.

Best climate and site Zones 5–10. Full sun to light shade.
Ideal soil conditions Well-drained, average garden soil; pH 6.0–7.0.
Growing guidelines Sow outdoors after danger of frost has passed. Plant in clumps 1 foot (30 cm) apart. Prune regularly for best shape. Since seedlings will not always produce the same flavor as the original plants, take cuttings or divide roots in spring or early autumn for best results. Lightly mulch each spring with organic matter. May not overwinter outdoors in cold climates. Replace every few years.
Growing habit Bushy perennial with purple-brown stems and woody base; height 1–2½ feet (30–75 cm).
Flowering time Summer; tubular, rose-purple or, rarely, white blossoms in broad terminal clusters.
Pest and disease prevention Usually trouble free.
Harvesting and storing Snip fresh sprigs as needed all summer; plants are cut when they begin flowering.
Special tips Like other strongly aromatic herbs, oregano has gained a reputation as a pest repellent. It is more often used dried rather than fresh.
Parts used Whole plant, leaves, oil.
Culinary uses Important in Mexican, Italian, Spanish and Greek cooking. Used in strongly flavored dishes.
Medicinal uses Internally for colds and stomach upsets. Externally for bronchitis and asthma.
Other uses Oil used in food flavoring and toiletries.
Other common names Wild marjoram.

Paeonia lactiflora
PAEONIACEAE

PEONY

Named after Paeon, the physician to the Greek gods, peony has been cultivated for centuries for its medicinal values. Although seldom used today for its clinical properties, it is still widely appreciated as a lovely garden plant.

Best climate and site Zones 6–8. Full sun to partial shade.
Ideal soil conditions Rich, well-drained soil; pH 4.3–7.8. Good drainage is important to avoid root rot.
Growing guidelines Propagate by seed sown in autumn (can take up to 3 years to germinate), plant divisions in spring or autumn, and by root cuttings in winter.
Growing habit Herbaceous perennial; height 2 feet (60 cm). Stems are erect and reddish, leaves are dark green and heavily divided. Roots are large and fleshy. Plants have been known to live for 100 years or more.
Flowering time Large, fragrant flowers 3–4 inches (7–10 cm) across occur in spring and summer. Flowers range in color from white, cream and yellow, to pink, rose, burgundy and scarlet. Flowers may be single, semidouble or double.
Pest and disease prevention Prone to leafspot, nematodes, viruses and the gray mold blight called peony wilt.
Harvesting and storing Roots of mature plants over 4 years old are lifted in autumn and boiled and dried for further use in powders and pills.
Precautions Should be used by qualified practitioners only. Not given to pregnant women.
Parts used Roots.
Medicinal uses Internally for menstrual problems, skin conditions and liver disorders. The peony is important in Chinese medicine, where it is highly valued as a yin tonic for the liver and circulation.

Panax ginseng
ARALIACEAE

GINSENG

Ginseng is the most famous of all Chinese medicines and is credited with the magical properties of long life, strength and happiness. It has been used for centuries as a cure-all and aphrodisiac.

Best climate and site Zones 6–10. Prefers shady position with ample warmth and humidity; frost resistant.
Ideal soil conditions Moist, well drained soil; pH 4.5–6.9.
Growing guidelines Propagate by seed in spring. Germination is slow.
Growing habit Perennial; height of 28–36 inches (70–90 cm). Erect, upright stems bear whorls of divided leaves with serrated edges. Rootstock is carrot shaped and aromatic.
Flowering time Small, greenish white flowers occur in spring and summer followed by small, bright red berries.
Pest and disease prevention Usually trouble free.
Harvesting and storing Roots from plants over 5 years old are lifted and used fresh or dried for use in powders and pills. Flowers are picked fresh for use in tonics.
Precautions Can cause headaches and raised blood pressure.
Parts used Roots, flowers.
Medicinal uses Internally for insomnia, stress and debility associated with old age; tonic for nerves and reputedly as an aphrodisiac. Ginseng is said to relax and stimulate the nervous system, encourage secretion of hormones, improve stamina, lower blood sugar and cholesterol levels and increase resistance.
Gardener's trivia Ginseng is now rarely found in the wild. It was used extensively by the Vietcong during the Vietnam War to speed recovery from gunshot wounds. Ginseng contains properties that have been patented for use in anti-tumor drugs.

Passiflora incarnata
PASSIFLORACEAE

PASSIONFLOWER

This climbing perennial with yellow, edible fruit has medicinal uses, but is usually grown as an ornamental for its unusual blossoms. Missionaries regarded these flowers as symbols of Christ's passion.

Best climate and site Zones 6–10. Full sun or greenhouse in very cold areas.
Ideal soil conditions Fertile, well-drained soil; pH 6.0–8.0.
Growing guidelines Propagate by seed or summer cuttings. Mulch the soil each spring with a thin layer of compost. Prune away old growth in winter or early spring.
Growing habit Height 25–30 feet (7.5–9 m); hairy vine grows from a woody stem. It has coiling tendrils which wrap around a support in order to climb. The leaves are deeply three-lobed.
Flowering time Early to late summer; sweet-scented, white or lavender petals and pink to purple banded filaments. The flowers are followed by an edible, oval fruit that ranges in color from yellow to orange.
Pest and disease prevention Usually free from pests and diseases. Check for thrips.
Harvesting and storing Collect the fruit in summer when ripe. It is best eaten fresh; the juice can be used to flavor drinks. The leaves and flowers are used medicinally but should not be taken without professional advice.
Precautions Not recommended during pregnancy.
Parts used Whole plant, fruits.
Culinary uses Fruits are eaten fresh; fruits pulped for jam; juice used to flavor drinks.
Medicinal uses Internally for insomnia, tension headaches, asthma, bowel problems, hypertension, premenstrual tension and shingles.
Other common names Maypops, apricot vine.

Pelargonium spp.
GERANIACEAE

GERANIUM, SCENTED

Scented geraniums have been cultivated in Europe since the 17th century. They are popular for their aromatic leaves and soft coloring. The many different species and cultivars offer a variety of flavors and scents.

Apple-scented geraniums are low-growing perennials with trailing stems and small, white, red-veined flowers which appear in spring and summer. The name comes from the pronounced apple aroma of its leaves. Add it to summer drinks, such as fruit punches, or use it in potpourris.

Best climate and site Zones 9–10 or greenhouse in cooler areas. Can be grown in pots and placed outside in summer.
Ideal soil conditions Rich, well-drained, loamy soil; pH 6.0–7.0.
Growing guidelines Softwood cuttings root quickly and easily from spring to autumn. Scented geraniums grow well in pots near a sunny window. Apply a liquid plant food, such as fish emulsion or compost tea, but hold back on the nitrogen for the best fragrance. Plants more than 1 year old tend to become straggly; take new cuttings and discard the old plants. Remove dead foliage regularly.
Growing habit Height up to 3 feet (90 cm); foliage and growth habit vary with species or cultivar. Leaves frilly, variegated, ruffled, velvety or smooth.
Flowering time Three or more months from rooting; flowers are sometimes inconspicuous.
Pest and disease prevention Vacuum whiteflies from foliage, or control with weekly sprays of insecticidal soap or a botanical insecticide. Garlic sprays may help repel pests. You can purchase parasitic wasps from suppliers of biological controls to help control whiteflies indoors. Avoid overwatering and use fast-draining potting mixes.
Harvesting and storing Pick leaves throughout the summer and dry them, storing in an airtight container, to use in winter potpourris.
Special tips Keep a pot of scented geraniums near walkways; passersby will brush against the foliage and release the fragrance. The showy flowering types of geranium are reputed to repel cabbageworms, corn earworms and Japanese beetles. The scented ones are thought to deter red spider mites and cotton aphids. Some gardeners believe that the white-flowered geraniums are effective as a trap crop for Japanese beetles; handpick the beetles from the leaves or destroy the plants.
Parts used Whole plant, leaves, oil.
Culinary uses Use fresh leaves in jellies, fruit dishes and tea, or as an aromatic garnish. Some species are used to flavor sauces, ice cream, cakes and vinegar.
Medicinal uses Some species are used internally for gastroenteritis, nausea, tonsillitis and poor circulation. Externally for skin complaints, acne, lice and ringworm. Oil used in aromatherapy for burns, shingles and skin sores.
Othe uses Dried leaves used in potpourri and herb pillows. Oil used in skin-care products and moth-repellent sachets.
Other species Apple-scented geranium *P. odoratissimum* is apple-scented, with sprawling growth and white flowers. Lemon-scented geranium *P. crispum* is a lemon-scented subshrub; height to 3 feet (90 cm). Leaves are small and three-lobed, with crinkled margins. Petals are rose or rosy white. Rose geranium *P. graveolens* is a rose-scented subshrub; height up to 3 feet (90 cm). Leaves are softly hairy, five- to seven-lobed and toothed. Flowers white to pale pink, marked purple. Also called sweet-scented geranium.

The flat, dark green foliage of Italian parsley has a stronger flavor than the curly variety. It is also hardier and more resistant to changes in the weather. It is also known as continental or flat-leaf parsley.

Petroselinum crispum
APIACEAE

PARSLEY

Parsley is required in so many recipes that it is a feature of most herb gardens. The delicate, dark green foliage makes it an excellent plant for borders or growing on sunny patios or windowsills.

Best climate and site Zones 5–10. Full sun but tolerates partial shade.
Ideal soil conditions Moderately rich, well-drained garden soil; pH 6.0–8.0.
Growing guidelines Sow parsley seed shallowly outdoors in early spring when soil reaches 50°F (10°C), thinning to 8 inches (20 cm) apart; germinates slowly. Alternatively, soak seeds overnight in warm water before sowing in peat pots indoors in early spring; transplants poorly. Remove all flower stalks that form and prune away dead leaves. For productive plants, side-dress with compost in midseason. Usually survives the winter, but quickly goes to seed in spring. In order to attract beneficial insects to the garden, let a few plants flower and go to seed. Plants may be grown in pots to bring indoors for winter harvests.
Growing habit Aromatic biennial grown as an annual with a white taproot and finely divided leaves on a long stalk; height 8–12 inches (20–30 cm).
Flowering time Early spring of second year; tiny, greenish yellow umbels followed by tiny, ribbed oval fruits.
Pest and disease prevention Follow proper spacing guidelines for best air circulation to prevent diseases. Carrot pests can attack parsley.
Harvesting and storing Cut leaf stalks at the base for fresh foliage all summer. Hang in bunches to dry in the shade, or freeze whole or chopped. Roots lifted in late autumn and dried. Seeds collected when ripe.
Special tips May go to seed prematurely if taproot is severely damaged during transplanting. Dried parsley quickly loses flavor. Save a winter's worth by chopping and freezing fresh parsley in zippered plastic bags. Parsley is handy in pots near the kitchen; after the new plant is established, you can harvest the bright green sprigs as needed.
Precautions Excess can cause abortion, gastrointestinal hemorrhage, liver and kidney damage. Not given to pregnant women or people with kidney problems.
Parts used Leaves, roots, seeds, oil.
Culinary uses Parsley is one of the most widely cultivated herbs around the world. The leaves are used to garnish and flavor savory dishes, soups, sauces, stuffing and meat dishes. It is eaten as a vegetable in some countries.
Medicinal uses Internally for menstrual problems, cystitis, kidney stones, indigestion, anemia, anorexia and arthritis. Used after delivery to help contract the uterus and promote lactation. Roots and seeds are in the pharmacopoeias of several countries.
Other uses Oil is used in commercial food flavoring, leaves and seeds used in perfumery.
Other species Italian parsley *Petroselinum crispum* 'Italian' is a cultivar with flat, dark green foliage, not curly, with a strong flavor. Plants are hardier, more resistant and larger than the curly variants.

Pimpinella anisum
APIACEAE

ANISE

Use these licorice-scented leaves and sweet, spicy seeds in salads, especially when combined with apples. The crushed, aromatic seeds enhance the fragrance of potpourris and are used to flavor candy and cakes.

Best climate and site Zones 6–10. Full sun.
Ideal soil conditions Thrives in poor, light, well-drained soil; pH 6.0–6.7.
Growing guidelines Sow seed outdoors in spring where plants will stand, then thin to 1 foot (30 cm) apart. Or sow several seeds in peat pots several months before the last frost. Transplants poorly. Stake to prevent sprawling.
Growing habit Annual with lacy foliage that resembles Queen Anne's lace; height up to 2 feet (60 cm).
Flowering time Summer; dainty white blossoms in umbels.
Pest and disease prevention Anise oil is said to have insect-repellent properties; the strong smell of the plant may repel aphids and fleas. Few pests bother this plant.
Harvesting and storing Seeds are ready to harvest when they fall easily from the head. Clip off the seed heads into a bag before the seedpods shatter, but leave a few on the plant so it will self-sow for next year. Dry seeds on sheets of paper for several sunny days outdoors; store in airtight containers. Snip foliage as needed.
Special tips Enhances the growth of cilantro (coriander). Anise was once used as a bait in mousetraps.
Parts used Leaves, seeds, oil.
Culinary uses Leaves added to salads; seeds used to flavor candy; oil used to flavor drinks such as Pernod and ouzo.
Medicinal uses Internally for coughs, bronchitis, indigestion and flatulence.
Externally for lice and used as a chest rub for bronchitis.

Piper nigrum
PIPERACEAE

PEPPER

Undoubtedly one of the most familiar and indispensable of cooking herbs, pepper comes from a vine native to the tropics. Pepper was once so highly valued that it was traded ounce for ounce with gold.

Best climate and site Zone 10. Prefers a protected, warm position with high humidity.
Ideal soil conditions Rich, moist soil; pH 4.7–7.9.
Growing guidelines Propagate by semiripe cuttings in summer or by seeds when available. Remove weak stems in early spring before new growth appears. Cut back young plants several times a year to stimulate shoot growth.
Growing habit Tropical, woody-stemmed climber; height 12 feet (3.6 m).
Flowering time Small, white flowers occur in spring, followed by long strings of 20–30 small berries, which ripen from green to dark red. The vine takes 7–8 years to reach maturity and then bears fruit for 15–20 years.
Pest and disease prevention Usually free from pests and diseases.
Harvesting and storing The berries are harvested in spring and summer. Different varieties vary in flavor and pungency. Black peppercorns are the dried, unripe berries; white peppercorns are the ripe red berries, which have been fermented, the skin and flesh removed and the corns dried; green peppercorns are fresh, unripe berries, pickled or freeze-dried. Tree-ripened red peppercorns are rarely found outside their country of origin. White and black peppercorns should be kept in an airtight container in a cool, dark place. Whole peppercorns will retain their pungency for much longer than ground pepper, which should also be stored in an airtight container away from light. Green peppercorns should be

The term pepper originally meant vine pepper from various plants of the genus Piper. The name was borrowed for hot and sweet peppers because of their similar pungency.

stored in an airtight container in the refrigerator. Various other seasonings commonly called pepper are unrelated to *Piper nigrum*. The berries known as pink peppercorns are the almost-ripe berries of a South American tree, *Schinus terebinthifolius*; Sichuan pepper is the dried berry of a Chinese variety of a small ash tree.
Parts used Fruits.
Culinary uses Used universally as a seasoning and condiment. Whole or ground pepper is used extensively in savory as well as in sweet dishes to enhance the flavor.
Medicinal uses Internally as an aid to digestion. Externally for skin conditions and for nasal congestion.
Gardener's trivia Pepper production accounts for one-fourth of the world spice trade. India is the main producer; pepper is also cultivated in Indonesia, Malaysia and Brazil. Pepper probably changed the course of history. It was the single most important reason for the European search for sea routes in the East; much of the exploration and colonization of new lands might not have occurred but for the European craving for pepper.

Plantago major
PLANTAGINACEAE

PLANTAIN

Plantain is a common weed found in lawns, fields and on roadsides. Try its tender, young leaves in salads, or steam and eat them like spinach. Plantain was once considered to be an indispensable cure-all.

Best climate and site Zones 5–10. Full sun to partial shade. Plantain is a cool-climate herb; it may not thrive in tropical or sub-tropical climates.
Ideal soil conditions Well-drained, moist soil; pH 5.0–8.0.
Growing guidelines Sow seed shallowly outdoors in early spring or autumn.
Growing habit Weedy perennial with broad, oval, ribbed leaves with blunted ends and prominent veins; height 6–18 inches (15–45 cm). It forms basal rosettes and spreads quickly. It is short lived and grows quickly from seed, so it can be treated as an annual.
Flowering time Summer; tall, cylindrical spikes of many small, purplish green to yellowish flowers. Bloom is followed by the appearance of small capsules, which may contain 25 seeds.
Pest and disease prevention Usually trouble free.
Harvesting and storing Dig the roots in autumn, scrub them well, and allow to dry until brittle. Chew the root to relieve toothache.
Parts used Leaves, roots.
Culinary uses Use fresh leaves in salads; steam and eat leaves like spinach. Was formerly eaten as a potherb.
Medicinal uses Internally for diarrhea, cystitis, bronchitis, asthma, hay fever, hemorrhage, catarrh and sinusitis. Externally for bee stings, insect bites, eye inflammations, shingles and ulcers. Also used to soothe stings from nettles.
Other uses Root and plant used for a gold dye.
Other common names Rat-tail plantain, white man's foot.

Polygonum bistorta (Syn. *Persicaria bistorta*)
POLYGONACEAE

KNOTWEED

Regarded as a weed in many places, this unusual small plant gets its name from the shape of its contorted, "knotted" rhizomes. Knotweeds have a long history in Chinese medicine where they are used as important tonic herbs.

Best climate and site Zones 3–8. Full sun to partial shade.
Ideal soil conditions Rich, moist soil; pH 4.5–7.5.
Growing guidelines Propagate by seed or by division in spring or autumn. Semiripe cuttings can also be taken in summer.
Growing habit Hardy perennial; height 2 feet (60 cm). Broad, oval leaves with prominent central veins; knobbly, twisted black-brown rhizomes. The plant grows from creeping stems and rapidly forms wide clumps. Frequent removal of some parts is necessary to keep this plant under control.
Flowering time Small, pink flowers tightly packed into dense, erect spikes appear late spring to early summer followed by numerous hard, nutlike seed capsules.
Pest and disease prevention Young growth is prone to attack by aphids.
Harvesting and storing Plants are lifted in autumn and the rhizomes collected and dried for further use in preparations.
Parts used Rhizomes, leaves.
Culinary uses Young raw leaves are pleasant to eat and can be added to salads.
Medicinal uses Internally for digestive disorders, diarrhea, catarrh and excessive menstruation.
Externally for sore throats and inflammations of the mouth.
Other common names Bistort, snakeweed, Easter ledges.
Other species Flowery knotweed *P. multiflorum* is a deciduous climber with small, white or pink-tinted flowers. Used to lower blood sugar levels and cholesterol. Also used in bacterial infections and as a Chinese tonic herb.

Portulaca oleracea
PORTULACACEAE

PURSLANE

Popular in Europe as a salad green, cultivated purslane is taller and more succulent than the weed, its cousin. It is a rich source of Omega-3 fatty acids, which help prevent heart disease.

Best climate and site Zones 4 and warmer. Full sun.
Ideal soil conditions Not fussy; will even grow in sand and is drought-resistant; pH 6.0–7.0.
Growing guidelines Grown from seed sown in spring. Keep moist until seeds germinate. Thin to 4–6 inches (10–15 cm) apart; use thinnings in salads. Water frequently.
Growing habit Annual, with trailing stems and fleshy leaves; height 8–18 inches (20–45 cm).
Flowering time Small yellow flowers in summer.
Pest and disease prevention Prone to aphids and slugs.
Harvesting and storing Harvest fresh leaves and stems with scissors as needed, leaving 1 inch (2.5 cm) or more above ground to sprout new leaves. May be harvested four or five times. Best used fresh; does not store well.
Special tips Cultivated purslane has a superior flavor to the common, weedy variety, although common purslane is also edible. Collect seeds of the best wild plants to grow in the garden, saving seeds each year from plants with the best flavor.
Precautions Not for pregnant or lactating women or people with digestive problems.
Parts used Whole plant, leaves.
Culinary uses Leaves cooked as a vegetable and added to sauces, soups and salads. Can also be pickled in vinegar.
Medicinal uses Internally for mastitis, hepatitis, hemorrhoids, dysentery and appendicitis. Also used to prevent heart disease. Can help to combat bacterial infections.
Externally for boils, snakebites and bee stings.

Primula vulgaris
PRIMULACEAE

PRIMROSE

This pretty flower has a long history of use as a medicinal herb. It was used by the ancient Romans for paralysis and rheumatism, and also by Culpeper as a wound healer. The pale yellow flowers go well with spring bulbs.

Best climate and site Zones 6–9. Full sun to partial shade. Native to temperate open woods and grassy places of western and southern Europe.
Ideal soil conditions Moist, humus-rich soil; pH 5.7–7.8.
Growing guidelines Easy to grow from fresh seed sown in autumn. Also by division in late spring or early autumn. Mulch plants in summer and winter. Divide clumps after flowering.
Growing habit Small, clump-forming perennial with broad, crinkled leaves rising directly from stout crowns; height 6 inches (15 cm). Thick, short rhizome.
Flowering time Flat, five-petaled, fragrant, yellow flowers occur in late winter to spring.
Pest and disease prevention Plants affected by rust, botrytis, leafspot and other fungal diseases. Aphids, caterpillars and weevils can attack the leaves.
Harvesting and storing Flowers are picked in spring and used fresh, or dried for further use. Whole plant cut when in flower and dried for use in infusions. Roots are lifted in autumn and used when dried for decoctions.
Precautions Can cause skin irritations and allergies. Not given to pregnant women or people on medications.
Parts used Whole plant, flowers, leaves, roots.
Culinary uses Young leaves and flowers are used in salads and as a garnish. Flowers are used to flavor desserts.
Medicinal uses Internally for chest and respiratory disorders, insomnia and headaches.
Externally for joint pain and minor wounds.

Pulsatilla vulgaris
RANUNCULACEAE

PASQUE FLOWER

The 16th century herbalist John Gerard gave this plant its common name due to its propensity to flower at Easter—Pasque means Easter. The flowers produce a green dye which was once used to color Easter eggs.

Best climate and site Zones 3–8. Full sun to partial shade.
Ideal soil conditions Average to humus-rich, well-drained soil; pH 6.7–8.3.
Growing guidelines Sow seed in autumn or spring. Self-sown seedlings are plentiful.
Growing habit Small, hairy perennial with bell-shaped flowers and rosettes of divided, pinnate leaves clothed in soft hairs; height 6–12 inches (15–30 cm). Plants grow from deep, fibrous roots.
Flowering time Flowers appear in spring and are pale or dark purple with five starry petals surrounding a central ring of fuzzy orange-yellow stamens. The flowers are followed by feathery seedheads. After seed is set, plants go dormant unless conditions are cool. Seldom needs division.
Pest and disease prevention Usually trouble free.
Harvesting and storing Harvest plants when flowering. Pasque flowers don't keep well.
Precautions Harmful if eaten. For use by qualified practitioners only. Can cause vomiting, convulsions and skin irritations. Not given to patients with colds.
Parts used Flowering plants.
Medicinal uses Internally for insomnia, disorders of the female reproductive system, coughs, asthma, bronchitis and skin infections.
Other uses Flowers yield a green dye.
Other species Prairie pasque flower *P. pratensis* has pale to dark violet flowers that are used in homeopathy.

Rhamnus purshiana
RHAMNACEAE

CASCARA SAGRADA

In Spanish, "cascara sagrada" means "sacred bark." This plant yields an extract that is an active ingredient in several commercial laxatives, for both people and their pets.

Best climate and site Zones 7–9. Full sun, but tolerates partial shade.
Ideal soil conditions Fertile, moist garden soil; pH 6.0–6.7.
Growing guidelines Propagate by seed sown in autumn, layering in late winter or early spring, or by semi-ripe cuttings in summer. Thin out branches and remove dead wood in late winter or early spring.
Growing habit Deciduous shrub with reddish gray bark and thin, elliptical leaves up to 8 inches (20 cm) long; height 10–20 feet (3–6 m).
Flowering time Spring; tiny greenish yellow flowers in clusters, followed by poisonous small red berries up to ½ inch (1 cm) in diameter that blacken when ripe.
Pest and disease prevention Usually free from pests and diseases.
Harvesting and storing In spring and autumn, strip bark from wood. Dry well before storing.
Special tips The bark must be aged for at least 1 year before use.
Precautions All parts are harmful if eaten. Infusions made from fresh bark tend to cause intestinal cramping and vomiting. Not given to pregnant or breastfeeding women.
Parts used Bark.
Medicinal uses Internally for constipation, digestive problems, hemorrhoids and jaundice.
Externally to stop nail biting because of its bitter taste.

Rheum palmatum
POLYGONACEAE

CHINESE RHUBARB

There are two main medicinal species of rhubarb. They contain laxative properties and are widely used in Chinese medicine. The familiar edible rhubarb was developed through hybridization during the 19th century.

Best climate and site Zones 6–9. Full sun. Native of Asia.
Ideal soil conditions Moist, deep, humus-rich soil; pH 5.0–7.0.
Growing guidelines Propagate by root division and root cuttings in colder months or (less effectively) by seed sown in spring. Need to water frequently. Rhubarb is a heavy feeder and needs regular fertilizing during the growing season.
Growing habit Large, hardy perennial with thick rhizome and round stalks with palmlike leaves; height 6 feet (2 m).
Flowering time Deep red flowers in summer followed by three-winged fruits.
Pest and disease prevention Usually trouble free.
Harvesting and storing Rhizomes are harvested in autumn from plants that are at least 3 years old, then dried.
Precautions Leaves are very poisonous if eaten as they contain high levels of oxalic acid and tannins. Roots not given to pregnant or breastfeeding women, or patients with intestinal obstructions.
Parts used Rhizomes.
Medicinal uses Internally for constipation, diarrhea, hemorrhoids and skin problems.
Externally for burns. Used in homeopathy for teething children.
Other uses Used in commercial food flavoring.
Other species Himalayan rhubarb *Rheum officinale* is the other species of medicinal rhubarb; height 10 feet (3 m). Edible rhubarb *Rheum* x *hybridum* syn. *R.* x *cultorum* has edible stems only; roots not used for medicinal purposes.

Ribes nigrum
GROSSULARIACEAE

BLACKCURRANT

The berries of this plant were once thought to breed worms in the stomach. Blackcurrants are an important source of vitamin C and have been used as a treatment for sore throats and colds for centuries.

Best climate and site Zones 5–8. Full sun to partial shade. Protect from cold or hot winds and late frost.
Ideal soil conditions Moist, well-drained soil; pH 4.3–7.2.
Growing guidelines Propagate by hardwood cuttings in winter. Benefits from an addition of mulch to protect shallow root system. Add compost and a potassium-rich fertilizer in early spring. Water regularly in dry weather. In the first season, cut the weakest stems to the ground in autumn. Remove one-quarter to one-third of older growth each year to maintain vigor in plant.
Growing habit Aromatic shrub; height 6 feet (1.8 m). Leaves are lobed and a deep green in color.
Flowering time In spring, nondescript, greenishwhite flowers occur in hanging clusters, followed by edible black berries.
Pest and disease prevention Prone to damage by aphids, birds and mites. Check for leafspot and mildew.
Harvesting and storing Fruits are picked in the summer when ripe. Leaves are picked during spring and summer.
Precautions This plant can host white pine blister rust, which can devastate coniferous forests. It is illegal in some areas to grow blackcurrant in the same vicinity as pine plantations.
Parts used Leaves, fruits.
Culinary uses Fruits eaten fresh or frozen; made into jams, cordials and desserts. Leaves used as a substitute for tea.
Medicinal uses Internally for colds, and mouth and throat infections.
Externally in gargles for sore throats.

Rosa spp.
ROSACEAE

ROSE

The fragrant flowers and aromatic fruits of these shrubs have medicinal properties and are used for making perfume. There are many different species and cultivars of varying colors, shapes, sizes and growing habits.

Best climate and site Zones 3–10 or warmer, depending on the species or variety. Prefers full sun. Avoid windy sites or sites with tree roots.
Ideal soil conditions Well-drained but moist, organic-rich soil; pH 6.0–7.5.
Growing guidelines Propagate from seed in autumn, by hardwood cuttings in autumn or by budding in summer. Purchase grafted nursery stock for best results. Work in plenty of compost or well-rotted manure when planting, and mulch roses each spring. Plant approximately 2½ feet (75 cm) apart in beds. Roses will be damaged if left standing in water, so they need good drainage. They need at least half a day of sun along with frequent watering and feeding. Prune in winter to maintain shape, and remove dead or damaged stems. Deadhead after flowering to prolong blooming period.
Growing habit Perennial; height varies with species and cultivars; stems thorned and upright to spreading.
Flowering time Spring to winter depending on type; single or double flowers, often clustered, with berry-like hips ripening in autumn. Most species and old roses flower on the previous year's growth and should not be pruned back hard.
Pest and disease prevention Space correctly; provide adequate sunshine and water in early morning when foliage will dry quickly to prevent blackspot. Check for rust and mildew. Knock aphids and mites from leaves with a spray of water. Handpick large pests daily. Rosehips are sometimes eaten by birds.

Roses were once called "gift of the angels." Some, such as the apothecary's rose, were used medicinally by the ancient Greeks, Romans and Persians. In AD 77, Pliny recorded 32 different disorders that responded well to treatment by rose preparations.

Rose essence is among the safest healing substances known and rosewater is excellent for cooking, flavoring candy and for skin care. Rosehips contain large amounts of vitamin C. Rosehip tea, made from the fruit, is a soothing drink that helps treat colds, influenza and scurvy.

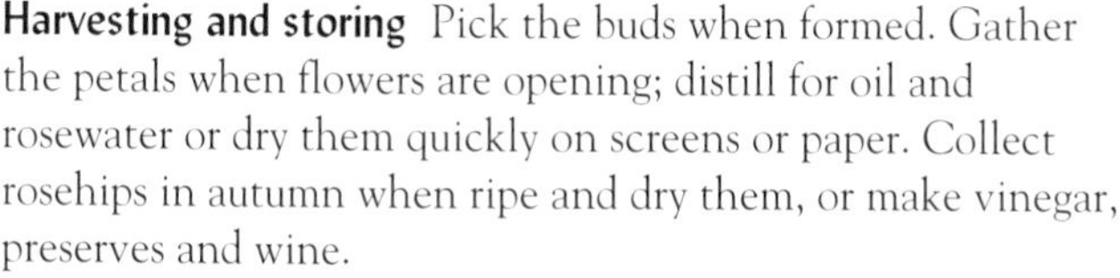

Harvesting and storing Pick the buds when formed. Gather the petals when flowers are opening; distill for oil and rosewater or dry them quickly on screens or paper. Collect rosehips in autumn when ripe and dry them, or make vinegar, preserves and wine.

Special tips As with all members of the rose family, never plant a new rose in an old rose's "grave." Disease pathogens or allelopathic substances that hinder the growth of a new plant of the same genus may still be in the soil.

Precautions Seeds contain irritant hairs. Most species have sharp thorns.

Parts used Petals, fruits (hips). Hips are used from *R. canina* and *R. laevigata*; flowers from *R. gallica* var. *officinalis*; flowers and hips from *R. rugosa*; and oil from seeds of *R. eglanteria*. Many other roses are used in various ways.

Culinary uses As a tea made from the fruit of roses (rosehip tea). Petals can be added to salads or crystallized for a sweet treat. Rosewater is used to flavor candy, especially Turkish delight and jellies.

Medicinal uses Internally for colds, influenza, scurvy, diarrhea, sore throats, eye irritations and minor infectious diseases. *R. eglanteria* used externally to treat burns, scars and wrinkles.

Other uses Fruits made into syrup as a nutritional supplement; syrup added to cough mixtures and to flavor medicine. Fruit extracts added to vitamin C tablets. Dried petals and rosebuds of *R. gallica* var. *officinalis* are important ingredients of northern African spice mixtures. Rose oil and rosewater used in skin care products and bath products. Used in aromatherapy for depression and anxiety. Rose oil used in women's and men's fragrances; also in cosmetics and soap. Dried petals and buds used in potpourris. Fresh flowers used in floral arrangements.

Other species Dog rose *R. canina* is a deciduous shrub with arching stems, curved prickles and blue-gray leaves; height 10 feet (3 m). Scented, single pink and white flowers with five petals in small clusters in summer, followed by long, scarlet hips.

Apothecary's rose *R. gallica* var. *officinalis* is a bushy deciduous shrub with prickly stems and leathery divided leaves; height to 3 feet (90 cm). Flowers in summer with semidouble, pink-red, fragrant flowers, followed by dark red hips.

Cherokee rose *R. laevigata* is a vigorous climbing rose; height 30 feet (9 m). Evergreen with glossy divided leaves; large, white, single flowers in spring, followed by orange-red hips.

Japanese rose *R. rugosa* is a deciduous shrub with prickly stems and dark green divided leaves; height 3–6 feet (90–180 cm). Purple, pink or white, clove-scented flowers in summer and autumn, followed by red hips with an obvious crown of sepals.

Sweet briar *R. eglanteria* is a dense, arching deciduous shrub; height 8 feet (2.5 m). Hooked thorns and divided apple-scented leaves with rust-colored sticky hairs on the underside; fragrant bright pink flowers in summer, followed by scarlet, round hips.

Rosmarinus officinalis
LAMIACEAE

White-flowered rosemary is an aromatic and ornamental herb with glossy green, needle-like leaves. Use it fresh or dry in cooking as you would use other types of rosemary.

ROSEMARY

The flowers and leaves of this highly scented herb are used to season and garnish meat, poultry and fish. Rosemary is also used as an insect repellent, a hair and scalp tonic and a breath freshener.

Best climate and site Zones 7–10. Grow outdoors where temperatures remain above 10°F (-12°C). Hardiness varies with cultivar. Full sun to partial shade.
Ideal soil conditions Light, well-drained soil; pH 6.0–6.7.
Growing guidelines Sow seed shallowly indoors in early spring, then transplant to pots outdoors; plant out in the garden for second season, spacing 3 feet (90 cm) apart. Or take cuttings from new growth in autumn, or layer young shoots in summer. Overwintering success varies with local conditions and cultivar; larger plants may overwinter better outdoors than small ones. Potted plants may be brought into a sunny greenhouse for the winter; or keep them at 45°F (7°C) in a sunny garage or enclosed porch, watering infrequently. Prune after flowering to encourage bushy growth.
Growing habit Evergreen shrub with scaly bark and aromatic, needle-like leaves; height 2–6 feet (60–180 cm).
Flowering time Spring and summer, varies according to climate and cultivar. Whorls of small pale blue to lilac or pink tubular flowers in clusters.
Pest and disease prevention Indoors, watch for scale pests and wipe them from foliage with a cloth soaked with rubbing alcohol. Can be susceptible to mildew, so provide good air circulation, especially in winter.
Harvesting and storing Leaves and flowering tops are collected in spring and early summer and distilled for oil or dried for extracts, spirits and infusions. Snip fresh foliage for culinary use as needed throughout the year.

Special tips Rosemary is a popular, attractive shrub for the garden. It is a good companion for cabbage, broccoli and related crops, as well as carrots and onions. The fragrance is said to repel insects; companion gardeners use it to discourage cabbage flies, root maggot flies and other flying pests. The small flowers will attract bees.
Parts used Leaves, flowering tops, oil.
Culinary uses Fresh or dried leaves are used to flavor meat, especially lamb; used in soups and stews and with vegetables; small amounts added to biscuits, bread and jam. Fresh sprigs used to flavor oil, vinegar and wine. Leaves used in a tea.
Medicinal uses Internally for headaches, migraines, depression, nervous tension, poor circulation and digestive problems. Externally for arthritis, neuralgia, rheumatism, wounds, dandruff and muscular injuries.
Other uses Used in hair, skin and bath preparations.
Other varieties Prostrate rosemary *R. officinalis* Prostratus Group in which some cultivars have deep blue flowers almost all year. Good for rock gardens and hanging baskets; not very winter-hardy.
White-flowered rosemary *R. officinalis* var. *albiflorus* is a choice plant for white gardens and floral tributes. Said to be the hardiest variety.
Gardener's trivia Rosemary is a symbol of friendship and remembrance and is traditionally carried at funerals and remembrance services. Greek scholars wore garlands of rosemary to aid memory and concentration.

Rubia tinctorum
RUBIACEAE

MADDER

The foliage and roots of madder are used to produce brown, orange, pink and red natural dyes. Madder needs space to sprawl, but will climb if planted beside a timber fence.

Best climate and site Zones 6–9. Thrives in full sun, but will tolerate light shade.
Ideal soil conditions Fertile, deep, well-drained soil with a neutral pH 6.7–7.0.
Growing guidelines If planting from seed, sow shallowly indoors in spring and set out in the garden in late spring or early autumn 1 foot (30 cm) apart. Once established, new plants will spring up from roots.
Growing habit Perennial; height up to 4 feet (1.2 m). Reddish brown rhizome with weak stems that lie along the ground without support. The stems are so weak that they can't support the weight of the plant when it climbs. The prickles help the plant to cling when climbing.
Flowering time Summer; loose spikes of small, yellow-green or honey-colored, starry flowers in second or third year, followed by small, round, red to black berries.
Pest and disease prevention Usually free from pests and diseases.
Harvesting and storing Dig the roots of the plant after about 3 years and after flowering; use the roots fresh or dry to make red or orange dye.
Parts used Roots, leaves.
Medicinal uses Internally as a diuretic, and as a laxative for kidney problems and bladder stones.
Externally for cuts and wounds.
Other uses The roots are used as a source of natural dyes. The prickly leaves can be used in facial scrubs.

Rubus fruticosus
ROSACEAE

BLACKBERRY

Rich in vitamin C, sugars and pectins, blackberries have been an important part of the human diet since prehistoric times. In ancient Greece, they were used to treat gout and the Romans found them invaluable for stomach aches.

Best climate and site Most blackberries grow well in Zones 6–10 with full sun, good air circulation and no high winds.
Ideal soil conditions Fertile, well-drained soil that hasn't been used to grow related plants, such as roses or tomatoes, as these plants leave behind soil-borne disease problems that attack blackberries.
Growing guidelines Can be grown from seed sown in spring, cuttings in summer or by tip layering in summer. However, due to the prevalence of viruses, it is recommended that only certified disease-free or quality nursery plants be used.
Growing habit Semi-evergreen shrub. Biennial canes grow the first season and flower the next. Each year, cut out the fruited canes and let in the new ones. Pruning each year will prevent an inhospitable and unattractive bramble.
Flowering time Small, white to pink flowers occur in spring followed by dark red to black juicy fruits in late summer.
Pest and disease prevention Prone to aphids, botrytis and viral diseases. Birds eat the fruits.
Harvesting and storing Leaves are picked just before flowering. Roots are harvested in summer and the fruits harvested when they turn black.
Parts used Leaves, roots, fruits.
Culinary uses Fruit eaten fresh or cooked, or made into syrups, cordials and wine. Leaves are used for herbal teas.
Medicinal uses Internally for stomach disorders, dysentery, hemorrhoids, cystitis and as a tonic.
Externally for inflammation of the mouth, gums and throat.

Rubus idaeus
ROSACEAE

RASPBERRY

This deciduous, woody-stemmed scrambler is native to the Northern hemisphere. Raspberries have heralded the onset of summer and all its bounty for centuries. They are delicious fresh or cooked in pies and jams.

Best climate and site Zones 3–9. Full sun and good air circulation in a sheltered position.
Ideal soil conditions Fertile, well-drained soil; pH 4.5–7.0.
Growing guidelines Propagate by division or layering of healthy stock. Due to the prevalence of diseases, it is advisable to only buy new, certified disease-free plants.
Growing habit Deciduous shrub; has suckering canes, prickly stems and dark green leaves. Apply compost in late winter for good growth and mulch to discourage weeds. Remove old stems after fruiting.
Flowering time Small, white flowers occur in drooping clusters in spring and summer followed by copious amounts of delicious, conical, red or orange-red berries.
Pest and disease prevention Botrytis (gray mold) can cause a gray coating on fruit. Cane blight can cause wilted shoot tips and dark spots on the canes. Anthracnose can cause red-bordered spots on canes and leaves. Viruses can cause stunted growth; curled, yellow leaves; and malformed berries.
Harvesting and storing Pick leaves just before flowering. Harvest berries when they are sweet and ripe.
Parts used Leaves, fruit.
Culinary uses Fruits are eaten fresh or cooked, and can be made into cordials, syrups, wines and vinegars.
Medicinal uses Internally for digestive disorders. Externally for mouth and gum infections, minor wounds and eye infections.

Rumex acetosa
POLYGONACEAE

SORREL

In the spring, use sorrel's tender new leaves to make a delicate soup, or add them to salads. When grown in meadows, the summer stalks of sorrel's flowers will make the whole area appear to be tinted reddish green.

Best climate and site Zones 5–9. Full sun or light shade.
Ideal soil conditions Fertile, moist garden soil; pH 3.0–9.0.
Growing guidelines Sow seed shallowly outdoors in late spring, thinning to 1½ feet (45 cm). Or divide older plants in early spring or autumn. If planting late, try to plant about 2 months before the first frost, to give the roots enough time to establish before the soil freezes. Water regularly; mulching will help soil retain moisture.
Growing habit Hardy perennial with wavy, green leaves; height 24 inches (60 cm). Replace every 3 or 4 years by letting a good plant run to seed.
Flowering time Midsummer; greenish to red flowers.
Pest and disease prevention Usually trouble free.
Harvesting and storing Harvest the outside leaves regularly to promote new growth. Sorrel leaves are best eaten fresh, but may also be blanched and frozen.
Precautions Sorrel is acidic and should not be eaten by people with rheumatism, arthritis or gout.
Parts used Leaves.
Culinary uses Fresh leaves added to salads, soups, cream cheese and egg dishes. Sorrel leaves can be cooked like spinach.
Medicinal uses Seldom used medicinally.
Other uses Juice from the leaves used to remove rust, mold, grass and ink stains from linen, wood and wicker.
Other species French sorrel *R. scutatus* is a lower-growing perennial; it has triangular pale green leaves with silvery patches. Has a less bitter flavor than *R. acetosa*.

Rumex crispus
POLYGONACEAE

Dock, Curled

Curled dock is a perennial weed with a large taproot, found in pastures and hayfields. The seed stalks mature to a rusty color in late summer. Only the roots are edible and are used medicinally.

Best climate and site Zones 5–9. Full sun.
Ideal soil conditions Any soil which is slightly acidic; pH 6.0–6.7.
Growing guidelines Sow seed in shallow beds in spring, then thin to 6 inches (15 cm). Weedy and hard to control, dock thrives despite neglect. Control its growth to prevent a future weed problem.
Growing habit Perennial; height 1–4 feet (30–120 cm). Forms a rosette the first year, then develops a large taproot and sends up a tall stem. From this central point come long, lance-shaped, wavy leaves.
Flowering time Summer; inconspicuous, greenish yellow flowers in spreading panicles followed by rusty brown seed capsules in autumn. Each plant produces over 3,000 seeds.
Pest and disease prevention Usually trouble free.
Harvesting and storing Dig roots in spring or autumn; clean and slice them before drying in the sun or artificially. Store in a tightly sealed container.
Special tips Most dock seeds fall close to the parent. Soil movement may distribute seeds. Cultivation of the soil may create root fragments, allowing new plants to form from each fragment.
Precautions Excess use may cause nausea and dermatitis.
Parts used Roots.
Medicinal uses Use an infusion as a laxative, astringent, or tonic, and to treat skin problems. Also used for jaundice, liver disorders and anemia.

Ruta graveolens
RUTACEAE

Rue

Rue has a pungent, skunklike odor. Rose growers recommend strong-smelling rue as a companion plant to repel insect pests. In the garden, its bluish, delicate foliage contrasts well with the greens of other plants.

Best climate and site Zones 5–9. Full sun.
Ideal soil conditions Poor, well-drained soil; pH 6.0–7.0.
Growing guidelines Sow seed shallowly indoors in late winter, transplanting outdoors in late spring 1½–2 feet (45–60 cm) apart. Take cuttings from new growth or divide older plants. Grows well in a pot and continues growing when wintered indoors by a sunny window. Mulch with compost or well-rotted manure each spring and prune away dead stems.
Growing habit Perennial with woody stems and greenish blue foliage; height 2–3 feet (60–90 cm).
Flowering time Summer to early autumn; yellow-green blossoms in terminal clusters.
Pest and disease prevention Usually trouble free.
Harvesting and storing Can be harvested several times each season, bunching foliage to dry.
Precautions Rue can be toxic when taken internally and in excess can affect the central nervous system and prove fatal. Contact with the skin can cause irritation.
Parts used Leaves.
Medicinal uses For use by qualified practitioners only. Externally for earache, sore eyes and rheumatism.
Other uses Leaves used to flavor the Italian liqueur grappa. Dried seedpods and leaves used in flower arrangements. A brush of rue was once used to sprinkle holy water—hence its other common name, herb of grace.
Gardener's trivia According to folklore, rue slows the growth of basil, sage and members of the cabbage family.

Salvia officinalis
LAMIACEAE

SAGE

Sage is an easy-to-grow, shrubby perennial with aromatic foliage that is used both fresh and dried in cooking and in herbal medicines. Its velvety texture and small blue flowers add a soft accent to the garden.

Purple sage is grown and used like common sage. It is a small shrub with reddish purple foliage. Sage was so valued by the Chinese in the 17th century that they would trade three chests of tea for one chest of sage.

Best climate and site Zones 5–10. Full sun to partial shade.
Ideal soil conditions Well-drained garden soil pH 6.0–7.0.
Growing guidelines Sow seed shallowly outdoors in spring or indoors in late winter; plant at 20–24 inch (50–60 cm) intervals. Trim back existing plants in spring to encourage vigorous, bushy new growth. Plants may decline after several years; take cuttings or divide in spring or autumn to have a steady supply. Yellowing leaves can mean roots need more space. Remove flowering spikes when young. Sage may improve the growth and flavor of cabbages, carrots, strawberries and tomatoes; it is also thought to grow well with marjoram. It may, however, stunt the growth of cucumbers, rue and onions.
Growing habit Perennial shrub; height 1–2 feet (30–60 cm); woody stems have wrinkled gray-green foliage.
Flowering time Spring; tubular pink to purple flowers in whorled spikes.
Pest and disease prevention Small green caterpillars can eat the leaves; remove by hand or prune off. Rarely bothered by pests and diseases except slugs and snails.
Harvesting and storing Snip fresh leaves as needed, or bunch them and hang to dry for use during winter months. A branch of strongly aromatic sage is a fragrant addition to a clothes drawer or blanket box, as it helps keep moths away. Refrain from harvesting the first year.
Special tips The plentiful, usually lilac-blue flowers attract bees and other beneficial insects. Use sage as a border plant, or dot among other plants as it is fast growing.

Precautions Toxic if used in excess or used over a long period of time.
Parts used Leaves, oil, flowers.
Culinary uses Leaves used in stuffing for poultry and meat; made into tea and used in Italian cooking. Also used to flavor vinegar, cheese and butter. Sage is an antioxidant.
Medicinal uses Internally for indigestion, flatulence, liver problems, night sweats, depression, female sterility and menopausal problems. Sage tea and sage wine are nerve and blood tonics; also used to reduce sweating.
Externally for insect bites, eyewash, mouthwash, vaginal discharges and skin infections.
Other uses Used in cosmetics as an astringent cleanser and facial wash. The oil is used as a fixative for perfumes and added to toothpaste. Used as a rinse to darken gray hair and to whiten teeth.
Other species and cultivars Golden sage *S. officinalis* 'Icterina' has variegated gold and green leaves; is an excellent bushy border plant.
S. officinalis 'Purpurascens' has leaves flushed reddish purple.
S. officinalis 'Tricolor' produces gray-green to cream foliage with tints of pink and purple; not quite so hardy.
Pineapple sage *S. elegans* has dark green, pineapple-scented leaves with brilliant red tubular flowers that bloom late summer, autumn or winter; height 2–3½ feet (60–105 cm). Prefers full sun; not hardy in Zones below 9. Pinch tops for bushier growth.

Salvia sclarea
LAMIACEAE

CLARY

Fresh clary has a bitter, warm aroma and flavor and makes an attractive flowering garden plant. Fresh and dried leaves are used for seasoning—it has the same culinary uses as sage.

Best climate and site Zones 5–10. Full sun.
Ideal soil conditions Average, well-drained soil; pH 4.8–7.5.
Growing guidelines Sow seed outdoors in spring; thin to 9 inches (23 cm). Can be propagated by division of 2-year-old plants in early spring, but best raised from seed annually.
Growing habit Biennial or short-lived perennial with upright, branched, square stems and broad, oblong, aromatic leaves; height 2–5 feet (60–150 cm).
Flowering time Spring and summer after first year; small pale blue to lavender blossoms that resemble garden sage.
Pest and disease prevention Usually trouble free.
Harvesting and storing Snip leaves for fresh use. Strip leaves and dry them on screens for potpourri. Oil can be distilled from the flowering tops.
Special tips Clary can be used as a substitute for garden sage. Use in potpourris with scents such as juniper, lavender, citrus, jasmine and sandalwood.
Precautions Clary may cause drowsiness and headaches. Not to be given in any form during pregnancy.
Parts used Leaves, flowers, seeds, oil.
Culinary uses Leaves cooked into fritters. Flowers can be added to salads and used as a tea.
Medicinal uses Internally for vomiting and nausea. Externally for ulcers, cuts and as an eye wash.
Other uses Used as a massage oil and as a fixative in perfumes. Also used in potpourris.

Sambucus nigra
CAPRIFOLIACEAE

ELDER

The elder has been highly valued for centuries and has been termed "the medicine chest of the people" due to its medicinal properties of lowering fevers, reducing inflammations and soothing irritations.

Best climate and site Zones 5–9. Full sun to partial shade.
Ideal soil conditions Moist, rich soil; pH 6.5–8.1.
Growing guidelines Propagate by softwood cuttings in summer or by seed sown in autumn. Prune back hard in winter to ensure good foliage and flowers for next season.
Growing habit Large, deciduous shrub or tree; height 30 feet (9 m). Leaves are dull green and pinnate in shape; they emit an unpleasant odor when crushed. Bark is gray-brown and corklike in texture.
Flowering time Very small, highly scented white flowers occur in early summer, followed by black berries.
Pest and disease prevention Prone to attack by aphids.
Harvesting and storing Leaves are picked in spring and summer and used fresh. Bark is stripped off the trunk in winter and dried for further use. Flowers are picked when fully open and dried. Fruits are picked when ripe and used fresh or dried.
Precautions Leaves, bark and raw berries are harmful if eaten.
Parts used Leaves, bark, flowers, fruit.
Culinary uses Flowers are used to add flavor to stewed fruits, jellies and jams; also used to make wine. Fruits are made into sauces. Juice is used to make liqueurs.
Medicinal uses Internally for colds, fever, rheumatic pain, arthritis and constipation. Externally for sore eyes, chilblains, minor burns and mouth infections.
Other uses Flowers are used in cosmetics, skin lotions, oils and ointments.

Sanguinaria canadensis
PAPAVERACEAE

BLOODROOT

Named for the blood red liquid extracted from the root, bloodroot was used by Native Americans as a dye for coloring skin and weapons. Recently it has become a source of sanguinarine, a dental plaque inhibitor.

Best climate and site Zones 3–9. Dappled to partial shade.
Ideal soil conditions Well-drained, rich soil; pH 4.5–6.9.
Growing guidelines Propagate by seed sown in autumn or by plant division after flowering. Self-sows easily.
Growing habit Perennial spring wildflower in woodlands with a single, deeply cut, palmately lobed leaf that emerges wrapped around a single flower bud; height 6–8 inches (15–20 cm). Plants grow from a thick, creeping rhizome with red sap.
Flowering time Solitary, snow white to pink flowers appear in spring; made up of 8–16 narrow petals with a striking cluster of yellow-orange stamens. Flowers last only a few days and are followed by an oblong seed capsule.
Pest and disease prevention Usually trouble free.
Harvesting and storing Rhizomes are dug up in autumn and dried for further use.
Precautions Use in small amounts and by qualified practitioners only. Excess can cause nausea and vomiting and can be fatal. Not to be taken by pregnant and breastfeeding women.
Parts used Rhizomes.
Medicinal uses Internally for respiratory tract infections but only in small amounts as it can be toxic.
Externally for warts and chilblains. Bloodroot acts as a local anesthetic and is thought to be effective against many pathogenic organisms.
Other uses Added to toothpaste and mouthwash as an anti-plaque agent.
Other common names Red puccoon, red Indian paint.

Santolina chamaecyparissus
ASTERACEAE

SANTOLINA

Santolina is an evergreen, aromatic shrub with cluster of yellow button-like flowers. Though it is also called lavender cotton, it is a member of the daisy family. It is useful as an insect repellent.

Best climate and site Zones 7–10. Full sun.
Ideal soil conditions Poor, well-drained soil; pH 7.0–8.0. If the soil is too rich or too wet, the foliage may be dull and growth of the whole plant may be extremely slow.
Growing guidelines Sow seed in late spring; germinates slowly. Take cuttings in late summer to early autumn; layer or divide older plants in spring. Set 2 feet (60 cm) apart; less for hedging. Shear or clip the plant in spring or summer, never in the colder months. Pinch off fading blooms; don't overwater. Plants root and spread.
Growing habit Evergreen shrub; height to 2 feet (60 cm). Leaves are silver-green, pinnately divided, long, narrow and highly aromatic when crushed. Forms low mounds.
Flowering time Summer; clusters of yellow button-like blooms rise above the foliage on 6-inch (15-cm) stalks; the fruit is brownish. May not flower the first year.
Pest and disease prevention Usually trouble free.
Harvesting and storing Harvest and bunch together the top 8–10 inches (20–25 cm) of foliage in summer and hang to dry. Collect flowers, with the stems, at full bloom; hang to dry.
Parts used Leaves, flowering stems.
Medicinal uses Internally for poor digestion, worms in children and jaundice.
Externally for stings, bites and skin inflammations.
Other uses Use as a backing for making aromatic wreaths and sprinkle into potpourri.
Other common names Lavender cotton.

Saponaria officinalis
CARYOPHYLLACEAE

SOAPWORT

This rhizomatous perennial, also called bouncing Bet, is a roadside and garden weed. It is a pretty plant with white or pink blossoms in spring. As its name implies, soapwort lathers and cleans like soap.

Best climate and site Zones 5–9. Full sun to light shade.
Ideal soil conditions Average to poor, well-drained soil; pH 6.0–7.0.
Growing guidelines Divide established plants in autumn or spring. Or sow soapwort indoors, about 6 weeks before last frost. Water regularly until the plants are established; it is very drought tolerant once it has matured. Clip back after flowering to encourage a second bloom. Don't plant next to fishponds as its lathering properties may seep into the water and poison the fish. Once established, soapwort self-sows and spreads rapidly.
Growing habit Rhizomatous perennial with sturdy branching stems that run to purple-green at the base; height 1–3 feet (30–90 cm). Soapwort spreads by seed and runners. Leaves are oval, pointed and pale green. Plant sap contains saponin, which is the substance that creates a lather when boiled.
Flowering time Summer to autumn; pink to white, five-petaled flowers in terminal clusters.
Pest and disease prevention Usually trouble free.
Harvesting and storing Clean, chop and boil the root to make a sudsy solution. The juice from fresh leaves can be used to relieve itching skin conditions.
Precautions Excess can destroy red blood cells; poisonous if eaten. Can cause eye irritation.
Parts used Leaves, leafy stems, rhizomes.
Medicinal uses Externally for skin problems.
Other uses As a soap substitute.

Sassafras albidum
LAURACEAE

SASSAFRAS

Sassafras is a tall, deciduous tree that produces an oil once used as a flavoring for cold and hot beverages. It has striking yellow, orange and red foliage in the autumn.

Best climate and site Zones 5–9. Full sun to partial shade.
Ideal soil conditions Well-drained acid to neutral garden soil; pH 6.7–7.3.
Growing guidelines Propagate by seed or by suckers; you can also take root cuttings. Only very small, young trees transplant successfully because the mature trees develop long taproots.
Growing habit Aromatic deciduous tree with deeply fissured bark; height 20–60 feet (6–18 m) or more. Variable leaves are mostly three-lobed, downy and different sizes. The young foliage smells of citrus; the roots and bark have a spicy scent like that of root beer.
Flowering time Spring; clusters of small, inconspicuous greenish yellow blossoms appear with the leaves. Male and female flowers are unisexual. The fruit that follows is a pea-sized, dark blue-black berry.
Pest and disease prevention Can be affected by Japanese beetles and gypsy moths.
Harvesting and storing Leaves are picked in spring; roots are lifted in autumn. Bark and root bark are used to produce oil.
Precautions Excess can cause vomiting. The volatile oil contains safrole, thought possibly to be carcinogenic. Should not be taken internally or only in very small quantities.
Parts used Leaves, roots, oil.
Culinary uses Leaves used to thicken soup.
Medicinal uses Externally for sore eyes, lice and insect bites.
Other uses As a flavoring for root beer using a safrole-free extract.

Satureja montana
LAMIACEAE

SAVORY, WINTER

This aromatic bushy, evergreen perennial has a peppery flavor and has been used in cooking for 2,000 years. It is also thought to be beneficial for digestion and skin problems. It is sometimes used as a salt substitute.

Best climate and site Zones 6–9. Full sun.
Ideal soil conditions Poor, well-drained soil, pH 6.7–7.3.
Growing guidelines Sow seed shallowly outdoors in late spring, thinning to 1 foot (30 cm). Germinates slowly. Take cuttings, or divide older plants in spring or autumn. Tip-prune to encourage bushiness.
Growing habit Evergreen perennial with woody stems and oblong, needle-like leaves; height 6–12 inches (15–30 cm).
Flowering time White to pale purple flowers in summer.
Pest and disease prevention Usually trouble free.
Harvesting and storing Harvest fresh as needed, or cut and dry the foliage just before flowering. Use as a flavoring in a variety of dishes, teas, herb butters and vinegars.
Special tips Winter savory can make a low hedge in the herb garden. Its thin leaves are a glossy dark green, adding some contrast to herb plantings.
Precautions Not given to pregnant women.
Parts used Leaves, shoots.
Culinary uses Leaves used to flavor processed meats, sausages, salami and Provençal dishes.
Medicinal uses Internally for indigestion, nausea and diarrhea. Externally for sore throat and insect bites.
Other uses Extracts used in liqueurs and used as a salt substitute. An infusion can also be used as a mouth wash.
Other species Summer savory *S. hortensis* is an aromatic annual with linear, downy leaves and pale lavender or white blossoms; height 12–18 inches (30–45 cm).

Simaba cedron
SIMAROUBACEAE

CEDRON (QUASSIA)

Cedron (quassia) is one of 14 species of shrubs and trees that are valued for their antimalarial compounds, found in the seeds. The related Quassia amara*, pictured above, also has medicinal properties.*

Best climate and site Zone 10 or more. Full sun. Native of Central America and northern Brazil.
Ideal soil conditions Well-drained soil; pH 4.5–7.8.
Growing guidelines Propagate by division of suckers or hardwood cuttings at the end of summer; also by seed when ripe.
Growing habit Deciduous tree; height 15–50 feet (5–15 m). Slender and erect with spreading branches. Leaves up to 3 feet (90 cm) in length divided into narrow leaflets.
Flowering time Dark yellow, fragrant, simple, five-petaled flowers appear in summer, followed by oval fruits each bearing one seed.
Pest and disease prevention Usually free from pests and diseases.
Harvesting and storing Seeds collected when ripe and used fresh or dried; powdered for use in infusions.
Special tips Once used to treat roundworm and lice, this plant is used today as a bitter or to denature alcohol. Sale and use of cedron quassia extracts are restricted in certain countries. Generally, "quassia" refers to a bitter compound extracted from the wood of a related tree species, *Quassia amara*, but not from *Simaba cedron*. Quassia chips, used as an animal repellent, are also from a related tree.
Parts used Seeds.
Medicinal uses Internally to lower fevers, reduce inflammation and to relax spasms.
Externally and internally for non-poisonous snakebite.

Solidago spp.
COMPOSITAE

GOLDENROD

Use the dried flowers of goldenrod for floral arrangements or to make a yellow dye. Also use medicinally to treat insect bites. It offers attractive shelter to praying mantids and other beneficial insects.

Best climate and site Zones 5–9, depending on the species. Thrives in full sun but tolerates partial shade.
Ideal soil conditions Average to poor, well-drained garden soil; pH 6.5–7.5.
Growing guidelines Easily grown from seed sown in early spring, or purchase plants from nurseries. Divide mature plants in spring or autumn. Can become weedy if the soil is too rich, so hold off on the nitrogen.
Growing habit Unbranched perennial with simple leaves; height 3–7 feet (90–210 cm).
Flowering time Late summer and autumn; yellow blossoms the second year.
Pest and disease prevention Usually free from pests and diseases, but watch for powdery mildew.
Harvesting and storing Collect the leaves and tops during the flowering period and dry in bunches or on screens; quickly turns black without adequate air circulation. Store in airtight containers. The leaves are used in a tea to treat flatulence.
Special tips Plant in masses or weave clumps into ornamental plantings near the vegetable garden to attract beneficial insects. Its blooming plumes are tightly clustered with small flowers rich in pollen and nectar. Many species self-sow freely or spread quickly by creeping roots, so thin regularly.
Parts used Leaves, flowering tops.
Medicinal uses Internally for urinary infections, catarrh, flatulence and kidney stones.
Externally for wounds, insect bites, ulcers and sore throats.

Stachys officinalis
LABIATAE

BETONY

Place betony, an attractive perennial, between the taller herbs and border plants that flower in midsummer, for a pretty garden arrangement. In the Middle Ages, people believed that betony kept away evil spirits.

Best climate and site Zones 5–9. Full sun but tolerates partial shade.
Ideal soil conditions Average soil with good drainage; pH 5.5–7.0.
Growing guidelines Easily started from seed sown outdoors in early spring. Spring cuttings will quickly root. Or divide established root systems for new plants. Control summer weeds. Every three to four years, dig up the plant and divide into several new clumps, adding compost or rotted manure to the soil.
Growing habit Rosette-forming perennial with deeply veined and toothed leaves; height up to 3 feet (90 cm).
Flowering time Summer; tubular red-purple flowers in dense spikes.
Pest and disease prevention Usually trouble free.
Harvesting and storing Collect leaves in summer or just before blooming; dry them quickly and store in an airtight container. The leaves can be used to make a pleasant tea and a chartreuse dye.
Precautions Excessive internal use irritates the stomach; can cause vomiting and diarrhea. Not given to pregnant women.
Parts used Whole plant.
Medicinal uses Internally for headaches, anxiety, hypertension and menopausal problems. Gargle tea made from the astringent leaves to treat throat irritations. Externally for wounds, bruises and ulcers.

Stellaria media
CARYOPHYLLACEAE

CHICKWEED

Chickweed is a hardy annual that has been used as a healing herb and as a source of wild food for centuries. Its leaves are a rich source of vitamin C and phosphorus, and domestic birds and fowls find it irresistible, hence its name.

Best climate and site Zones 5–10. Full sun but tolerates partial shade.
Ideal soil conditions Easy to grow but prefers moist soil; pH 5.8–7.9.
Growing guidelines Propagate by seed sown at any time; self-sows readily and in some areas is a serious weed problem.
Growing habit Vigorous, creeping annual, 4–16 inches (10–40 cm) long with a slender taproot. Succulent, oval leaves grow on weak, brittle, branched stems that are hairy on one side.
Flowering time Small, starlike white flowers with deeply notched petals appear throughout the year.
Pest and disease prevention Usually free from pests and diseases.
Harvesting and storing Plants are cut and used fresh or dried for infusions. Also used in liquid extracts, medicated oils, ointments and tinctures. It is an easy herb to use as it is available throughout the year and is readily infused in oil to use as a lotion.
Parts used Whole plant.
Culinary uses Sprigs can be added to salads and used as a vegetable.
Medicinal uses Internally for rheumatism and constipation. Fresh leaves can be used as a poultice to relieve inflammation and ulcers. Use whole plant to treat piles and skin wounds.
Other uses Sprigs used as food for domestic fowls and pet birds.

Symphytum officinale
BORAGINACEAE

COMFREY

Comfrey is an attractive plant with large, broad, deep green leaves and nodding clusters of tubular flowers. It has a colorful medicinal history, and was once thought to help repair broken bones.

Best climate and site Zones 5–10. Full sun to partial shade.
Ideal soil conditions Rich, moist garden soil; pH 6.7–7.3.
Growing guidelines Propagate by seed, division or cuttings; space new plants 3 feet (90 cm) apart. Establishes easily and requires little care. Remove dead leaves during the autumn cleanup. Divide every few years to prevent crowding.
Growing habit Perennial with broad leaves; height 2–4 feet (60–120 cm). New leaves sprout each spring from the roots.
Flowering time Spring to late summer; terminal clusters of drooping, bell-shaped purple, pink, white or cream flowers.
Pest and disease prevention Usually trouble free.
Harvesting and storing Pick the leaves and use fresh or dry. Leaves for drying are best picked in spring. Dig up the roots when the plant has died down in autumn and dry; store leaves and roots in airtight containers.
Special tips Comfrey can tolerate partial shade, but plants will be smaller, with few blossoms.
Precautions Comfrey is a suspected carcinogen and should not be taken internally. If used excessively, it may cause liver damage. Can also cause skin irritation. Comfrey is subject to legal restrictions in some countries.
Parts used Leaves, roots.
Medicinal uses Use roots and leaves to treat external bruises, wounds and sores. Externally for arthritis, fractures, sprains, psoriasis, bunions, and sore breasts during breastfeeding.
Other common names Knitbone, slippery root.

Tagetes patula
ASTERACEAE

FRENCH MARIGOLD

This aromatic annual is used in religious ceremonies in Mexico and India. The genus is named after an Etruscan god, Tages, who practiced the art of water divination. Marigolds add color to any sunny garden.

Best climate and site Zones 9–10. Full sun. Light afternoon shade can help prolong blooms in hot summer areas.
Ideal soil conditions Average, well-drained soil; pH 4.2–7.2.
Growing guidelines Propagate by seed sown in spring.
Growing habit Bushy annual; height 1 foot (30 cm). Leaves are deeply divided and toothed, and are highly aromatic when crushed.
Flowering time Yellow to orange or red-brown flowers appear from spring to autumn. Deadhead regularly.
Pest and disease prevention Usually free from pests and diseases.
Harvesting and storing Whole plants are harvested when flowering and dried for further use. Leaves and flowers are picked in summer and used fresh or dried. Oil is extracted from leaves picked during the growing season.
Special tips This plant is an excellent companion plant for vegetables as it is effective in repelling pests, such as soil nematodes, slugs and whiteflies, which target tomatoes and other vegetables.
Parts used Whole plant, leaves, flowers, oil.
Culinary uses Leaves used in salads and to flavor food. Oil is used as a food flavoring.
Medicinal uses Internally for stomach upsets.
Externally for rheumatic pain and eye inflammations.
Other uses Flowers used to give color to dairy products.
Other species Sweet mace *T. lucida* leaves are used to make a tea, popular in Latin America. Used as a substitute for tarragon.

Tamarindus indica
CAESALPINIACEAE

TAMARIND

This graceful, evergreen tree has been cultivated in India for centuries. The name tamarind comes from the Arabic word for "date of India" and refers to the datelike pulp inside the pods.

Best climate and site Zone 10 or warmer with full sun. Found widespread in the tropics. Drought and frost tender.
Ideal soil conditions Light, well-drained soil; pH 4.7–7.9.
Growing guidelines Propagate by seed sown when the temperature reaches 70°F (21°C) or by air layering or grafting.
Growing habit Evergreen tree with spreading branches and a stout, straight trunk covered with rough, grayish-black bark; height to 80 feet (24 m). Leaves are light green and consist of 8–32 pairs of lightly hairy leaflets to each leaf.
Flowering time Pale yellow, red-veined, fragrant flowers occur in summer, followed by brown fruit containing kidney-shaped seeds in an acid, sticky, brown pulp.
Pest and disease prevention Usually trouble free.
Harvesting and storing Fruits are picked when ripe and used fresh or dried. Young, tender pods are used as seasoning.
Special tips Tamarind fruits are available compressed into a block. To use, break off a piece and place in boiling water to soften. Strain and use the liquid; discard the debris.
Parts used Fruits.
Culinary uses Fruits are used freshly picked and made into a drink similar to lemonade. Pulp is used fresh or dried in curries, chutneys and sweets; also as a souring agent similar to lemon juice. Also in Worcestershire sauce.
Medicinal uses Internally for fevers, asthma, dysentery and to improve digestion.
Externally for ulcers and sore eyes. Has antiseptic properties.
Other uses Included in laxative preparations.

Tanacetum balsamita
ASTERACEAE

COSTMARY

In the summer, enjoy costmary's mint-scented leaves in your garden and add them to salads and vegetable dishes. In the autumn, harvest whole stems for weaving into fragrant herb baskets.

Best climate and site Zones 6–10. Full sun to partial shade.
Ideal soil conditions Well-drained, fertile, loamy soil; pH 6.0–6.7.
Growing guidelines Plants produce little or no seed, so propagate by dividing older plants in spring; space at 2-foot (60-cm) intervals. Divide plants every 2–3 years, since they spread quickly. Avoid shade, since costmary will not flower without sun. For more foliage production, discourage flowering by pruning away buds.
Growing habit Perennial with large, gray-green, silvery, hairy foliage; height 1–3 feet (60–90 cm). Dies back in cold climates during winter.
Flowering time Late summer, but may not bloom; very small, white daisy flowers in loose clusters with yellow button centers.
Pest and disease prevention Usually trouble free.
Harvesting and storing Collect leaves and dry as needed. To harvest foliage for baskets, harvest whole stems in late summer or autumn and hang to dry.
Special tips Add fresh leaves to salads for a minty flavor.
Parts used Leaves.
Culinary uses Fresh leaves added to salads, meat and vegetable dishes, and to iced drinks. Dried leaves infused as a tea.
Medicinal uses No longer used medicinally but once popular as a liver tonic and for insect stings.
Other uses Mainly for weaving into fragrant herb baskets and for potpourri; also for scenting drawers and cupboards.
Other common names Alecost, mint geranium.

Tanacetum cinerariifolium
ASTERACEAE

PYRETHRUM

This herb contains volatile oils that are extremely effective in repelling and killing insects. Dried flowers retain their insecticidal properties indefinitely and have been used around the home and garden for centuries.

Best climate and site Zones 6–10. Full sun. Tolerates seaside conditions but not waterlogged soil. Cold and heat tolerant.
Ideal soil conditions Average well-drained soil; pH 6.0–6.7.
Growing guidelines Propagate by seed in spring to summer. Divide plants in spring.
Growing habit Perennial with slender, hairy stems and leaves that are fine and heavily divided; height 1–2½ feet (30–75 cm). Plant can become woody and shrublike with age. Tends to spread abundantly, so prune back to control growth.
Flowering time Simple, small, daisy-like white flowers with bright yellow centers appear from early summer to autumn.
Pest and disease prevention Due to its insecticidal properties, rarely bothered by pests and diseases.
Harvesting and storing Flowers are picked as they open, dried and powdered. They contain volatile oils and other compounds.
Special tips Pyrethrum, which contains pyrethrin, deters all common insect pests such as bedbugs, aphids, mosquitoes and ants. Also kills beneficial insects, so spray at dusk, when bees and other beneficials are not active. It is also toxic to fish.
Precautions Handling this plant can cause allergic dermatitis and asthma. Acute exposure can be harmful. Wear protective clothing when using.
Parts used Flowers.
Other uses Extracts from dried flowers are used in fumigants and insecticides. Pyrethrin is less toxic in the environment than synthetic insecticides because it degrades quickly, and is valued as a natural, effective alternative to chemical pesticides.

Tanacetum vulgare
ASTERACEAE

TANSY

This easy-to-grow, aromatic, attractive perennial has brilliant green foliage and yellow button-like flowers. Companion gardeners recommend tansy to improve the vigor of roses and to repel pests.

Best climate and site Zones 4–10. Full sun to partial shade.
Ideal soil conditions Well-drained garden soil; pH 6.0–7.5.
Growing guidelines Sow seed indoors in late winter; transplant outdoors after danger of frost, 4 feet (1.2 m) apart. Divide established plants in spring or autumn. Spreads easily. Prune vigorously in midsummer for lush growth in late autumn. Plants may need support; they will stand upright when grown along fences.
Growing habit Erect perennial with branched stems and fern-like, aromatic leaves; height 3–4 feet (90–120 cm). Tansy grows and spreads very fast, even in poor soil.
Flowering time Summer to autumn; button-like, yellow blossoms in terminal clusters.
Pest and disease prevention Aphids can be a problem; to control, dislodge them with a spray of water.
Harvesting and storing Collect foliage anytime during summer. Flowers dry well but lose their bright yellow color.
Special tips Tansy is said to repel certain pest insects, while attracting the beneficials. Was used in the past as a flea and moth repellent.
Precautions The oil is highly toxic for both internal and external use and may prove fatal.
Parts used Leaves, flowers.
Culinary uses Leaves can be added to custard and cakes.
Other uses Flowers used in dried arrangements. Leaves and flowers used to make a green-gold dye.
Other common names Golden buttons.

Taraxacum officinale
ASTERACEAE

DANDELION

Some gardeners have learned to appreciate this brightly colored lawn weed. If your thumb is other than green, try planting dandelions to boost your self-confidence in the garden, as they are sure to thrive!

Best climate and site Zones 3–10. Full sun but tolerates partial shade.
Ideal soil conditions Any moderately fertile, moist soil; pH 6.0–7.5.
Growing guidelines It is best to obtain seed of a large-leafed variety from a specialist seed catalog and sow shallowly in early spring. For large roots that are easy to dig, work in plenty of compost or rotted manure to loosen the soil.
Growing habit Perennial with jagged leaves arising from a basal rosette; height 6–12 inches (15–30 cm).
Flowering time Late spring; the familiar golden-yellow flowers mature to puffballs of seeds.
Pest and disease prevention Usually free from pests and diseases.
Harvesting and storing Leaves can be picked throughout the year. Dig roots in autumn, and cut or slice them into small pieces, then air dry or roast in a slow oven.
Special tips Dandelion can become a problem in gardens if allowed to grow unchecked. Thin plantings regularly.
Parts used Whole plant, leaves, roots, flowers.
Culinary uses Use dried, roasted and ground roots to prepare a caffeine-free coffee substitute. Harvest young, fresh leaves for spring salads, soups and wine; less bitter if blanched first.
Medicinal uses Internally for jaundice, urinary tract infections, cirrhosis, gallstones and constipation. In Chinese medicine, used to treat mastitis, tumors and abscesses. Externally for non-poisonous snakebite.

Teucrium chamaedrys
LAMIACEAE

GERMANDER

Germander is grown for its boxy ornamental shape, and is well suited to the formal herb garden. The foliage is lightly aromatic and has been traditionally used as a treatment for gout, rheumatism and other ailments.

Best climate and site Zones 5–9. Full sun to partial shade.
Ideal soil conditions Well-drained garden soil; pH 6.0–8.0.
Growing guidelines Best propagated by cuttings, layering or division, since seed-raised plants are slow to germinate. Plant 1 foot (30 cm) apart; does well in pots. Can be pruned and trained like a dwarf hedge in knot gardens. Not fully frost-hardy in severe winters; protect with mulch or burlap.
Growing habit Perennial; height to 2 feet (60 cm). Leaves are short, dark green, oval and hairy; the square, hairy stalks are of a dirty green color and very weak. Variegated germander has irregular, clear gold splotches on dark green leaves; great for edging a perennial border.
Flowering time Early to late summer; small purple to purple-red flowers on leafy spikes, followed by egg-shaped nutlet fruits.
Pest and disease prevention Usually free from pests and diseases.
Harvesting and storing Harvest the leaves during spring and early summer. Dry and store them in an airtight container.
Precautions May cause liver damage.
Parts used Whole plant, leaves.
Culinary uses Leaves used to flavor alcoholic drinks such as liqueurs, wines and vermouth.
Medicinal uses Internally for loss of appetite, gout, rheumatoid arthritis, jaundice, catarrh and bronchitis. Externally for wounds, gum disease and skin problems.
Other common names Poor man's box, common germander, wall germander.

Thymus vulgaris
LAMIACEAE

THYME, COMMON OR GARDEN

Easy-to-grow thyme is a favorite of cooks and gardeners. Delicately pretty in leaf and flower, a carpet of thyme makes a beautiful underplanting for roses. The leaves enrich the flavor of meats and soups.

Best climate and site Zones 6–10. Ideally in full sun but partial shade tolerated.
Ideal soil conditions Ordinary, well-drained, neutral to alkaline soil; pH 6.0–8.0.
Growing guidelines Sow seed shallowly in late winter indoors, keeping the soil at 70° F (21°C) for best germination. Plant outdoors in late spring in clumps, 1 foot (30 cm) apart. You can divide older plants in spring or take cuttings in late summer or autumn. In winter, mulch with a light material such as straw. Replace plants every 3–4 years to control woody growth. Grow shrubs for low hedging and creepers for aromatic carpets.
Growing habit Variable shrub with gray-green leaves; height 1–1½ feet inches (30–45 cm). There are more than 350 species of thyme, mainly small, evergreen, aromatic, woody-based perennials. The different species of thyme vary in aroma, but most can be used to flavor food.
Flowering time Midsummer; flowers vary in color (lilac, rose-purple, mauve, white, pink, purple) depending on the cultivar; blossoms in clusters.
Pest and disease prevention Generally free from pests and diseases if soil is well drained.
Harvesting and storing Snip foliage as needed during summer, or harvest entirely twice per season, leaving at least 3 inches (7.5 cm) of growth. Best harvested while in bloom. Bunch sprigs together and hang to dry. Thyme foliage freezes well. Place in airtight containers for use during winter months.

The name thyme comes from the Greek word *thymon,* meaning "courage". Lemon thyme is one of the most common species and has pale lilac flowers. Its lemon-scented leaves are used in cooking, especially with chicken.

The powerful antiseptic and preserving properties of thyme were known to ancient Egyptians, who used it for embalming. Ancient Romans bathed in thyme water to give them good health and vigor.

Special tips Thyme is said to benefit the growth of vegetables such as potatoes, eggplants (aubergines) and tomatoes; it repels caterpillars and whiteflies. Thyme is also ideal for rock gardens and containers. The tiny, numerous flowers produce copious nectar that attracts beneficial insects. Thyme is rich in volatile oil, which has powerful antiseptic properties. Can be used as a household disinfectant.

Precautions Not to be used by for pregnant or breastfeeding women. The oil may cause skin irritations and allergic reactions in people with sensitive skin.

Parts used Whole plant, leaves, flowering tops, oil.

Culinary uses Thyme, when mixed with parsley and bay, is an essential ingredient of bouquet garni. It is important in French cooking. Used to flavor stock, marinades, stuffings, sauces and soup; it retains its flavor well in dishes that are cooked slowly in wine. Lemon-scented thyme is added to chicken, fish, vegetables, fruit salads and jam.

Medicinal uses Internally for coughs, bronchitis, asthma, laryngitis, indigestion and diarrhea.

Externally for tonsillitis, arthritis, gum disease and fungal infections. Oil used in aromatherapy for depression, exhaustion, upper respiratory tract infections and skin complaints.

Other uses Dried leaves are used in potpourri; also used in moth-repelling sachets. Leaves used in cosmetics, and in bath washes and facial steams. Essential oil used as an antiseptic in toothpastes and mouthwashes.

Other species Creeping thyme *T. praecox* is a mat-forming creeper with tiny hair-fringed leaves; height 2 inches (5 cm). Mauve to purple flowers in terminal clusters in summer. Not used for oil extracts.

Lemon thyme *T.* x *citriodorus* is a variable hybrid with glossy leaves that are dark green, white or yellow, variegated and lemon-scented; height 10–12 inches (25–30 cm). Pale lilac flowers in summer. Not grown from seed. Oil may be less of an irritant than other thyme oils.

Wild thyme *T. serpyllum* is a prostrate perennial with slender, creeping stems and tiny hairy leaves; height 3 inches (7 cm). Clusters of purple to pink flowers appear in summer. Reputedly effective in treating alcoholism and hangovers. The oil is used to treat stress but may cause allergies.

Caraway thyme *T. herba-barona* is a wiry, carpeting subshrub with tiny, dark green leaves which smell like caraway, nutmeg or lemon. Small clusters of pink to mauve flowers appear in summer; height 2–4 inches (5–10 cm).

Used mainly to flavor chicken, game and meat dishes with wine and garlic.

Mastic thyme *T. mastichina* is a hardy, erect shrub with wavy, downy leaves with a eucalyptus-like scent; height 8–12 inches (20–30 cm). Small, off-white flowers are produced in heads in summer. The oil is used commercially to flavor meat sauces.

Trifolium pratense
PAPILIONACEAE

RED CLOVER

Red clover is a member of the legume family. With the aid of microscopic soil organisms, legumes add nitrogen to the soil, an important element for all plant growth.

Best climate and site Zones 6–9. Full sun, but will tolerate partial shade.
Ideal soil conditions Light, moist, sandy, well-drained garden soil; pH 6.0–6.7.
Growing guidelines Broadcast seed shallowly outdoors in early spring. Thin plants to 1 foot (30 cm) apart. May need an inoculant or may be hard to control.
Growing habit Erect to sprawling, short-lived perennial with long-stalked, oval, hairy leaves; height 1–2 feet (30–60 cm).
Flowering time Summer; bright pink to purple, sometimes cream, tubular flowers, fragrant, in globose heads.
Pest and disease prevention Usually free from pests and diseases; can be susceptible to "clover sickness" in which toxins released by the roots stop the plant from growing.
Harvesting and storing Collect flowers at full bloom and dry on paper in the shade; store in airtight containers. Use dried for infusions, liquid extracts and ointments.
Special tips Sow as a living mulch or a green manure crop. The flowers attract beneficial insects, such as bees and butterflies, and the nitrogen-fixing bacteria on the roots work to enhance soil fertility. Can also be grown as a groundcover.
Parts used Flowering tops.
Medicinal uses Internally for eczema, psoriasis, gout, coughs and degenerative diseases. Used to make a slightly sweet tea that is said to purify the blood, relieve irritating coughs and be a mild sedative.

Trigonella foenum-graecum
PAPILIONACEAE

FENUGREEK

Fenugreek is a member of the same family as beans and clover. The seeds are used as a substitute for maple flavoring in baked goods and are also used in curries and to make a laxative tea.

Best climate and site Zones 6–10. Full sun.
Ideal soil conditions Rich garden soil; pH 6.0–7.0.
Growing guidelines When springtime soil temperatures reach 60°F (15°C), sow a thick band of seed outdoors. Avoid growing in cold, wet soils since seeds will rot before germinating. As a leguminous plant, fenugreek needs little nitrogen fertilizer; can enrich soils.
Growing habit Annual with clover-like stems and leaves; height 1–2 feet (30–60 cm).
Flowering time Summer; white flowers with distinctive pink or purple markings that resemble garden pea blossoms.
Pest and disease prevention Usually free from pests and diseases. Handpick snails from new growth.
Harvesting and storing Harvest pods when ripe but before they fall; leave seeds in the sun to dry. For culinary purposes, the dried seeds can be ground.
Special tips For a substitute for maple syrup, steep the seeds in boiling water and use the strained liquid.
Parts used Leaves, seeds.
Culinary uses Dried seeds used in Indian and Middle Eastern dishes; fresh leaves are added to vegetable curries; roasted seeds used in curry powder, also sprouted as a salad vegetable. Fenugreek is an important food in Africa.
Medicinal uses Internally for diabetes, gastric problems, bronchial complaints and allergies.
Externally for cellulitis and skin problems.
Other common names Bird's foot, Greek hayseed.

Tropaeolum majus
TROPAEOLACEAE

NASTURTIUM

Nasturtiums are a favorite of both gardeners and cooks. The blossoms are a reliable source of color all summer long and the spurred flowers attract nectar-eating birds. The flowers and leaves can be added to salads.

Best climate and site Zones 8–10. Blooms best in full sun.
Ideal soil conditions Average, moist, well-drained, nutrient-poor soil. Nasturtiums tend to produce more leaves than flowers if you plant them in rich soil; pH 6.0–8.0.
Growing guidelines Sow seed outdoors ¾ inch (2 cm) deep after the last frost, when the soil is warm in spring; thin plants to 6–9 inches (15–23 cm). For bushels of blooms, hold back the nitrogen. Also does well as a potted annual.
Growing habit Trailing or climbing annual; height 1–2 feet (30–60 cm) for dwarf bush cultivars. Height 10 feet (3 m) for climbers. Leaves are umbrella-like.
Flowering time Summer; red, orange or yellow funnel-shaped, sweet-smelling blossoms.
Pest and disease prevention Prone to aphids. Wash off with a spray of water. If persistent, spray with insecticidal soap.
Harvesting and storing Snip young, fresh leaves and blossoms all summer as needed for salads. In autumn, pickle the unopened buds for homemade capers.
Special tips Look for dwarf, vining and variegated types in seed catalogs.
Parts used Whole plant, leaves, flowers, seeds.
Culinary uses Leaves, flowers, flower buds and nectar spurs are added to salads. Chopped leaves add a peppery flavor to eggs and cream cheese. Flowers used to make vinegar.
Medicinal uses Internally for scurvy and hair problems. Externally for baldness.
Other common names Indian cress.

Urtica dioica
URTICACEAE

STINGING NETTLE

A noxious pest to gardeners, nettle is high in vitamins A and C and is used by practitioners of homeopathic medicine. The fibers can be used to make cloth, and the leaves can be cooked like spinach or used in soups.

Best climate and site Zones 5–9. Full sun to partial shade.
Ideal soil conditions Most soils; pH 5.0–8.0.
Growing guidelines Sow seed shallowly outdoors in early spring; self-sows readily and quickly multiplies.
Growing habit Herbaceous perennial; height 2–6 feet (60–180 cm); leaves have stinging hairs but provide food for butterfly caterpillars.
Flowering time Early to late summer; greenish male flowers in loose sprays; female flowers more densely clustered together.
Pest and disease prevention Usually trouble free.
Harvesting and storing Harvest whole plant above the root, just before flowering; hang in bunches to dry. Collect seeds and dry on paper. Wear heavy gloves when harvesting.
Precautions When touched, the hairs inject an irritating substance into the skin that will cause it to swell and sting for several hours. Rub dock leaves onto stings to soothe them.
Special tips Stinging nettle is a common wild herb and is considered to be a weed in the home garden. If you would prefer not to grow it but want to use it medicinally or in the kitchen, you can sometimes find it growing on waste ground.
Parts used Whole plants, leaves.
Culinary uses Young leaves are cooked like spinach, puréed for soups and used to make nettle beer.
Medicinal uses Internally for anemia, hemorrhage, arthritis and eczema.
Externally for gout, sciatica and scalp and hair problems.
Other uses In cosmetics, medicines and as a coloring agent.

Valeriana officinalis
VALERIANACEAE

VALERIAN

Formerly much used in Nordic countries, this plant has powerful medicinal properties. It has been prized for centuries as a tranquilizer, and drugs based upon the herb are still used today in some European countries.

Best climate and site Zones 4–9. Full sun to partial shade.
Ideal soil conditions Fertile, moist garden soil; pH 5.0–8.0.
Growing guidelines Sow seed shallowly outdoors in spring, transplanting to the garden when small plants are established. Germinates poorly. Propagate by division in spring or autumn, spacing new plants 1 foot (30 cm) apart. Dig and renew plants every 3 years.
Growing habit Herbaceous perennial with divided leaves and a fetid smell like old leather; height 3–5 feet (90–150 cm).
Flowering time Summer; small, tubular, pale pink, white or lavender flowers in dense terminal clusters.
Pest and disease prevention Usually trouble free.
Harvesting and storing Dig roots in autumn or spring, before new shoots form; wash and dry quickly at 120° F (49° C) until brittle. Stores well. Prepare a soothing bath by adding a decoction made from valerian.
Special tips The roots of valerian attract earthworms, so plant it in mixed borders and vegetable gardens. Cats and rats are attracted to the smell of valerian root, so use the plant to attract or catch them.
Precautions Not to be taken by people with liver problems.
Parts used Rhizomes, roots, oil.
Medicinal uses Internally for insomnia, migraine and anxiety. Externally for ulcers and minor injuries.
Other uses Extracts used to flavor ice cream, drinks, condiments and other food.
Other common names Garden heliotrope, cat's valerian.

Vanilla planifolia
ORCHIDACEAE

VANILLA

Vanilla is one of the world's most important flavorings. It was used by the Aztecs to flavor chocolate and was introduced into Europe in the 16th century. Vanilla flowers have to be pollinated by hand to produce the fruit pod.

Best climate and site Zone 10. Found in the tropics of both hemispheres. Requires ample moisture, shade and humidity.
Ideal soil conditions Vanilla is an epiphytic orchid and takes its nutrients from the air. It will not grow in soil but in a loose, friable compost mixture.
Growing guidelines Propagate from cuttings 6 feet (1.8 m) long at any time; leave to dry for 3 weeks before placing in loose compost.
Growing habit Climbing, evergreen perennial orchid with green stems and fleshy leaves. Grows on walls, trees or climbing posts, attaching itself with wormlike aerial roots.
Flowering time Pale yellow-green flowers in spring followed by long seed capsules which develop an aroma when cured.
Pest and disease prevention Plants damaged by scale insects, mildew, vanilla root rot and snails.
Harvesting and storing Fruits are picked when fully ripe and scalded before undergoing various stages of fermentation and drying. This whole process can take up to 6 months. Dried, cured fruit pods, known as vanilla pods or beans, are stored whole or processed commercially for vanilla extract (essence).
Parts used Fruits.
Culinary uses Extract used in the flavoring of ice cream, confectionery, soft drinks, liqueurs and tobacco.
Medicinal uses Internally as an aid to digestion.
Other uses In cosmetics, especially perfumes, and added to potpourri.

Verbascum thapsus
SCROPHULARIACEAE

MULLEIN

A stately plant with woolly leaves and large flower spikes, mullein has been used for centuries as a medicine for respiratory disorders. It is a frost-hardy biennial and will tolerate a diverse range of growing conditions.

Best climate and site Zones 4–8. Full sun to light shade. Tolerates a wide range of growing conditions.
Ideal soil conditions Well-drained to dry soil; pH 5.0–7.5.
Growing guidelines Propagate by seed sown in spring or by root cuttings taken in winter. Plants often self-seed in light soils. Thin or transplant to 2 feet (60 cm) apart. Stake plants in exposed sites.
Growing habit Tall biennial; height 6 feet (2 m). Leaves are large, soft and woolly, and a greenish gray.
Flowering time Small, five-petaled, yellow flowers packed into dense clusters on thick erect spikes appear in summer.
Pest and disease prevention Caterpillars may attack plants.
Harvesting and storing Whole plant is harvested when flowering. Flowers are collected as soon as they open and are used to make a pale yellow dye. Leaves are harvested in their first season.
Precautions All parts of mullein, except possibly the flowers, are slightly toxic. The fine hairs are an irritant. In some parts of the world, it is a noxious weed and is illegal to grow.
Parts used Whole plant, leaves, flowers.
Culinary uses Flowers used to flavor liqueurs.
Medicinal uses Internally for respiratory tract infections, coughs, colds, catarrh, tonsillitis and insomnia.
Externally for rheumatic pain, hemorrhoids, chilblains, earaches and sores.
Other common names Aaron's rod, great mullein, velvet plant, donkey's ears.

Verbena officinalis
VERBENACEAE

VERVAIN

This ancient perennial has a long religious and medicinal history. It was sacred to many cultures and it was used to treat tiredness, stress, minor cuts and bruises. Today it is still used in some medicinal preparations.

Best climate and site Zones 4–10. Full sun. Native to southern Europe but now found widely around the world.
Ideal soil conditions Ordinary, well-drained moist garden soil; pH 6.0–7.5.
Growing guidelines Easily grows from seed sown outdoors; thin to 1 foot (30 cm). Take stem cuttings in summer. Divide in winter to spring. Can self-sow. Mulching in spring will encourage better flowers and foliage.
Growing habit Loosely branched perennial with deeply lobed, oblong, slightly hairy leaves; height 1–2 feet (30–60 cm).
Flowering time Summer to autumn; small, tubular, pale lilac blossoms in spikes. The flowers have no scent.
Pest and disease prevention Usually trouble free.
Harvesting and storing Foliage can be picked as required. If using the whole plant, harvest it when it begins to flower.
Precautions Can be toxic and cause nausea and vomiting.
Parts used Whole plant.
Medicinal uses Internally for depression, asthma, migraine, jaundice and gall bladder problems.
Externally for gum disease, eczema and minor skin injuries.
Other uses A bath prepared with vervain soothes nervous exhaustion. Can be used as an eyewash and hair tonic.
Other species American vervain *V. hastata* is also called blue vervain. Has blue flowers; height 4–5 feet (1.2–1.5 m).
Gardener's trivia Legend has it that vervain should be harvested when neither sun nor moon is in the sky, and that pieces of honeycomb should be left in exchange.

Viola odorata
VIOLACEAE

VIOLET, SWEET

Violets are early fragrant bloomers that grow well in shaded locations during cool weather. With its wonderful perfume and rich color, sweet violet is a delightful inclusion in any garden.

Best climate and site Zones 6–10. Partial shade.
Ideal soil conditions Any well-drained but moist, rich soil.
Growing guidelines Sow seed shallowly outdoors or in a cold frame as soon as ripe in autumn or spring; cover seeds, which need darkness to germinate. Thin to 1 foot (30 cm). Divide mature plants in autumn, winter or early spring.
Growing habit Tufted perennial with kidney-shaped, downy leaves; height 4–6 inches (10–15 cm).
Flowering time Spring; fragrant purple, violet, white or pink blossoms.
Pest and disease prevention Prone to slugs, snails and fungal diseases. Check also for mites.
Harvesting and storing Leaves and flowers are collected during the flowering season. Thoroughly dry flowers for culinary use; store in airtight containers. Petals may be candied, or added to jams, flans and fruit salads.
Special tips When designing a garden for its fragrance, use sweet violets for a thick, scented groundcover under a bench or against a brick wall. Sweet violets don't grow well indoors.
Parts used Leaves, flowers, oil.
Culinary uses Flowers used sparingly in salads and as a garnish. Petals candied and used to decorate cakes and desserts.
Medicinal uses Internally for bronchitis, coughs, asthma and treatment for some cancers such as breast and lung cancer. Externally for mouth and throat infections.
Other uses Oil used in perfumes. Flowers used to flavor candy and in breath fresheners. Used in aromatherapy.

Wasabia japonica
BRASSICACEAE

WASABI

This native of Japan is generally found growing beside mountain streams. Wasabi is a condiment traditionally used to garnish raw fish and noodle dishes in Japan. It is also used as an antidote for fish poisoning.

Best climate and site Zones 3–6. Full shade.
Ideal soil conditions Wasabi is a mountain stream plant and requires rich, moist to wet soil; pH 4.5–7.4.
Growing guidelines Propagate in spring by seed kept moist or by division of rootstock in spring and autumn. Keep out of direct sun. Wasabi can acclimatize in cool gardens but may be difficult to grow.
Growing habit Attractive, hardy perennial herb; height 8–16 inches (20–40 cm). Has creeping rhizomes, upright stems and long-stalked, glossy, green, kidney-shaped leaves.
Flowering time Small, white flowers clustered along the stem are produced in spring, followed by twisted pods containing several large seeds.
Pest and disease prevention Usually trouble free.
Harvesting and storing Roots are lifted in spring or autumn and used fresh, dried, ground or preserved. Roots are mature 15–24 months after planting. Leaf stalks are also used.
Special tips Wasabi belongs to the same family as horseradish, radish and mustard, all of which are valued for the strong, pungent flavor of their roots. Good, fresh wasabi is not just spicy hot but also sweet with a gentle fragrance.
Parts used Roots, leaves, leaf stalks.
Culinary uses In Japanese cuisine, grated fresh roots are eaten with raw fish and used as seasoning. Powdered root is used to flavor meat and fish dishes. Leaves are used as a vegetable and garnish; also pickled.
Medicinal uses Internally as an antidote for fish poisoning.

Zea mays
POACEAE

SWEET CORN (MAIZE)

Tender and succulent, fresh sweet corn is a classic summer treat from the garden. It's well worth growing for its culinary and medicinal uses. The Aztecs used corn to clear excess heat from the heart.

Best climate and site Zones 7 and warmer. In colder areas, use early-maturing cultivars. Needs full sun. Avoid windy areas.
Ideal soil conditions Deep, well-manured soil; pH 6.0–6.8.
Growing guidelines Sow after last spring frost. Corn seed germinates poorly in cold, wet soil and may rot. Plant 1 inch (2.5 cm) deep and 4 inches (10 cm) apart in a block (several short, parallel rows) to ensure good wind pollination. Thin seedlings to 8–12 inches (20–30 cm). Corn grows rapidly and needs adequate fertilizer and plenty of water. Apply fish emulsion or compost tea after 1 month.
Growing habit Large annual, with lancelike leaves; height to 10 feet (3 m).
Pest and disease prevention Wireworms or caterpillars (earworms) may attack plants. Solarize soil before planting to discourage wireworms.
Harvesting and storing Harvest when the silks have turned brown and dry, and the kernels, if punctured, emit a milky (not watery) fluid. Quickly can or freeze corn that cannot be eaten immediately after picking, as it begins to turn starchy within hours.
Parts used Cobs, silks, oil.
Culinary uses As a vegetable. Used to make cornflour, cereals and polenta.
Medicinal uses Internally for cystitis and urethritis.
Other varieties *Z. mays* 'Gracillima Variegata' has yellow-seeded cobs, and creamy white and green striped foliage. It is an attractive plant for containers.

Zingiber officinale
ZINGIBERACEAE

GINGER

Fresh ginger has a zing that the powdered spice lacks. Grow your own in pots placed outdoors during the warm season. It has the double advantage of being both spicy and kind to your digestive system.

Best climate and site Zone 10 or warmer, or in a warm greenhouse. Full sun to partial shade.
Ideal soil conditions Fertile, moist, well-drained garden soil; pH 6.5–7.5 if planted in warm climates outside.
Growing guidelines Plant rhizomes in pots in a mix containing peat, sand and compost; keep indoors during winter, moving the pots outdoors in warm summers.
Growing habit Tropical perennial; height 2–5 feet (60–150 cm); leaves strap-shaped, 6–12 inches (15–30 cm) long.
Flowering time Ginger rarely flowers in containers; in the right conditions, it produces dense conelike spikes on a stalk with yellow-green and purple flowers.
Pest and disease prevention Usually free from pests and diseases. For healthy growth, water well during the hot summer months.
Harvesting and storing Dig the plant up after 1 year and remove the leaf stems, cutting away as much root as you need; replant the remaining root. Refrigerate harvested roots wrapped in paper toweling in a plastic bag for up to 1 month. Or dry shaved bits of root and store in an airtight container.
Parts used Rhizomes, oil.
Culinary uses Can be eaten raw, preserved in syrup or candied. Used in curries, chutneys, marinades, pickles and cakes. Can be combined with cinnamon to make tea.
Medicinal uses Internally for motion sickness, morning sickness, colds, coughs and indigestion.
Externally for muscle pain, lumbago and menstrual cramps.

Plant Hardiness Zone Maps

These maps of the United States, Canada and Europe are divided into ten zones. Each zone is based on a 10°F (5.6°C) difference in average annual minimum temperature. Some areas are considered too high in elevation for plant cultivation and so are not assigned to any zone. There are also island zones that are warmer or cooler than surrounding areas because of differences in elevation; they have been given a zone different from the surrounding areas. Many large urban areas, for example, are in a warmer zone than the surrounding land. Plants grow best within an optimum range of temperatures. The range may be wide for some species and narrow for others. Plants also differ in their ability to survive frost and in their sun or shade requirements.

The zone ratings indicate conditions where designated plants will grow well and not merely survive. Many plants may survive in zones warmer or colder than their recommended zone range. Remember that other factors, including wind, soil type, soil moisture, humidity, snow and winter sunshine, may have a great effect on growth.

Some nursery plants have been grown in greenhouses and they might not survive in your garden, so it's a waste of money, and a cause of heartache, to buy plants that aren't right for your climate zone.

Average annual minimum temperature °F (°C)

Zone 1	Below -50°F (Below -45°C)	Zone 6	-10° to 0°F (-23° to -18°C)
Zone 2	-50° to -40°F (-45° to -40°C)	Zone 7	0° to 10°F (-18° to -12°C)
Zone 3	-40° to -30°F (-40° to -34°C)	Zone 8	10° to 20°F (-12° to -7°C)
Zone 4	-30° to -20°F (-34° to -29°C)	Zone 9	20° to 30°F (-7° to -1°C)
Zone 5	-20° to -10°F (-29° to -23°C)	Zone 10	30° to 40°F (-1° to 4°C)

Australia and New Zealand

These maps divide Australia and New Zealand into seven climate zones which, as near as possible, correspond to the USDA climate zones used in the United States, Britain and Europe and in this book. The zones are based on the minimum temperatures usually, or possibly, experienced within each zone. Over the year, air temperatures heat then cool the soil and this is important to plants. Some cannot tolerate cold or even cool temperatures, while others require a period of low temperatures to grow properly. Although this book is designed primarily for cool-climate gardens, the information in it can be adapted for gardens in hotter climates. The text indicates the ideal zones in which to grow particular plants.

When you read that a plant is suitable for any of the zones 7 through to 10, you will know that it should grow successfully in those zones in Australia and New Zealand. There are other factors that affect plant growth, but temperature is one of the most important. Plants listed as being suitable for Zone 10 may also grow in hotter zones, but to be sure, consult a gardening guide specific to your area.

Australia

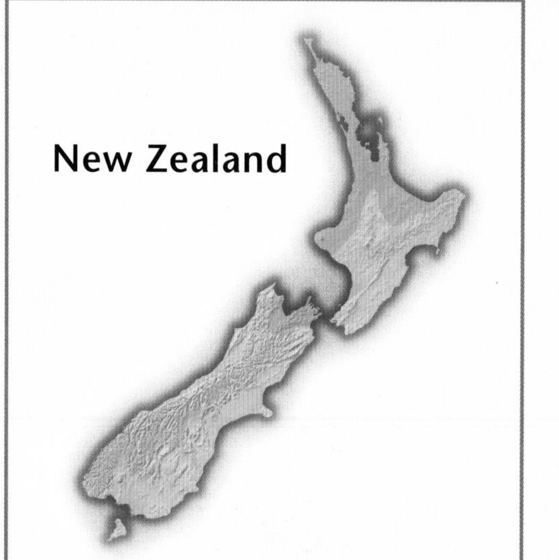

Minimum temperature °C (°F)

Zone 7 -15° to -10°C (5° to 14°F)

Zone 8 -10° to -5°C (14° to 23°F)

Zone 9 -5° to 0°C (23° to 32°F)

Zone 10 0° to 5°C (32° to 41°F)

Zone 11 5° to 10°C (41° to 50°F)

Zone 12 10° to 15°C (50° to 59°F)

Zone 13 15° to 20°C (59° to 68°F)

Glossary

acid A term used to describe soil with a pH value less than 7.

alkaline A term used to describe soil with a pH value more than 7. Many herbs thrive in alkaline soil.

alternate Describing leaves that occur on one side of the stem, then the other side, but are not opposite each other.

annual A plant that lives for one year, completing its life cycle—germination, flowering and dying—in a growing season.

axil Upper angle between a part of the plant and the stem that bears it.

biennial A plant that completes its life cycle in two years, growing in the first year and flowering and fruiting in the second, after which it dies.

bouquet garni A bunch of herbs, most commonly including a bay leaf, thyme and parsley or chervil, tied together with string, or placed in a muslin bag. It is used in the cooking of soups, stews and sauces and is removed before serving. The essential oils of the herbs provide a subtle flavor and aroma.

bract Modified leaf at the base of a flower or flower head. May be small and scale-like, or large and brightly colored, or petal- or leaflike.

compress A pad of soft material moistened with a warm herbal infusion or decoction and placed on a wound to promote healing.

corm A bulblike, underground storage organ often surrounded by a papery covering. Corms are replaced annually.

crown 1. Growing point of a plant from which new shoots arise, at or just below the soil surface at the junction with roots. 2. The upper, branched part of a tree. 3. A corona of a flower.

cultivar A cultivated variety. A plant raised or selected in cultivation, retaining distinctive characteristics when it is propagated. A cultivar is not usually found in wild populations.

cutting A section of leaf, stem or root separated from the plant and used to propagate it. Most herbs are easily propagated from cuttings.

deadhead To remove dead or withered flowers, either to prevent seeding or to destroy possible sites for pests and diseases; also to encourage more flowering.

deciduous Describing a tree or shrub that sheds its leaves annually at the end of the growing season.

decoction An extract of an herb made by simmering the herb or parts of it in water and then straining it. Best for tough plant parts such as roots and bark.

division The propagation of a plant by splitting it into two or more parts and replanting, each part having a section of the root system and one or more dormant shoots or buds.

evergreen Describing a plant that retains its growing leaves through more than one growing season.

fines herbes A mixture of chopped fresh herbs, such as parsley, tarragon, basil, chervil, chives, marjoram and thyme, stirred into foods at the end of cooking to add color as well as flavor.

fixative A substance that is added to a potpourri base mixture to help retain the essential oils and so preserve the fragrance. Fixatives can be of animal origin, such as ambergris and musk (now discouraged), or derived from plants, such as orris root, vetiver root, rose attar, dried rosemary, sweet flag or tonka beans. One tablespoon is used for each quart (liter) of dried base.

floret A tiny, individual flower in a head of many flowers; also known as floweret.

flower head A composite mass of flowers that appear together as one flower.

fruit The part of a plant that bears one or more seeds, such as a nut or berry.

genus A group of closely related species of plants that share a wide range of similar characteristics.

grafting A method of propagation where a part of one plant is artifically joined to another plant.

habit The characteristic mode of growth and appearance of a plant.

half hardy Not able to tolerate frost but able to withstand temperatures down to 32°F (0°C).

hardy Gardening term now generally used to describe plants able to withstand frost in cold climates without protection. The opposite of hardy is tender, taken to mean frost tenderness. However, the term hardy is also sometimes used in warm climates to indicate heat hardiness or drought tolerance.

herbaceous A non-woody perennial that dies back (losing its top growth) at the end of each growing season. Growth resumes again in spring.

hip The fleshy fruit of a rose.

humus The dark, decomposed organic content of soil, derived from decaying plant and animal matter.

hybrid The offspring of two genetically different parents produced either by accident or artificially in cultivation but sometimes arising in the wild.

inflorescence A cluster of flowers with a distinct arrangement such as an umbel.

infusion An extract made by steeping or soaking parts of an herb in boiling water, a method best used for flowers and leaves of plants.

lanceolate Narrow, lance-shaped leaves, widest below the middle and tapering at both ends.

layering Propagating a plant by burying a stem in the soil while it is still attached to the parent plant, to induce rooting. Works well with long, flexible stems.

loam Soil that is moisture-retentive, highly fertile and well-drained, containing roughly equal parts of clay, silt and sand.

maceration Steeping herbs in water at room temperature for 12 hours, then straining. Best used for herbs that may lose their benefit if heated.

marinade A liquid or paste in which foods are steeped to tenderize and flavor them. Commonly, meat or poultry is soaked in a marinade containing wine, vinegar and herbs for several hours.

mulch A layer of material spread on the surface of the soil to insulate roots, keeping them warmer in winter and cooler in summer, and to retain moisture and hinder weed growth. A mulch can be organic, such as compost, grass clippings or leaf mold, or inorganic, such as black plastic or landscaping fabric.

obovate Leaves that are inversely ovate, broader above than below the middle.

ovate Leaves that are egg shaped, more or less rounded at both ends and broadest below the middle.

overwintering The process of a plant surviving the winter. This may involve protection outside or being moved inside during a cold winter.

palmate Having three or more leaflets or lobes radiating fanwise from a common basal point of attachment.

panicle A compound, branched raceme where the flowers develop on stalks arising from the main stem.

perennial A plant that lives for more than two growing seasons; in gardening, usually applied to non-woody plants.

pH A measure of the alkalinity or acidity of the soil based on a scale of 1 (strongly acid) to 14 (strongly alkaline). 7 is neutral.

photosynthesis The chemical process in green plants that converts carbon dioxide and water into sugars and oxygen, using light energy from sunlight absorbed by chlorophyll.

pinch out To remove the soft growing tips of plants to encourage the bushy growth of sideshoots.

pinnate Constructed something like a feather, with the parts arranged along both sides of an axis. A pinnate leaf is compound, with leaflets arranged on both sides of a central axis.

potpourri Long-lasting, fragrant mixtures of dried herbs, flowers and other crushed plant material.

poultice A pulp or paste made of minced, dried or fresh herbs and hot water, sometimes with oats added. A poultice is applied directly on the skin, or between two layers of gauze, to promote healing.

propagate To increase plants by seed or vegetative means.

raceme Inflorescence of stalked flowers radiating from a single, unbranched axis with youngest flowers near the tip.

rhizome Usually a horizontal stem growing underground or at ground level, and usually branching and fleshy.

runner 1. A trailing stem growing along the soil surface and rooting at the nodes, producing plantlets. 2. Underground spreading shoot producing upright shoots that form new plants at intervals.

scarify To scar or scratch the coat of a seed by abrasion to speed up water intake and germination.

self-seed To regenerate from seed dispersed in the garden by the plant, without human intervention.

shrub A perennial with multiple woody stems or branches, generally bearing branches near its base.

species A category in plant classification, ranked below genus, consisting of similar individual plants that breed true in the wild. It is indicated by the second part of the scientific name.

stamen Male part of a flower, the pollen-bearing organ, composed of an anther, normally borne on a filament.

stolon A horizontally spreading stem, usually above ground, which roots at its tips to produce new plants.

stool layering The propagation of a plant by earthing up around the base of the parent plant, to stimulate rooting at the base of the stems. New plants are later removed and replanted.

subshrub A woody-based plant with soft-wooded stems, or a low-growing woody stemmed plant; often treated as a perennial.

sucker 1. A shoot arising from below ground level, usually from the roots of a plant. 2. A shoot that arises from the stock of a budded or grafted plant.

taproot Primary, sometimes swollen, downward growing root, from which the root system extends.

terminal Located at the end of a stem, shoot or other part.

tincture An extract of an herb made by soaking the dried plant in an alcohol and water mix. Tinctures are more concentrated than decoctions or infusions and their potency lasts longer.

topography The lay of an area of land, including hills, valleys and slopes.

toxic Harmful or poisonous.

transpiration Loss of water by evaporation from the surface of a plant.

trim To lightly prune.

tuber A swollen root or underground stem in which food is stored.

umbel A flat or round-topped inflorescence in which numerous stalked small flowers are terminally borne from a single point.

variegated Having irregular markings in various colors.

variety A naturally occurring variation of a species, as opposed to a cultivated variety.

whorl The arrangement of three or more leaves, flowers or other parts arising from the one node.

woody-stemmed Describes the fibrous stems of perennials such as trees and shrubs, that persist aboveground throughout the year.

x The sign used to indicate a hybrid plant, commonly the offspring of two genetically different species.

Index

Page references in *italics* indicate photos and illustrations.

G

H

Q

R

T

Acknowledgments

KEY l=left, r=right, c=center, t=top, b=bottom, f=far

AA=The Art Archive; APL=Australian Picture Library; AZ=A–Z Botanical Collection; CN=Clive Nichols; COR=Corel Corporation; DF=Derek Fell; DG=Denise Greig; DW=David Wallace; GDR=G. R. "Dick" Roberts; GI=Getty Images; GPL=Garden Picture Library; HA=Heather Angel; HSC=Harry Smith Collection; HSI=Holt Studios International; JC=John Callanan; JP=Jerry Pavia; JY=James Young; LC=Leigh Clapp; OSF=Oxford Scientific Films; PD=PhotoDisc; PH=Photos Horticultural; SOM=S. & O. Mathews; TE=Thomas Eltzroth; TPL=photolibrary.com; TR=Tony Rodd; WO=Weldon Owen; WR=Weldon Russell

1l LC; m GPL/Howard Rice; r JY **2**c JP **4–5**c GPL/Mark Bolton **6**c JP **10–11**c LC **12**b GPL/Linda Burgess **13**tl PH **15**tr JP **16**tr WO; bl LC/Rural Design; br PD **17**t GPL/Didier Willery **18**tc WO **19**tl GPL/John Glover; br CN **20**tc APL/Corbis/Darrell Gulin **21**t APL/Corbis/Gerry Sweeney **22**tr AA; bl APL/Corbis/Archivo Iconografico, S. A. **23**c TPL/Jean-Loup Charmet **24**br APL/Corbis/Burstein Collection **25**tr APL/Corbis/Christies Images **26–27**c JP **28**c CN; br GPL/CN **29**tc GPL/Steven Wooster **30**tc CN **31**tl GPL/John Glover **32**tr WO; bl GPL/Jacqui Hurst **33**c CN **34**tr GPL/Linda Burgess **35**tr LC **37**t GPL/David Askham; br DF **38**tl GPL/Neil Holmes **39**lc GPL/Gary Rogers; tr JP **40**tl DG; tr LC **41**t APL/Gerry Whitmont **42**r LC **43**br LC **44**b APL/Corbis/Layne Kennedy **45**c GPL/Juliet Wade **46**tr GPL/Michael Diggin; b DF **47**cr WO/Ad-Libitum/Stuart Bowey; b GPL/Juliette Wade **48**bl APL/Corbis/Michael Boys; br Gillian Beckett **49**t APL/Corbis/Michael Boys; b GPL/Brigitte Thomas **50**bl GPL/Steven Wooster; br JP **51**t GPL/Clay Perry; b LC **52**tc DW; tr JP **53**tr APL/Corbis/Peter Johnson **54**t GPL/Sunniva Harte; l, cr, br WO/DW **56**tr GPL/John Neubauer; bl GPL/John Glover **57**c LC **58**c LC **60**b APL/Corbis/Clay Perry **61**tl JY; r APL/Corbis/Eric Crichton **62**tr JY; bl LC **63**b LC **64**br DF **65**tc LC; br GPL/Michael Diggin **74**t Corbis; cl GPL/Neil Holmes; bl DW **75**tc WO **76–77**c GPL/Christopher Gallagher **78**tr APL/Premium Houses **79**bl WO/Ad-Libitum/Stuart Bowey **80**tc HSC; tr GPL/Brigitte Thomas; l, bl, br DF **81**tl APL/Corbis/Michael Boys **82**tr GPL/Linda Burgess; bl PH **83**tl PH; tc APL/Corbis/Bob Rowan; tr WO/JY; b TE **84**bl WR/DW; br PH **85**tr GPL/Howard Rice; bl GPL/Emma Peios **86**tr GPL/Michael Howes; bl PH **87**t GPL/Brian Carter; c PH; b HSC **88**b DW **89**br GPL/Jane Legate **90**bl DW **91**tl GPL/Michael Howes ; r DW **92**cl, b DW **93**t PD **94**t JC **95**tc WO/Kevin Candland; all others by DW **96**c LC **98**t GPL/Jane Legate **99**tl PD; tr PH **100**tc, bl LC **101**r APL/Corbis/Wolfgang Kaehler **102**tc, bl PH; br GPL/Lamontagne **103**tl GPL/Brigitte Thomas **104**t APL/Corbis/Eric Crichton **106**t WO **108** all images WO **109**tl DF; br WO **110**tr DF; bl WO **111**tl PH; tr WO **112**t GPL/Neil Holmes **113**t GPL/Lynne Brotchie **114**b GPL **115**br GPL/Lamontagne **116**bl CN **116**br GPL/Marie O'Hara; tc GPL/Mel Watson **118**tc WO **119**bl Getty Images **120**tr PH **121**t DF **122**tl WO/Leo Meier; tr APL/Corbis/Eric Crichton **123**tr DF; bl PH **124**tl PH; cl GPL/Michael Howes **125**t APL/Corbis/Eric Crichton **126**b JY **128**tr HSI/Nigel Cattlin; all others WO **129**t PH; bl WO; bcl HSC; bcr DF; br WO **130**tc WO **132** CN **133** SOM **134**tr APL/Corbis/Darrell Gulin **135**bl WO/Leo Meier **136**bl PD **137**tl LC **138**tl GPL/Georgia Glynn-Smith **139**b LC **140**c GPL **142**t GPL/Jane Legate; bl GPL/Lamontagne **143**tl GPL/Gary Rogers; b LC **144**c GI **145**t GPL; all others WO/JC/John Hollingshead **147**t APL/Corbis/Elizabeth Whiting; b WO/Ad-Libitum/Stuart Bowey **148**bc WO/JC **149**c WO/JC **150** all images WO/JC **151**tl, tr DW; all others WO/JC **152**tr GPL; bl WO/Chris Shorten; bc PH; br WO/Ad-Libitum/Stuart Bowey **156**br APL/Corbis/Bob Krist **157**br PD **162**tr APL/Corbis/Rick Gomez; br WO/Ad-Libitum/Stuart Bowey **163**tl TPL/Science Photo Library/Damian Lovegrove **163**tr APL/Corbis/Michelle Garrett **164**tr PD; bc WO/JC **165** all images WO/Ad-Libitum/Stuart Bowey **166**tr WO/Chris Shorten; bl GPL/Tim Spence **167**t GPL/Christel Rosenfeld; br WO/Ad-Libitum/Stuart Bowey **168**tc GPL/Michael Viard; bc WO/Ad-Libitum/Stuart Bowey **169**tl Corbis; tr DW; bl DW; br WO/Ad-Libitum/Stuart Bowey **171**c, br WO; tr WO/Michael Freeman **172–73**c LC **174**tl COR; tr JY **175**tl GPL/John Glover; tr JY **176**tl JY; tr GDR **177** all images DW **178**tl GPL/Juliet Wade; tr TE **179**tl DF; tr WO **180**tl JY; tr GPL/JP **181**tl JY; tr Random House **182**tl JY; tr DW **183**tl GPL/Brian Carter; tr Steven Foster Group Inc/Steven Foster **184**tl DW; tr TE **185**tl WO/DW; tr GDR **186**tl JY; tr HA **187**tl AZ/Malkolm Warrington; tr JY **188**tl JY; tr DW **189**tl JY; tr Cheryl Maddocks **190**tl WO; tr PH **191**tl GDR; tr AZ/Alan Gould **192**tl HSC; tr TR **193**tl WO/JY; tr GPL/Emma Peios **194**tl DW; tr TR **195**tl GDR; GPL/Densey Clyne **196**tl GPL/Lamontagne; tr WO/JY **197**tl WO/JY; tr TR **198**tl WO; tr TR **199**tl JY; tr WO **200**tl Ivy Hansen; tr Lorna Rose **201**tl Stirling Macoboy; tr OSF/Tom Leach **202**tl DW; tr WO **203**tl WO/JY; tr PH **204**tl WO; tr TR **205**tl Gillian Beckett; tr DW **206**tl CN; tr PH **207**tl PH; tr gardenphotos.com/Judy White **208**tl JY; tr JY **209**tl GPL/Brian Carter; tr GPL/Mayer/Le Scanff **210** all images JP **211**tl GPL/Howard Rice; tr GDR **212**tl GPL/Gary Rogers; tr TR **213**tl JP; tr PH **214**tl GDR; tr WO **215**tl PH; tr JY **216**tl WR/DW; tr TR **217**tl GPL/Jacqui Hurst; tr GPL/A. Lord **218**tl WO/JY; tr GDR **219**tl HSC; tr WO **220**tl TE; tr GPL/J. S. Sira **221**tl TE; tr HSC **222**tl TR; tr JP **223**tl GPL/Janet Sorrell; tr Bruce Coleman Limited/Dr. Eckart Pott **224**tl JY; tr TR **225**tl WO/JY; tr WO/Kylie Mulquin **226**tl WO/Kylie Mulquin; tr JP **227**tl HSC; tr GPL/John Glover **228** all images DW **229**tl WO; tr DW **230** all images WO/JY **231**tl GDR; tr WO/JY **232**tl JY; tr OSF/Deni Bown **233**tl GDR; tr DW **234**tl DW; tr JY **235** all images WO/JY **236**tl JP; tr DW **237** all images WO/JY **238**tl GPL/Michel Viard; tr GPL/Steven Wooster **239**tl WO/Kylie Mulquin; tr DW **240**tl JY; tr GDR **241**tl PH; tr JP **242**tl GPL/Michel Viard; tr DW **243**tl PH; tr JP **244** all images Gillian Beckett **245**tl JP; tr GDR **246**tl GPL/Michael Howes; tr DW **247**tl GPL/Howard Rice; tr GPL/Michael Diggin **248**tl DW; tr JY **249**tl Ardea/A. P. Paterson; tr PH **250**tl JY; tr GDR **251**tl GDR; tr JY **252**tl DW; tr WO/JY **253**tl AZ; tr GPL/Didier Willery **254**tl WO/JY; tr TR **255**tl TR; tr HA **256**tl DW; tr OSF/Deni Bown **257**tl TR; tr DW **258**tl GPL/Rex Butcher; tr WO **259**tl JY; tr GI **260**tl HSC; tr AZ/Bob Gibbons **261**tl JY; tr HA **262**tl PH; tr DW **263**tl DW; tr HSC **264**tl TR; tr AZ/Bob Gibbons **265**tl JY; tr PH **266**tl DW; tr GPL/Howard Rice **267**tl JP; tr HSC **268**tl TE; tr GDR **269**tl DW.

Illustrations by Artville, Anne Bowman, Tony Britt-Lewis, Helen Halliday, Angela Lober, David Mackay, Stuart McVicar, Oliver Rennert, Edwina Riddell, Barbara Rodanska, Jan Smith, Kathie Smith, Sharif Tarabay.

The publishers would like to thank Judy Moore, for the text of pages 12–25; Jenni Simpson, for research and caption writing; Bronwyn Sweeney, for proofreading; Tonia Johanson, for indexing.